A PRACTICAL GRAMMAR OF THE SANSKRIT LANGUAGE

A PRACTICAL GRAMMAR OF THE SANSKRIT LANGUAGE

FOR THE USE OF EARLY STUDENTS.

BY

THEODOR BENFEY.

SECOND EDITION.

CAREFULLY REVISED AND CORRECTED.

GYAN

Published by

Gyan Publishing House
5, Ansari Road
Daryaganj, New Delhi-110002
Phone: 011-47034999, 9811692060
E-mail: books@gyanbooks.com

Distribution Network
gyanbooks.com
India, USA, Canada, UK, Australia, France

ISBN : 978-81-212-2638-7 (HB)
First Published, 1868

2nd Impression 2021

Printed at: Gyan Press, Delhi.

A
Practical Grammar of the Sanskrit Language
Author: Theodor Benfey

A PRACTICAL GRAMMAR OF THE SANSKRIT LANGUAGE

FOR THE USE OF EARLY STUDENTS.

BY

THEODOR BENFEY.

SECOND EDITION.

CAREFULLY REVISED AND CORRECTED.

LONDON:
TRÜBNER & CO., 60, PATERNOSTER ROW.
1868.

PREFACE TO THE SECOND EDITION.

THE favour with which this little Grammar has been received, and my own experience of its usefulness as an introduction to the study of a difficult language, have led me to the conclusion that any material alterations in its form would be unadvisable. I have therefore limited myself to a careful review of the whole work, only supplying what appeared to be the deficiencies of the First Edition.

Some distinguished scholars have suggested that I should change the order of arrangement, and begin with the noun instead of the verb. With this suggestion I am unable to comply, for it seems to me that a real insight into the character of the Arian stock,—which should be aimed at from the very commencement of the study of its standard language,—can only be obtained by setting out from the verb. In order, however, to enable those who are of a different opinion to begin with the noun, I have carried the transliteration through the latter part of the Grammar; and for their convenience I recommend that the Grammar may be taken up in the following order: 1. § 1-36; 2. § 209-267; 3. § 62-186 and 188-190; 4. § 37-61, 187, and 191-208.

For the suggestion of additions or alterations, which may appear necessary to others, I shall feel grateful; and I assure those who are disposed thus to help me that I will endeavour, as far as possible, to profit by their friendly criticism.

TH. BENFEY.

GÖTTINGEN,
January, 1868.

CONTENTS.

PART THE FIRST.

LETTERS AND PHONETIC RULES.

CHAPTER I.—LETTERS.

§ 1. The Sanskrit alphabet, called *Devanâgarî*, comprises the following letters:—

I. Five short and five long vowels, viz.:

short: अ *a*, इ *i*, उ *u*, ऋ *ṛi*, ऌ *ḷi*.
long: आ *â*, ई *î*, ऊ *û*, ॠ *ṛî*, ॡ *ḷî*.

II. Four diphthongs: ए *e*, ऐ *ai*, ओ *o*, औ *au*.

Obs. ए *e* is in most cases a combination of *a* and *i*, ऐ *ai* of *â* and *i*, ओ *o* of *a* and *u*, औ *au* of *â* and *u*.

III. 1. Two slight nasals; the one, called *Anusvâra*, is denoted by a dot ं placed above the letter after which it is to be pronounced, *e.g.* अं *aṁ*; the other, called *Anunâsika*, is denoted by a half-moon with a dot in it ँ and placed either above or after the preceding letter, in the latter case with an oblique dash under it, *e.g.* अँ or अँ *a*ँ.

2. An aspirate, called *Visarga*, which is denoted by two dots, placed one above the other (:), *e.g.* अः *aḥ*.

IV. Thirty-three consonants:—

1. five gutturals:	क *ka*,	ख *kha*,	ग *ga*,	घ *gha*,	ङ *ṅa*,
2. five palatals:	च *cha*,	छ *chha*,	ज *ja*,	झ *jha*,	ञ *ńa*,
3. five linguals:	ट *ṭa*,	ठ *ṭha*,	ड *ḍa*,	ढ *ḍha*,	ण *ṇa*,
4. five dentals:	त *ta*,	थ *tha*,	द *da*,	ध *dha*,	न *na*,
5. five labials:	प *pa*,	फ *pha*,	ब *ba*,	भ *bha*,	म *ma*,
6. four semivowels:	य *ya*,	र *ra*,	ल *la*,	व *va*,	
7. three sibilants:	श *ça*,	ष *sha*,	स *sa*,		
8. the sonant aspirate:	ह *ha*.				

Obs. 1. The second and fourth letters of the five first classes are aspirated, *i.e.* combinations of the preceding unaspirated with *h.*

Obs. 2. The letter ह *ha* belongs to the guttural class, श *ça* to the palatal, ष *sha* to the lingual, and स *sa* to the dental.

Obs. 3. In some texts of Vedic works ळ *ḷa* and ळ्ह *ḷha* are used instead of ड *ḍa* and ढ *ḍha*, if preceded and followed by vowels or diphthongs, e.g. इळः *iḷaḥ* instead of इडः *iḍaḥ*.

Obs. 4. The *a* attached to the consonants only serves for the purpose of facilitating their utterance, as in English the *e* after *b*, *c*, *d*, etc.

Obs. 5. The words in the Dictionaries are arranged according to the order of letters in the above list.

§ 2. It is not possible to ascertain exactly the original pronunciation of the Sanskrit letters. However, the transcription of Hindu proper names in Greek and Latin works, as well as some other facts bearing upon this subject, allow us to establish the following rules with some confidence:—अ is to be pronounced like *a* in *apt*, आ like *a* in *far*, इ like *i* in *pin*, ई like *ee* in *feeble*, उ like *u* in *full*, ऊ like *o* in *move*, ऋ like *ri* in *rid*, ॠ like *rea* in *to read*, ऌ like *li* in *lid*, ॡ like *lea* in *to lead*, ए like *a* in *fate*, ऐ like the Italian *ai* in *mai*, ओ like *o* in *note*, औ like *ou* in *our*.

Anusvâra ं before the semivowels य *ya*, र *ra*, ल *la*, व *va*, the sibilants श *ça*, ष *sha*, स *sa*, and the aspirate ह *ha*, is pronounced like *ng* in *king*, before all other consonants like the nasal of the class to which the following letter belongs, *e.g.* before a guttural like the nasal of the guttural class (§ 1, IV. 1); कं गण *kang gaṇa*, कं जन *kañj jana*. The *Anunâsika* ँ seems to have been all but inaudible. *Visarga* (:) is to be pronounced like the Greek χ before क् *k* and ख् *kh*; like the Greek φ before प् *p* and फ् *ph*;[1] before श् *ç*, ष् *sh*, and स् *s*, perhaps like the Greek *spiritus lenis*.

[1] Cf. *A. Weber*, Ueber ein Fragment der *Bhagavatî* (On a Fragment of the *Bhagavatî*), Berlin, 1866 (Memoirs of the R. Acad. of Sc.), p. 386 sqq. The natives pronounce the *Visarga* everywhere almost inaudibly.

क like *k* in *king*, ख like *kh* in *inkhorn*, ग like *g* in *gun*, घ like *gh* in *loghouse*, ङ like *ng* in *to sing*.

च like *ch* in *church*. छ like *ch+h* in *churchhill*, ज like *j* in *jet*, झ like *j+h*, ञ like *n* in *singe*.

The linguals seem to have been pronounced originally like the corresponding dentals with the addition of a slight *r*.[1] But at present ट् *ṭ*, ड् *ḍ*, and ण् *ṇ*, sound quite like the English *t*, *d*, *n*;[2] in the aspirated an *h* must be added.

The true pronunciation of the dentals is very difficult for an European. It may be effected by bringing the tip of the tongue against the very edge of the upper front teeth.

The unaspirated labials, the स *sa* and the ह *ha*, are pronounced like the corresponding English letters; in the aspirated dentals and labials an *h* must be added. ष *sha* is to be pronounced like *sh* in *shun*, श *ça* like a sharp *s* as in *sit*, or perhaps like *ss* in *session*.

The pronunciation of the Vedic ळ *ḷa* is doubtful, perhaps it was sounded like a hollow *l*.

§ 3. The vowel ॠ *ṝ* never appears in the radical, but only in the derivative part of a real word; ऌ *ḷi* only in one verb; ॡ *ḹ* not at all in any real word. ं *Anusvâra*, ँ *Anunâsika*, and ः *Visarga*, never are primitive letters, but the two first are substitutes of an original *m* or *n*, and the last of an original *s* or *r*. The rules for these changes will be given later.

[1] This pronunciation is indicated by their origin. They are not primitive sounds of the Sanskrit language, but in most cases produced by the concurrence of a dental and *r*, e.g. चन्द्र *chandra* becomes चण्ड *chaṇḍa*, घूर्ण् *ghûrṇ* (originally *ghûr-n*) becomes घुण् *ghuṇ*, पत्त्र *patra* becomes पट्ट *paṭṭa*. The fact that *r* and *l* sometimes appear as substitutes for the lingual, as खोर *khora* and खोल *khola* instead of खोड *khoḍa*, seems to confirm this conjecture; cf. *Bühler*, on the Origin of the Sanskrit Linguals, in the Madras Lit. Soc. Journ. 1864, and *Justi*, in the Journ. Orient und Occident, vol. iii. pp. 379-83, Göttingen, 1865.

[2] Cf. the Hindu transliteration of English words, *e.g.* डिरेक्टर् *ḍirekṭar*, *i.e.* Director; गवर्ण्मेण्ट् *gavarṇmaṇṭ*, i.e. Government.

§ 4. When a vowel or diphthong stands in the beginning of a sentence or hemistich, or occurs after another vowel or diphthong, it retains the shape given in § 1, I. II. When it is preceded by a consonant, it is marked by a different sign, which is placed before or after, above or below the consonant after which it is to be pronounced. The vowel ऋ *ṛi*, however, if preceded by *r*, makes an exception and retains the form given in § 1, I. the sign for *r* being placed above the ऋ *ṛi* (र्ऋ *rṛi*, § 5).

A short *a* which follows a consonant, is left unwritten, being understood to be inherent in it, *e.g.* क *ka*. The forms of the vowels and diphthongs, if preceded by a consonant, are:

ा *â*, ि *i*, ी *î*, ु *u*, ू *û*, ृ *ṛi*, ॄ *ṛî*, ॢ *ḷi*, ॣ *ḷî*, *e.g.*
का *kâ*, कि *ki*, की *kî*, कु *ku*, कू *kû*, कृ *kṛi*, कॄ *kṛî*, कॢ *kḷi*, कॣ *kḷî*.

े *e*, ै *ai*, ो *o*, ौ *au*, *e.g.*
के *ke*, कै *kai*, को *ko*, कौ *kau*.

Some consonants alter their forms if combined with vowels. Thus:

र *ra*	with	ु *u*	becomes	रु *ru*
—	„	ू *û*	„	रू *rû*
ह *ha*	„	ु *u*	„	हु *hu*
—	„	ू *û*	„	हू *hû*
—	„	ृ *ṛi*	„	हृ *hṛi*
श *ça*	„	ु *u*	„	शु *çu*
—	„	ू *û*	„	शू *çû*
—	„	ृ *ṛi*, ॄ *ṛî*	„	शृ *çṛi*, शॄ *çṛî*.

Anusvâra ं and *Anunâsika* ँ when following a vowel are placed above the preceding consonant at the right side of the mark of the vowel, *e.g.* कां *kâṁ*, किं *kiṁ*, कीं *kîṁ*, कुं *kuṁ*, कूं *kûṁ*, कृं *kṛiṁ*, कें *keṁ*, कैं *kaiṁ*, कों *koṁ*, कौं *kauṁ*, काँ *kẫ*, किँ *kĩ*, कीँ *kî̃*, etc. *Anunâsika* may be placed separately after the vowel with a dash under it, *e.g.* काँ *kẫ*.

§ 5. Several consonants coming together without an intermediate vowel are combined, either by placing one consonant under the other and omitting the transverse line of the lower, as in ट्ट *ṭṭa* (ट्ट), or by placing one after the other and dropping the perpendicular line of the first, as in ज्य *jya* (ज य) ज्यि *jyi*, ज्यु *jyu*, etc.

When the र् *r* precedes a consonant or a combination of consonants it is placed on the top of it and assumes the shape of a crescent, *e.g.* र्य *rya*, र्ज्य *rjya*. If these consonants are accompanied by marks of vowels or nasals, ॅ is put at the right side of them, *e.g.* र्ये *rye*, र्यं *ryam̃*, र्ज्यैं *rjyaiṁ*.

When र् *r* is preceded by a consonant, it is written by a transverse line, or two divergent strokes at the foot of the preceding consonant or consonants, *e.g.* ग्र *gra*, ठ्र *ṭhra*. This sign denotes also *r* between two consonants, *e.g.* ध्र्य *dhrya*.

The shape of the single letters, when used in a combination, is sometimes considerably altered. The following is a list of those combinations which occur most frequently in our printed texts.

क्क *k-ka*, क्त *k-ta*, क्त्य *k-t-ya*, क्त्व *k-t-va*, क्न *k-na*, क्म *k-ma*, क्म्य *k-m-ya*, क्य *k-ya*, क्र *k-ra*, क्र्य *k-r-ya*, क्ल *k-la*, क्ल्य *k-l-ya*, क्व *k-va*, क्व्य *k-v-ya*, क्ष *k-sha*, क्ष्म *k-sh-ma*, क्ष्य *k-sh-ya*, क्ष्व *k-sh-va*, क्स *k-sa*;—ख्य *kh-ya*;—ग्ध *g-dha*, ग्न *g-na*, ग्य *g-ya*, ग्र *g-ra*, ग्र्य *g-r-ya*, ग्ल *g-la*, ग्व *g-va*;—घ्न *gh-na*, घ्म *gh-ma*, घ्य *gh-ya*, घ्र *gh-ra*;—ङ्क *ṅ-ka*, ङ्क्त *ṅ-k-ta*, ङ्क्त्य *ṅ-k-t-ya*, ङ्क्त्व *ṅ-k-t-va*, ङ्क्य *ṅ-k-ya*, ङ्क्र *ṅ-k-ra*, ङ्क्ष *ṅ-k-sha*, ङ्क्ष्व *ṅ-k-sh-va*, ङ्ख *ṅ-kha*, ङ्ख्य *ṅ-kh-ya*, ङ्ग *ṅ-ga*, ङ्ग्य *ṅ-g-ya*, ङ्ग्र *ṅ-g-ra*, ङ्घ *ṅ-gha*, ङ्घ्य *ṅ-gh-ya*, ङ्घ्र *ṅ-gh-ra*, ङ्ङ *ṅ-ṅa*, ङ्म *ṅ-ma*, ङ्य *ṅ-ya*, ङ्स *ṅ-sa*.

च्च *ch-cha*, च्छ *ch-chha*, च्छ्र *ch-chh-ra*, च्छ्व *ch-chh-va*, च्ञ *ch-ńa*, च्म *ch-ma*, च्य *ch-ya*;—छ्य *chh-ya*, छ्र *chh-ra*, छ्र्य *chh-r-ya*; ज्ज *j-ja*, ज्ज्व *j-j-va*, ज्झ *j-jha*, ज्ञ *j-ńa*, ज्म *j-ma*, ज्य *j-ya*, ज्र *j-ra*, ज्व *j-va*;—ञ्च *ń-cha*, ञ्च्म *ń-ch-ma*, ञ्च्य *ń-ch-ya*, ञ्छ *ń-chha*, ञ्छ्र *ń-chh-ra*, ञ्ज *ń-ja*, ञ्ज्म *ń-j-ma*, ञ्ज्य *ń-j-ya*.

ट्क *ṭ-ka*, ट्ट *ṭ-ṭa*, ट्ट्य *ṭ-ṭ-ya*, ट्य *ṭ-ya*, ट्स *ṭ-sa*;—ठ्य *ṭh-ya*, ठ्र *ṭh-ra*;—ड्ग *ḍ-ga*, ड्घ *ḍ-gha*, ड्ड *ḍ-ḍa*, ड्य *ḍ-ya*;—ढ्य *ḍh-ya*, ढ्र *ḍh-ra*;—ण्ट *ṇ-ṭa*, ण्ठ *ṇ-ṭha*, ण्ड *ṇ-ḍa*, ण्ड्र *ṇ-ḍ-ra*, ण्ड्र्य *ṇ-ḍ-r-ya*, ण्ढ *ṇ-ḍha*, ण्ण *ṇ-ṇa*, ण्य *ṇ-ya*, ण्व *ṇ-va*.

त्क *t-ka*, त्त *t-ta*, त्त्य *t-t-ya*, त्त्र *t-t-ra*, त्त्व *t-t-va*, त्थ *t-tha*, त्न *t-na*, त्प *t-pa*, त्प्र *t-p-ra*, त्फ *t-pha*, त्म *t-ma*, त्म्य *t-m-ya*, त्य *t-ya*, त्र *t-ra*, त्र्य *t-r-ya*, त्व *t-va*, त्स *t-sa*, त्स्न *t-s-na*, त्स्य *t-s-ya*;—थ्य *th-ya*;—द्ग *d-ga*, द्ग्र *d-g-ra*, द्घ *d-gha*, द्द *d-da*, द्द्ब *d-d-ba*, द्द्ब्र *d-d-b-ra*, द्द्य *d-d-ya*, द्द्र *d-d-ra*, द्द्व *d-d-va*, द्द्व्र *d-d-v-ra*, द्ध *d-dha*, द्ध्य *d-dh-ya*, द्ध्व *d-dh-va*, द्न *d-na*, द्ब *d-ba*, द्ब्र *d-b-ra*, द्भ *d-bha*, द्भ्य *d-bh-ya*, द्म *d-ma*, द्य *d-ya*, द्र *d-ra*, द्र्य *d-r-ya*, द्व *d-va*, द्व्य *d-v-ya*, द्व्र *d-v-ra*;—ध्न *dh-na*, ध्म *dh-ma*, ध्य *dh-ya*, ध्र *dh-ra*, ध्व *dh-va*;—न्घ्य *n-gh-ya*, न्त *n-ta*, न्त्य *n-t-ya*, न्त्र *n-t-ra*, न्थ *n-tha*, न्द *n-da*, न्द्र *n-d-ra*, न्ध *n-dha*, न्ध्य *n-dh-ya*, न्ध्र *n-dh-ra*, न्न *n-na*, न्न्य *n-n-ya*, न्प्र *n-p-ra*, न्फ *n-pha*, न्म *n-ma*, न्य *n-ya*, न्र *n-ra*, न्व *n-va*, न्स *n-sa*.

प्त *p-ta*, प्त्य *p-t-ya*, प्त्र्य *p-t-r-ya*, प्न *p-na*, प्प *p-pa*, प्ब *p-ba*, प्म *p-ma*, प्य *p-ya*, प्र *p-ra*, प्ल *p-la*, प्व *p-va*, प्स *p-sa*;—फ्य *ph-ya*;—ब्घ *b-gha*, ब्ज *b-ja*, ब्द *b-da*, ब्ध *b-dha*, ब्ब *b-ba*, ब्भ *b-bha*, ब्य *b-ya*, ब्र *b-ra*;—भ्य *bh-ya*, भ्र *bh-ra*, भ्व *bh-va*;—म्न *m-na*, म्प *m-pa*, म्प्र *m-p-ra*, म्ब *m-ba*, म्भ *m-bha*, म्भ्र *m-bh-ra*, म्म *m-ma*, म्य *m-ya*, म्र *m-ra*, म्ल *m-la*, म्व *m-va*.

य्य *y-ya*, य्र *y-ra*, य्व *y-va*;—ल्क *l-ka*, ल्ग *l-ga*, ल्प *l-pa*, ल्म *l-ma*, ल्य *l-ya*, ल्ल *l-la*, ल्व *l-va*;—व्य *v-ya*, व्र *v-ra*, व्व *v-va*.

श्च *ç-cha*, श्च्य *ç-ch-ya*, श्न *ç-na*, श्य *ç-ya*, श्र *ç-ra*, श्ल *ç-la*, श्व *ç-va*, श्श *ç-ça*;—ष्क *sh-ka*, ष्क्र *sh-k-ra*, ष्ट *sh-ṭa*, ष्ट्य *sh-ṭ-ya*, ष्ट्र *sh-ṭ-ra*, ष्ट्र्य *sh-ṭ-r-ya*, ष्ट्व *sh-ṭ-va*, ष्ठ *sh-ṭha*, ष्ठ्य *sh-ṭh-ya*, ष्ठ्र्य *sh-ṭh-r-ya*, ष्ण *sh-ṇa*, ष्प *sh-pa*, ष्प्र *sh-p-ra*, ष्म *sh-ma*, ष्य *sh-ya*, ष्व *sh-va*;—स्क *s-ka*, स्ख *s-kha*, स्त *s-ta*, स्त्र *s-t-ra*, स्थ *s-tha*, स्न *s-na*, स्प *s-pa*, स्फ *s-pha*, स्म *s-ma*, स्म्य *s-m-ya*, स्य *s-ya*, स्र *s-ra*, स्व *s-va*, स्स *s-sa*.

ह्ण *h-ṇa*, ह्न *h-na*, ह्म *h-ma*, ह्य *h-ya*, ह्र *h-ra*, ह्ल *h-la*, ह्व *h-va*.

§ 6. When a word standing at the end of a sentence or hemistich terminates in a consonant, the mark ् called *Virâma*, 'pause,' which denotes the absence of a vowel, is placed at the foot of the final, *e.g.* अभवत् *abhavat*. The want of types for the compound consonants compels us to use this mark sometimes in the middle of a word, sentence or hemistich, as in ण्ट्स *ṇ-ṭ-sa*. But this proceeding is at variance with the rules of Sanskrit orthography.

§ 7. The mark ऽ, called *Avagraha*, 'separation,' is inserted in the Vedic works between pure or nasalized vowels to denote the hiatus, *e.g.* यऽउवाच *ya uvâcha*, महाँऽअस्ति *mahẫ asti*; and to separate the parts of a compound, *e.g.* घृतऽस्रुत् *ghṛita-çchut*. In other works it serves to indicate the loss of a short अ *a* after a final ए *e* or ओ *o* (*cf.* § 23).

§ 8. The mark । indicates in prose the end of a sentence or part of a sentence, in poetry of a hemistich; ॥ denotes in prose the end of a longer period, in poetry of a whole verse.

The sign °, which may be placed before or after a word, indicates that one or several words must be repeated from a preceding sentence or part of the same sentence. Thus: स एकया स तिसृभिः पञ्चभ्यो हिं करोति। °सप्तभ्यो हिं करोति॥ *sa ekayâ sa tisṛibhiḥ pañchabhyo him̃ karoti* । °*saptabhyo him̃ karoti* ॥ is written instead of *sa ekayâ sa tisṛibhiḥ pañchabhyo him̃ karoti* । *sa ekayâ sa tisṛibhiḥ saptabhyo him̃ karoti* ।; or सविता शं नो भवतु । वरुणः° । इन्द्रः° ॥ *Savitâ çam̃ no bhavatu* । *Varuṇaḥ*° । *Indraḥ*° ॥ instead of *Savitâ çam̃ no bhavatu* । *Varuṇaḥ çam̃ no bhavatu* । *Indraḥ çam̃ no bhavatu*.

§ 9. The numerals are:—० १ २ ३ ४ ५ ६ ७ ८ ९ १० ११ etc. (*cf.* § 256).

ACCENT.

§ 10. The Sanskrit language has one principal accent only, the acute, called उदात्त *Udâtta*, 'high tone.' It distinguishes besides three different intonations, the *Svarita* स्वरित 'sounding tone,' *Anudâtta*, 'deep tone,' and the *Anudâttatara*, 'more than deep tone.'

1. The *Svarita* is the tone of a syllable which is immediately preceded by an acute, Udâtta, *e.g.* that of *hma* in ब्रह्म *Brahma*, where *bra* has the acute. When a vowel which has the acute is changed into a semivowel, the vowel which follows the semivowel generally retains the Svarita. For instance, when the

termination of the nominative plural अस् *as* is added to देवी *devî*, the final of which has the acute, the Svarita would fall on *a*, *devî́-às*. But as, according to a phonetic law, the *î* must be changed to *y*, which being a semivowel cannot have an accent, the acute, Udâtta, is lost, and the Svarita alone remains, *devyàs*. I shall call the latter kind of Svarita the independent Svarita, as the Udâtta on which it depends has disappeared.

2. The *Anudâtta* is the general intonation of speech, that is to say, of those syllables which are not distinguished by an Udâtta, Svarita, or Anudâttatara. Thus, in अतारिष्म *átârishma*, the first syllable has the Udâtta, consequently the second the Svarita, and the last two are pronounced in the general tone, *i.e.* with the Anudâtta.

3. The *Anudâttatara* falls on the syllable or syllables which precede an Udâtta or independent Svarita. For instance, in देव्यस् *devyàs*, *as* has the independent Svarita and *de* the Anudâttatara; in अग्निः *agníḥ* and आप्नुवानः *âpnuvânáḥ* the final syllables *gniḥ* and *naḥ* have the acute, and consequently the preceding *a* and *âpnuvâ* the Anudâttatara.

There are several systems in use for marking the accents. The most common is that which is adopted in the Rig-Veda. There the Svarita and Anudâttatara alone are indicated, the former by a perpendicular stroke placed above, the latter by a horizontal line placed below, *e.g.* इन्द्रः *indraḥ*, अग्निः *agniḥ*. As the independent Svarita is preceded by an Anudâttatara, and the इ *i* in इन्द्रः is not marked as such, the ॑ on द्रः can denote the dependent Svarita only, and this being preceded always by an acuted syllable, it follows that the इ *i* has the acute. In अग्निः the Anudâttatara under अ *a* and the absence of the mark of the Svarita over ग्निः show that the latter syllable is acuted, whilst in देव्यस् *devyas*, the mark of the Anudâttatara under the first syllable *de*, and that of the Svarita over the second, show that the word has the independent Svarita on its last syllable *vyas*.

In आप्नुवानः the mark of the Anudâttatara under the first three syllables, and the absence of any mark on the last, show that the word is an oxytonon, *âpnuvânâḥ*. In मित्रावरुणौ the Anudâttatara under the first syllable, and the Svarita over the fourth, show that the second and third must have the acute, *mitrắvárunau.* The unmarked syllables which are preceded by a Svarita are Anudâtta, *e.g.* in अतारिष्म *átárishma* the syllables *rishma*; if they had the acute, they would be preceded by an Anudâttatara, and if they were Svarita or Anudâttatara, they would be distinguished by the corresponding marks.

These two marks (_ '), therefore, are sufficient to indicate the accents of all words. An acute monosyllable has no mark at all, कः *káḥ;* if Svarita, it has the mark of this intonation, ह्यः *hyàḥ;* being without accent, it is distinguished by the sign of the Anudâttatara, *e.g.* च *cha.*

As for dissyllabic words: in अग्निः *agníḥ*, the first syllable having the Anudâttatara, the second has the Udâtta; in इन्द्रः *índraḥ*, the second syllable having the Svarita, the first has the Udâtta; in स्वर्वत् *svàrvat*, the first syllable has the independent Svarita, the second the Anudâtta; in देव्यस् *devyàs*, the first syllable has the Anudâttatara, the second the independent Svarita; in समः *samaḥ*, both syllables having the Anudâttatara, the word has no acute accent.

As for trisyllabic words: in आसीनः *âsínáḥ*, the first two syllables having the Anudâttatara, the last has the Udâtta; in अग्निना *agníná*, the first having the Anudâttatara, the last the Svarita, the middle has the Udâtta; in ब्रह्मणा *bráhmaṇá*, the second having the Svarita, the first has the Udâtta; in अपीच्यम् *apíchyàm*, the first two have the Anudâttatara, the third the independent Svarita; in सध्र्यञ्चः *sadhryàñchaḥ*, the second has the independent Svarita, the first the Anudâttatara; in स्वर्वते *svàrvate*, the first has the independent Svarita, the following two have the Anudâtta; in समस्य *samasya*, all the syllables having the Anudâttatara, the word has no acute accent.

As for words of four syllables: in आप्नुवानः *âpnuvânáh*, the first three syllables having the Anudâttatara, the last has the Udâtta; in आप्नुवते *âpnuváte*, the third has the Udâtta, and so on.

The Anudâtta, dependent Svarita, and Anudâttatara of words standing in the middle of a sentence or hemistich are subjected to several changes, which are caused by the influence of preceding or following words.

1. When a word which, when used singly, begins with more than one Anudâttatara, is preceded by an oxytonon, its first Anudâttatara is changed to a Svarita, and the rest, except the last, become Anudâttas. When it is preceded by a Svarita, all the Anudâttataras except the last are changed to Anudâttas, *e.g.* आप्नुवानः *âpnuvânáh* preceded by अग्निम् *agním*, becomes आप्नुवानः *ầpnuvânáh*; preceded by इन्द्रः *índrah*, आप्नुवानः *âpnuvânáh*.

2. A word ending in Anudâttas or in a dependent Svarita (*i.e.* a Svarita preceded by an Udâtta), and followed by a word beginning with a syllable having an acute or independent Svarita, changes its final Anudâtta or Svarita to Anudâttatara. Thus ब्रह्मणा *bráhmàṇâ* (ending with one Anudâtta), or शुचिबन्धुना *çúchìbandhunâ* (ending with three Anudâttas), or ब्रह्म *bráhmà* (ending with a dependent Svarita), before राज्ञा *rấjñâ* (beginning with an acute) or स्वः *svàh* (having an independent Svarita), are modified into ब्रह्मणा *bráhmàṇâ*, शुचिबन्धुना *çúchìbandhunâ*, ब्रह्म *bráhma*, with Anudâttatara on the final.

3 (*a*). When vowels combine by crasis or are changed:—

Udâtta with Udâtta or independent Svarita remains Udâtta, *e.g.* अद्य अत्र *adyá átra* become अद्यात्र *adyấtra*, क्व इत् *kvà ít* क्वेत् *kvét*.—Udâtta with dependent Svarita or Anudâttatara becomes optionally Udâtta or Svarita, *e.g.* अद्य अरुणः *adyá àruṇáh*, become either अद्यारुणः *adyấruṇáh* or अद्यारुणः *adyầruṇáh*, अद्य इदम् *adyá idám* either अद्येदम् *adyédám* or अद्येदम् *adyèdám*. If the Udâtta stands on ए *e* or ओ *o*, after which an original *a* has disappeared (§ 23), the Udâtta is changed to Svarita, *e.g.* ते अवदन् *té àvadan* become तें वदन् *tè vadan*, ते अद्य *té adyá* become तें द्य *tè dyá.*— Udâtta with a preceding Anudâttatara remains Udâtta, *e.g.* अत्र आ *átra ā́* become अत्रा *átrā́.*—If a vowel with Udâtta is changed to a semivowel, the Udâtta is lost, *e.g.* अभिऽअभि *abhí-àbhi* become अभ्यभि *abhyàbhi.*

Independent Svarita with Anudâtta or Anudâttatara remains Svarita, *e.g.* क्वऽइव *kvà-iva* become क्वेव *kvèva*, क्व इदम् *kvà idám* become क्वेदम् *kvèdám.*

Dependent Svarita with Anudâtta remains Svarita, *e.g.* अत्रं अभवत् *átrà abhavat* become अत्राभवत् *átrā̀bhavat*; with Anudâttatara it becomes Anudâttatara, *e.g.* अत्रं इदम् *átrà idám* become अत्रेदम् *átredám.*

Anudâtta with Anudâtta remains Anudâtta, *e.g.* ब्रह्मणा अभवत् *bráhmaṇâ abhavat* become ब्रह्मणाभवत् *bráhmaṇâbhavat*; with Anudâttatara it becomes Anudâttatara, *e.g.* ब्रह्मणा इदम् *bráhmaṇâ idám* become ब्रह्मणेदम् *bráhmaṇedám.* Anudâtta is changed to Svarita when a preceding Svarita by crasis is changed to Udâtta, *e.g.* अद्य अस्ति *adyá àsti* become अद्यास्ति *adyā́stì*; it is changed to Anudâttatara, if a following Anudâttatara is lost by crasis, *e.g.* इन्द्र अद्य *índrà adyá* become इन्द्राद्य *índrā̀dyá.*

(*b*) Two additional marks, the numerals १ and ३, are used to indicate the accent of words forming parts of a sentence or hemistich. When a syllable, which contains a short vowel and has an independent Svarita, or one produced by the loss of the Udâtta (*cf.* 3, *a*), is followed by an Udâtta or by an independent Svarita, or when it stands at the end of a sentence or hemistich, the sign १ is placed after it. When the Svarita vowel is long, the sign ३ is added under the same conditions; at the same time the mark of the Anudâttatara is placed under the accented syllable and the second Svarita is left unmarked, *e.g.* क्व१ तत् *kvà tát*, देव्यो३ मम *devyò máma*, यो३ ह्यो *yò hyò*, पक्वो३ ध्दीन्द्र *pakvò ddhī́ndra*, at the end वीर्य१म् *vī́ryàm.*

§ 11. Exercises in Reading.

I. Without Accents (Hitopadeça II. 4).

अस्त्यर्बुदशिखरनाम्नि पर्वते महाविक्रमो नाम सिंहः।
asty arbudaçikharanâmni parvate mahâvikramo nâma siñhaḥ.
तस्य पर्वतकुहरमधिशयानस्य केशराग्रं प्रत्यहं
tasya parvatakuharam adhiçayânasya keçarâgrañ pratyahañ
कश्चिन्मूषिकश्छिनत्ति। स सिंहः केशराग्रं लूनं
kaç chin mûshikaç chhinatti. sa siñhaḥ keçarâgrañ lûnañ
दृष्ट्वा कुपितस्तं विवरान्तर्गतं मूषिकमलभमानो
dṛishṭvâ kupitas tañ vivarântargatañ mûshikam alabhamâno
चिन्तयत् किमत्र विधेयम् यतः
chintayat: kim atra vidheyam. yataḥ:

क्षुद्रशत्रुर्भवेद्यस्तु विक्रमान्नैव लभ्यते।
kshudraçatrur bhaved yas tu vikramân naiva labhyate ।
तं निहन्तुं पुरस्कार्यः सदृशस्तस्य सैनिकः॥
tañ nihantuñ puraskâryaḥ sadṛiças tasya sainikaḥ ॥

इत्यालोच्य तेन सिंहेन ग्रामं गत्वा दधिकर्णनामा विडालो
ity âlochya tena siñhena grâmañ gatvâ dadhikarṇanâmâ viḍâlo
मांसाद्याहारं दत्त्वा प्रयत्नादानीय स्वकन्दरे धृतः।
mâñsâdyâhârañ dattvâ prayatnâd ânîya svakandare dhṛitaḥ.
ततस्तद्भयान्मूषिको न बहिर्निः सरति। तेनासौ सिंहो
tatas tadbhayân mûshiko na bahir niḥ sarati. tenâsau siñho
क्षतकेशरः सुखं स्वपिति। मूषिकशब्दं यदायदा शृणोति।
kshatakeçaraḥ sukhañ svapiti. mûshikaçabdañ yadâyadâ çṛiṇoti,
तदातदा मांसाहारदानेन तं विडालं सं वर्धयति। अथै-
tadâtadâ mâñsâhâradânena tañ viḍâlañ sañ vardhayati. athai-
कदा स मूषिकः क्षुधा पीडितो बहिश्चरन्मार्जारेण प्राप्तो
kadâ sa mûshikaḥ kshudhâ pîḍito bahiç charan mârjâreṇa prâpto
व्यापादितश्च। अनन्तरं स सिंहो यदा कदा चिदपि तस्य
vyâpâditaç cha. anantarañ sa siñho yadâ kadâ chid api tasya
मूषिकस्य शब्दं न शुश्राव। तदुपयोगाभावाद्विडालस्याहा-
mûshikasya çabdañ na çuçrâva, tadupayogâbhâvâd viḍâlasyâhâ-

रदाने मन्दादरो बभूव। ततो सौ दधिकर्णो प्याहाराभा-
radâne mandâdaro babhûva ; tato sau dadhikarṇo py âhârâbhâ-

वाद्दुर्बलो भवत् अतो हं ब्रवीमि।
vâd durbalo bhavat. ato ham̃ bravîmi :

निरपेक्षो न कर्तव्यो भृत्यैः स्वामी कदा चन।
nirapeksho na kartavyo bhṛityaiḥ svâmî kadâ chana ।

निरपेक्षं प्रभुं कृत्वा भृत्यः स्याद्दधिकर्णवत्॥
nirapeksham̃ prabhum̃ kṛitvâ bhṛityaḥ syâd dadhikarṇavat ॥

II. With Accents (Rig-Veda I. 62).

प्र मन्महे शवसानाय शूषमाङ्गूषं गिर्वणसे अङ्गिरस्वत्।
prá manmahe çavasânấya çûshám âṅgûshám̃ gírvaṇase aṅgirasvát

सुवृक्तिभिः स्तुवत ऋग्मियायार्चामार्कं नरे विश्रुताय॥ १॥
suvṛiktíbhiḥ stuvatá ṛigmiyấyấrchâmárkám̃ náre viçrutâya. 1.

प्र वो महे महि नमो भरध्वमाङ्गूष्यं शवसानाय साम।
prá vo mahé máhi námo bharadhvam âṅgûshyàm̃ çavasânấya sấma

येना नः पूर्वे पितरः पदज्ञा अर्चन्तो अङ्गिरसो गा अविन्दन्॥ २॥
yénâ naḥ pū́rve pitáraḥ padajñấ árchanto áṅgiraso gấ ávindan. 2.

इन्द्रस्याङ्गिरसां चेष्टौ विदत्सरमा तनयाय धासिम्।
índrasyấṅgirasâm̃ cheshṭaú vidát sarámâ tánayâya dhâsím

बृहस्पतिर्भिनदद्रिं विदद्गाः समुस्रियाभिर्वावशन्त नरः॥ ३॥
bṛiháspátir bhinád ádrim̃ vidád gấḥ sám usríyâbhir vâvaçanta náraḥ. 3.

स सुष्टुभा स स्तुभा सप्त विप्रैः स्वरेणाद्रिं स्वर्यो३ नवग्वैः।
sá sushṭúbhâ sá stubhấ saptá vípraiḥ svaréṇấdrim̃ svaryò návagvaiḥ

सरण्युभिः फलिगमिन्द्र शक्र वलं रवेण दरयो दशग्वैः॥ ४॥
saraṇyúbhiḥ phaligám indra çakra valám̃ ráveṇa darayo dáçagvaiḥ. 4.

गृणानो अङ्गिरोभिर्दस्म वि वरुषसा सूर्येण गोभिरन्धः
gṛiṇânó áṅgirobhir dasma ví var ushásâ sū́ryeṇa góbhir ándhaḥ

वि भूम्या अप्रथय इन्द्र सानु दिवो रज उपरमस्तभायः॥ ५॥
ví bhū́myâ aprathaya indra sấnu divó rája úparam astabhâyaḥ. 5.

तदु प्रयंचतममस्य कर्म दस्मस्य चारुतममस्ति दंसः ।
tád u práyakshatamam asya kárma dasmásya chárutamam asti dáṁsaḥ
उपह्वरे यदुपरा अपिन्वन्मध्वर्णसो नद्यश्चतस्रः ॥ ६ ॥
upahvaré yád úparâ ápinvan mádhvarṇaso nadyàç chátasraḥ. 6.

CHAPTER II.—PHONETIC RULES.

SECTION I.—GENERAL PHONETIC RULES.

§ 12. The letters are divided into two classes, soft letters or sonants, and hard letters or surds. To the former belong the vowels and diphthongs, the semivowels (§ 1, IV. 6), the last three letters of the first five classes (§ 1, IV.), and the aspirate (§ 1, IV. 8); to the latter, the first two letters of the first five classes and the sibilants (§ 1, IV. 7), viz.:

hard or surd letters: क ख च छ ट ठ त थ प फ and श ष स
k kh ch chh ṭ ṭh t th p ph ç sh s

soft or sonant: ग घ ज झ ड ढ द ध ब भ
g gh j jh ḍ ḍh d dh b bh
and ङ ञ ण न म य र ल व ह
ṅ ń ṇ n m y r l v h

with all the vowels and diphthongs.

The first ten of each class correspond with each other, viz. क *k* with ग *g*, and so on up to फ *ph* with भ *bh*.

§ 13. A Sanskrit word may end in any vowel (except ॠ *ṛí*, ऌ *ḷi*, ॡ *ḷí*), a diphthong, the Visarga ः, the Anusvara ं, Anunâsika ँ, the consonants ङ् *ṅ*, ण् *ṇ*, न् *n*, म् *m*, क् *k*, ट् *ṭ*, त् *t*, प् *p*, and the compound consonants र्क् *rk*, र्ट् *rṭ*, र्त् *rt*, र्प् *rp*, but in the latter only when both are radical, or changed from radical ones.

§ 14. छ *chh* between two vowels becomes च्छ *chchh;* for instance, when the termination अति *ati* is added to the base गछ् *gachh,* it becomes गच्छति *gachchh-ati.*

§ 15. When two र् *r* meet together, one is rejected and a preceding short vowel made long, *e.g.* the crude form of the frequentative अर्ऋ *arṛi* together with the termination अति *ati,* which ought to be अर्रति *arrati* according to the general rule in § 91, becomes आरति *ârati;* दुर् *dur* compounded with रोहण *rohaṇa* makes दूरोहण *dûrohaṇa;* पुनर् *punar* followed by रामः *râmaḥ* becomes पुना रामः *punâ râmaḥ.*

§ 16. When न् *n,* followed by a vowel, diphthong, or न् *n,* म् *m,* य् *y,* or व् *v,* is preceded by a ऋ *ṛi,* ॠ *ṛî,* र् *r,* or ष् *sh,* either immediately or separated by intermediate vowels or diphthongs, guttural or labial consonants, म् *m,* य् *y,* व् *v,* or ह् *h,* it is changed to the lingual ण् *ṇ, e.g.* पूर्+न *pûr+na* becomes पूर्ण *pûrṇa;* कर्+अन *kar+ana,* करण *karaṇa;* कार्य+मान *kârya+mâna,* कार्यमाण *kâryamâṇa;* गामिनी *gâminî* combined with preceding वृष *vṛisha* becomes वृषगामिणी *vṛishagâmiṇî;* नीयते *nîyate* preceded by प्र *pra* becomes प्र णीयते *pra ṇîyate.*

Under the same condition a double न् *n* is changed to ण् *ṇṇ, e.g.* विषण्ण *vishaṇṇa,* where ण्ण *ṇṇ* is substituted for original न्न *nn.*

§ 17. If a dental sibilant स् *s,* followed by a vowel or diphthong, or त् *t,* थ् *th,* न् *n,* म् *m,* or य् *y,* is preceded by any vowel (except अ *a* or आ *â*), or by a diphthong, or क् *k,* र् *r,* or ल् *l,* it is changed to ष् *sh,* though an Anusvâra ं, Anunâsika ँ, or Visarga ः may intervene, and the following त् *t,* थ् *th,* and न् *n* become ट् *ṭ,* ठ् *ṭh,* and ण् *ṇ, e.g.*

अग्नि *agni* compounded with स्थ *stha* become अग्निष्ठ *agnishṭha.*

नि स्थास्यामि *ni sthâsyâmi*	„	नि ष्ठास्यामि *ni shṭhâsyâmi.*
हविस्+आ *havis+â*	„	हविषा *havishâ.*
वक्+स्यति *vak+syati*	„	वक्ष्यति *vakshyati.*
बिभर्+सि *bibhar+si*	„	बिभर्षि *bibharshi.*
सुवल्+सु *suval+su*	„	सुवल्षु *suvalshu.*

Observ. to §§ 16, 17. These two rules apply to nearly all the simple words, but in compounds and in sentences and hemistichs they suffer many restrictions (*cf.* my Vollständige Grammatik, § 22-51).

§ 18. The vowels इ *i* and उ *u* preceding a radical र् *r* or व् *v* are made long if another consonant follows, *e.g.*

गुर्+न *gur+na* becomes गूर्ण *gûrṇa* (cf. § 16).
दिव्+यामि *div+yâmi* „ दीव्यामि *dîvyâmi*.

The same rule applies to verbs, which in our Dictionaries or collections of roots (Dhâtupâṭhas) have a short *i* or *u* before *r*. These, if followed by a consonant, lengthen their vowels, *e.g.* कुर्द्+अति *kurd+ati* becomes कूर्दति *kûrdati*.

SECTION II.—CHANGES OF LETTERS AT THE END AND AT THE BEGINNING OF WORDS IN A SENTENCE OR HEMISTICH.

§ 19. The following rules, from §§ 20 to 36, apply not only to separate words, but also to the component parts of compounds (§ 196), and those from § 25 to the bases and affixes in secondary derivatives (*cf.* § 193), if these affixes begin with any consonant except य् *y*.

§ 20. Homogeneous vowels concurring at the end and the beginning either of separate words or parts of a compound, combine into one long homogeneous vowel, whether they be both short or both long, or one be long and the other short; *a+a* makes *â*; *i+i* makes *î*; *u+u* makes *û*; *ṛi+ṛi* makes *ṛî*, *e.g.*:

अत्र । अस्ति *atra asti*	become	अत्रास्ति *atrâsti*.
गता । अस्ति *gatâ asti*	„	गतास्ति *gatâsti*.
अत्र । आसीत् *atra âsît*	„	अत्रासीत् *atrâsît*.
गता । आसीत् *gatâ âsit*	„	गतासीत् *gatâsît*.
इति । इदम् *iti idam*	„	इतीदम् *itîdam*.
इति । ईहा *iti îha*	„	इतीहा *itîha*.
स्वादु । उत *svâdu uta*	„	स्वादूत *svâdûta*.
पितृऋति *pitṛi-ṛiti* (a compound)	„	पितॄति *pitṛîti*.

§ 21. When a word, or first part of a compound, ends in अ *a* or आ *â*, and the following begins—1. with इ *i* or ई *î*, the two vowels become ए *e*, *e.g.* इह । इदम् *iha idam* and likewise ईहा । इदम् *îhâ idam* become इहेदम् *ihedam*, ईहेदम् *îhedam*,—2. with उ *u* or ऊ *û* they become ओ *o*, *e.g.* इह । उत *iha uta* become इहोत *ihota*, त्वाऽऊत *tvâ-ûta* (a compound) becomes त्वोत *tvota*,—3. with ऋ *ṛi* (ॠ *ṛî*) they become अर् *ar*, *e.g.* इह । ऋतुः *iha ṛituḥ* become इहर्तुः *ihartuḥ*, गता । ऋतुः *gatâ ṛituḥ* become गतर्तुः *gatartuḥ*,—4. (with ऌ *ḷi* or ॡ *ḷî* they become अल् *al*),—5. with ए *e* or ऐ *ai* they become ऐ *ai*, *e.g.* इह । एव *iha eva* become इहैव *ihaiva*, इह । ऐन्द्रः *iha aindraḥ* become इहैन्द्रः *ihaîndraḥ*,—6. with ओ *o* or औ *au* they become औ *au*, *e.g.* इह । ओजः *iha ojaḥ* become इहौजः *ihaujaḥ*, गता । औरसा *gatâ aurasâ* become गतौरसा *gataurasâ*.

Exceptions :—1. A final अ *a* and आ *â* are rejected, if the following word begins with ए *e* or ओ *o* which has been produced by a combination of a radical *i* or *u* with the preposition आ *â* (§ 189), *e.g.* अद्य । ओढः *adya oḍhaḥ* (compounded from *â* and *ûḍhaḥ*) become अद्योढः *adyoḍhaḥ*.

2. The final अ *a* or आ *â* of a preposition (1) combines with the beginning ऋ *ṛi* of a verb to आर् *âr*, *e.g.* प्र । ऋच्छति *pra ṛichchhati* make प्रार्च्छति *prârchchhati*; (2) is rejected before the beginning ए *e* or ओ *o* of a verb (except forms of इ *i*, 'to go,' beginning with ए *e*, and एध् *edh*, 'to increase'); for instance, प्र । एजते *pra ejate* become प्रेजते *prejate*, but प्र । एमि *pra emi* become प्रैमि *praimi*.

For other exceptions to these exceptions, *cf.* my Vollständige Grammatik, § 86, Exc. 7, 8, 9.

§ 22. When a word, or first part of a compound, ends in इ *i* or ई *î*, उ *u* or ऊ *û*, ऋ *ṛi* (or ॠ *ṛî*, ऌ *ḷi* or ॡ *ḷî*), and the following begins with a heterogeneous vowel or a diphthong, इ *i* and ई *î* are changed to य् *y*, उ *u* and ऊ *û* to व् *v*, ऋ *ṛi* (ॠ *ṛî*) to र् *r*, (ऌ *ḷi* and ॡ *ḷî* to ल् *l*). Thus :

इति । अत्र *iti atra*	make	इत्यत्र *ity atra.*
मही । अत्र *mahí atra*	„	मह्यत्र *mahy atra.*
इति । उत *iti uta*	„	इत्युत *ity uta.*
इति । ऋतम् *iti ṛitam*	„	इत्यृतम् *ity ṛitam.*
इति । एव *iti eva*	„	इत्येव *ity eva.*
पितृऽअर्थ *pitṛi-artha* (a compound)	„	पित्रर्थ *pitrartha.*

§ 23. When a word ending in ए *e* or ओ *o* is followed by a word beginning with अ *a*, the latter vowel is rejected, and this elision is sometimes indicated by ऽ (called *Avagraha*, 'separation,' *cf.* § 7), *e.g.*:

गजो अभवत् *gajo abhavat* make गजो भवत्, or गजो ऽभवत् *gajo bhavat.*

Followed by any other vowel or diphthong, a final ए *e* may be changed to अय् *ay*, and ओ *o* to अव् *av*, or both may become अ *a*. For instance:

वने । आस्ते *vane âste* become either वनयास्ते *vanay âste*, or वन आस्ते *vana âste.*

विष्णो आस्स्व *vishṇo âssva* either विष्णवास्स्व *vishṇav âssva*, or विष्ण आस्स्व *vishṇa âssva.*

A final अ *a*, thus deduced from ए *e* or ओ *o*, does not undergo the modifications prescribed in § 20, 21; thus, वन आस्ते *vana âste* cannot become वनास्ते *vanâste.*

§ 24. Concurring with a vowel or diphthong, a final ऐ *ai* may be changed to आय् *ây*, and a final औ *au* to आव् *âv*, or both become आ *â*; *e.g.* तस्मै । अवेदयत् *tasmai avedayat* make either तस्मायवेदयत् *tasmây avedayat* or तस्मा अवेदयत् *tasmâ avedayat*, तौ । उभौ *tau ubhau* either तावुभौ *tâv ubhau* or ता उभौ *tâ ubhau.*

The final आ *â* being thus the substitute of ऐ *ai* or औ *au*, does not undergo the modifications taught in §§ 20, 21.

Exceptions:—1. Final ई *í*, ऊ *ú*, and ए *e*, when terminations of the dual of a noun, pronoun or verb, and अमी *amí*, the nom. plur. masc. of the pronoun अदस् *adas*, are left unchanged before the vowels and diphthongs, nor does such an ए *e* cause the elision of a following अ *a*. Thus, मती इह *matí iha*, धेनू अत्र *dhenû atra*, पचेते अत्र *pachete atra* (cf. §§ 20, 22, 23, 80, and 229).

2. Some monosyllabic particles remain unchanged, *e.g.* इ इन्द्र *i indra*, 'O Indra.'

3. For other anomalies, particularly in the Vedas, *cf.* my Vollständige Grammatik, § 86, Exc. and § 92.

§ 25. A final Visarga (:), when followed by क् *k*, ख् *kh*, प् *p*, फ् *ph*, is left unchanged, *e.g.* गजः क्रामति *gajaḥ krâmati.*

Exc.—Sometimes, especially in the Vedic language, the final Visarga of a preposition or first part of a compound, if preceded by अ *a*, is changed to स् *s*, and if preceded by इ *i* or उ *u*, to ष् *sh*, *e.g.* निः । क्रामति *niḥ krâmati* (cf. § 188) become निष्क्रामति *nish krâmati*.

§ 26. Visarga (:) followed by श् *ç*, ष् *sh*, or स् *s*, may either be left unchanged or may be assimilated to the following sibilant, *e.g.* गजः । शेते *gajaḥ çete* make either गजः शेते *gajaḥ çete* or गजश्शेते *gajaç çete*; गजाः । षट् *gajâḥ shaṭ* either गजाः षट् *gajâḥ shaṭ* or गजाष्षट् *gajâsh shaṭ*; गजाः सप्त *gajâḥ sapta* or गजास्सप्त *gajâs sapta.*

§ 27. Visarga (:) followed by च् *ch* or छ् *chh*, becomes श् *ç*, *e.g.* गजः । चरति *gajaḥ charati* = गजश्चरति *gajaç charati.* If it precedes ट् *ṭ* or ठ् *ṭh* it is changed to ष् *sh*, *e.g.* गजः । टिट्टिभः *gajaḥ ṭiṭṭibhaḥ* = गजष्टिट्टिभः *gajash ṭiṭṭibhaḥ*; preceding त् *t* or थ् *th* it is changed to स् *s*, *e.g.* गजः । तरति *gajaḥ tarati* = गजस्तरति *gajas tarati.*

§ 28. Before a soft or sonant letter (*cf.* § 12) Visarga (:) is changed to र् *r*. Thus:

ज्योतिः *jyotiḥ*			
	अस्ति *asti*	make	ज्योतिरस्ति *jyotir asti.*
	गच्छति *gachchhati*	,,	ज्योतिर्गच्छति *jyotir gachchhati.*
	महत् *mahat*	,,	ज्योतिर्महत् *jyotir mahat.*

Exc.—1. If Visarga, being the substitute of an स् *s* (§ 3) and preceded by a short अ *a*, be followed by an initial अ *a* or a sonant consonant (§ 12), it forms, together with the penultimate, the diphthong ओ *o*. An initial अ *a* which follows an ओ *o* so produced is dropped, according to § 23, *e.g.* गजः । अभवत् *gajaḥ* (with

Visarga (:) *ḥ* for original स् *s*) *abhavat* become गजो भवत् (or ऽभवत्, § 7) *gajo bhavat*, गजः । महान् *gajaḥ mahân* become गजो महान् *gajo mahân*. If the following word begins with any other vowel than अ *a*, or with a diphthong, such a Visarga is rejected and the concurring vowels do not undergo any further alteration, *e.g.* गजः । आसीत् *gajaḥ âsît* become गज आसीत् *gaja âsît*.

2. The Visarga (:) for original स् *s*, preceded by आ *â*, is dropped before sonant letters (§ 12). Here also (*cf.* Exc. 1) concurring vowels are not changed, *e.g.* गजाः । अभवन् *gajâḥ abhavan* become गजा अभवन् *gajâ abhavan*, गजाः । भवन्ति *gajâḥ bhavanti* become गजा भवन्ति *gajâ bhavanti*.

Obs. On account of the foregoing exceptions, it being necessary to know whether Visarga be the substitute of an स् *s* or र् *r*, the forms which ought to be written with a final Visarga (:) will be given in this grammar (against § 13) in their original shape terminating in र् *r* or स् *s*, *e.g.* शिवस् *çivas* (Nominative Singular), अबिभर् *abibhar* (2[d] and 3[d] person of the Imperfect Parasmaipada), instead of शिवः *çivaḥ*, अबिभः *abibhaḥ*.

§ 29. Final ङ् *ṅ*, ण् *ṇ*, and न् *n*, if preceded by a short vowel and followed by any initial vowel or diphthong, are doubled, *e.g.* प्रत्यङ् । आस्ते *pratyaṅ âste* become प्रत्यङ्ङास्ते *pratyaṅṅ âste*, अभवन् । अत्र *abhavan atra* become अभवन्नत्र *abhavann atra*.

§ 30. A final dental nasal न् *n* followed by ज् *j*, झ् *jh*, ञ् *ñ*, or श् *ç*, becomes ञ् *ñ*, *e.g.* प्रशान् । जायते *praçân jâyate* make प्रशाञ्जायते *praçâñ jâyate*; followed by ड् *ḍ*, ढ् *ḍh*, or ण् *ṇ*, it becomes ण् *ṇ*, *e.g.* तान् । डामरान् *tân ḍâmarân* make ताण्डामरान् *tâṇ ḍâmarân*; followed by ल् *l*, it becomes ल्ँ, of which the ̃ may indicate a slight nasalization, *e.g.* तान् । लभते *tân labhate* become ताल्ँलभते *tâl̃ labhate*.

§ 31. When a final न् *n* is followed by the surd consonants (§ 12) of the 2[d], 3[d], or 4th class (§ 1, IV.), viz. च् *ch*, छ् *chh*, ट् *ṭ*, ठ् *ṭh*, त् *t*, or थ् *th*, the sibilant of the class to which the following letter belongs, viz. श् *ç*, ष् *sh*, स् *s* (§ 1, Obs. 2), must be inserted after it, and the न् *n* is changed to Anusvâra ं or Anunâsika ँ; *e.g.* अभवन् । च *abhavan cha* make अभवंश्च *abhavaṁç cha*, तान् । ठक्कुरान् *tân ṭhakkurân*, तांष्ठक्कुरान् *tâṁsh ṭhakkurân*, तान् । तत्र *tân tatra*, तांस्तत्र *tâṁs tatra*. When followed by स् *s*, a त् *t* may be inserted, *e.g.* तान् सः *tân saḥ* may become तान्त्सः *tânt saḥ*, or remain unchanged.

§ 32.—1. A final म् *m* is changed to Anusvâra ं or Anunâsika ँ, when followed by र् *r*, the sibilants श् *ç*, ष् *sh*, स् *s*, or the aspirate ह् *h*, *e.g.* तम् । रथम् *tam ratham* make तं रथम् *taṁ ratham*, गजम् । हन्ति *gajam hanti*, गजं हन्ति *gajaṁ hanti*.

2. Before य् *y*, ल् *l*, and व् *v*, it may either become Anusvâra, or may be assimilated to the following letter, retaining perhaps at the same time a slight nasalization, marked by the sign of the Anunâsika, *e.g.* तम् । यवम् *tam yavam* make either तं यवम् *taṁ yavam* or तय्ँयवम् *tayঁ yavam*, तम् । लभमानम् *tam labhamânam* either तं ल॰ *taṁ labh.* or तल्ँलभ॰ *talঁ labhamânam*.

3. Preceding any other consonant, final म् *m* may either be changed to Anusvâra ं, or to the nasal of that class to which the following consonant belongs, *e.g.* तम् । गणम् *tam gaṇam* make either तं गणम् *taṁ gaṇam* or तङ्गणम् *taṅ gaṇam*, तम् । डामरम् *tam ḍâmaram* either तं डा॰ *taṁ ḍâ॰* or तण्डा॰ *taṇ ḍâ॰*.

Obs. When the following word begins with the conjunct consonants ह्न *hn*, ह्म *hm*, ह्य *hy*, ह्ल *hl*, or ह्व *hv*, a preceding final म् *m* may undergo the changes prescribed in § 32, 1, or may be treated as if it preceded the second member of the combination, *e.g.* तम् । ह्यः *tam hyaḥ* may become, according to § 32, 1, तं ह्यः *taṁ hyaḥ*, or, according to § 32, 2, तय्ँह्यः *tayঁ hyaḥ*.

§ 33. A final क् *k*, ट् *ṭ*, त् *t*, or प् *p*, followed by a sonant letter (§ 12), is changed to the corresponding sonant, viz. ग् *g*, ड् *ḍ*, द् *d*, and ब् *b* (§ 12), *e.g.* वाक् । अभूत् *vâk abhût* become वागभूत् *vâg abhût*, षट् । गच्छन्ति *shaṭ gachchhanti* become षड्गच्छन्ति *shaḍ gachchhanti*. But if the following sonant letter be a nasal, the final क् *k*, ट् *ṭ*, त् *t*, and प् *p* may be changed also to the nasals of their own classes (§ 1, IV.), viz. ङ् *ṅ*, ण् *ṇ*, न् *n*, म् *m*; thus, वाक् । मम *vâk mama* may become either वाग्मम *vâg mama* or वाङ्मम *vâṅ mama*, तत् । न *tat na* either तद्न *tad na* or तन्न *tan na*. The latter change is generally preferred, and before secondary suffixes it is obligatory; *e.g.* वाक्+मय *vâk+maya* only वाङ्मय *vâṅmaya*.

§ 34.—1. A final त् *t* before च् *ch*, छ् *chh*, or श् *ç* is changed to च् *ch*, *e.g.* तत् । च *tat cha* become तच्च *tach cha*.

2. Before ज् *j* or झ् *jh* it is changed to ज् *j*, *e.g.* तत् । जायते *tat jâyate* become तज्जायते *taj jâyate*.

3. Before ट् *ṭ* or ठ् *ṭh* it becomes ट् *ṭ*, *e.g.* तत् । टङ्कम् *tat taṅkam* make तट्टङ्कम् *taṭ ṭaṅkam*.

4. Before *ḍ* ड् or ढ् *ḍh* it becomes ड् *ḍ*, *e.g.* तस्मात् । डामरात् *tasmât ḍâm°* make तस्माड्डा° *tasmâḍ ḍâ°*.

5. Before the nasal of the palatal class, ञ् *ñ*, it is either changed to the unaspirated sonant or the nasal of this class, viz. to ज् *j* or ञ् *ñ*, and likewise before the nasal of the lingual class either to ड् *ḍ* or to ण् *ṇ*, *e.g.* तस्मात् । ण्यात् *tasmât ṇyât* either become तस्माड् ण्यात् *tasmâḍ ṇyât* or तस्माण्ण्यात् *tasmâṇ ṇyât*.

6. Before ल् *l* it becomes ल् *l*, *e.g.* तत् । लभते *tat labhate* become तल्लभते *tal labhate*.

§ 35. An initial ह् *h* which follows a word or part of a compound, the final of which, according to § 33, has been changed to ग् *g*, ड् *ḍ*, द् *d*, or ब् *b*, is commonly changed to the aspirated sonant of the class to which the preceding consonant belongs: after ग् *g* to घ् *gh*, after ड् *ḍ* to ढ् *ḍh*, after द् *d* to ध् *dh*, after ब् *b* to भ् *bh*, *e.g.* वाक् । ह *vâk ha* may become, according to § 33, वाग्ह *vâg ha*, but commonly it is changed to वाग्घ *vâg gha*, वेदवित् । हन्ति *vedavit hanti* may become वेदविद् हन्ति *vedavid hanti* or वेदविद्धन्ति *vedavid dhanti*.

§ 36. An initial श् *ç* is optionally changed to छ् *chh* after क् *k*, च् *ch* (cf. § 34, 1), ञ् *ñ* (cf. § 30), ट् *ṭ*, or प् *p*. This rule is nearly absolute in the case of a preceding च् *ch* or ञ् *ñ*, *e.g.* तत् । शत्रुः *tat çatruḥ*, where the final त् *t* must be changed to च् *ch* (§ 34, 1), may become तच्शत्रुः *tach çatruḥ*, or, according to the common use, तच्छत्रुः *tach chhatruḥ*.

At the same time a च् *ch* may be inserted after ञ् *ń*. Thus तान् । शत्रून् *tân çatrûn*, where, according to § 30, the final न् *n* ought to be changed to ञ् *ń*, may become ताञ्शत्रून् *tâń çatrûn* or, with छ् *chh* instead of श् *ç*, ताञ्छत्रून् *tâń chhatrûn*, or with inserted च् *ch* either ताञ्च्शत्रून् *tâńch çatrûn* or ताञ्च्छत्रून् *tâńch chhatrûn*; the last change is the usual one.

PART THE SECOND.

FORMATION OF WORDS.

---

§ 37. Under this head are comprised the rules concerning the crude forms and those concerning the inflexion. We shall begin with the verb.

CHAPTER I.—THE VERB.

SECTION I.—CRUDE FORMS OF THE VERB.

§ 38. The crude forms of the verbs are either primitive or derivative. The primitive verbs may be learned from the collections of roots, the so-called *Dhâtupâṭhas* (*dhâtu* meaning 'fundamental form, element'), or from our dictionaries. All of them are given in the Glossary to my 'Sanskrit Chresthomathie.' I shall quote them under the forms which are assigned to them by the Hindu Grammarians.[1] The same practice has been followed in Wilson's and Goldstücker's Dictionaries and in my Glossary. In the Sanskrit Lexicon of Böhtlingk and Roth, which is published at St. Petersburgh, the roots containing ऋ *ṛi* or terminating in ॠ *ṛî* are spelt with अर् *ar*, those with a medial ॠ *ṛî* with ईर् *îr*, those terminating in ए *e*, ऐ *ai*, ओ *o*, with आ *â* instead of these diphthongs, and the only one which contains ऌ *ḷi* with अल् *al*.

[1] With some slight exceptions, adopted by almost all European grammarians; *e.g.* I do not use, like the Hindu grammarians, ण् *ṇ* and ष् *sh* for original न् *n* and स् *s* at the beginning of a verb: I write नम् *nam*, not णम् *ṇam*; सु *su*, not षु *shu*.

The derivative verbs are—1. the frequentative or intensive; 2. the desiderative; 3. the causal; 4. the verbs of the tenth conjugational class; 5. the denominatives. The formation of these will be taught in the following paragraphs.

1. Frequentative or Intensive.

§ 39. The Frequentative or Intensive is generally used in order to signify the repetition or intensity of the action or condition denoted by the verb from which it is derived.

§ 40. With few exceptions, the frequentative is formed only from primitive verbs, which consist of a single syllable and begin with a consonant (and do not belong to the tenth conjugational class, *cf.* §§ 38 and 61).

§ 41. There are two kinds of frequentatives. The one is formed by reduplication, the other by reduplication and the affix य *ya*; for instance, from गम् *gam*, 'to go,' by reduplication जंगम् *jaṁ-gam*, and by reduplication and affix जंगम्य *jaṁ-gam-ya*.

General rules of reduplication.

§ 42. Before proceeding to the details of the formation of the frequentatives, I shall give some general rules which apply to all reduplicated forms, viz. the frequentative, the desiderative, the third conjugational class, the Perfect, and the third Aorist.

§ 43. If primitive verbs undergo any changes in the form which is to be reduplicated, the modified form is reduplicated instead of the original. Thus तॄ *tṛí* in the second frequentative being changed to तीर् *tír*, on account of the affix य *ya* being added (§ 50, 3), the modified form तीर् *tír* is reduplicated instead of तॄ *tṛí*.

§ 44. The reduplication is effected by doubling the initial consonant together with the first vowel, *e.g.* तुद् *tud* becomes, by doubling तु *tu*, तुतुद् *tutud*.

§ 45. This rule, however, as far as it affects consonants, is modified in the following cases:—

1. The verb beginning with an aspirated consonant, the corresponding unaspirated (§ 1, IV.) is substituted for it in the reduplication, *e.g.* च् *ch* for छ् *chh*, ज् *j* for झ् *jh*, त् *t* for थ् *th*, द् *d* for ध् *dh*, प् *p* for फ् *ph*, ब् *b* for भ् *bh*. Thus भिद् *bhid*, 'to split,' by reduplication becomes बिभिद् *bibhid*.

2. A guttural is represented by the corresponding unaspirated palatal, viz. क् *k* and ख् *kh* by च् *ch*, ग् *g*, घ् *gh*, and ह् *h* by ज् *j*, as कम् *kam*, 'to love,' red. चकम् *chakam*.

3. If a verb begins with a compound consonant, in compliance with § 44, the first consonant only is reduplicated, *e.g.* श्रु *çru*, 'to hear,' शुश्रु *çuçru*; क्रम् *kram*, 'to go,' चक्रम् *chakram*. But if the first be a sibilant (श् *ç*, ष् *sh*, or स् *s*) and the second a surd consonant (§ 12), the second only is repeated, *e.g.* स्तन् *stan*, 'to thunder,' तस्तन् *tastan*; स्फुर् *sphur*, 'to throb,' पुस्फुर् *pusphur*; स्खल् *skhal*, 'to slip,' चस्खल् *chaskhal*.

Obs.—The verbs हन् *han*, 'to kill,' and हि *hi*, 'to go,' when reduplicated, change their ह् *h* to घ् *gh*, as जघन् *jaghan*, जिघि *jighi*.

§ 46. A long vowel is made short in the reduplicated syllable, *e.g.* भी *bhí*, 'to fear,' बिभी *bibhí*. A diphthong is represented by its last element (§ 1, II. Obs.), ए *e* and ऐ *ai* by इ *i*, ओ *o* and औ *au* by उ *u*, *e.g.* रेक् *rek*, 'to suspect,' रिरेक् *rirek*; लोक् *lok*, 'to see,' लुलोक् *lulok*.

Obs.—द्युत् *dyut*, 'to shine,' has दि *di* as syllable of the reduplication, दिद्युत् *didyut*.

§ 47. A reduplicated form cannot be reduplicated a second time. Thus, if a desiderative, which ought to be formed by reduplication (§ 53), is to be derived from a frequentative which is formed also by reduplication, the desiderative is not reduplicated again, *e.g.* लोलूय *lolúya* (frequentative of लू *lú*, 'to cut'), makes in the desiderative लोलूयिष *lolúyisha*.

Special rules for the Reduplication of the Frequentative.

§ 48. The reduplication of the frequentative differs from the preceding rules in the following points :—

1. अ *a* is inserted before the vowel of the reduplicated syllable. This अ *a* with अ *a* combines to आ *á*, with इ *i* to ए *e*, with उ *u* to ओ *o* (cf. § 1, II. Obs.), with ऋ *ṛi* to अर् *ar*, with ऌ *ḷi* to अल् *al*. Thus, बिभी *bibhí* (§ 46) becomes in the first frequentative बेभी *bebhí*, in the second बेभीय *bebhíya* (§ 41), रिरेक् *rirek* (§ 46) in the frequentatives रेरेक् *rerek*, रेरेक्य *rerekya*; लुलोक् *lulok* (§ 46), लोलोक् *lolok*, लोलोक्य *lolokya*; दिद्युत् *didyut* (§ 46, Obs.), देद्युत् *dedyut*, देद्युत्य *dedyutya*.

2. In the first frequentative an इ *i* or ई *í* may be optionally added to a reduplicate अर् *ar* or अल् *al*. In the second frequentative ई *í* must be added, *e.g.* दृश् *dṛiç*, 'to see,' in the first frequentative may become दर्दृश् *dardṛiç* (cf. 1) or दरिदृश् *dari-dṛiç* or दरीदृश् *darí-dṛiç*, but in the second it must become दरीदृश्य *darí-dṛiçya*; क्लृप् *kḷip*, 'to be able,' in the first frequentative चल्क्लृप् *chalkḷip*, चलिक्लृप् *chali-kḷip* or चलीक्लृप् *chalí-kḷip*, in the second चलीक्लृप्य *chalí-kḷipya*.

3. ॠ *ṛí* is represented by आ *á* (even where इर् *ir* appears in its place), *e.g.* तॄ *tṛí*, तातॄ *tátṛí* (Present Sing. 1. तातर्मि *tá-tar-mi*, Plur. 3. तातिरति *tá-tir-ati*).

Exception.—1. If the primitive verb ends in a nasal, the whole verb is repeated, in accordance with the general rules given in §§ 42-47, and the reduplicated nasal is treated like a final म् *m*, according to § 32, *e.g.* शम् *çam*, 'to be tranquil,' शंशम् *çamçam*, शंशम्य *çamçamya* (§ 32, 1); यम् *yam*, 'to restrain,' यंयम् *yamyam* or यँय्यम् *yayyam*, यंयम्य *yamyamya* or यँय्यम्य *yayyamya* (§ 32, 2); भ्रम् *bhram*, 'to whirl,' बंभ्रम् *bambhram* (§ 45) or बम्भ्रम् *bambhram*, बंभ्रम्य *bambhramya* or बम्भ्रम्य *bambhramya* (§ 32, 3); क्रम् *kram*, 'to go,' चंक्रम् *chamkram* or चङ्क्रम् *chankram*, चंक्रम्य *chamkramya* or चङ्क्रम्य *chankramya*; क्षण् *kshaṇ*, 'to kill,' although ending in

ण् *ṇ*, and हन् *han*, 'to kill,' although ending in न् *n*, as if these letters were म् *m*, form चंचण् *chaṁkshaṇ* or चङ्क्षण् *chaṅkshaṇ*, etc., जंघन् *jaṁghan* (§ 45, Obs.) or जङ्घन् *jaṅghan*, etc.

2. Verbs ending in य् *y*, ल् *l*, or व् *v*, and having a medial अ *a*, may follow the general rule (§ 48, 1), or insert after the अ *a* of the reduplicated syllable a nasal, which is treated like a final म् *m*, *e.g.* दय् *day*, 'to give,' makes either दादय् *dâday*, दादय्य *dâdayya*, or दंदय् *daṁday*, दंदय्य *daṁdayya*, दन्दय् *danday*, दन्दय्य *dandayya*.

3. Other exceptions are enumerated in the list, § 51.

§ 49. A final ए *e*, ऐ *ai*, or ओ *o* of the primitive verb is changed to आ *â*, and the latter vowel is repeated in the reduplication, *e.g.* वे *ve*, 'to weave,' becomes वावा *vâvâ*, वावाय *vâvâya*; ग्लै *glai*, 'to be weary,' जाग्ला *jâglâ*, जाग्लाय *jâglâya*; शो *ço*, 'to sharpen,' शाशा *çâçâ*, शाशाय *çâçâya*.

§ 50. In the second frequentative, previous to their being reduplicated, the primitive verbs undergo the following changes:—

1. A final इ *i* or उ *u* is lengthened, *e.g.* चि *chi*, 'to collect,' चेचीय *chechíya*; स्तु *stu*, 'to praise,' तोष्टूय *toshṭûya* (*cf.* § 17).

2. री *rí* is substituted for a final ऋ *ṛi*, preceded by a single consonant. Thus कृ *kṛi*, 'to make,' changed to क्री *krí*, makes चेक्रीय *chekríya*, according to §§ 43 and 48, 1. But when ऋ *ṛi* is preceded by more than one consonant, it becomes अर् *ar*, *e.g.* स्मृ *smṛi*, 'to recollect,' changed to स्मर् *smar*, makes सास्मर्य *sâsmarya* (*cf.* § 48, 1).

3. ॠ *ṛí* is changed to ईर् *ír*, and if preceded by a labial (प् *p*, फ् *ph*, ब् *b*, भ् *bh*, म् *m*) or व् *v*, to ऊर् *úr*, *e.g.* तॄ *tṛí*, 'to cross,' changed to तीर् *tír*, makes तेतीर्य *tetírya*; पॄ *pṛí*, 'to fill,' changed to पूर् *púr*, makes पोपूर्य *popúrya* (§ 48, 1).

4. A nasal before a final consonant is frequently rejected, *e.g.* तञ्च् *tañch*, 'to shrink,' तातच्य *tâtachya*. A list of the verbs undergoing this change is given in my 'Vollständige Grammatik,' § 154, 2, 2.

§ 51. Alphabetical List of Anomalous Frequentatives.

अटाट् अटाट्य		freq. of	अट् 'to roam.'
अरार्य or Vedic अलार्य		„ „	ऋ 'to go.'
अशाश् अशाश्य		„ „	अश् 'to pervade,' and 'to eat.'
ऊर्णोनु ऊर्णोनूय		„ „	ऊर्णु 'to cover.'
कनिक्रन्द्	Vedic	„ „	क्रन्द् 'to roar.'
कनीकश् कनीकश्य		„ „	कश् 'to sound.'
कनीकस् कनीकस्य		„ „	कस् 'to go.'
करिकृ	Vedic	„ „	कृ 'to make.'
करीकृष्	Vedic	„ „	कृष् 'to draw.'
कोकु कोकूय (also regularly चोकु चोकूय)		„ „	कु 'to cry.'
गनिगम् or गनीगम्	Vedic	„ „	गम् 'to go.'
घनिघन्	Vedic	„ „	हन् 'to strike.'
चञ्चुर् चञ्चूर्य		„ „	चर् 'to go.'
चनिश्चन्द्	Vedic	„ „	चन्द् 'to shine.'
चनिष्कन्द्	Vedic	„ „	स्कन्द् 'to jump.'
चनीस्कन्द् चनीस्कद्य		„ „	स्कन्द्
चाकन्	Vedic	„ „	कन् 'to love.'
चाखाय (also regularly चंखन्य)	second	„ „	खन् 'to dig.'
चेकीय	second	„ „	चाय् 'to worship.'
जञ्जप् जञ्जप्य		„ „	जप् 'to murmur (prayers).'
जञ्जभ् जञ्जभ्य		„ „	जभ् 'to gape.'
जरीगृह्य	second	„ „	ग्रह् 'to take.'
जर्भुर्	Vedic	„ „	हृ 'to convey.'
जल्गुल्	Vedic	„ „	गॄ 'to swallow.'
जाजाय (also regularly जंजन्य)	second	„ „	जन् 'to bring forth.'
जेगिल्य	second	„ „	गॄ 'to swallow.'
जेगीय	second	„ „	गा 'to go,' and गै 'to sing.'
जेघ्नीय	second	„ „	हन् 'to strike.'

जेघ्रीय	second freq. of	घ्रा 'to smell.'
जेज्नीय	second „ „	ज्या 'to overpower,' etc., ज्यो 'to restrain,' and जि 'to overpower.'
जेहीय	second „ „	हा 'to go' and 'to abandon.'
जोहू जोहूय	„ „	ह्वे 'to call.'
तरितृ and तर्तुर्	Vedic „ „	तृ 'to pass over.'
तवीतु	Vedic „ „	तु 'to be powerful.'
तेष्ठीय	second „ „	स्था 'to stand.'
दनीध्वंस् दनीध्वस्य	„ „	ध्वंस् 'to fall to pieces.'
दंदंश् दंदश्य	„ „	दंश् 'to bite.'
दर्दृ	Vedic „ „	दृ 'to burst.'
दविद्युत् दविद्युत्य	Vedic „ „	द्युत् 'to shine.'
दविधु	Vedic „ „	धु 'to shake.'
दाधृ	Vedic „ „	धृ 'to bear.'
देदीय	second „ „	दा 'to give,' दे 'to protect,' and दो 'to cut.'
देद्युत् देद्युत्य	„ „	द्युत् 'to shine.'
देधीय	second „ „	धा 'to put,' and धे 'to drink.'
देध्मीय	second „ „	ध्मा 'to blow.'
नन्नम्	Vedic „ „	नम् 'to bow to.'
नवीनु	Vedic „ „	नु 'to praise.'
पणीफण्	Vedic „ „	फण् 'to go.'
पनिपन्	Vedic „ „	पन् 'to be praiseworthy.'
पनीपत् पनीपत्य	„ „	पत् 'to fall.'
पनीपद् पनीपद्य	„ „	पद् 'to go.'
पंफुल् पंफुल्य	„ „	फल् 'to burst.'

परीपृच्छ्य	second freq. of			प्रच्छ् 'to ask.'
पापत्	Vedic	„	„	पत् 'to fall.'
पेपी		„	„	प्याय् 'to be exuberant.'
पेपीय	second	„	„	पा 'to drink,' and प्याय् 'to be exuberant.'
बद्बध्	Vedic	„	„	बन्ध् 'to bind.'
बनीभ्रंश् बनीभ्रश्य		„	„	भ्रंश् } 'to fall.'
बनीभ्रंस् बनीभ्रस्य		„	„	भ्रंस् } 'to fall.'
बंभञ्ज् बंभज्य		„	„	भञ्ज् 'to break.'
बरीभृज्ज्य	second	„	„	भ्रज्ज् 'to fry.'
भरिभृ	Vedic	„	„	भृ 'to bear.'
मेमीय	second	„	„	मा 'to mete' and 'to sound,' and मे 'to barter.'
यम्यम्	Vedic	„	„	यम् 'to restrain.'
रारम्	Vedic	„	„	रम् 'to rest.'
वनीवञ्च् वनीवच्य		„	„	वञ्च् 'to go.'
वरीवृश्च्य	second	„	„	व्रश्च् 'to tear.'
वेविच्य	second	„	„	व्यच् 'to surround.'
वेवी वेवीय		„	„	व्ये 'to cover.'
शंशप् शंशप्य		„	„	शप् 'to execrate.'
शाशय्य	second	„	„	शी 'to lie down.'
शेशिष्य	second	„	„	शास् 'to teach.'
शोशु शोशूय		„	„	श्वि 'to swell.'
सनिषन्	Vedic	„	„	सन् 'to obtain.'
सनिष्वन्	Vedic	„	„	स्वन् 'to sound.'
सनीस्रंस् सनीस्रस्य		„	„	स्रंस् 'to fall.'
सासाय (also regularly संसन्य)	second	„	„	सन् 'to obtain.'
सेषीय	second	„	„	सै 'to waste' and सो 'to destroy.'
सेसिम्य	second	„	„	स्यम् 'to sound.'
सोषुप्य	second	„	„	स्वप् 'to sleep.'

2. Desiderative.

§ 52. The desiderative form indicates that the agent wishes to perform the action or be in the condition which the verb implies, from which it is derived. Any verb, whether primitive or derivative, except a desiderative, admits of this modification.

§ 53. The desiderative is formed by the reduplication of the base and by adding the affix स *sa*, which is changed to ष *sha* where § 17 applies. Thus from क्षिप् *kship*, 'to throw,' is formed चिक्षिप्स *chi-kship-sa*; but from भू *bhû*, 'to be,' बुभूष *bu-bhû-sha*.

§ 54. The rules for the reduplication differ in the following points from those given in §§ 42-47 :—

I. In the reduplicated syllable इ *i* is substituted for radical अ *a*, आ *â*, ऋ *ṛi*, and ऌ *ḷi*, *e.g.* शप् *çap*, 'to execrate,' शिशप्स *çi-çap-sa*; या *yâ*, 'to go,' यियास *yi-yâ-sa*; वृत् *vṛit*, 'to be,' विवृत्स *vi-vṛit-sa*; क्लृप् *kḷip*, 'to be able,' चिक्लृप्स *chi-kḷip-sa*.

Exceptions. 1. When the अ *a* or आ *â* of the base has been produced by a change of उ *u* and is preceded by any consonant except ज् *j*, a labial (प् *p*, फ् *ph*, ब् *b*, भ् *bh*, म् *m*), or a semivowel, it is represented by उ *u* in the syllable of reduplication, for instance, नावय *nâvaya*, the causal of नु *nu*, 'to praise,' where the आ *â* is produced by the change of उ *u* to आव् *âv* (§ 59, 2), makes नुनावयिष *nu-nâvay-isha*; but पावय *pâvaya*, although the आ *â* has the same origin (causal of पू *pû*, 'to purify'), makes पिपावयिष *pi-pâvay-isha*, because it is preceded by a labial.

2. The अ *a* or आ *â* of a desiderative from च्यु *chyu*, 'to move,' द्रु *dru*, 'to run,' प्रु *pru*, and प्लु *plu*, 'to go,' श्रु *çru*, 'to hear,' स्नु *snu* and स्रु *sru*, 'to flow,' is optionally represented by उ *u* or इ *i*, *e.g.* चिच्यावयिष *chi-chyâvay-isha*, or चुच्यावयिष *chu-chyâvay-isha*, desiderative of the causal of च्यु *chyu*.

II. When the verb begins with a vowel or diphthong, and ends in a single consonant or a combination of consonants, the first part of which is any other consonant than र् *r* or a nasal, the first consonant following the vowel or diphthong is reduplicated with इ *i*, inserted after the reduplicated letter, *e.g.* अश् *aç*, 'to pervade,' forms अशिशिष *a-çiç-isha*; अभ्र् *abhr*, 'to go,' अबिभ्रिष *a-bibhr-isha.*

When the beginning vowel or diphthong is followed by a compound consonant, the first part of which is a nasal or र् *r*, the second element is reduplicated with inserted इ *i*, *e.g.* अर्च् *arch*, 'to worship,' अर्चिचिष *ar-chich-isha*; इन्ध् *indh*, 'to kindle,' इन्दिधिष *in-didh-isha.*

§ 55. When the affix is to be added to a derivative verb, or to a primitive verb ending in a consonant, the vowel इ *i* is inserted between the verb and the affix which, according to §§ 17, 53, is changed to ष *sha;* if the derivative verb ends in a vowel, it is rejected, *e.g.* बोधय *bodhaya* (causal of बुध् *budh*, 'to know') makes बुबोधयिष *bu-bodhay-i-sha*, श्नथ् *çnath*, 'to slay,' शिश्नथिष *çi-çnath-i-sha.*

After a primitive verb with final ॠ *ṛí*, इ *i* or ई *í* may be optionally inserted: if the insertion takes place, ॠ *ṛí* is changed to अर् *ar*; if not, to ईर् *ír*, or ऊर् *úr*, (see § 56, II. 2), *e.g.* शॄ *çṛí*, 'to hurt,' makes शिशरिष *çi-çar-i-sha* or शिशरीष *çi-çar-í-sha* or शिशीर्ष *çi-çír-sha.*

Exception. There are some verbs ending in क् *k*, च् *ch*, ज् *j*, त् *t*, द् *d*, ध् *dh*, न् *n*, प् *p*, भ् *bh*, म् *m*, श् *ç*, ष् *sh*, स् *s*, and ह् *h*, which either must or may add the affix without insertion of इ *i*. They are enumerated in my 'Kurze Grammatik,' § 116, II.; *e.g.* तप् *tap*, 'to burn,' makes तितप्स *ti-tap-sa*; त्रप् *trap*, 'to be ashamed,' तित्रप्स *ti-trap-sa* or तित्रपिष *ti-trap-i-sha.* Besides the insertion of इ *i* is optional in verbs ending in इव् *iv*, *e.g.* दिव् *div* (*cf.* § 56, I. and II. 10).

§ 56. The verb from which the desiderative is derived is subject to the following changes:—

I. When इ *i* or ई *í* is inserted before the affix, a final ॠ *ṛí* is changed to अर् *ar* (*cf.* § 55), and an initial or medial इ *i* followed by a single radical consonant to ए *e*, उ *u* to ओ *o*, ऋ *ṛi* to अर् *ar*, ऌ *ḷi* to अल् *al*,[1] *e.g.*—

तॄ *tṛī*, 'to cross,' becomes तितरिष *titar-i-sha*, तितरीष *titar-ī-sha* (§ 55)

दिव *div*, 'to play' (§ 55, Exc.) „ दिदेविष *didev-i-sha*.

उख् *ukh*, 'to go,' „ ओचिखिष *ochikh-i-sha* (§ 54, II.)

चृत् *chṛit*, 'to connect,' „ चिचर्तिष *chichart-i-sha*.

Exc. 1. There are many verbs which are not subject to these changes; they are enumerated in my 'Kurze Grammatik,' p. 53, *e.g.* कुच् *kuch*, 'to be crooked,' makes चुकुचिष *chu-kuch-i-sha*.—Medial इ *i* and उ *u* are optionally changed, for instance, क्लिद् *klid*, 'to become wet,' makes चिक्लिदिष *chi-klid-i-sha* or चिक्लेदिष *chi-kled-i-sha*.

2. A final अ *a* is rejected (*cf.* § 55).

3. The final य *ya* of the second frequentative, if preceded by a consonant, is rejected, *e.g.* बेभिद्य *bebhidya* (second freq. of भिद् *bhid*, 'to split'), makes बेभिदिष *bebhid-i-sha*. In denominatives ending in य *ya*, preceded by a consonant, the rejection is optional, *e.g.* नमस्य *namasya*, 'to honour' (§ 62, III.), makes निनमस्यिष *ninamasy-i-sha* or निनमसिष *ninamas-i-sha*.

II. When स *sa* or ष *sha* (§ 53) is added without the insertion of इ *i*:—

1. Final इ *i* and उ *u* are lengthened, *e.g.* शि *çi*, 'to sharpen,' शिशीष *çiçī-sha*.

2. Final ऋ *ṛi* and final or medial ॠ *ṛī* are changed to ईर् *īr*, or when preceded by a labial (प् *p*, फ् *ph*, ब् *b*, भ् *bh*, म् *m*) or व् *v*,

[1] This change is generally called *guṇa*. A long or short radical *i*, *u*, *ṛi*, is generally gunated if final; short *i*, *u*, *ṛi*, *ḷi*, if followed by *one* radical consonant, *e.g.* *bobhū* (frequentative of *bhū*) with *mi* becomes *bobho-mi*, *bebhid* (freq. of *bhid*) *bebhed-mi*, but *memīl* (freq. of *mīl*) *memīl-mi*, *tarītṛimp* (freq. of *tṛimp*) *tarītṛimp-mi*. The guṇa *e* becomes before vowels *ay*, and *o av*, *e.g.* *sidh* with *a* becomes *sedha*, but *ji* with *a* is changed instead of *je-a* to *jay-a*, and *bhū* instead of *bho-a* to *bhav-a*.

to ऊर् *úr*, *e.g.* कृ *kṛi*, 'to do,' चिकीर्ष *chi-kír-sha*, तॄ *tṛí*, 'to cross,' तितीर्ष *ti-tír-sha*, स्मृ *smṛi*, 'to recollect,' सुस्मूर्ष *su-smúr-sha*, स्तृह् *stṛih*, 'to hurt,' तिस्तीर्क्ष *ti-stírk-sha* (*cf.* 4).

3. A final ए *e*, ऐ *ai*, or ओ *o* is changed to आ *á* (*cf.* § 49), *e.g.* शो *ço*, 'to sharpen,' शिशास *çi-çá-sa*.

4. Final च् *ch*, ज् *j*, श् *ç*, ष् *sh*, and ह् *h* are changed to क् *k*, as पच् *pach*, 'to cook,' पिपक्ष *pi-pak-sha* (*cf.* § 17).

5. Final द् *d* and ध् *dh*, to त् *t*, as भिद् *bhid*, 'to split,' बिभित्स *bi-bhit-sa* (*cf.* 9).

6. Final न् *n* and म् *m* are changed to Anusvâra ं or Anunâsika ँ *e.g.* क्रम् *kram*, 'to go,' चिक्रंस *chi-kraṁ-sa*.

7. Final भ् *bh* to प् *p*, *e.g.* यभ् *yabh*, 'to copulate,' यियप्स *yi-yap-sa*.

8. Final स् *s* to त् *t*, *e.g.* वस् *vas*, 'to dwell,' विवत्स *vi-vat-sa*.

9. When a verb ending in ध् *dh*, भ् *bh*, or ह् *h* begins with ग् *g*, द् *d*, or ब् *b*, these letters are changed to घ् *gh*, ध् *dh*, भ् *bh*, *e.g.* बुध् *budh*, 'to know,' बुभुत्स *bu-bhut-sa*; दिह् *dih*, 'to smear,' दिधिक्ष *di-dhik-sha*.

10. Final इव् *iv* is changed to यू *yú*, *e.g.* दिव् *div*, 'to play,' दुद्यूष *du-dyú-sha* (*cf.* § 55).

§ 57. Alphabetical List of Anomalous Desideratives.

अट्टिटिष (अतिट्टिष and regularly अटिट्टिष) . . . . desid. of अट्ट् 'to transgress.'
अड्डिडिष (regularly अडिड्डिष) . . „ „ अड्ड् 'to attach.'
अरिरिष . . . . „ „ ऋ 'to go.'
ईप्स . . . . „ „ आप् 'to attain.'
ईर्त्स (also regularly अर्दिधिष) . . „ „ ऋध् 'to prosper.'
ईषिष . . . . „ „ इ and ई 'to go.'
ऊर्णूनूष . . . . „ „ ऊर्णु 'to cover.'
चिकमिष (also regularly चिकामयिष) „ „ कामय (X[th] conj. cl. of कम्, § 61) 'to love.'
चिकीष (also regularly चिचीष) . „ „ चि 'to arrange.'

जिगांस (also regularly जिगमिष) . desid. of गम् 'to go.'
जिगलिष . . . . „ „ गॄ 'to swallow.'
जिगीष . . . . „ „ जि 'to overpower' and गा 'to go.'
जिघांस . . . . „ „ हन् 'to strike.'
जिघीष . . . . „ „ हि 'to go.'
जिघृच . . . . „ „ ग्रह् 'to take.'
जुहावयिष . . . . „ „ the causal of ह्वे 'to call,' as if it were ह्वावय (*cf.* § 60).
जुहूष . . . . „ „ ह्वे 'to call.'
ज्ञीप्स (also regularly जिज्ञापयिष or जिज्ञपयिष) . . . . „ „ ज्ञापय or ज्ञपय, causal of ज्ञा 'to know.'
तितांस (also regularly तितनिष) . „ „ तन् 'to draw.'
तितृच . . . . „ „ तृंह् 'to hurt.'
दित्स . . . . „ „ दा 'to give,' दे 'to protect,' or दो 'to cut.'
दिदरिद्रास or दिदरिद्रिष . . . . „ „ दरिद्रा 'to be in distress.'
दिदरिष . . . . „ „ दृ 'to consider.'
दिद्युतिष or दिद्योतिष . . . . „ „ द्युत् 'to shine.'
दिधरिष . . . . „ „ धृ 'to bear.'
दिप्स . . . . Vedic „ „ दम्भ् 'to hurt.'
धित्स . . . . „ „ धा 'to put,' or धे 'to drink.'
धिप्स or धीप्स . . . . „ „ दम्भ् 'to hurt.'
निनङ्क्ष (also regularly निनशिष) . „ „ नश् 'to be lost.'
निनत्स . . . . „ „ नह् 'to bind.'
पित्स . . . . „ „ पद् 'to go.'
पित्स (also regularly पिपतिष) . . „ „ पत् 'to fall.'
पिपविष . . . . „ „ पू 'to purify.'

पिपीष	Vedic desid. of पा 'to drink.'
पिपृच्छिष	„ „ प्रच्छ् 'to ask.'
बिभरिष (also regularly बुभूर्ष) .	„ „ भृ 'to bear.'
बिभर्क्ष or बिभर्ज्जिष (also regularly बिभ्रक्ष or बिभ्रज्जिष)	„ „ भ्रज्ज् 'to fry.'
मित्स	„ „ मा 'to mete,' मि 'to throw,' मी 'to hurt,' or मे 'to barter.'
मिमङ्क्ष (also regularly मिमज्जिष) .	„ „ मज्ज् 'to dive.'
मिमार्जिष or मिमृक्ष	„ „ मृज् 'to wipe.'
यियविष (also regularly युयूष) .	„ „ यु 'to bind.'
रित्स	„ „ राध् 'to make merciful.'
रिप्स	„ „ रभ् 'to desire vehemently.'
लिप्स	„ „ लभ् to obtain.'
विवरिष or विवरीष or वुवूर्ष	„ „ वृ 'to screen,' etc.
विव्रक्ष (also regularly विव्रश्चिष) .	„ „ व्रश्च् 'to tear.'
शिश्रयिष (also regularly शिश्रीष) .	„ „ श्रि 'to go to.'
शुशावयिष (also regularly शिश्वाययिष)	„ „ the causal (श्वायय) of श्वि 'to swell.'
सिषास (also regularly सिसनिष) .	„ „ सन् 'to obtain.'
सिस्मयिष	„ „ स्मि 'to smile.'
सिस्वरिष (also regularly सुस्वूर्ष) .	„ „ स्वृ 'to sound.'
सुषुप्स	„ „ स्वप् 'to sleep.'
सुष्वापयिष	„ „ the causal (स्वापय) of स्वप् 'to sleep.'

Obs.—There are besides seven verbs which, although originally desideratives, on account of some anomalies are considered as primitive ones, viz., चिकित्स *chi-kit-sa*, 'to cure,' जुगुप्स *ju-gup-sa*, 'to despise,' तितिक्ष *titiksha* (vb. *tij*), 'to bear,' दीदांस *dîdâṁsa*, 'to straighten,' बीभत्स *bîbhatsa* (vb. *bâdh*), 'to loathe,' मीमांस *mîmâṁsa* (vb. *man*), 'to investigate,' शीशांस *çîçâṁsa* (*cf.* vb. *ço, çi*), 'to sharpen.' Therefore they are capable of forming desideratives against § 52, but without reduplicating again, conform to § 47, *e.g.* from जुगुप्स *jugupsa*, जुगुप्सिष *jugups-isha*.

3. Causal.

§ 58. The causal implies that a person is caused to do the action, or to be in the condition, which the verb expresses, as in English 'to fell' = 'to cause to fall,' 'to lay' = 'to cause to lie.' All verbs, primitive as well as derivative, admit of this modification.

The causal is formed: I. By adding to the verb the affix अय *aya*, *e.g.* गम् *gam*, 'to go,' गमय *gam-aya*, 'to cause to go.'

II. In many instances by changing the vowel of the base.

Exception from I.: Verbs ending in आ *â*, ए *e*, ऐ *ai*, or ओ *o*, which must be changed to आ *â* (*cf.* § 56, II. 3), take पय *paya* as affix, *e.g.* दा *dâ*, 'to give,' दापय *dâ-paya*, 'to cause to give.' In some instances the final आ *â* of the base is shortened, *e.g.* श्रा *çrâ* or श्रै *çrai*, 'to cook,' makes श्रापय *çrâ-paya* or श्रपय *çra-paya*.

§ 59. The changes of the vowel of the base mentioned in § 58, II. are the following:—

1. Primitive verbs ending in a single consonant lengthen a preceding अ *a*, for instance पद् *pad*, 'to go,' पादय *pâd-aya*.—There are many exceptions to this rule; almost all verbs ending in म् *m* retain the short अ *a*; as क्लम् *klam*, 'to be sad,' क्लमय *klam-aya*. A list of these exceptions is given in my 'Kurze Grammatik,' § 130.

2. Final इ *i* and ई *î* are changed to आय् *ây*, उ *u* and ऊ *û* to आव् *âv*, ऋ *ṛi* and ॠ *ṛî* to आर् *âr*,[1] *e.g.* श्वि *çvi*, 'to go,' श्वायय

[1] This change is called *Vṛiddhi*; concerning *i* and *u* it is taught that they are changed first to *ai*, *au*, which become *ây*, *âv*, before the following *a*, as in § 24.

çvây-aya; नी *nî*, 'to lead,' नायय *nây-aya*; प्लु *plu*, 'to move,' प्लावय *plâv-aya*; पू *pû*, 'to purify,' पावय *pâv-aya*; कृ *kṛi*, 'to make,' and कॄ *kṛî*, 'to throw,' कारय *kâr-aya*.

3. Verbs ending in a single consonant change a preceding इ *i* to ए *e*, उ *u* to ओ *o*, ऋ *ṛi* to अर् *ar*, ऌ *ḷi* to अल् *al*,[1] *e.g.* भिद् *bhid*, 'to split,' makes भेदय *bhed-aya*; बुध् *budh*, 'to know,' बोधय *bodh-aya*; कृत् *kṛit*, 'to cut,' कर्तय *kart-aya*; कॢप् *kḷip*, 'to be able,' कल्पय *kalp-aya*.

Exc. The इ *i* before the ष *sha* of the desiderative is not changed (*cf.* 5).

4. A medial ॠ *ṛî* becomes ईर् *îr*, *e.g.* स्तॄह् *stṛîh*, 'to hurt,' स्तीर्हय *stîrh-aya*.

5. Verbs ending in अ *a* reject that vowel, *e.g.* बुबोधिष *bubodhisha* (desiderative of बुध् *budh*) makes बुबोधिषय *bubodhish-aya* (*cf.* 3, Exc.). The final य *ya* of the second frequentative, if preceded by a consonant, is rejected, *e.g.* बेभिद्य *bebhidya* makes बेभिदय *bebhid-aya*. In the case of a denominative ending in य *ya* preceded by a consonant the rejection is optional, *e.g.* नमस्य *namasya* makes नमस्यय *namasy-aya* or नमसय *namas-aya* (*cf.* § 56, I. 3).

6. Verbs ending in अय *aya*, viz., causals, verbs of the tenth conjugational class (§ 61) and denominatives derived by the affix अय *aya* (§ 62, II.) are left unchanged. Thus the causal from पादय *pâdaya*, causal of पद् *pad*, is also पादय *pâdaya*.

§ 60. Alphabetical List of Anomalous Causals.

अर्पय	causal of ऋ 'to go.'
(अधि) आपय	„ „ (अधि) इ 'to read.'
क्षपय	„ „ क्षप् 'to pity.'
क्नोपय	„ „ क्नू 'to sound.'
क्रापय	„ „ क्री 'to buy.'

[1] *Guṇa*, *cf.* p. 34, note.

क्षपय	causal of क्षि 'to decrease.'
क्ष्मापय	" " क्ष्माय् 'to tremble.'
गूहय	" " गुह् 'to conceal.'
ग्लपय (also regularly ग्लापय)	" " ग्लै 'to become exhausted.'
चापय (also regularly चायय)	" " चि 'to arrange.'
छायय	" " छो 'to cut.'
जम्भय	" " जभ् 'to gape.'
जरय	" " जॄ 'to grow old.'
जागरय	" " जागृ 'to wake.'
जापय	" " जि 'to overpower.'
ज्ञपय (also regularly ज्ञापय)	" " ज्ञा 'to know.'
दरय	" " दॄ 'to burst.'
दरिद्रय	" " दरिद्रा 'to be in distress.'
दापय	" " दी 'to go to ruin' (or दा 'to give,' दे 'to protect,' दो 'to cut').
दीधय	" " दीधी 'to shine.'
दूषय (the regular दोषय only in one signification)	" " दुष् 'to be depraved.'
धूनय	" " धू 'to shake.'
नरय	" " नॄ 'to lead.'
पायय	" " पा 'to drink,' and पै 'to dry.'
पालय	" " पा 'to protect.'
प्रीणय	" " प्री 'to delight.'
भर्ज्जय (also regularly भ्रज्जय)	" " भ्रज्ज् 'to fry.'
भापय, भीषय (also regularly भायय)	" " भी 'to fear.'
मापय	" " मि 'to throw,' मी 'to hurt,' मा 'to mete,' मे 'to barter.'

मार्जय	causal of	मृज् 'to wipe.'
रजय (also regularly रञ्जय). .	„ „	रञ्ज् 'to colour.'
रन्धय	„ „	रध् 'to perish.'
रम्भय	„ „	रभ् 'to desire vehemently.'
रेपय	„ „	री 'to howl' and 'to distil.'
रोपय (also regularly रोहय) .	„ „	रुह् 'to grow.'
लम्भय	„ „	लभ् 'to obtain.'
लापय / लालय / लीनय (and regularly लायय).	„ „	ली 'to adhere.'
वर्हय (and regularly बृंहय) . .	„ „	बृंह् 'to grow.'
वाजय 'to shake'	„ „	वा 'to blow,' etc.
वापय (also regularly वायय) .	„ „	वी 'to lie with.'
वायय	„ „	वे 'to weave.'
वेवय	„ „	वेवी 'to go.'
व्यायय	„ „	व्ये 'to cover.'
व्लेपय (? or ब्लेपय or व्रेपय) .	„ „	व्ली (? or ब्ली or व्री) 'to select.'
शातय	„ „	शद् 'to fall.'
शायय	„ „	शो or शि 'to sharpen,' शी 'to lie down.'
श्रपय (also regularly श्रापय) .	„ „	श्रा or श्रै 'to cook.'
श्रापय . . . . . Vedic	„ „	श्रि 'to go to' (Yajur-V. 23, 26).
श्रापय . . . . regular	„ „	श्रा or श्रै 'to cook.'
साधय (also regularly सेधय) .	„ „	सिध् 'to be accomplished.'
सायय	„ „	सो 'to destroy.'
स्नपय (also regularly स्नापय) .	„ „	स्ना 'to bathe.'
स्फारय (also regularly स्फोरय).	„ „	स्फुर् 'to tremble.'
स्फावय	„ „	स्फाय् 'to swell.'

स्मरय . . . . causal of स्मृ 'to recollect.'
स्मापय (also regularly स्मायय) . „ „ स्मि 'to smile.'
हिडय . . . . „ „ हेड् 'to disregard.'
ह्रेपय . . . . „ „ ह्री 'to be ashamed.'
ह्वायय . . . . „ „ ह्वे 'to call.'

4. Verbs of the Tenth Conjugational Class.

§ 61. In the collections of roots and in the native grammarians and dictionaries about 150 verbs are marked as belonging to the tenth conjugational class (*cf.* § 69). These verbs, before taking the inflectional terminations or affixes, are dealt with according to the rules for the formation of the causal (§§ 58, 59). Thus चुर् *chur*, 'to steal,' which belongs to this class, according to § 58, takes the affix अय *aya*, and, according to § 59, 3, changes its medial उ *u* to ओ *o*. The crude form of the verb therefore, properly speaking, is not चुर् *chur*, but चोरय *choraya*; and in fact almost[1] all these verbs, though called primitive, are in reality derivative, partly causals, partly denominatives, formed by the affix अय *aya* (§ 62, II.). For instance, the verb यन्त्र् *yantr*, 'to restrain,' or properly यन्त्रय *yantraya*, is derived from यन्त्र *yantra*, a subst., 'restraining, restraint.'

As they follow strictly the rules for the formation of the causal, it will suffice to give a few examples: भल् *bhal*, 'to describe,' makes, according to § 59, 1, भालय *bhâl-aya*, श्लिष् *çlish*, 'to adhere,' according to § 59, श्लेषय *çlesh-aya*, कृत् *kṛit*, 'to glorify,' according to § 59, 4, कीर्तय *kîrt-aya*.

Exc. There is a small number of verbs belonging to this class, which do not alter the medial vowel of the base. They are given in my 'Kurze Grammatik,' § 134, and in my 'Vollständige Grammatik,' § 208.

[1] Some may have been produced by the influence of the Prâkṛit (*cf.* Lassen, Inst. Ling. Pracr. p. 339, § 120, 3).

Observ. Some verbs of this class optionally take the affix आपय *âpaya, e.g.* अर्थ् *arth,* 'to ask,' may become अर्थय *arth-aya* or अर्थापय *arth-âpaya.* For the list of these exceptions see my 'Vollständige Grammatik,' § 209.

5. Denominatives.

§ 62. There are five classes of Denominatives:—

I. The first class comprises those which are formed by simply adding the inflectional formations to the noun, according to the rules which will be given afterwards, *cf. e.g.* § 71, II. 4. Thus कृष्ण *kṛishṇa,* a proper name, may, without undergoing any change, be used as the crude form of a verb, in the sense of 'to treat somebody as if he was Kṛishṇa.'

II. The second class consists of those which add the affix अय *aya* to the noun and change its final vowel agreeably to § 59, 2, *e.g.* श्री *çrí,* 'happiness,' makes श्रायय *çrây-aya.* Many nouns must or may optionally take आपय *âpaya* instead of अय *aya, e.g.* from सत्य *satya,* 'truth,' सत्यापय *satyâpaya,* 'to tell the truth.' For many special rules see my 'Vollständige Grammatik,' §§ 213-223.

III. The denominatives of the third class subjoin य *ya* to the noun, as नमस् *namas,* 'veneration,' नमस्य *namas-ya,* 'to venerate;' तपस् *tapas,* 'penance,' तपस्य *tapas-ya,* 'to do penance.'

A final अ *a,* इ *i,* or उ *u* of the noun is made long, as पुत्र *putra,* 'a son,' पुत्राय *putrâ-ya,* 'to wish for a son;' कवि *kavi,* 'a poet,' कवीय *kaví-ya;* विष्णु *vishṇu,* 'a proper name,' विष्णूय *vishṇú-ya.* But if the denominative takes the terminations of the first form of the active voice (called Parasmaipada, § 64), आ *â* before य *ya* is changed to ई *í, e.g.* पुत्रीयति *putrí-ya-ti,* 3d pers. sing. pres. of the Parasmaipada.

A final ऋ *ṛi* is changed to री *rí, e.g.* मातृ *mâtṛi,* 'mother,' मात्रीय *mâtrí-ya.*

A final ओ *o* is changed to अव् *av,* and औ *au* to आव् *âv, e.g.* गो *go,* 'a cow,' गव्य *gav-ya,* 'to wish for a cow;' नौ *nau,* 'a ship,'

नाव्य *nâv-ya.* For further details see my 'Kurze Grammatik,' § 140, and 'Vollständige Grammatik,' §§ 224-232 and 234.

IV. The denominatives of the fourth class add the affix स्य *sya* or अस्य *asya;* before the latter a final अ *a* is dropped, इ *i* and ई *î* are changed to य् *y,* उ *u* and ऊ *û* to व *v,* ऋ *ṛi* to र् *r, e.g.* मधु *madhu,* 'honey,' मधुस्य *madhu-sya* or मध्वस्य *madhv-asya,* 'to long after honey;' क्षीर *kshîra,* 'milk,' क्षीरस्य *kshîr-asya* 'to long after milk.'

V. Those of the fifth class compound the noun with काम्य *kâmya, e.g.* पुत्रकाम्य *putra-kâmya,* 'to wish for a son.'

SECTION II.—INFLEXION OF THE VERB: CONJUGATION.

§ 63. The verb has an active and a passive voice. We shall first treat of the active.

I. Active Voice.

§ 64. The active voice in Sanskrit, as in Greek, has two forms; the one, which is called *Parasmaipada,* corresponds to the Greek active, and implies that the action of the verb tends to another person or thing than the agent (transitive or objective): the other, *Âtmanepada,* corresponds to the Greek middle voice and expresses that the action of the verb is confined to the agent (subjective).

§ 65. The use of the two forms of the active is regulated by the following rules:—

1. The active verb is generally conjugated in the Parasmaipada. But if two or more agents mutually affect each other by doing the same action, or do the same action by turns, the verb is conjugated in the Âtmanepada.

2. Causals (§ 58-60) take the termination of the Âtmanepada, when they are reflexive. Thus रोहय *rohaya,* 'to cause to mount,' is generally conjugated in the Parasmaipada; but when it is used

in the sense of 'to cause one's-self to be mounted,' the Âtmanepada is used, *e.g.* गजो रोहयते *gajo rohaya-te*, 'the elephant causes himself to be mounted.'

3. All the verbs ending in अय *aya*, viz., the causals (§ 58-60), the verbs of the tenth conjugational class (§ 61), and the denominatives formed according to § 62, II., are conjugated in the Âtmanepada, when the agent performs the action for himself. This rule also applies to some primitive verbs, *e.g.* यजति *yaj-a-ti*, 3rd pers. sing. pres. Parasmaip., 'he offers a sacrifice,' यजते *yaj-a-te*, 3rd pers. sing. pres. Âtmanep., 'he offers a sacrifice for himself,' from the verb यज् *yaj*, 'to sacrifice.'

4. There are some primitive verbs which are conjugated in the Âtmanepeda only, *e.g.* शी *çí*, 'to lie down.'

5. The frequentatives of the second form, and some denominatives, likewise take the terminations of the Âtmanepada only.

6. The desiderative, with very few exceptions, is conjugated in the same form in which its base is conjugated.

§ 66. In the Dictionaries these differences, as far as they regard the primitive verbs, are indicated in the following manner:—A verb with the mark Par. (Parasmaipada) follows § 65, 1; a verb with Par. Âtm. (Parasmaipada and Âtmanepada) follows § 65, 3, and the second part of the rule given in § 65, 1; a verb marked with Âtm. (Âtmanepada) follows § 65, 4.

TENSES AND MOODS.

§ 67. The conjugation of the verb comprises ten forms, partly tenses partly moods, which we shall arrange in the following order:—

1. Present,	6. Aorist,
2. Imperfect,	7. Future I,
3. Imperative,	8. Future II,
4. Potential,	9. Conditional,
5. Perfect,	10. Precative.

CONJUGATION OF THE FIRST FOUR VERBAL FORMS.

§ 68. The terminations of the first four forms, viz. present, imperfect, imperative, and potential, are very seldom attached immediately to the crude form of a primitive verb. In most cases they are added to special inflective bases derived from the crude form. The terminations of the last six forms, on the contrary, are generally attached immediately to the crude form.

§ 69. The class of verbs which receive the affixes of the first four forms immediately, together with eight classes which add eight different conjugational characteristics before those affixes, and finally the so-called tenth conjugational class (for which see § 61), constitute the ten classes of conjugation under which the Hindu Grammarians have arranged the *dhâtus* (§ 38), *i.e.* the verbs of the Sanskrit language, which they take for primitive ones.

§ 70. These ten classes are again distributed into two, called the two conjugations, the first of which comprises by far the greater part of the primitive verbs (about 1340), the verbs of the tenth conjugational class (about 150) and all the derivative verbs, except the first form of the frequentative. The second consists of about 230 primitive verbs and the frequentatives of the first form.

In the Dictionaries the conjugational classes are indicated by numbers added to the verbs. Where the conjugations are marked likewise, the Roman number refers to the conjugation and the Arabic to the class.

§ 71. The First Conjugation comprises:—

I. Three classes of primitive verbs (§§ 38, 69), viz., the first, fourth, and sixth, and besides the tenth conjugational class (§ 61).

1. The verbs of the first class form their special base, to which the terminations of the first four forms are attached, by adding अ *a* to the root and subjecting the radical vowel to different

changes. A final radical इ *i*, ई *í*, or ए *e* becomes अय् *ay*; उ *u*, ऊ *ú*, or ओ *o* becomes अव् *av*; ऋ *ṛi* or ॠ *ṛí* becomes अर् *ar*; ऐ *ai* becomes आय् *áy*. Verbs ending in a single consonant change a preceding इ *i* to ए *e*, उ *u* to ओ *o*, ऋ *ṛi* to अर् *ar* (guṇa), *e.g.* जि *ji*, 'to conquer,' makes जय *jay-a*; नी *ní*, 'to lead,' नय *nay-a*; दे *de*, 'to protect,' दय *day-a*; च्यु *chyu*, 'to move,' च्यव *chyav-a*; भू *bhú*, 'to become,' भव *bhav-a*; ज्यो *jyo*, 'to restrain,' ज्यव *jyav-a*; हृ *hṛi*, 'to take,' हर *har-a*; तॄ *tṛí*, 'to pass over,' तर *tar-a*; ग्लै *glai*, 'to wane,' ग्लाय *gláy-a*; सिध् *sidh*, 'to go,' सेध *sedh-a*; बुध् *budh*, 'to know,' बोध *bodh-a*; वृत् *vṛit*, 'to be,' वर्त *vart-a*.

The last radical vowel or its substitute has the accent (acute), जयं *jáya*, सेधं *sédha*.

2. The fourth class adds य *ya* to the crude form of the verb, as नह् *nah*, 'to bind,' नह्य *nah-ya*. The last radical vowel has the acute, नह्यं *náhya*.

3. The sixth class adds an accented अ *a*, *e.g.* तुद् *tud*, 'to strike,' makes तुद *tud-á*. A final radical vowel इ *i* or ई *í* is changed to इय् *iy*, *e.g.* रि *ri*, 'to go,' makes रिय *riy-á*; in the same position उ *u* or ऊ *ú* becomes उव् *uv*, *e.g.* नु *nu* or नू *nú*, 'to praise,' नुव *nuv-á*; a final ऋ *ṛi* is changed to रिय् *riy*, *e.g.* मृ *mṛi*, 'to die,' म्रिय *mriy-á*; a final ॠ *ṛí* to इर् *ir*, *e.g.* कॄ *kṛí*, 'to throw,' किर *kir-á*. When the accented अ *a* is dropped before, or combined with, a following vowel, the accent passes over to the latter.

4. Of the tenth class we have treated in § 61. The form there given is left unchanged; the accent falls on the अ *a* which precedes the य *ya*, *e.g.* चोरयं *choráya*, 'to steal.'

II. The first Conjugation comprises secondly all the derivative verbs, except the frequentatives of the first form, viz.:—

1. The derivative verbs ending in अय *aya*, viz., the causals (§ 58-60) and the denominatives in अय *aya* (§ 62, II.).

2. The desideratives (§ 52-57).

3. The frequentatives of the second form (in य *ya*, § 40-51),

the denominatives in य *ya* (§ 62, III.-V.), and the verbs in आय *áya*, ईय *íya* (enumerated in my 'Kurze Grammatik,' § 168, 6, 6, and in my 'Vollständige Grammatik,' § 211, and quoted further on in the alphabetical list of anomalous bases, § 81).

These three classes do not undergo any further changes; those ending in अय *aya* (No. 1) accent the penultimate, *e.g.* बोधयं *bodháya* (causal of बुध् *budh*), श्वेतयं *çvetáya*, 'to be mounted on a white horse' (derived from श्वेत *çveta*, 'white'); the desiderative has the accent on the first syllable, *e.g.* चिचिंक्षिप्स *chíkshipsa* (desiderative from क्षिप् *kship*, 'to throw'); those ending in य *ya* (No. 3) have the accent on the final य *ya*, *e.g.* बेभिद्य *bebhidyá* (frequentative from भिद् *bhid*, 'to split'), तपस्य *tapasyá* (denominative from तपस् *tapas*, 'penance'), पुत्राय *putráyá* (from पुत्र *putra*, 'a son'), मधुस्य *madhusyá* (from मधु *madhu*, 'honey'), पुत्रकाम्य *putrakámyá* (from पुत्र *putra*, *cf.* § 62, III. IV. V.), and धूपाय *dhúpáyá* (from धूप् *dhúp*, 'to fumigate').

4. The denominatives without affix (*cf.* § 62, I.). These add अ *a* before which a final अ *a* of the noun is dropped, and change their last vowel according to § 71, I. 1, *e.g.* कृष्ण *kṛishṇa* remains *kṛishṇa*, but पितृ *pitṛi* becomes पितरं *pitára*. The accent is on the last vowel of the base.

§ 72. It appears from the rules given in the last paragraph, that all the special bases of the verbs which belong to the first conjugation terminate in अ *a*.

The Hindu grammarians, however, state that one primitive verb of the first conjugational class ending in आ *á*, forms, by combining this vowel with the conjugational characteristic अ *a*, a special base ending in आ *á*. It is likewise allowed to derive denominatives without affix from words ending in आ *á*, the final आ *á* of which, combined with the conjugational characteristic, remains आ *á*.

But as I never have met with such forms in the course of my reading, nor have found those statements supported by quotations from literature, I shall take no notice of them. The student may therefore take it for granted that in the first conjugation the inflective base of the first four verbal forms ends in अ *a*.

§ 73. In the PRESENT, which, like all the conjugational forms of the verb, has three numbers, with three persons in each, the following terminations are attached to the special bases:—

	In the Parasmaipada.			In the Âtmanepada.		
	SINGULAR.	DUAL.	PLURAL.	SINGULAR.	DUAL.	PLURAL.
1.	मि *mi*	वस् *vas*	मस् *mas* (in the Veda also मसि *masi*)	ए *e*	वहे *vahe*	महे *mahe*
2.	सि *si*	थस् *thas*	थ *tha*	से *se*	आथे *âthe*	ध्वे *dhve*
3.	ति *ti*	तस् *tas*	अन्ति *anti*	ते *te*	आते *âte*	अन्ते *ante*

Observation. 1. The present in connexion with the particle स्म *sma* assumes the signification of the preterite.

2. In the Vedas the final अ *a* of the base and the beginning त् *t* of the termination of the third person sing. Âtmanep. are often dropped, *e.g.* शोभे *çobh-e* instead of शोभते *çobh-a-t-e*.

§ 74. In the IMPERFECT:

1. The accented temporal *augment* अ *a* is prefixed. If the base begins with a consonant, no change takes place, *e.g.* बोध *bodha* (special base of बुध् *budh*, I. 1, 'to know,' § 71, I. 1) makes अबोध *ábodha*; but with an initial अ *a* or आ *â* the augment combines to accented आ *â*; with इ *i*, ई *î*, ए *e*, or ऐ *ai* to accented ऐ *ai*; with उ *u*, ऊ *û*, ओ *o*, or औ *au* to accented औ *au*; and with ऋ *ṛi* or ॠ *ṛî* to आर् *âr* with the acute on *â*, *e.g.* अर्च *árcha* (base of अर्च् *arch*, I. 1, 'to worship') becomes आर्च *ârcha*; आञ्छ *âṅchha* (base of आञ्छ् *âṅchh*, I. 1, 'to stretch'), आञ्छ *âṅchha*; इष्य *íshya* (base of इष् *ish*, I. 4, § 71, I. 2), ऐष्य *aíshya*; ईक्ष *îksha* (base of ईक्ष् *îksh*, I, 1, 'to see'), ऐक्ष *aíksha*; एध *édha* (base of एध् *edh*, I, 1, 'to thrive'), ऐध *aídha*; उक्ष *ukshá* (base of उक्ष् *uksh*, I. 6, 'to sprinkle,' § 71, I. 3), औक्ष *aúksha*; ऋष *ṛishá* (base of ऋष् *ṛish*, I. 6, 'to flow'), आर्ष *ârsha*.

Observation. An *imperfect* preceded by the prohibitive particle

मा *mâ*, followed by स्म *sma*, rejects the augment and takes the signification of an imperative. In the Veda it is dropped also in many other instances. The accent then falls on the same vowel as in the present.

2. The following terminations are subjoined to the base:—

	In the Parasmaipada.			In the Âtmanepada.		
	SINGULAR.	DUAL.	PLURAL.	SINGULAR.	DUAL.	PLURAL.
1.	अम् *am*	व *va*	म *ma*	इ *i*	वहि *vahi*	महि *mahi*
2.	स् *s*	तम् *tam*	त *ta*	थास् *thâs*	आथाम् *âthâm*	ध्वम् *dhvam*
3.	त् *t*	ताम् *tâm*	अन् *an*	त *ta*	आताम् *âtâm*	अन्त *anta*

§ 75. The IMPERATIVE is formed by affixing the following terminations to the base:—

	In the Parasmaipada.			In the Âtmanepada.		
	SINGULAR.	DUAL.	PLURAL.	SINGULAR.	DUAL.	PLURAL.
1.	आनि *âni*	आव *âva*	आम *âma*	ऐ *ai*	आवहै *âvahai*	आमहै *âmahai*
2.	no termination, or तात् *tât*	तम् *tam*	त *ta*, or तात् *tât*	स्व *sva*	आथाम् *âthâm*	ध्वम् *dhvam*
3.	तु *tu*, or तात् *tât*	ताम् *tâm*	अन्तु *antu*	ताम् *tâm*	आताम् *âtâm*	अन्ताम् *antâm*

§ 76. The original terminations of the POTENTIAL are:—

	In the Parasmaipada.			In the Âtmanepada.		
	SINGULAR.	DUAL.	PLURAL.	SINGULAR.	DUAL.	PLURAL.
1.	याम् *yâm*	याव *yâva*	याम *yâma*	ईय *îya*	ईवहि *îvahi*	ईमहि *îmahi*
2.	यास् *yâs*	यातम् *yâtam*	यात *yâta*	ईथास् *îthâs*	ईयाथाम् *îyâthâm*	ईध्वम् *îdhvam*
3.	यात् *yât*	याताम् *yâtâm*	युस् *yus*	ईत *îta*	ईयाताम् *îyâtâm*	ईरन् *îran*

§ 77. But as the initial या *yâ* and ई *î* of these affixes combine with the final अ *a* of the base to ए *e*, and in the first person singular and the third person plural of the Parasmaipada anomalous changes take place, the potential of the first conjugation ends in the following terminations, before which the final अ *a* of the base is rejected:—

	In the Parasmaipada.			In the Âtmanepada.		
	SINGULAR.	DUAL.	PLURAL.	SINGULAR.	DUAL.	PLURAL.
1.	एयम् *eyam*	एव *eva*	एम *ema*	एय *eya*	एवहि *evahi*	एमहि *emahi*
2.	एस् *es*	एतम् *etam*	एत *eta*	एथास् *ethâs*	एयाथाम् *eyâthâm*	एध्वम् *edhvam*
3.	एत् *et*	एताम् *etâm*	एयुस् *eyus*	एत *eta*	एयाताम् *eyâtâm*	एरन् *eran*

Observation. In the Veda न *na* is often added to the थ *tha* and त *ta* of the second person plural Parasmaipada.

§ 78. Before these terminations the final अ *a* of the base undergoes the following changes:—

1. It is lengthened when followed by a termination beginning with व् *v*, or म् *m*, *e.g.* बोध + मि *bódha + mi*, 1st pers. sing. pres. Par., or + वस् *vas*, 1st pers. dual pres. Par. becomes बोधामि *bódhâmi*, बोधावस् *bódhâvas*.

2. It is dropped before any termination beginning with a vowel or diphthong, *e.g.* अबोध + अम् *ábodha+am* becomes अबोधम् *ábodham*, first sing. imperf. Par.

Exception to rule 2. With the इ *i* of the first person singular of the imperfect Âtmanepada and with the आ *â* of the second and third persons dual of the present, imperfect, and imperative Âtm. it coalesces to ए *e*, *e.g.* अबोध + इ *ábodha+i* becomes अबोधे *ábodhe*, बोध + आथे *bódha+âthe* (2d du. pres. Âtmanep.) बोधेथे *bódhethe*.

§ 79. In forming the special bases the general phonetic rules, § 14-18, must be remembered, *e.g.* कुर्द् *kurd*, I. 1, 'to play,' according to § 18 makes कूर्द *kûrda*; दिव् *div*, I. 4, दीव्य *dívya*.

§ 80. Paradigms of the First Conjugation.

1. Of the first class: बुध् *budh*, 'to know,' special base बोध *bódha*.

PRESENT.

Parasmaipada.			Âtmanepada.		
बोधामि *bódhâmi* I know	बोधावस् *bódhâvas* We two know	बोधामस् *bódhâmas* We know	बोधे *bódhe*	बोधावहे *bódhâvahe*	बोधामहे *bódhâmahe*
			I know, etc., as in the Parasmaipada.		
बोधसि *bódhasi* Thou knowest	बोधथस् *bódhathas* You two know	बोधथ *bódhatha* You know	बोधसे *bódhase*	बोधेथे *bódhethe*	बोधध्वे *bódhadhve*
बोधति *bódhati* He knows	बोधतस् *bódhatas* They two know	बोधन्ति *bódhanti* They know	बोधते *bódhate*	बोधेते *bódhete*	बोधन्ते *bódhante*

Parasmaipada.		IMPERFECT.	Âtmanepada.		
अबोधम् *ábodham* I knew	अबोधाव *ábodhâva*	अबोधाम *ábodhâma*	अबोधे *ábodhe* I knew	अबोधावहि *ábodhâvahi*	अबोधामहि *ábodhâmahi*
अबोधस् *ábodhas*	अबोधतम् *ábodhatam*	अबोधत *ábodhata*	अबोधथास् *ábodhathâs*	अबोधेथाम् *ábodhethâm*	अबोधध्वम् *ábodhadhvam*
अबोधत् *ábodhat*	अबोधताम् *ábodhatâm*	अबोधन् *ábodhan*	अबोधत *ábodhata*	अबोधेताम् *ábodhetâm*	अबोधन्त *ábodhanta*

IMPERATIVE.

बोधानि *bódhâni* May I know	बोधाव *bódhâva*	बोधाम *bódhâma*	बोधै *bódhai*	बोधावहै *bódhâvahai*	बोधामहै *bódhâmahai*
बोध or *bódha* बोधतात् *bódhatât*	बोधतम् *bódhatam*	बोधत or *bódhata* बोधतात् *bódhatât*	बोधस्व *bódhasva*	बोधेथाम् *bódhethâm*	बोधध्वम् *bódhadhvam*
बोधतु or *bódhatu* बोधतात् *bódhatât*	बोधताम् *bódhatâm*	बोधन्तु *bódhantu*	बोधताम् *bódhatâm*	बोधेताम् *bódhetâm*	बोधन्ताम् *bódhantâm*

POTENTIAL.

बोधेयम् *bódheyam* I may, or I might know	बोधेव *bódheva*	बोधेम *bódhema*	बोधेय *bódheya*	बोधेवहि *bódhevahi*	बोधेमहि *bódhemahi*
बोधेस् *bódhes*	बोधेतम् *bódhetam*	बोधेत *bódheta*	बोधेथास् *bódhethâs*	बोधेयाथाम् *bódheyâthâm*	बोधेध्वम् *bódhedvam*
बोधेत् *bódhet*	बोधेताम् *bódhetâm*	बोधेयुस् *bódheyus*	बोधेत *bódheta*	बोधेयाताम् *bódheyâtâm*	बोधेरन् *bódheran*

In the same way are inflected *e.g.* जि *ji*, 'to overpower,' special base जय *jáya*, 1st sing. pres. Par. जयामि *jáyâmi*, etc.; भू *bhû*, 'to become,' special base भव *bháva*, 1st sing. pres. Par. भवामि *bhávâmi*, etc.; सृ *sṛi*, 'to go,' special base सर *sára*, 1st sing. pres. Par. सरामि *sárâmi*, etc.; धे *dhe*, 'to drink,' special base धय *dháya*, 1st sing. pres. Par. धयामि *dháyâmi*, etc.; दै *dai*, 'to purify,' special base दाय *dấya*, 1st sing. pres. Par. दायामि *dấyâmi*, etc.; ज्यो *jyo*, Âtm. 'to restrain,' special base ज्यव *jyáva*, 1st sing. pres. Âtm. ज्यवे *jyáve*, etc.; गद् *gad*, 'to speak,' special base गद *gáda*, 1st sing. pres. Par. गदामि *gádâmi*; चित् *chit*, 'to think,' special base चेत *chéta*, 1st sing. pres. Par. चेतामि *chétâmi*, etc.

2. Fourth class: नह् *nah*, 'to bind,' special base नह्य *náhya*.

PRESENT.

Parasmaipada.			Âtmanepada.		
नह्यामि *náhyâmi*	नह्यावस् *náhyâvas*	नह्यामस् *náhyâmas*	नह्ये *náhye*	नह्यावहे *náhyâvahe*	नह्यामहे *náhyâmahe*
नह्यसि *náhyasi*	नह्यथस् *náhyathas*	नह्यथ *náhyatha*	नह्यसे *náhyase*	नह्येथे *náhyethe*	नह्यध्वे *náhyadhve*
नह्यति *náhyati*	नह्यतस् *náhyatas*	नह्यन्ति *náhyanti*	नह्यते *náhyate*	नह्येते *náhyete*	नह्यन्ते *náhyante*

IMPERFECT.

अनह्यम् *ánahyam*	अनह्याव *ánahyâva*	अनह्याम *ánahyâma*	अनह्ये *ánahye*	अनह्यावहि *ánahyâvahi*	अनह्यामहि *ánahyâmahi*
अनह्यस् *ánahyas*	अनह्यतम् *ánahyatam*	अनह्यत *ánahyata*	अनह्यथास् *ánahyathâs*	अनह्येथाम् *ánahyethâm*	अनह्यध्वम् *ánahyadhvam*
अनह्यत् *ánahyat*	अनह्यताम् *ánahyatâm*	अनह्यन् *ánahyan*	अनह्यत *ánahyata*	अनह्येताम् *ánahyetâm*	अनह्यन्त *ánahyanta*

IMPERATIVE.

नह्यानि *náhyâni*	नह्याव *náhyâva*	नह्याम *náhyâma*	नह्यै *náhyai*	नह्यावहै *náhyâvahai*	नह्यामहै *náhyâmahai*
नह्य or *náhya* नह्यतात् *náhyatât*	नह्यतम् *náhyatam*	नह्यत or *náhyata* नह्यतात् *náhyatât*	नह्यस्व *náhyasva*	नह्येथाम् *náhyethâm*	नह्यध्वम् *náhyadhvam*
नह्यतु or *náhyatu* नह्यतात् *náhyatât*	नह्यताम् *náhyatâm*	नह्यन्तु *náhyantu*	नह्यताम् *náhyatâm*	नह्येताम् *náhyetâm*	नह्यन्ताम् *náhyantâm*

POTENTIAL.

नह्येयम् *náhyeyam*	नह्येव *náhyeva*	नह्येम *náhyema*	नह्येय *náhyeya*	नह्येवहि *náhyevahi*	नह्येमहि *náhyemahi*
नह्येस् *náhyes*	नह्येतम् *náhyetam*	नह्येत *náhyeta*	नह्येथास् *náhyethâs*	नह्येयाथाम् *náhyeyâthâm*	नह्येध्वम् *náhyedhvam*
नह्येत् *náhyet*	नह्येताम् *náhyetâm*	नह्येयुस् *náhyeyus*	नह्येत *náhyeta*	नह्येयाताम् *náhyeyâtâm*	नह्येरन् *náhyeran*

नृत् *nṛit*, special base नृत्य *nṛítya*, 1st sing. pres. Par. नृत्यामि *nṛ́tyâmi*, etc.; जॄ *jṝi*, 'to grow old,' special base जीर्य *jī́rya*, 1st sing. pres. Par. जीर्यामि *jī́ryâmi*, etc.

3. Sixth class : तुद् *tud*, 'to strike,' special base तुद *tudá*.

PRESENT.

Parasmaipada.			Âtmanepada.		
तुदामि *tudā́mi*	तुदावस् *tudā́vas*	तुदामस् *tudā́mas*	तुदे *tudé*	तुदावहे *tudā́vahe*	तुदामहे *tudā́mahe*
तुदसि *tudási*	तुदथस् *tudáthas*	तुदथ *tudátha*	तुदसे *tudáse*	तुदेथे *tudéthe*	तुदध्वे *tudádhve*
तुदति *tudáti*	तुदतस् *tudátas*	तुदन्ति *tudánti*	तुदते *tudáte*	तुदेते *tudéte*	तुदन्ते *tudánte*

IMPERFECT.

अतुदम् *átudam*	अतुदाव *átudâva*	अतुदाम *átudâma*	अतुदे *átude*	अतुदावहि *átudâvahi*	अतुदामहि *átudâmahi*
अतुदस् *átudas*	अतुदतम् *átudatam*	अतुदत *átudata*	अतुदथास् *átudathâs*	अतुदेथाम् *átudethâm*	अतुदध्वम् *átudadhvam*
अतुदत् *átudat*	अतुदताम् *átudatâm*	अतुदन् *átudan*	अतुदत *átudata*	अतुदेताम् *átudetâm*	अतुदन्त *átudanta*

IMPERATIVE.

तुदानि *tudā́ni*	तुदाव *tudā́va*	तुदाम *tudā́ma*	तुदै *tudái*	तुदावहै *tudā́vahai*	तुदामहै *tudā́mahai*
तुद or *tudá* तुदतात् *tudátât*	तुदतम् *tudátam*	तुदत or *tudáta* तुदतात् *tudátât*	तुदस्व *tudásva*	तुदेथाम् *tudéthâm*	तुदध्वम् *tudádhvam*
तुदतु or *tudátu* तुदतात् *tudátât*	तुदताम् *tudátâm*	तुदन्तु *tudántu*	तुदताम् *tudátâm*	तुदेताम् *tudétâm*	तुदन्ताम् *tudántâm*

POTENTIAL.

तुदेयम् *tudéyam*	तुदेव *tudéva*	तुदेम *tudéma*	तुदेय *tudéya*	तुदेवहि *tudévahi*	तुदेमहि *tudémahi*
तुदेस् *tudés*	तुदेतम् *tudétam*	तुदेत *tudéta*	तुदेथास् *tudéthâs*	तुदेयाथाम् *tudéyâthâm*	तुदेध्वम् *tudédhvam*
तुदेत् *tudét*	तुदेताम् *tudétâm*	तुदेयुस् *tudéyus*	तुदेत *tudéta*	तुदेयाताम् *tudéyâtâm*	तुदेरन् *tudéran*

स्पृश् *spṛç* 'to touch,' special base स्पृश *spṛçá*, 1st sing. pres. Par. स्पृशामि *spṛçā́mi*, etc.

4. Verbs ending in the affix अय *aya* (tenth conjugational class, causals and denominatives): बोधय *bodháya*, causal of बुध् *budh*, 'to know.'

PRESENT.

Parasmaipada.			Âtmanepada.		
बोधयामि *bodháyâmi*	बोधयावस् *bodháyâvas*	बोधयामस् *bodháyâmas*	बोधये *bodháye*	बोधयावहे *bodháyâvahe*	बोधयामहे *bodháyâmahe*
बोधयसि *bodháyasi*	बोधयथस् *bodháyathas*	बोधयथ *bodháyatha*	बोधयसे *bodháyase*	बोधयेथे *bodháyethe*	बोधयध्वे *bodháyadhve*
बोधयति *bodháyati*	बोधयतस् *bodháyatas*	बोधयन्ति *bodháyanti*	बोधयते *bodháyate*	बोधयेते *bodháyete*	बोधयन्ते *bodháyante*

IMPERFECT.

अबोधयम् *ábodhayam*	अबोधयाव *ábodhayâva*	अबोधयाम *ábodhayâma*	अबोधये *ábodhaye*	अबोधयावहि *ábodhayâvahi*	अबोधयामहि *ábodhayâmahi*
अबोधयस् *ábodhayas*	अबोधयतम् *ábodhayatam*	अबोधयत *ábodhayata*	अबोधयथास् *ábodhayathâs*	अबोधयेथाम् *ábodhayethâm*	अबोधयध्वम् *ábodhayadhvam*
अबोधयत् *ábodhayat*	अबोधयताम् *ábodhayatâm*	अबोधयन् *ábodhayan*	अबोधयत *ábodhayata*	अबोधयेताम् *ábodhayetâm*	अबोधयन्त *ábodhayanta*

IMPERATIVE.

बोधयानि *bodháyâni*	बोधयाव *bodháyâva*	बोधयाम *bodháyâma*	बोधयै *bodháyai*	बोधयावहै *bodháyâvahai*	बोधयामहै *bodháyâmahai*
बोधय or *bodháya* बोधयतात् *bodháyatât*	बोधयतम् *bodháyatam*	बोधयत or *bodháyata* बोधयतात् *bodháyatât*	बोधयस्व *bodháyasva*	बोधयेथाम् *bodháyethâm*	बोधयध्वम् *bodháyadhvam*
बोधयतु or *bodháyatu* बोधयतात् *bodháyatât*	बोधयताम् *bodháyatâm*	बोधयन्तु *bodháyantu*	बोधयताम् *bodháyatâm*	बोधयेताम् *bodháyetâm*	बोधयन्ताम् *bodháyantâm*

POTENTIAL.

बोधयेयम् *bodháyeyam*	बोधयेव *bodháyeva*	बोधयेम *bodháyema*	बोधयेय *bodháyeya*	बोधयेवहि *bodháyevahi*	बोधयेमहि *bodháyemahi*
बोधयेस् *bodháyes*	बोधयेतम् *bodháyetam*	बोधयेत *bodháyeta*	बोधयेथास् *bodháyethâs*	बोधयेयाथाम् *bodháyeyâthâm*	बोधयेध्वम् *bodháyedhvam*
बोधयेत् *bodháyet*	बोधयेताम् *bodháyetâm*	बोधयेयुस् *bodháyeyus*	बोधयेत *bodháyeta*	बोधयेयाताम् *bodháyeyâtâm*	बोधयेरन् *bodháyeran*

चुर् *chur*, 'to steal,' base of the conjugation चोरय *choráya*, 1st sing. pres. Par. चोरयामि *choráyâmi*, etc.

5. Desiderative: बुबोधिष *búbodhisha*, from बुध् *budh*, 'to know.'

Parasmaipada.			Âtmanepada.		
PRESENT.					
बुबोधिषामि *búbodhishâmi*	बुबोधिषावस् *búbodhishâvas*	बुबोधिषामस् *búbodhishâmas*	बुबोधिषे *búbodhishe*	बुबोधिषावहे *búbodhishâvahe*	बुबोधिषामहे *búbodhishâmahe*
बुबोधिषसि *búbodhishasi*	बुबोधिषथस् *búbodhishathas*	बुबोधिषथ *búbodhishatha*	बुबोधिषसे *búbodhishase*	बुबोधिषेथे *búbhodhishethe*	बुबोधिषध्वे *búbodhishadhve*
बुबोधिषति *búbodhishati*	बुबोधिषतस् *búbodhishatas*	बुबोधिषन्ति *búbodhishanti*	बुबोधिषते *búbodhishate*	बुबोधिषेते *búbodhishete*	बुबोधिषन्ते *búbodhishante*
IMPERFECT.					
अबुबोधिषम् *ábubodhisham*	अबुबोधिषाव *ábubodhishâva*	अबुबोधिषाम *ábubodhishâma*	अबुबोधिषे *ábubodhishe*	अबुबोधिषावहि *ábubodhishâvahi*	अबुबोधिषामहि *ábubodhishâmahi*
अबुबोधिषस् *ábubodhishas*	अबुबोधिषतम् *ábubodhishatam*	अबुबोधिषत *ábubodhishata*	अबुबोधिषथास् *ábubodhishathâs*	अबुबोधिषेथाम् *ábubodhishethâm*	अबुबोधिषध्वम् *ábubodhishadhvam*
अबुबोधिषत् *ábubodhishat*	अबुबोधिषताम् *ábubodhishatâm*	अबुबोधिषन् *ábubodhishan*	अबुबोधिषत *ábubodhishata*	अबुबोधिषेताम् *ábubodhishetâm*	अबुबोधिषन्त *ábubodhishanta*
IMPERATIVE.					
बुबोधिषाणि *búbodhishâṇi* (Cf. § 16.)	बुबोधिषाव *búbodhishâva*	बुबोधिषाम *búbodhishâma*	बुबोधिषै *búbodhishai*	बुबोधिषावहै *búbodhishâvahai*	बुबोधिषामहै *búbodhishâmahai*
बुबोधिष *búbodhisha* or बुबोधिषतात् *búbodhishatât*	बुबोधिषतम् *búbodhishatam*	बुबोधिषत *búbodhishata* or बुबोधिषतात् *búbodhishatât*	बुबोधिषस्व *búbodhishasva*	बुबोधिषेथाम् *búbodhishethâm*	बुबोधिषध्वम् *búbodhishadhvam*
बुबोधिषतु *búbodhishatu* or बुबोधिषतात् *búbodhishatât*	बुबोधिषताम् *búbodhishatâm*	बुबोधिषन्तु *búbodhishantu*	बुबोधिषताम् *búbodhishatâm*	बुबोधिषेताम् *búbodhishetâm*	बुबोधिषन्ताम् *búbodhishantâm*
POTENTIAL.					
बुबोधिषेयम् *búbodhisheyam*	बुबोधिषेव *búbodhisheva*	बुबोधिषेम *búbodhishema*	बुबोधिषेय *búbodhisheya*	बुबोधिषेवहि *búbodhishevahi*	बुबोधिषेमहि *búbodhishemahi*
बुबोधिषेस् *búbodhishes*	बुबोधिषेतम् *búbodhishetam*	बुबोधिषेत *búbodhisheta*	बुबोधिषेथास् *búbodhishethâs*	बुबोधिषेयाथाम् *búbodhisheyâthâm*	बुबोधिषेध्वम् *búbodhishedhvam*
बुबोधिषेत् *búbodhishet*	बुबोधिषेताम् *búbodhishetâm*	बुबोधिषेयुस् *búbodhisheyus*	बुबोधिषेत *búbodhisheta*	बुबोधिषेयाताम् *búbodhisheyâtâm*	बुबोधिषेरन् *búbodhisheran*

6. **Verbs ending in derivative** य *ya* **(denominatives and frequentatives of the second form, and verbs in** आय *âyá*, ईय, *íyá*) : नमस्य *namasyá* 'to worship' (denominative from नमस् *namas*, 'veneration').

PRESENT.

Parasmaipada.			Âtmanepada.		
नमस्यामि *namasyấmi*	नमस्यावस् *namasyấvas*	नमस्यामस् *namasyấmas*	नमस्ये *namasyé*	नमस्यावहे *namasyấvahe*	नमस्यामहे *namasyấmahe*
नमस्यसि *namasyási*	नमस्यथस् *namasyáthas*	नमस्यथ *namasyátha*	नमस्यसे *namasyáse*	नमस्येथे *namasyéthe*	नमस्यध्वे *namasyádhve*
नमस्यति *namasyáti*	नमस्यतस् *namasyátas*	नमस्यन्ति *namasyánti*	नमस्यते *namasyáte*	नमस्येते *namasyéte*	नमस्यन्ते *namasyánte*

IMPERFECT.

अनमस्यम् *ánamasyam*	अनमस्याव *ánamasyâva*	अनमस्याम *ánamasyâma*	अनमस्ये *ánamasye*	अनमस्यावहि *ánamasyâvahi*	अनमस्यामहि *ánamasyâmahi*
अनमस्यस् *ánamasyas*	अनमस्यतम् *ánamasyatam*	अनमस्यत *ánamasyata*	अनमस्यथास् *ánamasyathâs*	अनमस्येथाम् *ánamasyethâm*	अनमस्यध्वम् *ánamasyadhvam*
अनमस्यत् *ánamasyat*	अनमस्यताम् *ánamasyatâm*	अनमस्यन् *ánamasyan*	अनमस्यत *ánamasyata*	अनमस्येताम् *ánamasyetâm*	अनमस्यन्त *ánamasyanta*

IMPERATIVE.

नमस्यानि *namasyấni*	नमस्याव *namasyấva*	नमस्याम *namasyấma*	नमस्यै *namasyái*	नमस्यावहै *namasyấvahai*	नमस्यामहै *namasyấmahai*
नमस्य or *namasyá* नमस्यतात् *namasyátât*	नमस्यतम् *namasyátam*	नमस्यत or *namasyáta* नमस्यतात् *namasyátât*	नमस्यस्व *namasyásva*	नमस्येथाम् *namasyéthâm*	नमस्यध्वम् *namasyádhvam*
नमस्यतु or *namasyátu* नमस्यतात् *namasyátât*	नमस्यताम् *namasyátâm*	नमस्यन्तु *namasyántu*	नमस्यताम् *namasyátâm*	नमस्येताम् *namasyétâm*	नमस्यन्ताम् *namasyántâm*

POTENTIAL.

नमस्येयम् *namasyéyam*	नमस्येव *namasyéva*	नमस्येम *namasyéma*	नमस्येय *namasyéya*	नमस्येवहि *namasyévahi*	नमस्येमहि *namasyémahi*
नमस्येस् *namasyés*	नमस्येतम् *namasyétam*	नमस्येत *namasyéta*	नमस्येथास् *namasyéthâs*	नमस्येयाथाम् *namasyéyâthâm*	नमस्येध्वम् *namasyédhvam*
नमस्येत् *namasyét*	नमस्येताम् *namasyétâm*	नमस्येयुस् *namasyéyus*	नमस्येत *namasyéta*	नमस्येयाताम् *namasyéyâtâm*	नमस्येरन् *namasyéran*

7. Denominatives without affix: पितृ *pitṛi*, 'to behave like a father' (denominative from पितृ *pitṛi*, 'father'), special base पितर *pitára*.

PRESENT.

Parasmaipada.			Âtmanepada.		
पितरामि *pitárâmi*	पितरावस् *pitárâvas*	पितरामस् *pitárâmas*	पितरे *pitáre*	पितरावहे *pitárâvahe*	पितरामहे *pitárâmahe*
पितरसि *pitárasi*	पितरथस् *pitárathas*	पितरथ *pitáratha*	पितरसे *pitárase*	पितरेथे *pitárethe*	पितरध्वे *pitáradhve*
पितरति *pitárati*	पितरतस् *pitáratas*	पितरन्ति *pitáranti*	पितरते *pitárate*	पितरेते *pitárete*	पितरन्ते *pitárante*

IMPERFECT.

अपितरम् *ápitaram*	अपितराव *ápitarâva*	अपितराम *ápitarâma*	अपितरे *ápitare*	अपितरावहि *ápitarâvahi*	अपितरामहि *ápitarâmahi*
अपितरस् *ápitaras*	अपितरतम् *ápitaratam*	अपितरत *ápitarata*	अपितरथास् *ápitarathâs*	अपितरेथाम् *ápitarethâm*	अपितरध्वम् *ápitaradhvam*
अपितरत् *ápitarat*	अपितरताम् *ápitaratâm*	अपितरन् *ápitaran*	अपितरत *ápitarata*	अपितरेताम् *ápitaretâm*	अपितरन्त *ápitaranta*

IMPERATIVE.

पितराणि[1] *pitárâṇi*	पितराव *pitárâva*	पितराम *pitárâma*	पितरै *pitárai*	पितरावहै *pitárâvahai*	पितरामहै *pitárâmahai*
पितर or पितरतात् *pitára* or *pitáratât*	पितरतम् *pitáratam*	पितरत or पितरतात् *pitárata* or *pitáratât*	पितरस्व *pitárasva*	पितरेथाम् *pitárethâm*	पितरध्वम् *pitáradhvam*
पितरतु or पितरतात् *pitáratu* or *pitáratât*	पितरताम् *pitáratâm*	पितरन्तु *pitárantu*	पितरताम् *pitáratâm*	पितरेताम् *pitáretâm*	पितरन्ताम् *pitárantâm*

POTENTIAL.

पितरेयम् *pitáreyam*	पितरेव *pitáreva*	पितरेम *pitárema*	पितरेय *pitáreya*	पितरेवहि *pitárevahi*	पितरेमहि *pitáremahi*
पितरेस् *pitáres*	पितरेतम् *pitáretam*	पितरेत *pitáreta*	पितरेथास् *pitárethâs*	पितरेयाथाम् *pitáreyâthâm*	पितरेध्वम् *pitáredhvam*
पितरेत् *pitáret*	पितरेताम् *pitáretâm*	पितरेयुस् *pitáreyus*	पितरेत *pitáreta*	पितरेयाताम् *pitáreyâtâm*	पितरेरन् *pitáreran*

[1] Cf. § 16.

Observation. The intelligent reader will not fail to notice that the six last Paradigms differ almost in the accent only from the first.

§ 81. Alphabetical List of Anomalous Bases.

Base		Root
इच्छ I. 6	from the verb	इष् 'to wish.'
ऋच्छ I. 1 (? in the Veda I. 6)	from the verb	ऋ 'to go.'
ऋतीय I. 1	from the verb	ऋत् 'to blame.'
कामय I. 10	from the verb	कम् 'to love.'
कृन्त I. 6	from the verb	कृत् 'to cut.'
क्राम I. 1, क्राम्य I. 4	from the verb	क्रम् 'to go.'
क्लाम I. 1, क्लाम्य I. 4	from the verb	क्लम् 'to be sad.'
क्षाम्य I. 4	from the verb	क्षम् 'to endure.'
खिन्द I. 6	from the verb	खिद् 'to be distressed.'
गच्छ I. 1	from the verb	गम् 'to go.'
गिल (also regularly गिर) I. 6	from the verb	गॄ 'to swallow.'
गूह I. 1	from the verb	गुह् 'to hide.'
गोपाय I. 1	from the verb	गुप् 'to protect.'
(आ) चाम I. 1	from the verb	चम् 'to drink' (but only when preceded by the preposition आ *â*).
छ्य I. 4	from the verb	छो 'to cut.'
जम्भ I. 1	from the verb	जभ् 'to gape.'
जाय I. 4	from the verb	जन् 'to be born.'
जिघ्न I. 1 (Vedic)	from the verb	हन् 'to kill.'
जिघ्र I. 1	from the verb	घ्रा 'to smell.'
ताम्य I. 4	from the verb	तम् 'to be distressed.'
तिष्ठ I. 1	from the verb	स्था 'to stand.'
तृह I. 6	from the verb	तृंह् 'to hurt.'
दश I. 1	from the verb	दंश् 'to bite.'
दाम्य I. 4	from the verb	दम् 'to tame.'
द्य I. 4	from the verb	दो 'to tie.'

धम I. 1 . . . . from the verb ध्मा 'to blow.'
धाव I. 1 optionally . . . „ „ „ सृ 'to go.'
धूपाय I. 1 . . . . „ „ „ धूप् 'to fumigate.'
पणाय I. 1 . . . . „ „ „ पण् } 'to praise.'
पनाय I. 1 . . . . „ „ „ पन् }
पश्य I. 1 . . . . „ „ „ दृश् 'to see.'
पिंश I. 6 . . . . „ „ „ पिश् 'to form.'
पिब } I. 1 . . . . „ „ „ पा 'to drink.'
पिव }
पृच्छ I. 6 . . . . „ „ „ प्रछ् 'to ask.'
भृज्ज I. 6 . . . . „ „ „ भ्रज्ज् 'to fry.'
भ्रश्य I. 4 . . . . „ „ „ भ्रंश् } 'to fall.'
भ्रस्य I. 4 . . . . „ „ „ भ्रंस् }
भ्राम्य (also regularly भ्रम्य) I. 4 „ „ „ भ्रम् 'to whirl.'
मन I. 1 . . . . „ „ „ म्ना 'to think.'
माद्य I. 4 . . . . „ „ „ मद् 'to be glad.'
मेद्य I. 4 . . . . „ „ „ मिद् 'to be unctuous.'
मार्ज I. 1 . . . . „ „ „ मृज् 'to clean.'
यच्छ I. 1 . . . . „ „ „ { यम् 'to lift up,' and दा 'to give.'
रज I. 1 } . . . . „ „ „ रञ्ज् 'to colour.'
रज्य I. 4 }
लिम्प I. 6 . . . . „ „ „ लिप् 'to anoint.'
लुम्प I. 6 . . . . „ „ „ लुप् 'to cut.'
विच I. 6 . . . . „ „ „ व्यच् 'to deceive.'
विच्छाय I. 1 . . . . „ „ „ विछ् 'to go.'
विध्य I. 6 . . . . „ „ „ व्यध् 'to hurt.'
विन्द I. 6 . . . . „ „ „ विद् 'to find.'
शाम्य I. 4 . . . . „ „ „ शम् 'to be tranquil.'
श्य I. 4 . . . . „ „ „ शो 'to sharpen.'
शीय I. 1 } . . . . „ „ „ शद् 'to fall.'
शीय I. 6 }
श्राम्य I. 4 . . . . „ „ „ श्रम् 'to be weary.'

ष्ठीव I. 1 . . . . from the verb ष्ठिव् 'to spit.'
सज I. 1 . . . . " " " सञ्ज् 'to adhere.'
सिञ्च I. 6 . . . . " " " सिच् 'to sprinkle.'
सीद I. 1 } सीद I. 6 } . . . . " " " सद् 'to sit.'
स्य I. 4 . . . . " " " सो 'to destroy.'
स्वज I. 1 . . . . " " " स्वञ्ज् 'to embrace.'

SECOND CONJUGATION.

§ 82. It is a characteristic peculiarity of the second conjugation, that the accent (acute) in most inflexions falls on the first syllable of the termination, and in the Potential of the Âtmanepada on the second, *e.g.* द्विष् *dvish*, II. 2, 'to hate,' with the termination of the 1st pl. pres. Parasmaip. (*cf.* § 73) द्विष्मस् *dvish-más*, with that of the 1st pl. pres. Âtmanep. द्विष्महे *dvish-máhe*, 1st sing. poten. Âtm. द्विषीय *dvish-íyá*.

There are, however, the following exceptions:—

1. The verbs which are conjugated in the Âtmanepada only never have the accent on the termination, *e.g.* शी *çí*, II. 2, Âtm. 'to lie down,' in the 1st pl. pres. शेमहे *çé-mahe*.

2. In the augmented forms, according to § 74, the accent falls on the augment, *e.g.* 1st pl. imperf. Par. from द्विष् *dvish*, II. 2, अद्विष्म *á-dvish-ma*.

3. In the *present* and *imperfect singular* of the *Parasmaipada*, in the *first persons* singular, dual, and plural of the *imperative Parasmaipada* and *Âtmanepada*, and in the third person singular of the imperative of the Parasmaipada, formed by the termination तु *tu* (in the Veda optionally also in the second person singular and plural Parasmaipada, if not formed by तात् *tất*) the accent generally falls (except the third conjugational class and the frequentatives of the first form, *cf.* § 83, II. A. 2) on the syllable which precedes the termination and causes its vowel to be strengthened, *e.g.* द्विष् *dvish*, II. 2, in the 1st singular present

becomes, by changing इ *i* to the diphthong ए *e*, द्वेष्मि *dvésh-mi*, in the 1st sing. imperfect, when without augment, द्वेषम् *dvésh-am*, but when with augment, according to 2, अद्वेषम् *á-dvesh-am*. We shall call these forms strong forms.

§ 83. This conjugation comprises:—

I. The second, third, fifth, seventh, eighth, and ninth conjugational classes of the primitive verbs.

II. The frequentatives of the first form.

A. 1. In the second class the terminations of the first four verbal forms are attached immediately to the crude form of the verb. Thus the root द्विष् *dvish* is also the special base for the present, imperfect, imperative and potential. In the strong forms (*cf.* § 82, 3), a final radical इ *i* or ई *î* before an affix beginning with a consonant is changed to ए *e*, before an affix beginning with a vowel to अय् *ay*,[1] *e.g.* वी *vî*, 'to go,' in 1st sing. pres. Par. वेमि *vé-mi*, in 1st sing. imperative Par. वयानि *váy-âni* (*cf.* § 75); a final उ *u* before consonants becomes औ *au*,[2] before vowels अव् *av*,[1] *e.g.* यु *yu*, 'to join,' यौमि *yaú-mi*, यवानि *yáv-âni*; a final ऋ *ṛi* becomes अर् *ar*,[1] *e.g.* जागृ *jâgṛi*, 'to wake,' जागर्मि *jâgár-mi*, जागराणि *jâgár-âṇi* (with ण् *ṇ* instead of न् *n*, agreeably to § 16). इ *i*, उ *u*, and ऋ *ṛi*, when followed by a single radical consonant only, are changed to ए *e*, ओ *o*, and अर् *ar*,[1] *e.g.* द्विष् *dvish*, 1st sing. pres. Par. द्वेष्मि *dvésh-mi*, 1st sing. imperat. Par. द्वेषाणि *dvésh-âṇi*.

Observ. The verbs with final ऊ *û*, which belong to this class, are irregular (*cf.* § 108).

2. The third class forms its special base for the present, imperfect, imperative, and potential, by reduplicating the verb, according to the general rules given in § 42-46, *e.g.* दा *dâ*, 'to give,' ददा *dadâ*. A radical ऋ *ṛi* or ॠ *ṛî*, however, is repre-

[1] *Guṇa*, p. 34, n. [2] *Vṛiddhi*, p. 38, n.

sented in the reduplicated syllable by इ *i*, *e.g.* भृ *bhṛi*, 'to bear,' makes बिभृ *bi-bhṛi*; पॄ *pṛî*, 'to fill,' पिपॄ *pi-pṛî*.

In the strong forms (§ 82, 3) the verbs of this class as well as the frequentatives of the first form (§ 41) change final इ *i* and ई *î* before consonants to ए *e*, before vowels to अय् *ay*,[1] *e.g.* भी *bhî*, 'to fear,' special base बिभी *bibhî*, in the 1st sing. pres. Par. बिभेमि *bibhe-mi*, in the 1st sing. imperative Par. बिभयानि *bibhay-âni*; final उ *u* and ऊ *û* before consonants become ओ *o*, before vowels अव् *av*,[1] *e.g.* बोभू *bobhû*, frequentative of भू *bhû*, 'to become,' 1st sing. pres. Par. बोभोमि *bobho-mi*, 1st sing. imperative Par. बोभवानि *bobhav-âni*; final ऋ *ṛi* and ॠ *ṛî* become अर् *ar*,[1] *e.g.* भृ *bhṛi*, special base बिभृ *bibhṛi*, 1st sing. pres. Par. बिभर्मि *bibhar-mi*, 1st sing. imperative Par. बिभराणि *bibhar-âṇi* (*cf.* § 16). इ *i*, उ *u*, and ऋ *ṛi*, when followed by a single radical consonant, are changed to ए *e*, ओ *o*, and अर् *ar*,[1] when the termination begins with a consonant, *e.g.* बेभिद् *bebhid*, frequentative of भिद् *bhid*, 'to split,' in the 1st sing. pres. Par. बेभेद्मि *bebhed-mi*; but when the termination begins with a vowel, or a vowel is inserted before it, they are left unchanged, *e.g.* 1st sing. imperative Par. बेभिदानि *bebhid-âni*, 1st sing. pres. Par. with inserted ई *î* (*cf.* § 84, 5) बेभिदीमि *bebhid-î-mi*.

In the forms which do not belong to the strong ones, that is to say, in all others except those which are enumerated § 82, 3:—

(*a*) A final radical आ *â*, when followed by a termination beginning with a consonant, is changed to ई *î*, *e.g.* हा *hâ*, 'to leave,' special base जहा *jahâ*, becomes in the 1st plur. pres. Par. जहीमस् *jahî-más*; when followed by a termination beginning with a vowel, the आ *â* is rejected, *e.g.* जहा *jahâ* with the termination अति *ati* (3d plur. pres. Par. § 84, 2) becomes जहति *jah-ati*.

(*b*) Some verbs, enumerated in my 'Vollständige Grammatik,' § 154, 2, 2, ending in a compound consonant, the first member

[1] *Guṇa.*

of which is a nasal, drop the nasal, *e.g.* चोकुञ्च् *chokuñch*, frequentative of कुञ्च् *kuñch*, 'to contract,' becomes in the 3[d] dual pres. Par. चोकुक्तस् *chokuk-tás* (with the termination तस् *tas*, § 73, before which च् *ch* is changed to क् *k* conformably to § 98, 1), in the 3[d] plur. pres. Par. चोकुचति *chokuch-ati.*

In the strong forms and in all those forms the terminations of which begin with a vowel, the accent (acute) generally falls on the reduplicated syllable, *e.g.* दा *dâ*, 'to give,' special base ददा *dadâ*, 1st sing. pres. Par. ददामि *dádâ-mi*; भृ *bhṛi*, special base बिभृ *bibhṛi*, 3[d] plur. pres. Par. बिभ्रति *bíbhr-ati.*

3. The fifth class forms its special base by adding नु *nu* to the verb, *e.g.* चि *chi*, 'to arrange,' special base चिनु *chi-nu*. In many cases नु *nu* becomes णु *ṇu*, according to § 16.

In the strong forms the final उ *u* is changed before a consonant to ओ *o* (guṇa), चिनोमि *chi-no-mi*, before a vowel to अव् *av*, चिनवानि *chi-nav-âni.*

In the other forms the final उ *u* before vowels becomes व् *v*, and, if preceded by more than one consonant उव् *uv*, *e.g.* चिनु+अन्ति *chinu+anti* (3[d] plur. pres. Par.) becomes चिन्वन्ति *chinv-anti*; आप्नु *âpnu*, special base of the verb आप् *âp*, 'to obtain,' with अन्ति *anti*, makes आप्नुवन्ति *âpnuv-anti.*

4. The verbs of the seventh class form their special bases by inserting न *na* before the final radical in the strong forms, and न् *n* in all the others. In many cases न *na* becomes ण *ṇa*, according to § 16. न् *n* before sibilants and ह् *h* is changed to Anusvâra ं, before gutturals to ङ् *ṅ*, before palatals to ञ् *ñ*, before linguals to ण् *ṇ*, before labials to म् *m*. In the strong forms the acute falls on न *na* (ण *ṇa*). For instance the special base of शिष् *çish*, 'to leave,' is in the strong forms शिनष् *çinash*, in others शिंष् *çiṁsh*, *e.g.* शिनष्मि *çinásh-mi*, 1st sing. pres. Par., शिंष्मस् *çiṁsh-más*, 1st plur.; युज् *yuj*, 'to join,' makes in the strong forms युनज् *yunaj*, in others युञ्ज् *yuñj*, *e.g.* युनज्मि *yunáj-mi*, युञ्ज्मस् *yuñj-más*,

in the 2[d] plur. pres. Par. युङ्क्थ *yuṅk-thá* (क् *k* instead of ज् *j* according to § 98, 1).

Observ. Verbs ending in a compound consonant the first element of which is a nasal, reject the latter in the strong forms, *e.g.* भञ्ज् *bhañj*, 'to break,' भनज्मि *bhanáj-mi*; in all the other forms they have of course only one nasal, *e.g.* भञ्ज्मस् *bhañj-más*.

5. The eighth class forms its special base by adding उ *u* to the verb, which, as in the fifth, in the strong forms before consonants is changed to ओ *o*, before vowels to अव् *av* (guṇa), *e.g.* तन् *tan*, 'to stretch,' special base तनु *tan-u*, in the 1st sing. pres. Par. तनोमि *tanó-mi*, in the 1st sing. imperative Par. तनवानि *tanáv-âni*. In the other forms the final उ *u* is changed before vowels to व् *v*, *e.g.* तनु+अन्ति *tanu+anti* becomes तन्वन्ति *tanv-ánti*.

Observ. Verbs ending in single consonants optionally change a preceding इ *i* to ए *e*, उ *u* to ओ *o*, ऋ *ṛi* to अर् *ar* (guṇa), *e.g.* ऋण् *ṛiṇ*, 'to go,' special base ऋणु *ṛiṇu*, or अर्णु *arṇu*.

6. The verbs of the ninth class form their special bases by subjoining ना *nâ* or णा *ṇâ* (according to § 16, and when preceded by ड् *ḍ*, as मृड् *mṛiḍ*, 'to pardon,' मृड्णा *mṛiḍ-ṇâ*) in the strong forms, नी *nî* (or णी *ṇî*) in the other, when the termination begins with a consonant, and न् *n* or ण् *ṇ*, when it begins with a vowel, *e.g.* यु *yu*, 'to join,' 1st sing. pres. Par. युनामि *yu-nấ-mi*, 1st plur. pres. Par. युनीमस् *yu-nî-más*, 3[d] plur. pres. Par. युनन्ति *yu-n-ánti*.

Observ. 1. A penultimate nasal of the root is rejected, *e.g.* मन्थ् *manth*, 'to churn,' special bases मथ्ना *math-nâ*, मथ्नी *math-nî*, and मथ्न् *math-n*. A final long vowel is made short, except in क्री *krî*, 'to buy;' प्री *prî*, 'to love;' श्री *çrî*, 'to cook;' क्नू *knû*, 'to sound;' द्रू *drû*, 'to hurt;' *e.g.* पू *pû*, 'to purify,' makes पुना *pu-nâ*, पुनी *pu-nî*, पुन् *pu-n*; but क्री *krî*, क्रीणा *krî-ṇâ* (§ 16), क्रीणी *krî-ṇî*, क्रीण् *krî-ṇ*.

Observ. 2. In the Vedas the verbs belonging to this class often take the affix आय *âyá*, instead of ना *nâ*, नी *nî*, न् *n*, and follow the first conjugation, *e.g.* मन्थ् *manth* (*cf.* Observ. 1), मथाय *math-áyá.*

B. Nearly all the changes to which the frequentatives of the first form are subjected before the conjugational terminations, have been described in § 83 II. A. 2. We may add now that in the forms which do not belong to the strong forms, the frequentatives, ending in nasals, lengthen a preceding short vowel, if the termination begins with त् *t*, थ् *th*, or ह् *h*, *e.g.* शंशम् *çamçam*, frequentative of शम् *çam*, 'to be tranquil,' with तस् *tas*, the termination of the 3[d] dual pres. Par., makes शंशान्तस् *çamçân-tas*, (*cf.* § 95, 3). Some reject their final nasal (*cf.* my 'Kurze Sanskrit Grammatik,' § 206, 2, *c*, *β*).

§ 84. In the second conjugation the temporal augment has the same form and is prefixed according to the same rules as in the first (§ 74, I). The inflectional terminations differ from those given above (§§ 73-76) in the following particulars: —

1. In the third person plural of the present, imperfect, and imperative Âtmanepada, the न् *n* of the termination is dropped, *e.g.* द्विषते *dvish-áte*, अद्विषत *á-dvish-ata*, द्विषताम् *dvish-átâm.*

2. In the third class and in the frequentatives:—

(*a*) The third person plural of the present and imperative Parasmaipada rejects the न् *n* of the termination, *e.g.* बेभिदति *bébhid-ati*, बेभिदतु *bébhid-atu*, from the frequentative of the verb भिद् *bhid.*

(*b*) The third person plural of the imperfect Parasmaipada substitutes उस् *us* for अन् *an*, before which a final radical इ *i* or ई *î* is changed to अय् *ay*; उ *u* or ऊ *û* to अव् *av*; ऋ *ṛi* or ॠ *ṛî* to अर् *ar* (guṇa), *e.g.* अबिभरुस् *á-bibhar-us* from भृ *bhṛi*, II. 3.

Observ. The verbs of the second conjugational class, which end in आ *â*, optionally take उस् *us*, instead of अन् *an*, in the third person plural of the imperfect Parasmaipada, *e.g.* या *yâ*, 'to go,' may form with अन् *an*, अयान् *á-yân*, or with उस् *us*, अयुस् *á-yus* (*cf.* § 88).

3. In the second person singular of the imperative Parasmaipada, the verbs of the second, third, and seventh classes, and the frequentatives, if ending in any consonant except a nasal, र् *r*, or ल् *l*, attach to the special base the termination धि *dhi*, as अद् *ad*, II. 2, 'to eat,' अद्धि *ad-dhí*; युज् *yuj*, II. 7, 'to join,' युङ्ग्धि *yuṅg-dhí* (with ग् *g* instead of ज् *j*, according to § 99, 1).

The verbs of the second and third classes and the frequentatives ending in vowels or nasals, र् *r*, or ल् *l*, the verbs of the fifth class ending in consonants, and the verbs of the ninth class ending in vowels, attach हि *hi* to the special base, *e.g.* या *yâ*, II. 2, 'to go,' याहि *yâ-hí*; आप् *âp*, II. 5, 'to obtain,' आप्नुहि *âpnu-hí*; यु *yu*, II. 9, 'to join,' युनीहि *yuní-hí*.

The verbs of the eighth class and those of the fifth, the crude forms of which end in vowels, reject the termination, *e.g.* तन् *tan*, II. 8, 'to stretch;' चि *chi*, II. 5, 'to arrange;' special base and 2[d] sing. imperative Parasm. तनु *tanú*, चिनु *chinú*.

The verbs of the ninth class, ending in consonants, attach no termination in the 2[d] pers. sing. imperat. Parasm. and substitute आन *âná* (where § 16 applies, आण *âṇá*), for the characteristic of their class, *e.g.* मन्थ् *manth*, 'to churn,' मथान *math-âná* (the penultimate nasal of the verb is dropped according to § 83, II. A. 6, Observ. 1).

4. The potential Parasmaipada takes the original terminations given in § 76, याम् *yâm*, यास् *yâs*, यात् *yât*, etc.

5. In the first frequentative the vowel ई *í* is optionally inserted before the terminations of the singular present, of the second and third persons singular of the imperfect, and of the third person singular of the imperative Parasmaipada in तु *tu*, *e.g.* बेभिद् *bebhid* makes in the 1st sing. pres. either बेभेद्मि *bébhed-mi*, or बेभिदीमि *bébhid-í-mi* (*cf.* § 83, II. A. 2), बोभू *bobhú*, frequentative from भू *bhú*, 'to become,' बोभोमि *bóbho-mi*, or बोभवीमि *bóbhav-í-mi*.

6. In the Vedas the त् *t* of the third person of the singular and plural Âtmanepada is often dropped, *e.g.* ईशे *íç-e* instead of ईश्+ते

íç + te, which would become ईष्टे *ísh-ṭe* (§ 98, 2, *cf.* my 'Vollständige Grammatik,' § 813, IV.).

7. The उ *u* of the characteristics of the fifth and eighth classes, when preceded by a single consonant, may be rejected before the terminations beginning with व् *v* or म् *m*, *e.g.* the special base of तन् *tan*, II. 8, तनु + वस् *tanu + vas*, makes तनुवस् *tanuvás*, or तन्वस् *tanvás*; the special base of चि *chi*, II. 5, चिनु + मस् *chinu+mas*, makes चिनुमस् *chinumás* or चिन्मस् *chinmás*.

8. An initial स् *s* of the termination is changed to ष् *sh* agreeably to the rules given in § 17, *e.g.* बिभृ + स्व *bibhṛi + sva* becomes बिभृष्व *bibhṛishva*, 2[d] sing. imperative Âtm. of भृ *bhṛi*, II. 3.

§ 85. The rules given in §§ 82-84, will enable the student to conjugate the verbs of the fifth, eighth, and ninth classes. We therefore proceed to give the paradigms:—

PARADIGMS OF THE FIFTH CONJUGATIONAL CLASS: चि *chi*, 'to arrange,' and आप् *âp*, 'to obtain.'

PRESENT.

Parasmaipada.			Âtmanepada.		
चिनोमि *chinómi*	चिनुवस् *chinuvás* or चिन्वस् *chinvás*	चिनुमस् *chinumás* or चिन्मस् *chinmás*	चिन्वे *chinvé*	चिनुवहे *chinuváhe* or चिन्वहे *chinváhe*	चिनुमहे *chinumáhe* or चिन्महे *chinmáhe*
चिनोषि *chinóshi*	चिनुथस् *chinuthás*	चिनुथ *chinuthá*	चिनुषे *chinushé*	चिन्वाथे *chinvā́the*	चिनुध्वे *chinudhvé*
चिनोति *chinóti*	चिनुतस् *chinutás*	चिन्वन्ति *chinvánti*	चिनुते *chinuté*	चिन्वाते *chinvā́te*	चिन्वते *chinváte*

IMPERFECT.

अचिनवम् *áchinavam*	अचिनुव *áchinuva* or अचिन्व *áchinva*	अचिनुम *áchinuma* or अचिन्म *áchinma*	अचिन्वि *áchinvi*	अचिनुवहि *áchinuvahi* or अचिन्वहि *áchinvahi*	अचिनुमहि *áchinumahi* or अचिन्महि *áchinmahi*
अचिनोस् *áchinos*	अचिनुतम् *áchinutam*	अचिनुत *áchinuta*	अचिनुथास् *áchinuthâs*	अचिन्वाथाम् *áchinvâthâm*	अचिनुध्वम् *áchinudhvam*
अचिनोत् *áchinot*	अचिनुताम् *áchinutâm*	अचिन्वन् *áchinvan*	अचिनुत *áchinuta*	अचिन्वाताम् *áchinvâtâm*	अचिन्वत *áchinvata*

IMPERATIVE.

Parasmaipada.			Âtmanepada.		
चिनवानि chinávâni	चिनवाव chinávâva	चिनवाम chinávâma	चिनवै chinávai	चिनवावहै chinávâvahai	चिनवामहै chinávâmahai
चिनु chinú	चिनुतम् chinutám	चिनुत chinutá	चिनुष्व chinushvá	चिन्वाथाम् chinvấthâm	चिनुध्वम् chinudhvám
or चिनुतात् chinutất		or चिनुतात् chinutất			
चिनोतु chinótu	चिनुताम् chinutấm	चिन्वन्तु chinvántu	चिनुताम् chinutấm	चिन्वाताम् chinvấtâm	चिन्वताम् chinvátâm
or चिनुतात् chinutất					

POTENTIAL.

चिनुयाम् chinuyấm	चिनुयाव chinuyấva	चिनुयाम chinuyấma	चिन्वीय chinvîyá	चिन्वीवहि chinvîváhi	चिन्वीमहि chinvîmáhi
चिनुयास् chinuyấs	चिनुयातम् chinuyấtam	चिनुयात chinuyấta	चिन्वीथास् chinvîthấs	चिन्वीयाथाम् chinvîyấthâm	चिन्वीध्वम् chinvîdhvám
चिनुयात् chinuyất	चिनुयाताम् chinuyấtâm	चिनुयुस् chinuyús	चिन्वीत chinvîtá	चिन्वीयाताम् chinvîyấtâm	चिन्वीरन् chinvîrán

सु *su*, 'to distil,' 1 sing. pres. Par. सुनोमि *sunómi*, Âtm. सुन्वे *sunvé*.

I shall give only those forms of the second paradigm, which differ from the preceding.

Present dual 1. Parasm. only आप्नुवस् *âpnuvás* (§ 84, 7), plur. 1. आप्नुमस् *âpnumás*, 3. आप्नुवन्ति *âpnuvánti* (§ 83, 3). Âtman. sing. 1. आप्नुवे *âpnuvé*, dual 1. आप्नुवहे *âpnuváhe*, 2. आप्नुवाथे *âpnuvấthe*, 3. आप्नुवाते *âpnuvấte*, plur. 1. आप्नुमहे *âpnumáhe*, 3. आप्नुवते *âpnuváte*.

Imperfect dual 1. Parasm. आप्नुव *ấpnuva*, plu. 1. आप्नुम *ấpnuma* 3. आप्नुवन् *ấpnuvan*; Âtm. sing. 1. आप्नुवि *ấpnuvi*, dual. 1. आप्नुवहि *ấpnuvahi*, 2. आप्नुवाथाम् *ấpnuvâthâm*, 3. आप्नुवाताम् *ấpnuvâtâm*, plur. 1. आप्नुमहि *ấpnumahi*, 3. आप्नुवत *ấpnuvata*.

Imperative sing. 2. Parasm. आप्नुहि *âpnuhí*, plur. 3. आप्नुवन्तु *âpnuvántu*; Âtman. dual 2. आप्नुवाथाम् *âpnuvấthâm*, 3. आप्नुवाताम् *âpnuvấtâm*, plur. 3. आप्नुवताम् *âpnuvátâm*.

Potential Âtmanep. sing. 1. आप्नुवीय *âpnuvîyá*, 2. आप्नुवीथास् *âpnuvîthâs*, etc., according to § 83, 3.

शक् *çak*, 'to be able,' 1 sing. pres. Par. शक्नोमि *çaknómi*, Âtm. शक्नुवे *çaknuvé*.

PARADIGM OF THE EIGHTH CLASS: तन् *tan*, 'to stretch.'

The verb तन् *tan* follows so strictly the analogy of the first paradigm of the fifth class, that it will be sufficient to give the first two persons.

	PRESENT.		IMPERFECT.	
	Parasm.	Âtmanep.	Parasm.	Âtmanep.
Sing. 1.	तनोमि *tanómi*	तन्वे *tanvé*	अतनवम् *átanavam*	अतन्वि *átanvi*
2.	तनोषि *tanóshi*	तनुषे *tanushé*	अतनोस् *átanos*	अतनुथास् *átanuthâs*
	IMPERATIVE.		POTENTIAL.	
Sing. 1.	तनवानि *tanávâni*	तनवै *tanávai*	तनुयाम् *tanuyâm*	तन्वीय *tanvîyá*
2.	तनु तनुतात् *tanú, tanutât*	तनुष्व *tanushvá*	तनुयास् *tanuyâs*	तन्वीथास् *tanvîthâs*

सन् *san*, 'to obtain,' 1 sing. pres. Par. सनोमि *sanómi*, Âtm. सन्वे *sanvé*.

PARADIGMS OF THE NINTH CLASS: यु *yu*, 'to join,' बन्ध् *bandh*, 'to bind.'

PRESENT.

Parasmaipada.			Âtmanepada.		
युनामि *yunâmi*	युनीवस् *yunîvás*	युनीमस् *yunîmás*	युने *yuné*	युनीवहे *yunîvdhe*	युनीमहे *yunîmáhe*
युनासि *yunâsi*	युनीथस् *yunîthás*	युनीथ *yunîthá*	युनीषे *yunîshé*	युनाथे *yunâthe*	युनीध्वे *yunîdhvé*
युनाति *yunâti*	युनीतस् *yunîtás*	युनन्ति *yunánti*	युनीते *yunîté*	युनाते *yunâte*	युनते *yunáte*

IMPERFECT.

अयुनाम् *áyunâm*	अयुनीव *áyunîva*	अयुनीम *áyunîma*	अयुनि *áyuni*	अयुनीवहि *áyunîvahi*	अयुनीमहि *áyunîmahi*
अयुनास् *áyunâs*	अयुनीतम् *áyunîtam*	अयुनीत *áyunîta*	अयुनीथास् *áyunîthâs*	अयुनाथाम् *áyunâthâm*	अयुनीध्वम् *áyunîdhvam*
अयुनात् *áyunât*	अयुनीताम् *áyunîtâm*	अयुनन् *áyunan*	अयुनीत *áyunîta*	अयुनाताम् *áyunâtâm*	अयुनत *áyunata*

Parasmaipada.		IMPERATIVE.		Âtmanepada.	
युनानि *yunā́ni*	युनाव *yunā́va*	युनाम *yunā́ma*	युनै *yunái*	युनावहै *yunā́vahai*	युनामहै *yunā́mahai*
युनीहि *yunīhí* or युनीतात् *yunītā́t*	युनीतम् *yunītám*	युनीत *yunītá* or युनीतात् *yunītā́t*	युनीष्व *yunīshvá*	युनाथाम् *yunā́thâm*	युनीध्वम् *yunīdhvám*
युनातु *yunā́tu* or युनीतात् *yunītā́t*	युनीताम् *yunītā́m*	युनन्तु *yunántu*	युनीताम् *yunītā́m*	युनाताम् *yunā́tâm*	युनताम् *yunátâm*

POTENTIAL.

युनीयाम् *yunīyā́m*	युनीयाव *yunīyā́va*	युनीयाम *yunīyā́ma*	युनीय *yunīyá*	युनीवहि *yunīváhi*	युनीमहि *yunīmáhi*
युनीयास् *yunīyā́s*	युनीयातम् *yunīyā́tam*	युनीयात *yunīyā́ta*	युनीथास् *yunīthā́s*	युनीयाथाम् *yunīyā́thâm*	युनीध्वम् *yunīdhvám*
युनीयात् *yunīyā́t*	युनीयाताम् *yunīyā́tâm*	युनीयुस् *yunīyús*	युनीत *yunītá*	युनीयाताम् *yunīyā́tâm*	युनीरन् *yunīrán*

For other paradigms look to § 83, II. A. 6, Observ.

The second paradigm बन्ध् *bandh* differs from the foregoing only in the first form of the second person singular of the imperative Parasmaipada, *e.g.* pres. sing. 1. Par. बध्नामि *badhnā́mi* (*cf.* § 83, 6, Obs. 1), 2. बध्नासि *badhnā́si*; Âtm. 1. बध्ने *badhné*, 2. बध्नीषे *badhníshé*, imperfect Par. sing. 1. अबध्नाम् *ábadhnâm*, 2. अबध्नास् *ábadhnâs*, Âtman. 1. अबध्नि *ábadhni*, imperative Par. sing. 1. बध्नानि *badhnā́ni*, but 2. बधान *badhâná*, or बध्नीतात् *badhnītā́t*.

स्तम्भ् *stambh*, 'to stop,' 1. sing. pres. Par. स्तभ्नामि *stabhnā́mi*, Âtm. स्तभ्ने *stabhné*; 2 sing. imper. Par. स्तभान *stabhâná*.

§ 86. Alphabetical List of the Anomalous Bases of the Fifth, Eighth, and Ninth Classes.

करो special base in the strong forms, for all the other forms कुरु, except before terminations beginning with म, व, or य, where कुर्,	of the verb कृ II. 8 'to make,' *e.g.* pres. sing. 1. करोमि 2. करोषि, 3. करोति, dual 1. कुर्वस्, 2. कुरुथस्, 3. कुरुतस्, plur. 1. कुर्मस् 2. कुरुथ, 3. कुर्वन्ति, potential 1. कुर्याम्, etc.

कृणु, कृणो	special bases of the verb				कृण्व् II. 8 'to do.'
क्षुभ्ना, क्षुभ्नी, क्षुभ्न्, without changing न् to ण् (§ 16)	„	„	„	„	क्षुभ् II. 9 'to shake.'
खौना, खौनी, खौन्, or खुना, खुनी, खुन् . .	„	„	„	„	खव् II. 9 (?)
गृह्णा, गृह्णी, गृह्ण् . . .	„	„	„	„	ग्रह् II. 9 'to take.'
जाना, जानी, जान् . .	„	„	„	„	ज्ञा II. 9 'to know.'
जिना, जिनी, जिन् . .	„	„	„	„	ज्या II. 9 'to grow old.'
तृप्नु, तृप्नो without changing न् to ण् (§ 16), but in the Veda regularly तृप्णु, तृप्णो . . .	„	„	„	„	तृप् II. 5 'to satisfy.
दभ्नु, दभ्नो	„	„	„	„	दम्भ् II. 5 'to hurt.'
धिनु, धिनो	„	„	„	„	धिन्व् II. 8 'to satisfy.'
शृणु, शृणो	„	„	„	„	श्रु II. 5 'to hear.'
स्कभ्नु, स्कभ्नो . . .	„	„	„	„	स्कम्भ् II. 5 } 'to stop.'
स्कुभ्नु, स्कुभ्नो . . .	„	„	„	„	स्कुम्भ् II. 5 } 'to stop.'
स्तभ्नु, स्तभ्नो	„	„	„	„	स्तम्भ् II. 5 } 'to stop.'
स्तुभ्नु, स्तुभ्नो	„	„	„	„	स्तुम्भ् II. 5 } 'to stop.'

PARADIGMS OF THE SECOND, THIRD AND SEVENTH CLASSES, AND OF THE FREQUENTATIVES OF THE FIRST FORM.

§ 87. As the special bases of these verbs end in all letters, except अ *a*, ऌ *ḷi*, or ॡ *ḹi*, ए *e*, ऐ *ai*, and ओ *o* (*cf.* § 93 Obs.), it will be necessary, before giving the paradigms, to lay down the rules for the numerous phonetic changes which they undergo in receiving the inflectional terminations.

§ 88. A final आ *á* combines with an initial अ *a* or आ *á* to आ *á*, *e.g.* अया+अम् *áyá+am* makes अयाम् *áyám* (sing. 1. imperfect Parasm. from या *yá* II. 2, 'to go'), and with इ *i*, or ई *í*, to ए *e*. Before उ *u*, ए *e*, or ऐ *ai* it is rejected, *e.g.* अया+उस *áyâ+us* makes अयुस् *áyus* (*cf.* § 84, 2, Obs.)

§ 89. Monosyllabic bases ending in इ *i* or ई *î* change their final to इय् *iy* before the terminations beginning with vowels, *e.g.* वी *vî*, II. 2, 'to go,' + अन्ति *anti* makes वियन्ति *viy-anti*. This rule applies also to those reduplicated bases, in which the इ *i* or ई *î* is preceded by a compound consonant: thus the special base of ह्री *hrî*, II. 3, 'to be ashamed,' जिह्री *jihrî*+अति *ati* makes जिह्रियति *jíhriy-ati*, 3 plur. pres. Par. In all other reduplicated bases the final इ *i* or ई *î* is changed to य् *y*. Thus the special base of भी *bhî*, II. 3, 'to fear,' बिभी+अति *bibhî+ati* makes बिभ्यति *bíbhy-ati*.

§ 90. Final उ *u* and ऊ *û* before vowels are changed to उव् *uv*, *e.g.* नु *nu*, II. 2, 'to praise,' + अन्ति *anti*, नुवन्ति *nuv-ánti*, 3d plur. pres. Par.

§ 91. A final ऋ *ṛi* before vowels becomes र् *r*, *e.g.* बिभृ *bibhṛi* (special base of भृ *bhṛi*, II. 3, 'to bear') + अति *ati*, बिभ्रति *bíbhr-ati*.

§ 92. A final ॠ *ṛî* before vowels becomes इर् *ir*, or, if preceded by labials or व् *v*, उर् *ur*, *e.g.* तातॄ *tâtṛî*, first frequentative from तॄ *tṛî*, 'to cross,' + अति *ati* becomes तातिरति *tâtir-ati*, पिपॄ *pipṛî*, special base of पॄ *pṛî*, II. 3, 'to fill,' + अति *ati* would become पिपुरति *pípur-ati*.

§ 93. ऐ *ai* and औ *au*, produced by the combination of the temporal augment with a uniliteral base (§ 74, 1), are changed before vowels to आय् *ây* and आव् *âv*, *e.g.* ऐ *ai* (from the verb इ *i*, II. 2, 'to go') + अम् *am* becomes आयम् *ây-am*.

Observ. In common Sanskrit, verbs ending in radical ए *e*, ऐ *ai*, or ओ *o* do not belong to the second conjugation. In the Vedas and in the Epic poetry, however, they sometimes do. In this case their finals are changed to आ *â* and follow § 88.

§ 94. Radical इ *i* and उ *u* before a consonantal group beginning with र् *r* are lengthened, *e.g.* चञ्चुर् *chañchur*, frequentative of चर् *char* (§ 51) + मस् *mas* = चञ्चूर्मस् *chañchûr-más*.

§ 95. 1. A final ॠ *ṛî* before consonants becomes ईर् *îr* or, if preceded by labials or व् *v*, ऊर् *úr*, *e.g.* तातृ *tâtṛí*, frequentative of तॄ *tṛí*, + मस् *mas*, तातीर्मस् *tâtír-más*; पिपृ *pipṛí*, special base of पृ *pṛí*, II. 3, would become पिपूर्मस् *pipúr-más*.

2. Final य् *y* and व् *v* are rejected before any consonant, except य् *y*, *e.g.* तोतुर्व् *toturv*, frequentative from तुर्व् *turv*, 'to overcome,' + मस् *mas*, तोतूर्मस् *totúr-más* (*cf.* § 94).

3. A final म् *m* is changed to न् *n* before any consonant, except य् *y*, स् *s*, or ह् *h*, *e.g.* जंगम् *jam̃gam* (frequentative of गम् *gam*, 'to go') + मस् *mas* becomes जंगन्मस् *jam̃gan-más*.

§ 96. Before terminations beginning with स् *s*, त् *t*, थ् *th*, or ध् *dh*:—

1. Final aspirated consonants reject the aspiration, *e.g.* मामथ् *mâmath*, first frequentative of मथ् *math*, 'to churn,' + सि *si* becomes मामत्सि *mâmat-si*, लोलुभ् *lolubh*, frequentative of लुभ् *lubh*, 'to desire,' + धि *dhi* लोलुब्धि *lolub-dhi*.

2. Before ध् *dh* the surds क् *k* and ख् *kh* are changed to ग् *g*, ट् *ṭ* and ठ् *ṭh* to ड् *ḍ* (*cf.* § 101), त् *t* and थ् *th* to द् *d*, प् *p* and फ् *ph* to ब् *b*; स् *s* may either become द् *d* or be rejected, *e.g.* चिकित् *chikit* (special base of कित् *kit*, II. 3, 'to perceive') + धि *dhi* makes चिकिद्धि *chikid-dhí*; आस् *ás*, II. 2, 'to sit,' + ध्वम् *dhvam* either आद्ध्वम् *âd-dhvam* or आध्वम् *â-dhvam*.

3. Before स् *s*, त् *t*, and थ् *th* the sonants ग् *g* and घ् *gh* are changed to क् *k*, ड् *ḍ* and ढ् *ḍh* to ट् *ṭ* (*cf.* § 101), द् *d* and ध् *dh* to त् *t*, ब् *b* and भ् *bh* to प् *p*, *e.g.* अद् *ad*, II. 2, 'to eat,' + सि *si* makes अत्सि *át-si*. But when the verb ends in घ् *gh*, ध् *dh*, भ् *bh*, and the affix begins with त् *t* or थ् *th*, the former (according to 1) are changed to the corresponding unaspirated sonants, and the latter to ध् *dh*, *e.g.* लोलुभ् *lolubh* (frequentative of लुभ् *lubh*, 'to desire') + थस् *thas* or + तस् *tas* makes लोलुब्धस् *lolub-dhás*.

4. When a final aspirated sonant, agreeably to 1-3, rejects its aspiration before स् *s* or ध्व् *dhv*, and the syllable containing the final aspirate begins with ग् *g*, ड् *ḍ*, द् *d*, or ब् *b*, the latter are changed to the corresponding aspirated घ् *gh*, ढ् *ḍh*, ध् *dh*, and

भ् *bh, e.g.* बोबोध् *bobodh* (strong form, § 83, II. A. 2, of बोबुध् *bobudh,* frequentative of बुध् *budh*) + सि *si* makes बोभोत्सि *bó-bhot-si.*

§ 97. Before a termination beginning with स् *s*:—

1. Final क्ष् *ksh,* च् *ch,* छ् *chh,* ज् *j,* झ् *jh,* श् *ç,* ष् *sh,* and ह् *h* are changed to क् *k,* and the following स् *s,* agreeably to § 17, becomes ष् *sh, e.g.* चक्ष् *chaksh,* II. 2, 'to see,' + से *se* becomes चक्षे *chák-she*; वच् *vach,* II. 2, 'to speak,' + सि *si* वक्षि *vák-shi.* When the syllable, ending in ह् *h,* begins with ग् *g,* द् *d,* or ब् *b,* these letters become aspirated, *e.g.* दोह् *doh* (strong form, § 83, II. A. 1, of दुह् *duh,* II. 2, 'to milk') + सि *si* makes धोक्षि *dhók-shi.*

2. Final न् *n* and म् *m* become Anusvâra ं, or Anunâsika ँ, *e.g.* हन् *han,* II. 2, 'to kill,' + सि *si* makes हंसि *hám̃-si,* or हँसि *há-si.*

§ 98. Before terminations beginning with त् *t* or थ् *th*:—

1. Final च् *ch,* ज् *j,* and झ् *jh* are changed to क् *k, e.g.* वच् *vach* + ति *ti* = वक्ति *vák-ti,* युञ्ज् *yuñj,* special base of युज् *yuj,* II. 7, + थ *tha,* युङ्क्थ *yuṅk-thá.*

2. Final क्ष् *ksh,* छ् *chh,* and श् *ç* become ष् *sh,* after which त् *t* and थ् *th* are changed to the corresponding linguals ट् *ṭ* and ठ् *ṭh, e.g.* चक्ष् *chaksh* + ते *te,* चष्टे *chásh-ṭe*; पाप्रछ् *páprachh,* frequentative of प्रछ् *prachh,* 'to ask,' + थ *tha,* पाप्रष्ठ *pâprash-ṭhá.*

3. A final ह् *h* is rejected, but the following त् *t* or थ् *th* is changed to ढ् *ḍh,* and a preceding अ *a,* इ *i,* or उ *u* is lengthened, *e.g.* लेह् *leh,* strong form of लिह् *lih,* II. 2, 'to lick,' + ति *ti* makes लेढि *léḍhi*; लिह् *lih* + थस् *thas,* or तस् *tas,* make लीढस् *líḍhás.*

Exception. If the syllable ending in ह् *h,* begins with द् *d,* the ह् *h* is changed to ग् *g,* and the beginning त् *t* or थ् *th* to ध् *dh, e.g.* दुह् *duh* + थस् *thas,* or तस् *tas,* makes दुग्धस् *dug-dhás*; in other words ह् *h* is treated as if it was घ् *gh* (*cf.* § 96, 3).

§ 99. Before terminations beginning with ध् *dh*:—

1. Final च् *ch,* ज् *j,* and झ् *jh* are changed to ग् *g, e.g.* वच् *vach,* + धि *dhi* makes वग्धि *vag-dhí.*

2. Final क्ष् *ksh,* छ् *chh,* श् *ç,* and ष् *sh* become ड् *ḍ,* after which

ध् *dh* is changed to its corresponding lingual ढ् *ḍh*, *e.g.* चक्ष् *chaksh* + ध्वे *dhve* makes चड्ढ्वे *cháḍ-ḍhve*; द्विष् *dvish* + धि *dhi* द्विड्ढि *dviḍ-ḍhí*.

3. A final ह् *h* is rejected, but the following ध् *dh* is changed to ढ् *ḍh*, and a preceding अ *a*, इ *i*, or उ *u* is lengthened, *e.g.* लिह् *lih* + धि *dhi* makes लीढि *líḍhí*. The special rule for syllables beginning with द् *d* (§ 98, 3, Exc.) applies also here, *e.g.* दुह् *duh* + धि *dhi* makes दुग्धि *dugdhí*. When the termination begins with ध्व् *dhv*, and the syllable ending in ह् *h* with ग् *g*, द् *d*, or ब् *b*, these letters become aspirated, *e.g.* दुह् *duh* + ध्वे *dhve* makes धुग्ध्वे *dhug-dhvé*.

§ 100. Before the termination हि *hi* of the second person of the imperative Parasmaipada a final न् *n* or म् *m* is changed to Anusvâra ं *e.g.* शंशम् *çaṁçam*, frequentative of शम् *çam*, 'to be tranquil,' makes शंशांहि *çaṁçâṁ-hí* (§ 83, II. B).

§ 101. If a termination beginning with त् *t*, थ् *th*, or ध् *dh* is attached to a base ending in ट् *ṭ*, ड् *ḍ*, or ण् *ṇ*, त् *t* is changed to ट् *ṭ*, थ् *th* to ठ् *ṭh*, ध *dh* to ढ् *ḍh*, *e.g.* चोकोट् *chokoṭ*, strong form of चोकुट् *chokuṭ*, frequentative of कुट् *kuṭ*, 'to make crooked,' + ति *ti* makes चोकोट्टि *chókoṭ-ṭi*; चोकुट् *chokuṭ* + थस् *thas*, चोकुट्ठस् *chokuṭ-ṭhás*, + धि *dhi*, चोकुड्ढि *chokuḍ-ḍhí* (*cf.* § 96, 2); ईड् *íḍ*, 'to praise,' + ध्वे *dhve*, ईड्ढ्वे *íḍ-ḍhve*, + ते *te*, ईट्टे *íṭ-ṭe* (*cf.* § 96, 3); पंपण् *paṁpaṇ*, frequentative of पण् *paṇ*, 'to praise,' + ति *ti*, पंपण्टि *páṁpaṇ-ṭi*, + धि *dhi*, पंपण्ढि *paṁpaṇ-ḍhí* (*cf.* § 98, 2 and 99, 2 and 3).

§ 102. Alphabetical List of Exceptions to the Rules given in §§ 96-101.

द्रुह् I. 4, 'to hurt,' optionally follows either the general rule, §§ 98, 3; 99, 3, or the special rule for roots beginning with द् *d*, § 98, 3, Exc., § 99, 3, *e.g.* दोद्रुह् *dodruh*, frequentative, + थस् *thas* or तस् *tas* may become दोद्रूढस् *dodrúḍhás* or दोद्रुग्धस् *dodrug-dhás*, with the termination धि *dhi* दोद्रूढि *dodrúḍhí* or दोद्रुग्धि *dodrug-dhí*.

नह् I. 4, 'to bind,' changes ह् *h* before स् *s* to त् *t*, *e.g.* नानह् *nânah*, frequentative, + सि *si* makes नानत्सि *nânat-si*; before त् *t*, थ् *th*, and ध् *dh* to द् *d*, after which त् *t* and थ् *th* become ध् *dh*, *e.g.* नानह् *nânah* + थस् *thas* or तस् *tas* makes नानद्धस् *nânad-dhás*. In other words ह् *h* is treated as if it was ध् *dh*, *cf* § 96, 1, 3.

भ्रज्ज् I. 6, 'to fry,' changes ज्ज् *jj* before स् *s* to क् *k*, after which स् *s* becomes ष् *sh* (§ 17); before त् *t* or थ् *th* to ष् *sh*, after which त् *t* and थ् *th* are changed to ट् *ṭ* and ठ् *ṭh* (§ 98, 2); and before ध् *dh* to ड् *ḍ*, after which ध् *dh* becomes ढ् *ḍh* (§ 101), *e.g.* बाभ्रज्ज् *bâbhrajj*, frequentative, + सि *si* makes बाभ्रक्षि *bâbhrak-shi*, + थस् *thas* बाभ्रष्ठस् *bâbhrash-ṭhás*, + तस् *tas* बाभ्रष्टस् *bâbhrash-ṭás*, + धि *dhi* बाभ्रड्ढि *bâbhraḍ-ḍhí*.

भ्राज् I. 1, Âtm. 'to shine,' following the analogy of the preceding verb, changes ज् *j* before त् *t* and थ् *th* to ष् *sh*, before ध् *dh* to ड् *ḍ*.

मुह् I. 4, 'to be foolish,' follows the analogy of द्रुह्.

मृज् II. 2, 'to wipe,'
यज् I. 1, 'to sacrifice.' } follow the analogy of भ्राज्.
राज् I. 1, 'to shine,'

लज्ज् I. 6, 'to be ashamed,' rejects the last consonant before terminations beginning with स् *s*, त् *t*, थ् *th*, or ध् *dh*, *e.g.* लालज्ज् *lâlajj*, frequentative, + ति *ti* makes लालक्ति *lâlakti* (*cf.* § 97, 1).

वह् I. 1, 'to bear,' instead of lengthening अ *a*, agreeably to §§ 98, 3 and 99, 3, changes it to ओ *o*, *e.g.* वावह्, frequentative, + ति वावोढि.

व्रश्च् I. 6, 'to cut,' rejects the last consonant before terminations beginning with स् *s*, त् *t*, थ् *th*, or ध् *dh*.

सह् I. 1, 'to bear,' changes अ to ओ, like वह्.

सृज् I. 6, 'to abandon,' follows the analogy of राज्.

स्निह् I. 4, 'to love,'
स्नुह् I. 4, 'to vomit,' } follow the analogy of मुह्.

§ 103. After bases ending in consonants, agreeably to § 13, the terminations of the second and third persons singular of the imperfect Parasmaipada, viz. *s* and *t*, are rejected. But the final letters of the base undergo the following changes:—

I. A final consonant, preceded by a vowel or र् *r*, generally undergoes the same changes as before an affix beginning with स् *s* (*cf.* §§ 96 and 97), *e.g.* अयुनज् *ayunaj*, strong form (§ 83, II. A. 4) of युज् *yuj*, II. 7, with the temporal augment, becomes in both persons अयुनक् *ayunak* (*cf.* युनज् + सि *yunaj* + *si* = युनक्षि *yunak-shi*, § 97, 1), अवर्वर्ज् *avarvarj*, strong form of the frequentative वर्वृज् *varvṛij* (from वृज् *vṛij*, 'to exclude') with the temporal augment, makes in both persons अवर्वर्क् *avarvark*, अदर्दर्भ् *adardarbh* (from the frequentative दर्दृभ् *dardṛibh*, of दृभ् *dṛibh*, 'to string') would become अदर्धर्प् *adardharp* (*cf.* § 96, 1, 3, 4).

Exceptions. 1. The verbs ending in त् *t*, थ् *th*, द् *d*, or ध् *dh* in the second person may follow the general rule, or affix स् *s* after having rejected the dental, *e.g.* अवेद् *aved*, strong form of विद् *vid*, II. 2, 'to know,' with the augment, may become अवेत् *avet* or अवेस् *aves*, *i.e.* अवेः *aveḥ*, *cf.* §§ 13 and 28, Obs.; अपास्पर्ध् *apâspardh*, frequentative of स्पर्ध् *spardh*, 'to contend with,' with the augment, either, according to the general rule, अपास्पर्त् *apâspart*, or अपास्पार् *apâspâr* (based on *apâspars* = *apâsparr*, *cf.* § 15), अपास्पाः *apâspâḥ*, §§ 13 and 28, Observ.

2. Verbs ending in स् *s*, in forming the second person, may follow the general rule, or change their final to त् *t*, *e.g.* from चकास् *chakâs*, II. 2, 'to shine,' either अचकास् *áchakâs* (अचकाः *áchakâḥ*, §§ 13 and 28, Obs.) or अचकात् *áchakât*. In the third person the latter change must be effected, अचकात् *áchakât*.

3. Final क्ष् *ksh*, छ् *chh*, श् *ç*, ष् *sh*, and ह् *h* are changed to ट् *ṭ*, *e.g.* अपाप्रछ् *apâprachh*, frequentative of प्रछ् *prachh*, 'to ask,' with the augment, makes in the second and third persons of the imperfect Parasm. अपाप्रट् *ápâpraṭ*. If the syllable ending in ह् *h*, begins with द् *d*, the ह् *h* is changed to क् *k* (*cf.* § 98, 3, Exc.), and if it begins with ग् *g*, द् *d*, or ब् *b*, these letters become aspirated (*cf.* § 97, 1), *e.g.* अलेह् *aleh*, strong form of लिह् *lih*, II. 2,

with the temporal augment, becomes अलेट् *áleṭ*, अदोह् *adoh* of दुह् *duh*, II. 2, अधोक् *ádhok*. द्रुह् *druh*, मुह् *muh*, स्निह् *snih*, and स्नुह् *snuh*, optionally change ह् *h* to ट् *ṭ* or क् *k*, and नह् *nah* changes it to त् *t* (*cf.* § 102). The verbs दिश् *diç*, 'to show,' दृश् *dṛiç*, 'to see,' मृश् *mṛiç*, and स्पृश् *spṛiç*, 'to touch,' must, and नश् *naç*, 'to perish,' may optionally change श् *ç* to क् *k*, *e.g.* अदर्दर्श् *adardarç*, from दर्दृश् *dardṛiç*, frequentative of दृश् *dṛiç*, becomes अदर्दर्क् *ádardark*. The verbs भ्रज्ज् *bhrajj*, भ्राज् *bhrâj*, मृज् *mṛij*, यज् *yaj*, राज् *râj*, सृज् *sṛij*, change their finals to ट् *ṭ* (*cf.* § 102).

4. A final म् *m* is changed to न् *n*, *e.g.* अजंगम् *ajam̃gam*, frequentative of गम् *gam*, with the augment, makes अजंगन् *ájam̃gan*.

II. When the base ends in a compound consonant—except क्ष् *ksh* (for which *cf.* I. Exc. 3) or those which contain an र् *r* before any consonant of the first five classes except nasals (§ 1, IV.; *cf.* § 103, I.)—its final element is rejected, and the preceding undergoes the changes prescribed by the rules in I., *e.g.* अवावल्ग् *avâvalg*, frequentative of वल्ग् *valg*, 'to go by leaps,' with the augment, becomes अवावल् *avâval*; अजोघूर्ण् *ajoghûrṇ*, frequentative of घूर्ण् *ghûrṇ*, 'to reel,' becomes अजोघूर् *ajoghûr*, *i.e.* अजोघूः *ajoghûḥ*, §§ 13 and 28, Obs. A nasal, thus becoming the final, is changed to न् *n*, *e.g.* अजेहिंस् *ajehim̃s*, frequentative of हिंस् *him̃s*, 'to hurt,' with the augment, becomes अजेहिन् *ajehin*. But the verbs ध्वंस् *dhvam̃s* and स्रंस् *sram̃s*, 'to fall,' substitute त् *t* for it, *e.g.* असंनीस्रत् *ásanîsrat*, second and third persons of the imperfect Parasm. of the first frequentative of स्रंस् *sram̃s* (*cf.* § 51).

§ 104. Paradigm of the Second Conjugational Class: लिह् *lih*, 'to lick.'

PRESENT.

Parasmaipada.			Âtmanepada.		
लेह्मि *léhmi*	लिह्वस् *lih̄vás*	लिह्मस् *lih̄más*	लिहे *lih̄é*	लिह्वहे *lih̄váhe*	लिह्महे *lih̄máhe*
लेक्षि *lékshi*	लीढस् *lîḍhás*	लीढ *lîḍhá*	लिक्षे *likshé*	लिहाथे *lih̄âthe*	लीढ्वे *lîḍhvé*
लेढि *léḍhi*	लीढस् *lîḍhás*	लिहन्ति *lih̄ánti*	लीढे *lîḍhé*	लिहाते *lih̄âte*	लिहते *lih̄áte*

IMPERFECT.

Parasmaipada.			Âtmanepada.		
अलेहम् *áleham*	अलिह्व *álihva*	अलिह्म *álihma*	अलिहि *álihi*	अलिह्वहि *álihvahi*	अलिह्महि *álihmahi*
अलेट् *áleṭ*	अलीढम् *álîḍham*	अलीढ *álîḍha*	अलीढास् *álîḍhâs*	अलिहाथाम् *álihâthâm*	अलीढ्वम् *álîḍhvam*
अलेट् *áleṭ*	अलीढाम् *álîḍhâm*	अलिहन् *álihan*	अलीढ *álîḍha*	अलिहाताम् *álihâtâm*	अलिहत *álihata*

IMPERATIVE.

लेहानि *léhâni*	लेहाव *léhâva*	लेहाम *léhâma*	लेहै *léhai*	लेहावहै *léhâvahai*	लेहामहै *léhâmahai*
लीढि or *lîḍhí* लीढात् *lîḍhất*	लीढम् *lîḍhám*	लीढ or *lîḍhá* लीढात् *lîḍhất*	लिक्ष्व *likshvá*	लिहाथाम् *lihấthâm*	लीढ्वम् *lîḍhvám*
लेढु or *léḍhu* लीढात् *lîḍhất*	लीढाम् *lîḍhấm*	लिहन्तु *lihántu*	लीढाम् *lîḍhấm*	लिहाताम् *lihấtâm*	लिहताम् *lihátâm*

POTENTIAL.

लिह्याम् *lihyấm*	लिह्याव *lihyấva*	लिह्याम *lihyấma*	लिहीय *lihîyá*	लिहीवहि *lihîváhi*	लिहीमहि *lihîmáhi*
लिह्यास् *lihyấs*	लिह्यातम् *lihyấtam*	लिह्यात *lihyấta*	लिहीथास् *lihîthấs*	लिहीयाथाम् *lihîyấthâm*	लिहीध्वम् *lihîdhvám*
लिह्यात् *lihyất*	लिह्याताम् *lihyấtâm*	लिह्युस् *lihyús*	लिहीत *lihîtá*	लिहीयाताम् *lihîyấtâm*	लिहीरन् *lihîrán*

दुह् *duh*, 'to milk,' 1 sing. pres. Par. दोह्मि *dóhmi*, Âtm. दुहे *duhé*.

§ 105. Paradigm of the Third Conjugational Class: पॄ *pṛi*, 'to fill.'

PRESENT.

पिपर्मि *píparmi*	पिपृवस् *pipṛivás*	पिपृमस् *pipṛimás*	पिप्रे *pípre*	पिपृवहे *pipṛiváhe*	पिपृमहे *pipṛimáhe*
पिपर्षि *píparshi*	पिपृथस् *pipṛithás*	पिपृथ *pipṛithá*	पिपृषे *pipṛishé*	पिप्राथे *píprâthe*	पिपृध्वे *pipṛidhvé*
पिपर्ति *píparti*	पिपृतस् *pipṛitás*	पिप्रति *píprati*	पिपृते *pipṛité*	पिप्राते *píprâte*	पिप्रते *píprate*

IMPERFECT.

Parasmaipada.			Âtmanepada.		
अपिपरम् *ápiparam*	अपिपृव *ápipṛiva*	अपिपृम *ápipṛima*	अपिप्रि *ápipri*	अपिपृवहि *ápipṛivahi*	अपिपृमहि *ápipṛimahi*
अपिपर् (॰पः) *ápipar, °paḥ*	अपिपृतम् *ápipṛitam*	अपिपृत *ápipṛita*	अपिपृथास् *ápipṛithâs*	अपिप्राथाम् *ápiprâthâm*	अपिपृध्वम् *ápipṛidhvam*
अपिपर् (॰पः) *ápipar, °paḥ*	अपिपृताम् *ápipṛitâm*	अपिपरुस् *ápiparus*	अपिपृत *ápipṛita*	अपिप्राताम् *ápiprâtâm*	अपिप्रत *ápiprata*

IMPERATIVE.

पिपराणि[1] *piparâṇi*	पिपराव *piparâva*	पिपराम *piparâma*	पिपरै *piparai*	पिपरावहै *piparâvahai*	पिपरामहै *piparâmahai*
पिपृहि or पिपृतात् *pipṛihí* or *pipṛitất*	पिपृतम् *pipṛitám*	पिपृत or पिपृतात् *pipṛitá* or *pipṛitất*	पिपृष्व *pipṛishvá*	पिप्राथाम् *piprâthâm*	पिपृध्वम् *pipṛidhvám*
पिपर्तु or पिपृतात् *pipartu* or *pipṛitất*	पिपृताम् *pipṛitấm*	पिप्रतु *pipratu*	पिपृताम् *pipṛitấm*	पिप्राताम् *piprâtâm*	पिप्रताम् *pipratâm*

POTENTIAL.

पिपृयाम् *pipṛiyấm*	पिपृयाव *pipṛiyấva*	पिपृयाम *pipṛiyấma*	पिप्रीय *piprîya*	पिप्रीवहि *piprîvahi*	पिप्रीमहि *piprîmahi*
पिपृयास् *pipṛiyấs*	पिपृयातम् *pipṛiyấtam*	पिपृयात *pipṛiyấta*	पिप्रीथास् *piprîthâs*	पिप्रीयाथाम् *piprîyâthâm*	पिप्रीध्वम् *piprîdhvam*
पिपृयात् *pipṛiyất*	पिपृयाताम् *pipṛiyấtâm*	पिपृयुस् *pipṛiyús*	पिप्रीत *piprîta*	पिप्रीयाताम् *piprîyâtâm*	पिप्रीरन् *piprîran*

ह्री *hrî́*, 'to be ashamed,' 1 sing. pres. Par. जिह्रेमि *jihrémi*, 3 plur. जिह्रियति *jíhriyati*. पॄ *pṝ́*, 'to fill,' 1 sing. pres. Par. पिपर्मि *píparmi*, 1 dual पिपूर्वस् *pipûrvás*, 3 plur. पिपुरति *pípurati*.

§ 106. Paradigm of the Frequentative बोभू *bobhû́* (from भू *bhû́*, 'to become').

Parasmaipada.

PRESENT.

बोभोमि or बोभवीमि *bóbhomi* *bóbhavîmi*	बोभूवस् *bobhûvás*	बोभूमस् *bobhûmás*
बोभोषि or बोभवीषि *bóbhoshi* *bóbhavîshi*	बोभूथस् *bobhûthás*	बोभूथ *bobhûthá*
बोभोति or बोभवीति *bóbhoti* *bóbhavîti*	बोभूतस् *bobhûtás*	बोभुवति *bóbhuvati*

[1] Cf. § 16.

Parasmaipada.

IMPERFECT.

अबोभवम् *ábobhavam*	अबोभूव *ábobhûva*	अबोभूम *ábobhûma*
अबोभोस् or अबोभवीस् *ábobhos* *ábobhavîs*	अबोभूतम् *ábobhûtam*	अबोभूत *ábobhûta*
अबोभोत् or अबोभवीत् *ábobhot* *ábobhavît*	अबोभूताम् *ábobhûtâm*	अबोभवुस् *ábobhavus*

IMPERATIVE.

बोभवानि *bóbhavâni*	बोभवाव *bóbhavâva*	बोभवाम *bóbhavâma*
बोभूहि or बोभूतात् *bobhûhí* *bobhûtất*	बोभूतम् *bobhûtám*	बोभूत, बोभूतात् *bobhûtá* *bobhûtất*
बोभोतु or बोभवीतु or बोभूतात् *bóbhotu* *bóbhavîtu* *bobhûtất*	बोभूताम् *bobhûtấm*	बोभुवतु *bóbhuvatu*

POTENTIAL.

बोभूयाम् *bobhûyấm*	बोभूयाव *bobhûyấva*	बोभूयाम *bobhûyấma*
बोभूयास् *bobhûyấs*	बोभूयातम् *bobhûyấtam*	बोभूयात *bobhûyấta*
बोभूयात् *bobhûyất*	बोभूयाताम् *bobhûyấtâm*	बोभूयुस् *bobhûyús*

§ 107. Paradigm of the Seventh Conjugational Class: युज् *yuj*, 'to join.'

PRESENT.

Parasmaipada.			Âtmanepada.		
युनज्मि *yunájmi*	युञ्ज्वस् *yuńjvás*	युञ्ज्मस् *yuńjmás*	युञ्जे *yuńjé*	युञ्ज्वहे *yuńjváhe*	युञ्ज्महे *yuńjmáhe*
युनक्षि *yunákshi*	युङ्क्थस् *yuńkthás*	युङ्क्थ *yuńkthá*	युङ्क्षे *yuńkshé*	युञ्जाथे *yuńjấthe*	युङ्ग्ध्वे *yuṅgdhvé*
युनक्ति *yunákti*	युङ्क्तस् *yuńktás*	युञ्जन्ति *yuńjánti*	युङ्क्ते *yuńkté*	युञ्जाते *yuńjấte*	युञ्जते *yuńjáte*

IMPERFECT.

अयुनजम् *áyunajam*	अयुञ्ज्व *áyuńjva*	अयुञ्ज्म *áyuńjma*	अयुञ्जि *áyuńji*	अयुञ्ज्वहि *áyuńjvahi*	अयुञ्ज्महि *áyuńjmahi*
अयुनक् *áyunak*	अयुङ्क्तम् *áyuńktam*	अयुङ्क्त *áyuńkta*	अयुङ्क्थास् *áyuńkthâs*	अयुञ्जाथाम् *áyuńjâthâm*	अयुङ्ग्ध्वम् *áyuṅgdhvam*
अयुनक् *áyunak*	अयुङ्क्ताम् *áyuńktâm*	अयुञ्जन् *áyuńjan*	अयुङ्क्त *áyuńkta*	अयुञ्जाताम् *áyuńjâtâm*	अयुञ्जत *áyuńjata*

IMPERATIVE.

Parasmaipada.			Âtmanepada.		
युनजानि *yunájâni*	युनजाव *yunájâva*	युनजाम *yunájâma*	युनजै *yunájai*	युनजावहै *yunájâvahai*	युनजामहै *yunájâmahai*
युङ्ग्धि or *yuṅgdhí*	युङ्क्तम् *yuṅktám*	युङ्क्त or *yuṅktá*	युङ्क्ष्व *yuṅkshvá*	युञ्जाथाम् *yuñjā́thâm*	युङ्ग्ध्वम् *yuṅgdhvám*
युङ्क्तात् *yuṅktā́t*		युङ्क्तात् *yuṅktā́t*			
युनक्तु or *yunáktu*	युङ्क्ताम् *yuṅktā́m*	युञ्जन्तु *yuñjántu*	युङ्क्ताम् *yuṅktā́m*	युञ्जाताम् *yuñjā́tâm*	युञ्जताम् *yuñjátâm*
युङ्क्तात् *yuṅktā́t*					

POTENTIAL.

युञ्ज्याम् *yuñjyā́m*	युञ्ज्याव *yuñjyā́va*	युञ्ज्याम *yuñjyā́ma*	युञ्जीय *yuñjīyá*	युञ्जीवहि *yuñjīváhi*	युञ्जीमहि *yuñjīmáhi*
युञ्ज्यास् *yuñjyā́s*	युञ्ज्यातम् *yuñjyā́tam*	युञ्ज्यात *yuñjyā́ta*	युञ्जीथास् *yuñjīthā́s*	युञ्जीयाथाम् *yuñjīyā́thâm*	युञ्जीध्वम् *yuñjīdhvám*
युञ्ज्यात् *yuñjyā́t*	युञ्ज्याताम् *yuñjyā́tâm*	युञ्ज्युस् *yuñjyús*	युञ्जीत *yuñjītá*	युञ्जीयाताम् *yuñjīyā́tâm*	युञ्जीरन् *yuñjīrán*

रुध् *rudh*, 'to obstruct,' 1 sing. pres. Par. रुणध्मि *ruṇádhmi*, 1 dual रुन्ध्वस् *rundhvás*. 2, 3 sing. imperf. अरुणत् *áruṇat*.

शिष् *çish*, 'to leave,' 1 sing. pres. Par. शिनष्मि *çináshmi*, 1 dual शिंष्वस् *çiṁshvás*, 2, 3 sing. imperf. अशिनट् *áçinaṭ*.

हिंस् *hiṁs*, 'to strike,' 1 sing. pres. Par. हिनस्मि *hinásmi*, 1 dual हिंस्वस् *hiṁsvás*, 2 sing. imperf. अहिनस् *áhinas* (॰नः °*naḥ*) or अहिनत् *áhinat*, 3 अहिनत् *áhinat*.

§ 108. Alphabetical List of the Most Remarkable Anomalous Verbs, Special Bases, Connective Vowels, Forms of the Second, Third, and Seventh Conjugational Classes, and of the Frequentatives (*cf.* § 102).

अ, connective vowel, see अद्, अन्, रुद्, श्वस्, and स्वप्.

अद्, II. 2, 'to eat,' inserts अ before the terminations of the second and third persons singular of the imperfect Parasmaipada, आदस् *ā́d-a-s*, आदत् *ā́d-a-t*.

अन्, II. 2, 'to breathe,' 1. inserts इ *i* before any consonant except यु, and अ *a* or ई *ī* in the second and third persons sing. of the imperfect Parasm., *e.g.* अनिमि *án-i-mi*, आनीस् *ā́n-ī-s*, or आनस् *ā́n-a-s*.

2. After prepositions containing र् *r* changes its न् to ण्, *e.g.* प्र अनिति = प्राणिति (*cf.* § 16).

अस्, II. 2, 'to be,' 1. drops its vowel in any inflexion, except the singular present Parasmaipada, the whole imperfect, the first persons of the imperative, and the third person sing. of the imperative Parasmaipada in तु, *e.g.* 1 dual pres. Par. स्वस् (*cf.* § 82, 3).

2. Drops its स *s* before the terminations of the second person beginning with स् or ध्, *e.g.* 2 sing. pres. असि.

3. Inserts ई before the terminations of the second and third persons singular of the imperfect Parasm., *e.g.* आसीस्.

4. Makes एधि in the second person singular of the imperative Parasmaipada.

5. Changes its स् *s* to ह् *h* before the termination of the first person sing. of the present Âtmanep., which becomes हे (*cf.* 1).

As this verb is of frequent occurrence I shall give the inflexions in detail.

PRESENT.

Parasmaipada.			Âtmanepada.		
अस्मि *ásmi*	स्वस् *svás*	स्मस् *smás*	हे *hé*	स्वहे *sváhe*	स्महे *smáhe*
असि *ási*	स्थस् *sthás*	स्थ *sthá*	से *sé*	साथे *sā́the*	ध्वे *dhvé*
अस्ति *ásti*	स्तस् *stás*	सन्ति *sánti*	स्ते *sté*	साते *sā́te*	सते *sáte*

IMPERFECT.

आसम् *ā́sam*	आस्व *ā́sva*	आस्म *ā́sma*	आसि *ā́si*	आस्वहि *ā́svahi*	आस्महि *ā́smahi*
आसीस् *ā́sīs*	आस्तम् *ā́stam*	आस्त *ā́sta*	आस्थास् *ā́sthās*	आसाथाम् *ā́sāthām*	आध्वम् *ā́dhvam*
आसीत् *ā́sīt*	आस्ताम् *ā́stām*	आसन् *ā́san*	आस्त *ā́sta*	आसाताम् *ā́sātām*	आसत *ā́sata*

IMPERATIVE.

Parasmaipada.			Âtmanepada.		
असानि	असाव	असाम	असै	असावहै	असामहै
dsâni	*dsâva*	*dsâma*	*dsai*	*dsâvahai*	*dsâmahai*
एधि or स्तात्	स्तम्	स्त or स्तात्	स्व	साथाम्	ध्वम्
edhi *stât*	*stdm*	*stá* *stât*	*svd*	*sâthâm*	*dhvdm*
अस्तु or स्तात्	स्ताम्	सन्तु	स्ताम्	साताम्	सताम्
dstu *stât*	*stâm*	*sántu*	*stâm*	*sâtâm*	*sdtâm*

POTENTIAL.

स्याम्	स्याव	स्याम	सीय	सीवहि	सीमहि
syâm	*syâva*	*syâma*	*sîyd*	*sîvdhi*	*sîmdhi*
स्यास्	स्यातम्	स्यात	सीथास्	सीयाथाम्	सीध्वम्
syâs	*syâtam*	*syâta*	*sîthâs*	*sîyâthâm*	*sîdhvdm*
स्यात्	स्याताम्	स्युस्	सीत	सीयाताम्	सीरन्
syât	*syâtâm*	*syús*	*sîtd*	*sîyâtâm*	*sîrán*

इ, connective vowel, see अन्, ईड्, ईश्, जक्ष्, दरिद्रा, रुद्, श्वस्, स्वप्.

इ, II. 2, 'to go,' is changed to य् (against § 89) before terminations beginning with a vowel, *e.g.* इ + अन्ति becomes यन्ति. But when combined with the preposition अधि, and in the signification 'to read' (Âtmanepada), it follows the rule prescribed in § 89, *e.g.* अधि + इये, 1 sing. present Âtm., अधीये.

इयर्, special base of the strong
इयृ, " " of the other
} forms of ऋ II. 3, 'to go;' य् is inserted in order to avoid the hiatus (*cf.* § 223).

ई, connective vowel, see अन्, अस्, तु, ब्रू, रु, रुद्, श्वस्, स्तु, स्वप्.

ईड्, II. 2, Âtmanepada, 'to praise,' and ईश्, II. 2, Âtm., 'to govern,' insert इ before the terminations से, स्व, ध्वे, and ध्वम्, *e.g.* ईडिषे, ईशिषे (*cf.* § 17).

ईश्, see the preceding.

उष्, see वस्.

ऊर्णो or ऊर्णौ, base of the strong forms of ऊर्णु, II. 2, 'to cover,' in the singular present: the imperfect has only और्णो in the singular, *e.g.* 1 pres. ऊर्णोमि or ऊर्णौमि, but 2 imperfect only और्णोस् (*cf.* § 83, II. A. 1̄).

एधि, see अस्.

घ्न, see हन्.

चकास्, II. 2, 'to shine,' rejects the न् of the termination of the third persons plural in the present and imperative Parasmaipada, and substitutes उस् for अन् in the third person plural of the imperfect Parasm., *e.g.* चकासति, चकासतु, अचकासुस् (*cf.* § 84, 2).

चंखन्, frequentative of खन्, 'to dig,' follows the rules for the frequentative of जन् given under जजन्.

चंखा, see under जजन्.

चंचुर्, frequentative of चर्, 'to go,' leaves the उ unchanged in the first persons singular, dual, and plural of the imperative, and in the first person singular of the imperfect Parasmaipada; in the other strong forms (*i.e.* in the singular present Parasm., in the second and third persons of the imperfect Parasm., and in the third person of the imperative Parasm.) उ follows § 94, *e.g.* 1 sing. of the imperative Par. चञ्चुराणि, 1 sing. present Par. चञ्चूर्मि.

चंख्न्, see under जजन्.

जक्ष्, II. 2, 'to eat,' 1. rejects न् and takes उस् like चकास्, *e.g.* जक्षति, अजक्षुस्.—2. Inserts the vowels इ, ई, and अ like अन्, *e.g.* जक्षिमि, अजक्षीस् or अजक्षस्.

जंग, see जंगम्.

जंगम्, frequentative of गम्, 'to go,' 1. drops the radical अ before terminations beginning with a vowel, except the first persons of the imperative and the first person singular of the imperfect Parasm., *e.g.* जंगम् + अति = जंग्मति, 3 plur. pres. Par.—2. Rejects its final म् before terminations beginning with त्, थ्, or ह्, except in the third person sing. of the present, *e.g.* जंगम् + थस् = जंगथस्, 2 dual pres. Par.

जंग्म्, see जंगम्.

जंघ, जंघन्, जंघ्न्, see हन्.

जजन्, special base of जन्, II. 3, 'to bring forth,' 1. drops its final न् and lengthens at the same time the preceding अ before terminations beginning with a consonant, except those of the singular present and imperfect Parasmaipada and the termination

तु of the third person singular of the imperative Parasm., *e.g.* जजाथस्, 2 dual pres. Parasm.—In the potential this change is optional, *e.g.* जजन्याम् or जजायाम्.—2. Rejects the radical अ before terminations beginning with a vowel, except the first persons singular, dual, and plural of the imperative and the first person singular of the imperative Parasmaipada. The न् after ज् is changed to ञ् *e.g.* जजन् + अति = जज्ञति 3 plur. pres. Parasm.

The same rules apply to जंजन्, the frequentative of जन्, *e.g.* जंजाथस्, जंजन्याम् or जंजायाम्, जंज्ञति; also—except the changing of न् to ञ्—to चंखन्, frequentative of खन्, *e.g.* चंखाथस्, चंखन्याम् or चंखायाम्, चंख्नति.

जजा, जज्ञ्, जंजन्, जंजा, जंज्ञ्, see जजन्.

जह्, see जहा.

जहा, special base of हा, II. 3, 'to leave.' 1. In the second person singular of the imperative Parasmaipada आ may be left unchanged or be modified, according to the rule given in § 83, II. A. 2, or be changed to इ, जहाहि, जहीहि or जहिहि. 2. In the potential आ is rejected, जह्याम्.

जहि, see जहा and हन्.

जागृ, II. 2, 'to wake,' drops the न् and takes उस् like चकास्; before उस् the final ऋ is changed to अर् (*cf.* § 84, 2), *e.g.* 3 plur. of the pres. Parasm. जाग्रति, 3 plur. of the imperf. Par. अजागरुस्.

जागृह्, see जाग्रह्.

जाग्रह्, frequentative of ग्रह्, 'to take,' changes its medial र to ऋ, except in the singular of the present and imperfect Parasmaipada, the first persons singular, dual, and plural of the imperative, and the third person singular of the imperative Parasmaipada, if formed by the termination तु (*cf.* § 82, 3), *e.g.* 1 dual pres. Par. जागृह्वस्.

जाजी, see जाज्या.

जाज्या, frequentative of ज्या, 'to become old,' and of ज्यो 'to restrain,' changes या and यो to ई, except in the inflexions enumerated under जाग्रह्, *e.g.* 1 dual pres. Par. जाजीवस्.

जिहा, special base of हा, II. 3, 'to go,' with anomalous reduplication.

जुहु, special base of हु, II. 3, 'to sacrifice,' takes in the second person singular of the imperative Parasmaipada the termination धि, जुहुधि (against § 84, 3).

तवी, see तु.

तु, II. 2, 'to be strong,' may optionally insert ई before any termination beginning with a consonant, *e.g.* 1 sing. pres. Par. तौमि or तवीमि *tav-î-mi*, potential तुयाम् or तुवीयाम् (*cf.* §§ 83, II. A. 2 and 90).

तृणेह्, strong form of the special base of तृह्, II. 7, 'to injure,' before terminations beginning with a consonant, *e.g.* तृणेह्मि, तृणेक्षि, तृणेढि, but तृणहानि, तृंह्वस्, तृण्ढस्, etc.

तृह्, see तृणेह्.

दद्, see ददा.

ददा, special base, and दादा, frequentative, of दा, II. 3, 'to give.' The final आ of these bases is rejected in all forms, except in the singular of the present and imperfect and the third person singular of the imperative Parasmaipada, formed by तु, *e.g.* 1 dual pres. दद्वस्, दाद्वस्, but 1 sing. pres. ददामि, दादामि.—In the second person sing. of the imperative Par. ददा makes देहि.

दध्, see दधा.

दधा, special base, and दाधा, frequentative, of धा, II. 3, 'to hold,' follow the analogy of ददा and दादा, *e.g.* दध्वस्, दाध्वस्; दधामि, दाधामि. Before terminations beginning with त् or थ् the ध् of दध् and दाध् is changed to त् and the beginning द् to ध्, *e.g.* धत्थस् (2 dual present Par.); regarding the change before स् and ध्व् *cf.* § 96, 1, 3, and 4, *e.g.* धत्से (2 sing. pres. Âtm.), धद्ध्वे (2 plur. pres. Âtm.).—In the second person sing. of the imperative Par. दधा makes धेहि.

दरिद्र्, see दरिद्रा.

दरिद्रा, II. 2, 'to be in distress,' 1. rejects its final आ before any termination beginning with or attached by a vowel, except in the first person singular of the imperfect Parasmaipada.—2. Rejects the न् of the third persons plural of the present and imperative Parasmaipada and takes उस् in the third person plural of the imperfect Parasm. like चकास्, *e.g.* दरिद्रति, अदरिद्रुस्.—3. Prefixes इ to the terminations beginning with a consonant, except in the singular of the present and imperfect Parasm. and in the third person singular of the imperative Par. in तु, *e.g.* 1 dual pres. Par. दरिद्रिवस् *daridr-i-vas* (*cf.* 1).

दरिद्रि, see दरिद्रा.

दर्दृश्, दरिदृश्, or दरीदृश्, frequentative of दृश् 'to see,' changes ऋ (against § 83, II. A. 2) in the second and third persons singular present and the third person singular imperative Parasmaipada, when formed by तु, to र, *e.g.* दर्द्रष्टि, दरिद्रष्टि, or दरीद्रष्टि (3 sing. pres. Par.)

दर्द्रश्, दरिद्रश्, दरीद्रश्, see दर्दृश्.

दादा, see ददा.

दाधा, see दधा.

दीधी, II. 2 Âtm., 'to shine,' changes its final ई before vowels to य् and drops it before the terminations of the potential, *e.g.* दीध्यते (3 plur. of the pres.), दीधीय (1 sing. of the potential).

देहि, see ददा.

द्विष्, II. 2, 'to hate,' in the third plural of the imperfect Parasm. optionally takes उस् instead of अन्, *e.g.* अद्विषुस् or अद्विषन्.

धेहि, see दधा.

नानश्, frequentative of नश्, 'to perish,' in the second person singular of the present Parasm. makes नानङ्क्षि, in the third नानंष्टि, and in the third person singular of the imperative Parasm. नानंष्टु.

नेनिज्, special base of निज् II. 3, 'to clean,' with anomalous reduplication.

पंफुल्, frequentative of फल्, 'to burst.' The उ is left unchanged in the strong forms (against § 83, II. A. 2), *e.g.* first sing. of the pres. Par. पंफुल्मि.

बप्स्, बब्, see बभस्.

बभस्, special base of **भस्**, II. 3, 'to eat,' drops the radical **अ**, and changes **भ्** to **प्**, when the termination begins with a vowel, except in the first person singular of the imperfect Parasmaipada and in the first persons of the imperative, *e.g.* **बप्सति**, 3 plur. pres. Par.—In the Veda **अ** is rejected also before terminations beginning with a consonant, except in the singular of the present and imperfect Parasm. and before **तु** of the third person sing. of the imperative Par., and then **स्** also is lost, thus **बभस्** + **तम्** makes **बब्धम्** (*cf.* § 96, 3).

बिभि, see **बिभी**.

बिभी, special base of **भी**, II. 3, 'to fear,' may optionally shorten the **ई** before the terminations beginning with a consonant, except in the singular of the present and imperfect Par. and before **तु** of the third person sing. imperative Par., where it is changed according to § 83, II. A. 2, *e.g.* **बिभीवस्** or **बिभिवस्**, 1 dual pres. Par.

ब्रू, II. 2, 'to speak,' prefixes **ई** to the terminations of the singular of the present, and the second and third persons singular of the imperfect Parasmaipada and the termination **तु** of the third person sing. of the imperative Par. *e.g.* **ब्रवीमि** (*cf.* § 83, II. A. 1).

मर्मृज्, see **मृज्**.

मामज्ज्, frequentative of **मज्ज्**, 'to dive,' makes in the second person singular of the pres. Par. **मामङ्क्षि**, in the third **मामङ्क्ति**, and in the third person singular of the imperative Par. **मामङ्क्तु**.

मार्ज्, see **मृज्**.

मिमा, special base of **मा**, II. 3, 'to measure, to sound,' with anomalous reduplication.

मृज्, II. 2, 'to wipe,' and its frequentative **मर्मृज्**, **मरिमृज्**, or **मरीमृज्**, change **ऋ** to **आर्** in the singular of the present and imperfect Parasmaipada, in the first persons of the imperative, and before the termination **तु** of the third person of the imperative Parasmaipada; optionally also before all the other inflexions if the termination begins with a vowel, *e.g.* **मार्ज्मि**, **मर्मार्ज्मि**, **मृजन्ति** or **मार्जन्ति**, **मर्मृजति** or **मर्मार्जति** (*cf.* § 102).

य्, see **इ** 'to go.'

रवी, see **रु**.

रु, II. 2, 'to roar,' like **तु**, optionally inserts **ई** before the terminations beginning with a consonant, *e.g.* **रौमि** or **रवीमि**, **रुयाम्** or **रुवीयाम्**.

रुद्, II. 2, 'to cry,' like **अन्**, prefixes **इ** to the terminations beginning with a consonant, except those of the potential, and **ई** or **अ** to the second and third persons of the imperfect Parasmaipada, *e.g.* **रोदिमि**, **अरोदीस्** or **अरोदस्**.

वच्, II. 2, 'to speak,' is deficient of the third person plural of the present, according to others of all the third persons plural, or even of the whole plural.

वश्, II. 2, 'to desire,' changes **व** to **उ**, except in the strong forms (§ 82, 3), *e.g.* 1 dual of the pres. Par. **उश्वस्**, of the imperfect **औश्व**; but 1 sing. pres. **वश्मि**.

वाविध्, see **वाव्यध्**.

वाव्यध्, frequentative of **व्यध्**, 'to pierce,' substitutes **वाविध्**, except in the strong forms (§ 82, 3), *e.g.* **वाविध्वस्**, **अवाविध्व**, but **वाव्यध्मि**.

विद्, II. 2, 'to know.' The present may be expressed by the perfect, but without reduplication, *e.g.* sing. 1. **वेद**, 2. **वेत्थ**, 3. **वेद**, dual 1. **विद्व**, 2. **विदथुस्**, etc. (*cf.* § 118). The third person plural of the imperfect takes the termination **उस्**, instead of **अन्**, *e.g.* **अविदुस्**.—The imperative Parasmaipada may be expressed by a periphrastic form, viz., by **विदाम्** combined with the imperative Parasmaipada of **कृ**, II. 8, 'to make,' *e.g.* 1 sing. **विदां करवाणि** (*cf.* § 86).—Before the terminations of the third persons plural of the present, imperfect, and imperative Âtmanepada **र्** *r* may be inserted optionally, *e.g.* **विदते** *vid-ate* or **विद्रते** *vid-r-ate*, **अविदत** *avid-ata* or **अविद्रत** *avid-r-ata*.

विद्र्, see **विद्**.

वी, II. 2, 'to go,' changes (against § 89) **ई** to **य्** in the third person plural of the imperfect Parasmaipada, *e.g.* **अव्यन्**.

वेविज्, special base of **विज्**, II. 3, 'to separate,' with anomalous reduplication.

वेविष्, special base of **विष्**, II. 3, 'to pervade,' with anomalous reduplication.

वेवी, II. 2, Âtm. 'to go,' changes, like **दीधी**, the final **ई** to **य्** before vowels and rejects it in the potential, *e.g.* **वेव्यते**, **वेवीय**.

शय्, see **शी**.

शाशास्, see **शास्**.

शास्, II. 2, 'to instruct,' 1. rejects, like **चकास्**, the **न्** in the terminations of the third person plural and takes in the third person plural of the imperfect **उस्**, instead of **अन्**, *e.g.* **शासति**, **अशासुस्**.—2. **शास्** and its frequentative **शाशास्**, are changed to **शिष्** and **शाशिष्** before terminations beginning with a consonant, except in the singular of the present and imperfect, and before **तु** of the third person singular of the imperative, *e.g.* **शिष्वस्**, **शाशिष्वस्**.—3. The second person singular of the imperative is **शाधि**, **शाशाधि**.—**आ शास्**, that is to say **शास्**, combined with the preposition **आ** (§ 189), 'to bless,' is regular, *e.g.* 1 dual of the pres. Par. **आ शास्वस्**.

शी, II. 2, Âtm. 'to lie,' 1. changes its **ई** before terminations beginning with a consonant to **ए**, before vowels to **अय्** (Guṇa), *e.g.* 1 sing. pres. **शये**, 2 **शेषे**, 3 **शेते**, etc.—2. Before the terminations of the third persons plural of the present, imperfect, and imperative **र्** is inserted, *e.g.* **शेरते** *çe-r-ate* (3 plur. pres.), **अशेरत** *açe-r-ata*.

श्वस्, II. 2, 'to breathe,' like **अन्**, prefixes **इ** to the terminations beginning with a consonant, except in the potential, and **ई** or **अ** in the second and third persons of the imperfect Parasm., *e.g.* **श्वसिमि**, **अश्वसीस्** or **अश्वसस्**.—The third person singular of the potential Parasmaipada follows the analogy of the first conjugation, **श्वसेत्** (*cf.* § 77).

स्, see **अस्**.

संसन्, frequentative of **सन्**, 'to obtain,' follows the analogy of

जंजन् (*cf.* जजन्) in rejecting the न् and lengthening the radical अ, except in the potential, *e.g.* संसाथस्.

सर्सृज्, सरिसृज् or सरीसृज्, frequentative of सृज्, 'to abandon,' changes ऋ to र् in the second and third persons singular of the present and before the termination तु of the third person of the imperative Parasmaipada, *e.g.* सर्स्रष्टि (*cf.* दर्द्दर्म् and § 102).

सू, II. 2, Âtm. 'to bring forth,' changes ऊ in the first persons of the imperative to उव् (against § 83, II. A. I), *e.g.* सुवै.

स्तवी, see स्तु.

स्तु, II. 2, 'to praise,' like रु, optionally prefixes ई to the terminations beginning with a consonant, *e.g.* स्तौमि or स्तवीमि, स्तुयाम् or स्तुवीयाम्.

स्वप्, II. 2, 'to sleep,' like अन्, prefixes इ to the terminations beginning with a consonant, except in the potential, and ई or अ to those of the second and third persons of the imperfect Parasmaipada, *e.g.* स्वपिमि, अस्वपीस् or अस्वपस्.

ह्, see हन्.

हन्, II. 2, 'to kill,' and जंघन्, its frequentative:

I. 1. Drop the final न् before terminations beginning with consonants (except म्, व्, य्, the singular of the present and imperfect, and the termination तु of the third person singular of the imperative Parasmaipada), *e.g.* हथस्, जंघथस्, 2 dual pres. Par.

2. Reject the radical अ before terminations beginning with a vowel, except in the first person singular of the imperfect Parasm. and the first persons of the imperative, changing at the same time ह् to घ्, *e.g.* घ्नन्ति, जंघ्नति, 3 plur. of the pres. Par.

II. The second person singular of the imperative Parasmaipada of हन् is जहि.

III. After a preposition containing र् the न्, followed by व् or म् may optionally be changed to ण्, *e.g.* प्र हण्वस् or प्र हन्वस् (*cf.* § 16).

CONJUGATION OF THE LAST SIX VERBAL FORMS.

§ 109. These forms are derived from the crude forms of the primitive verbs, which are given in the Dictionaries, and from the derivative verbs, for which see §§ 39-62. We shall begin with the perfect.

FIFTH VERBAL FORM: PERFECT.

§ 110. There are two forms of the perfect, a reduplicated one and a periphrastic.

1. REDUPLICATED PERFECT.

§ 111. The reduplication of the base is effected according to the general rules given in §§ 42-46 and the following special rules:—

I. ऋ *ṛi*, ॠ *ṛí*, ऌ *ḷi*, and a final ए *e*, ऐ *ai*, and ओ *o* are represented in the reduplicated syllable by अ *a*, *e.g.* भृ *bhṛi*, 'to bear,' बभृ *babhṛi*; दृश् *dṛiç*, 'to see,' ददृश् *dadṛiç*; पॄ *pṛí*, 'to fill,' पपॄ *papṛí*; क्लृप् *kḷip*, 'to be able,' चक्लृप् *chakḷip*; धे *dhe*, 'to drink,' दधे *dadhe*; गै *gai*, 'to sing,' जगै *jagai*; शो *ço*, 'to sharpen,' शशो *çaço*.

Except. स्तॄह् *stṛíh*, 'to hurt,' when conjugated, is changed to स्तीर्ह् *stírh*; the reduplicated form therefore, according to § 43, is तिस्तीर्ह् *tistírh*.

II. Verbs beginning with अ *a* followed by a single final consonant, lengthen this vowel, *e.g.* अन् *an*, 'to breathe,' makes आन् *ân* (instead of *a-an*).

An initial आ *ậ* is left unchanged, आप् *âp*, 'to obtain,' is also the base of the reduplicated perfect (for *a-âp*).

Initial इ *i* and उ *u* are lengthened, except in the strong forms, for which *cf.* § 114, *e.g.* इष् *ish*, 'to wish,' makes ईष् *ísh* (for *i-ish*); उष् *ush*, 'to burn,' ऊष् *úsh* (for *u-ush*). But in the strong forms, in which the radical इ *i* is changed to ए *e*, or अय् *ay*, or आय् *ây*, उ *u* to ओ *o*, or अव् *av*, or आव् *âv*, इ *i* is reduplicated to

इय् *iy*, and उ *u* to उव् *uv*, *e.g.* इयेष् *iy-esh* (for *i-esh*), उवोष् *uv-osh* (for *u-osh*).

An initial अ *a* followed by more than one radical consonant, and an initial ऋ *ṛi*, are represented in the syllable of reduplication by आन् *ân*, *e.g.* अङ्ग् *ang*, 'to go,' makes आनङ्ग् *ân-ang* (for *a-ang* with न् *n* inserted in order to avoid the hiatus, and the vowel lengthened before the nasal, *cf.* the numerous analogies in the declension §§ 223, 4, and 229, 2 and 10, etc.) ऋध् *ṛidh*, 'to grow,' आनृध् *ân-ṛidh* (for *a-ṛidh*).

Verbs with an initial ई *î*, ऊ *û*, ॠ *ṛî*, ए *e*, ऐ *ai*, ओ *o*, or इ *i*, उ *u*, ऋ *ṛi* followed by more than one consonant, have no reduplicated perfect (*cf.* § 119).

§ 112. The following personal terminations are affixed to the base reduplicated according to the rules given in § 111.

Parasmaipada.

SINGULAR.	DUAL.	PLURAL.
अ *a* (औ *au*, *cf.* Obs. 1)	इव *iva* (व *va*, *cf.* Obs. 2)	इम *ima* (म *ma*, *cf.* Obs. 2)
इथ *itha* (थ *tha*, *cf.* Obs. 2)	अथुस् *athus*	अ *a*
अ *a* (औ *au*, *cf.* Obs. 1)	अतुस् *atus*	उस् *us*

Âtmanepada.

ए *e*	इवहे *ivahe* (वहे *vahe*, *cf.* Obs. 2)	इमहे *imahe* (महे *mahe*, *cf.* Obs. 2)
इषे *ishe* (से *se*, *cf.* Obs. 2)	आथे *âthe*	इध्वे *idhve*, इढ्वे *iḍhve* (ध्वे *dhve*, ढ्वे *ḍhve*, *cf.* Observ. 2 and § 116)
ए *e*	आते *âte*	इरे *ire* (रे *re*, *cf.* Obs. 2)

Observ. 1. In the first and third pers. sing. Parasm. the termination औ *au* is subjoined to the verbs ending in आ *â*, ए *e*, ऐ *ai*, or ओ *o*, these vowels being rejected before it, *e.g.* दा *dâ*, 'to give,' ददौ *dadau*, धे *dhe* दधौ *dadhau*, गै *gai* जगौ *jagau*, शो *ço* शशौ *çaçau* (*cf.* § 111, I).

Observ. 2. Many verbs must or may reject the इ *i* prefixed to the terminations of the second person singular, the first persons dual and plural in the Parasmaipada and Âtmanepada, and of the second person plural Âtmanepada. When इ *i* is rejected, the termination of the second person singular in the Âtmanepada becomes से *se*, or, according to § 17, षे *she*, e.g. कृ *kṛi*, 'to make,' चकृव *chakṛi-va* (1 dual Par.), चकृषे *chakṛi-she* (2 sing. Âtm.), क्लिद् *klid*, 'to be moist,' चिक्लिदिध्वे *chiklid-i-dhve*, or चिक्लिद्ध्वे *chiklid-dhve* (2 plur. Âtm.), चिक्लिदिषे *chiklid-i-she*, or चिक्लित्से *chiklit-se* (2 sing. Âtm., conformably to § 96, 3).

In the second person singular Parasmaipada इ must be dropped after the verbs ending in ऋ *ṛi*. After verbs ending in आ *â*, ए *e*, ऐ *ai*, ओ *o*, इ *i*, ई *î*, उ *u*, and some others (*cf.* my 'Kurze Grammatik,' § 213) it is rejected optionally.

When इ *i* is retained, final आ *â*, ए *e*, ऐ *ai*, and ओ *o* are rejected, *e.g.* दा *dâ* makes ददाथ *dadâ-tha* or ददिथ *dad-i-tha*. If the termination is subjoined without इ *i*, ए *e* ऐ *ai* and ओ *o* are changed to आ *â*, *e.g.* गै *gai* makes जगाथ *jagâtha* or जगिथ *jag-i-tha*. Final consonants undergo the changes prescribed in §§ 96-102, and penultimate nasals those prescribed in § 83, II. A. 4, *e.g.* तञ्च् *tañch*, 'to contract,' ततङ्कथ *tatañk-tha* (2 sing. Par.), ततङ्क्षे *tatañk-she* (2 sing. Âtm.), ततङ्ग्ध्वे *tatañg-dhve* (2 plur. Âtm.).

The rejection of इ *i* in the third person plural Âtmanepada occurs in the Vedic writings only.

§ 113. In the first and third persons singular Parasmaipada the accent (acute) falls on the radical syllable, in the forms ending in औ *au* on this diphthong, because it contains the radical vowel, *e.g.* भ्रंश् *bhraṁç*, 'to fall,' बभ्रंश *ba-bhráṁç-a*; दा *dâ* ददौ *da-daú*. In the second person sing. Parasm. it likewise falls on the radical syllable, when इ *i* is rejected, *e.g.* ददाथ *dadátha*; शक् *çak*, 'to be able,' शशकथ *çaçáktha*; but when इ *i* is retained, the accent may fall on any syllable, *e.g.* ददिथ *dáditha*, ददिथ *dadítha*, or ददिथ *dadithá*.—In all other inflexions the accent falls on the first syllable of the termination, इ *i* not being counted, *e.g.* 1 dual Par. from तुद् *tud* 'to hurt,' तुतुदिव *tutud-i-vá*.

In consequence of this accentuation, the radical syllable when it has the accent, that is to say in the singular Parasmaipada, is generally strengthened; when without it, that is to say in the dual and plural Parasmaipada and the whole Âtmanepada, it is very often weakened.

§ 114. I. In the strong forms, *i.e.* the singular Parasmaipada, the base undergoes the following changes:—

1. A medial अ *a,* when followed by a single radical consonant, ought to be lengthened in the third person singular Parasmaipada. In the first person this change is optional, *e.g.* पत् *pat,* 'to fall,' 3rd पपात *papắta,* 1st पपत *papáta,* or पपात *papắta.*

2. A final इ *i* or ई *î* is changed in the third person to आय् *ây,* in the first to अय् *ay* or आय् *ây,* in the second to ए *e,* or, when इ *i* is retained, अय् *ay, e.g.* चि *chi,* 'to arrange,' 3rd चिचाय *chichắy-a,* 1st चिचय *chicháy-a* or चिचाय *chichắy-a,* 2nd चिचेथ *chiché-tha* or चिचयिथ *chichay-i-tha.*

3. A final उ *u* or ऊ *û* is changed in the third person to आव् *âv,* in the first to अव् *av,* or आव् *âv,* in the second to ओ *o,* or when इ *i* is retained (*cf.* § 117, 3), to अव् *av, e.g.* दु *du,* 'to go,' 3rd दुदाव *dudắv-a,* 1st दुदव *dudáv-a* or दुदाव *dudắv-a,* 2nd दुदोथ *dudó-tha* or दुदविथ *dudav-i-tha.*

4. A final ऋ *ṛi* or ॠ *ṛî* becomes in the third person आर् *âr,* in the first अर् *ar* or आर् *âr,* in the second अर् *ar, e.g.* कृ *kṛi,* 'to make,' 3rd चकार *chakắr-a,* 1st चकर *chakár-a,* or चकार *chakắr-a,* 2nd चकर्थ *chakár-tha.*

5. A medial इ *i* followed by a single radical consonant is changed in the singular of the Parasmaipada to ए *e,* उ *u* to ओ *o,* ऋ *ṛi* to अर् *ar* (Guṇa), *e.g.* तुद् *tud,* 1st तुतोद *tutód-a,* 2nd तुतोदिथ *tutod-i-tha,* 3rd तुतोद *tutód-a.*

II. When the accent falls on the terminations, that is to say in the dual and plural Parasmaipada, in the whole Âtmanepada, and in the second person singular Parasmaipada, provided the termination is preceded by इ *i,* the base is weakened:—

1. In such instances as may be gathered from the alphabetical list of the anomalous forms in § 118.

2. In the verbs which contain a medial अ *a* between two single consonants, provided the first consonant is not व् *v*, and does not belong to those which are liable to be altered in the reduplicated syllable (§ 45, 1 and 2). These reject the reduplicated syllable and substitute ए *e* for the radical अ *a* in the whole Âtmanepada, in the dual and plural Parasm., and in the second pers. sing. Parasm. when the termination is preceded by इ *i*, *e.g.* पच् *pach*, 1st sing. Âtm. पेचे *pech-é*, 2nd पेचिषे *pech-ishé*, 1st dual Parasm. पेचिव *pech-ivá*, 2nd sing. Parasm. पेचिथ *pech-itha* (or पपक्थ *papák-tha*).

§ 115. The finals of the base undergo the following changes before the terminations:—

1. Final आ *á*, ए *e*, ऐ *ai*, and ओ *o* are rejected before terminations beginning with a vowel, *e.g.* दा *dá*, in 2nd dual Par. ददथुस् *dad-áthus*, in 1st dual ददिव *dad-ivá*.

2. Final इ *i* and ई *í* before terminations beginning with a vowel, are changed to य् *y*, but when preceded by a compound consonant to इय् *iy*, *e.g.* नी *ní*, 'to lead,' 1st dual Par. निन्यिव *niny-ivá*, क्री *krí*, 'to buy,' चिक्रियिव *chikriy-ivá*.

3. Final उ *u* and ऊ *ú* before vowels become उव् *uv*, *e.g.* लू *lú*, 'to cut,' लुलुविव *luluv-ivá*.

4. A final ऋ *ṛi* before vowels becomes र् *r*, but, when preceded by a compound consonant, अर् *ar*; *e.g.* कृ *kṛi*, 2nd dual Par. चक्रथुस् *chakr-áthus*, but स्मृ *smṛi*, 'to remember,' सस्मरथुस् *sasmar-áthus*.

5. A final ॠ *ṛí* becomes अर् *ar*, *e.g.* कॄ *kṛí*, 'to throw,' 2nd dual Par. चकरथुस् *chakar-áthus*, 1st dual चकरिव *chakar-ivá*.

6. For the changes of final consonants *cf.* § 112, Obs. 2.

§ 116. Concerning the terminations :—

I. *Cf.* § 112, Obs. 2.

II. ध्वे *dhve*, the termination of the second person plural Âtman. without इ *i*, becomes ढ्वे *ḍhve* :—1. When preceded by ड् *ḍ*, *e.g.* व्रश्

vraçch, which, according to §§ 112, Obs. 2; 102 and 99, 2, is changed to व्रड् *vraḍ*, makes वव्रड्ढ्वे *vavraḍ-ḍhve*.—2. After the verbs द्रु *dru*, 'to run,' स्रु *sru*, 'to flow,' स्तु *stu*, 'to praise,' कृ *kṛi*, 'to make,' भृ *bhṛi*, 'to bear,' वृ *vṛi*, 'to choose, etc.', and सृ *sṛi*, 'to go,' *e.g.* from कृ *kṛi* चकृढ्वे *chakṛi-ḍhvé*.—3. This change is optional, when the इ *i*, by which this termination is generally preceded, follows य् *y*, or र् *r*, ल् *l*, व् *v*, or ह् *h*, *e.g.* लू *lû* लुलुविध्वे *luluv-idhve*, or लुलुविढ्वे *luluv-iḍhve*.

§ 117. Paradigms:—

1. Of verbs ending in आ *â*, ए *e*, ऐ *ai*, or ओ *o*: दा *dâ*, 'to give.'

Parasmaipada.			Âtmanepada.		
ददौ *dadáu*, I have given.	ददिव *dadivá*	ददिम *dadimá*	ददे *dadé*	ददिवहे *dadivádhe*	ददिमहे *dadimádhe*
ददाथ or ददिथ *dadâtha* *daditha*	ददथुस् *dadáthus*	दद *dadá*	ददिषे *dadishé*	ददाथे *dadâthe*	ददिध्वे *dadidhvé*
ददौ *dadáu*	ददतुस् *dadátus*	ददुस् *dadús*	ददे *dadé*	ददाते *dadâte*	ददिरे *dadiré*

ख्या *khyâ*, 'to proclaim,' चख्यौ *chakhyáu*, चख्ये *chakhyé*.

The verbs ending in ए *e*, ऐ *ai*, or ओ *o* follow strictly the analogy of the preceding, *e.g.* from गै, जगौ, जगाथ or जगिथ, etc.

2. Of verbs ending in इ *i*, or ई *î*, (*a*) preceded by a single consonant: शि *çi*, 'to sharpen.'

Parasmaipada.			Âtmanepada.		
शिशय *çiçáya* or शिशाय *çiçâya*	शिश्यिव *çiçyivá*	शिश्यिम *çiçyimá*	शिश्ये *çiçyé*	शिश्यिवहे *çiçyivádhe*	शिश्यिमहे *çiçyimádhe*
शिशेथ *çiçétha* or शिशयिथ *çiçayitha*	शिश्यथुस् *çiçyáthus*	शिश्य *çiçyá*	शिश्यिषे *çiçyishé*	शिश्याथे *çiçyâthe*	शिश्यिध्वे *çiçyidhvé* or शिश्यिढ्वे *çiçyiḍhvé*
शिशाय *çiçâya*	शिश्यतुस् *çiçyátus*	शिश्युस् *çiçyús*	शिश्ये *çiçyé*	शिश्याते *çiçyâte*	शिश्यिरे *çiçyiré*

नी 'to lead,' निनय or निनाय *ninâya*, निन्ये *ninyé*.

(*b*) Preceded by a compound consonant: क्री *krí*, 'to buy.'

Parasmaipada.			Âtmanepada.		
चिक्रय *chikráya* or चिक्राय *chikrā́ya*	चिक्रियिव *chikriyivá*	चिक्रियिम *chikriyimá*	चिक्रिये *chikriyé*	चिक्रियिवहे *chikriyiváhe*	चिक्रियिमहे *chikriyimáhe*
चिक्रेथ *chikrétha* or चिक्रयिथ *chikrayitha*	चिक्रियथुस् *chikriyáthus*	चिक्रिय *chikriyá*	चिक्रियिषे *chikriyishé*	चिक्रियाथे *chikriyā́the*	चिक्रियिध्वे *chikriyidhvé* or चिक्रियिढ्वे *chikriyiḍhvé*
चिक्राय *chikrā́ya*	चिक्रियतुस् *chikriyátus*	चिक्रियुस् *chikriyús*	चिक्रिये *chikriyé*	चिक्रियाते *chikriyā́te*	चिक्रियिरे *chikriyiré*

श्री *çrí*, 'to cook,' शिश्रय or शिश्राय *çiçrā́ya*, शिश्रिये *çiçriyé*.

3. Of verbs ending in उ *u* or ऊ *ú*: दु *du* 'to go.'

दुदव *dudáva* or दुदाव *dudā́va*	दुदुविव *duduvivá*	दुदुविम *duduvimá*	दुदुवे *duduvé*	दुदुविवहे *duduviváhe*	दुदुविमहे *duduvimáhe*
दुदोथ *dudótha* or दुदविथ *dudavitha*	दुदुवथुस् *duduváthus*	दुदुव *duduvá*	दुदुविषे *duduvishé*	दुदुवाथे *duduvā́the*	दुदुविध्वे *duduvidhvé* or दुदुविढ्वे *duduviḍhvé*
दुदाव *dudā́va*	दुदुवतुस् *duduvátus*	दुदुवुस् *duduvús*	दुदुवे *duduvé*	दुदुवाते *duduvā́te*	दुदुविरे *duduviré*

Those which end in ऊ *ú* differ only in the second person singular Parasmaipada, where इ *i* must be retained, *e.g.* लू *lú*, लुलविथ *lulav-i-tha*.

यु *yu*, 'to join,' युयव or युयाव, *yuyā́va*, युयुवे *yuyuvé*; पू *pú*, 'to purify,' पुपव or पुपाव, *pupā́va*, पुपुवे *pupuve*.

4. Of verbs ending in ऋ *ṛi*, (*a*) preceded by a single consonant: धृ *dhṛi*, 'to hold.'

दधर or दधार *dadhára* *dadhā́ra*	दध्रिव *dadhrivá*	दध्रिम *dadhrimá*	दध्रे *dadhré*	दध्रिवहे *dadhriváhe*	दध्रिमहे *dadhrimáhe*
दधर्थ *dadhártha*	दध्रथुस् *dadhráthus*	दध्र *dadhrá*	दध्रिषे *dadhrishé*	दध्राथे *dadhrā́the*	दध्रिध्वे or दध्रिढ्वे *dadhridhvé* *dadhriḍhvé*
दधार *dadhā́ra*	दध्रतुस् *dadhrátus*	दध्रुस् *dadhrús*	दध्रे *dadhré*	दध्राते *dadhrā́te*	दध्रिरे *dadhriré*

हृ *hṛi*, 'to take,' जहर or जहार *jahā́ra*, जह्रे *jahre*.

(*b*) Preceded by a compound consonant: स्मृ *smṛi*, 'to remember.'

Parasmaipada.			Âtmanepada.		
सस्मर *sasmára* or सस्मार *sasmā́ra*	सस्मरिव *sasmarivá*	सस्मरिम *sasmarimá*	सस्मरे *sasmaré*	सस्मरिवहे *sasmarivádhe*	सस्मरिमहे *sasmarimádhe*
सस्मर्थ *sasmártha*	सस्मरथुस् *sasmaráthus*	सस्मर *sasmará*	सस्मरिषे *sasmarishé*	सस्माराथे *sasmarā́the*	सस्मरिध्वे *sasmaridhvé* or सस्मरिढ्वे *sasmariḍhvé*
सस्मार *sasmā́ra*	सस्मरतुस् *sasmarátus*	सस्मरुस् *sasmarús*	सस्मरे *sasmaré*	सस्माराते *sasmarā́te*	सस्मरिरे *sasmariré*

स्तृ *stṛi*, 'to spread,' तस्तर or तस्तार *tastā́ra*, तस्तरे *tastare.*

5. Of verbs ending in ॠ *ṝ*: कॄ *kṝ*, 'to throw.'

चकर *chakára* or चकार *chakā́ra*	चकरिव *chakarivá*	चकरिम *chakarimá*	चकरे *chakaré*	चकरिवहे *chakarivádhe*	चकरिमहे *chakarimádhe*
चकरिथ *chakaritha*	चकरथुस् *chakaráthus*	चकर *chakará*	चकरिषे *chakarishé*	चकराथे *chakarā́the*	चकरिध्वे *chakaridhvé* or चकरिढ्वे *chakariḍhvé*
चकार *chakā́ra*	चकरतुस् *chakarátus*	चकरुस् *chakarús*	चकरे *chakaré*	चकराते *chakarā́te*	चकरिरे *chakariré*

6. Of verbs ending in consonants: शुच् *çuch*, 'to grieve.'

शुशोच *çuçócha*	शुशुचिव *çuçuchivá*	शुशुचिम *çuçuchimá*	शुशुचे *çuçuché*	शुशुचिवहे *çuçuchivádhe*	शुशुचिमहे *çuçuchimádhe*
शुशोचिथ *çuçochitha*	शुशुचथुस् *çuçucháthus*	शुशुच *çuçuchá*	शुशुचिषे *çuçuchishé*	शुशुचाथे *çuçuchā́the*	शुशुचिध्वे *çuçuchidhvé*
शुशोच *çuçócha*	शुशुचतुस् *çuçuchátus*	शुशुचुस् *çuçuchús*	शुशुचे *çuçuché*	शुशुचाते *çuçuchā́te*	शुशुचिरे *çuçuchiré*

बुध् *budh*, 'to know,' बुबोध *bubodha*, बुबुधे *bubudhe.*

7. Of verbs changing अ *a* to ए *e*, agreeably to § 114, II. 2: तन् *tan*, 'to stretch.'

Parasmaipada.			Âtmanepada.		
ततन or तताने *tatána* *tatā́na*	तेनिव *tenivá*	तेनिम *tenimá*	तेने *tené*	तेनिवहे *tenivā́he*	तेनिमहे *tenimáhe*
तेनिथ[1] *tenitha*	तेनथुस् *tenáthus*	तेन *tená*	तेनिषे *tenishé*	तेनाथे *tenā́the*	तेनिध्वे *tenidhvé*
तताने *tatā́na*	तेनतुस *tenátus*	तेनुस *tenús*	तेने *tené*	तेनाते *tenā́te*	तेनिरे *teniré*

पच् *pach*, 'to cook,' पपच or पपाच *papắcha*, पेचे *peche.*

§ 118. ALPHABETICAL LIST OF ANOMALOUS FORMS.

आनज् in the Veda is optionally used for आनञ्ज् (reduplicated base of अञ्ज् 'to anoint') in the weak forms (§ 114, II).

आनर्छ्, reduplicated base of ऋछ् 'to go,' *e.g.* 1 dual Parasmaipada आनर्छिव.

आनश्, reduplicated base of अश् 'to pervade,' *e.g.* 1 singular Âtmanepada आनशे.

आर्, reduplicated base of ऋ 'to go,' *e.g.* 1 dual Par. आरिव.

आह्, reduplicated form of a lost verb (अह्), which furnishes only some persons of the reduplicated perfect of ब्रू 'to speak,' viz. Parasmaipada, singular 2. आत्थ (*cf.* § 102, नह्), 3. आह, dual 2. आहथुस्, 3. आहतुस्, plur. 3. आहुस्.

इयज्, reduplicated base of यज् 'to sacrifice,' in strong forms (§ 114, I.), *i.e.* the first and third persons singular Parasmaipada and optionally in the second, 1st इयज or इयाज (*cf.* ईज् and येज्).

ईज्, reduplicated base of यज्, in weak forms (§ 114, II), *i.e.*, the whole Âtmanepada, the dual and plural Parasmaipada, and optionally in the second person singular Parasmaipada, *e.g.* 1st dual Par. ईजिव (*cf.* इयज्).

ईध्, reduplicated base of इन्ध् Âtman. 'to kindle,' in the Veda, 1st or 3rd sing. ईधे.

ईय्, reduplicated base of इ 'to go,' in the weak forms (§ 114, II), *e.g.* 1st dual Par. ईयिव *íy-ivá*; in the singular Par. regularly (*cf.* § 111, II., and 114, I. 2), *e.g.* in the 3rd person इयाय *iyā́y-a*.

[1] In the Veda also ततन्थ *tatántha.*

उवच्, reduplicated base of वच् 'to speak,' in the singular of the Parasmaipada (*cf.* ऊच्), 3rd उवाच.

उवद्, like the preceding, of वद् 'to speak,' उवाद (*cf.* ऊद्).

उवप्, like the preceding, of वप् 'to sow,' उवाप (*cf.* ऊप् and वेप्).

उवय्, like the preceding, of वे 'to weave,' but also regularly ववे *e.g.* 1st person उवय or उवाय or ववौ (*cf.* ऊव् and ऊय्).

उवश्, like the preceding, of वश् 'to desire' (*cf.* ऊश्).

उवस्, like the preceding, of वस् I. 1 'to dwell' (*cf.* ऊष्).

उवह्, like the preceding, of वह् 'to bear;' remember § 102 (*cf.* ऊह्).

ऊच्, reduplicated base of वच् 'to speak,' in the weak forms (§ 114, II.), 1st dual Par. ऊचिव (*cf.* उवच्),

ऊद्, reduplicated base of वद् 'to speak' (*cf.* उवद्), } in the weak forms.
ऊप्, reduplicated base of वप् 'to sow' (*cf.* उवप्), }

ऊय्, reduplicated base of वे 'to weave,' in the weak forms, but also regularly, 1st dual Par. ऊयिव or वविव (*cf.* उवय् and ऊव्).

ऊर्णुनु, reduplicated base of ऊर्णु 'to cover.' In the second person singular Parasmaipada the termination is only इथ, and the final उ may optionally be changed to अव् or उव्, ऊर्णुनविथ or ऊर्णुनुविथ; in the other forms उ is changed regularly, in the first person singular Parasmaipada to अव् or आव्, in the third to आव्, in all the rest to उव्; 3rd sing. Par. ऊर्णुनाव, 1st dual ऊर्णुनुविव.

ऊव्, reduplicated base of वे 'to weave,' in the weak forms (§ 114, II.), 1st dual Par. ऊविव (*cf.* ऊय् and उवय्).

ऊश्, redupl. base of वश् (*cf.* उवश्). } in the
ऊष्, redupl. base of वस् (*cf.* उवस्), 1st dual Par. ऊषिव. } weak
ऊह्, redupl. base of वह् (*cf.* उवह्). } forms.

ग्रेथ् may optionally be used as base of the perfect of ग्रन्थ् 'to tie,' in the weak forms (§ 113, II.), 1st dual Par. ग्रेथिव, or regularly जग्रन्थिव.

चक्र्, reduplicated base of कृ 'to make,' has the initial इ of the personal terminations only in the third person plural Âtmanepada, *e.g.* 1st dual Par. चकृव, but चक्रिरे *chakr-iré*.

चख्न्, reduplicated base of खन् 'to dig,' in the weak forms (§ 114, II.), *e.g.* चख्निव, 1st dual Par.

चस्कर्, reduplicated base of कृ 'to make,' when combined with certain prepositions, after which it becomes स्कृ (*cf.* § 189, Observ. 4), *e.g.* 3rd sing. Par. सं चस्कार, 1st dual सं चस्करिव.

चिकि (and regularly चिचि), reduplicated base of चि 'to arrange,' 3rd singular Parasmaipada चिकाय or चिचाय.

जक्ष्, reduplicated base of घस् 'to eat,' in the weak forms (§ 114, II.), 1st dual Par. जक्षिव.

जगल् or जगर्, reduplicated base of गॄ 'to swallow.'

जगृह्, reduplicated base of ग्रह् 'to take,' in the weak forms (§ 114, II.), जगृहिव, 1st dual Par.

जग्म्, like the preceding of गम् 'to go,' जग्मिव.

जघन्, reduplicated base of हन् 'to kill,' in the singular Parasmaipada, *e.g.* 3rd person जघान (*cf.* जघ्न्).

जघ्न् of हन् 'to kill,' in the weak forms (§ 114, II.), *e.g.* 1st dual Parasmaip. जघ्निव (*cf.* जघन्).

जजम्भ्, reduplicated base of जभ् Âtm. 'to gape,' 1st sing. जजम्भे.

जजागर्, and without reduplication (*cf.* § 47), जागर्, redupl. base of जागृ 'to wake,' 3rd sing. Par. जजागार or जागार, 1st dual जजागरिव or जागरिव.

जज्ञ्, reduplicated base of जन् 'to bring forth,' in the weak forms (§ 114, II), जज्ञिव, 1st dual Parasmaipada.

जागर्, see जजागर्.

जिगि, reduplicated base of जि 'to conquer,' 3rd sing. Par. जिगाय 1st dual Par. जिग्यिव.

जिघि of हि 'to go,' जिघाय, जिघ्यिव.

जिज्या of ज्या, 'to become old,' जिज्यौ, जिज्यिव.

जिज्यो of ज्यो, Âtm. 'to restrain,' 1st sing. Âtm. जिज्ये.

जुगूह् of गुह्, 'to hide,' in the first and third persons singular Parasmaipada, and in the second if ह् is retained, 1st and 3rd sing. Par. जुगूह, 2nd जुगूहिथ or जुगोढ.

जुहू of ह्वे, 'to call,' *e.g.* 3rd singular Par. जुहाव, 1st dual जुहुविव.

जेर् of जॄ, 'to grow old,' may optionally be used as base of the weak forms (§ 114, II.), 1st dual Parasm. जजरिव or जेरिव.

तत्, Vedic reduplicated base of तन्, 'to stretch,' in the weak forms (§ 114, II.), *e.g.* 2nd sing. Âtm. तत्निषे.

तत्रप्, reduplicated base of तृप् 'to satisfy,' in the second person singular Parasmaipada, when without इ, तत्रप्थ, or regularly ततर्प्थ and ततर्पिथ.

तस्तभ्, Vedic reduplicated base of स्तम्भ् 'to stop,' in the weak forms (§ 114, II.), तस्तभतुस्, 3rd dual Par.

तिष्ठिव्, reduplicated base of ष्ठिव् 'to spit,' also regularly टिष्ठिव्.

तिष्ठीव्, reduplicated base of ष्ठीव् 'to spit,' also regularly टिष्ठीव्.

तुष्टु, reduplicated base of स्तु 'to praise,' retains इ only in the termination of the third person plural Âtmanepada, *e.g.* 1st dual Par. तुष्टुव.

तेर्, reduplicated base of तॄ 'to cross,' in the weak forms (§ 114, II.), तेरिव, 1st dual Par.

त्रेप्, reduplicated base of त्रप् 'to be ashamed,' in the same inflexions, त्रेपिव.

त्रेस् (?), reduplicated base of त्रस् 'to fear,' optionally in the same inflexions, तत्रसिव or त्रेसिव.

दद्द्, reduplicated base of दद् 'to give' (against § 114, II. 2), दद्दिव.

ददश्, reduplicated base of दंश् 'to bite,' optionally in the weak forms (§ 114, II.), ददंशिव or ददशिव.

दद्र्, reduplicated base of दॄ 'to burst,' optionally in the weak forms (§ 114, II.), *e.g.*, ददरिव or दद्रिव.

दद्रप्, reduplicated base of दृप् 'to be proud,' optionally in the second person singular Parasmaipada, when without इ, दद्रप्थ or ददर्प्थ or ददर्पिथ.

दद्रश्, reduplicated base of दृश् 'to see,' in the second person singular Parasmaipada, when without इ, दद्रष्ठ (or ददर्शिथ).

दिगि, reduplicated base of दे Âtm. 'to protect,' 1st sing. दिग्ये.

दिदीय्, reduplicated base of दी Âtm. 'to go to ruin,' 1st sing. दिदीये.

दिद्युत्, reduplicated base of द्युत् Âtm. 'to shine,' दिद्युते.

दुद्रु, reduplicated base of द्रु 'to run,' retains the इ of the terminations only in the 3rd pers. plural Âtm.; *e.g.* दुद्रुव, but दुद्रुविरे.

देभ्, reduplicated base of दम्भ् 'to hurt,' optionally in the weak forms (§ 114, II.), देभिव or ददम्भिव.

ननंश्, reduplicated base of नश् 'to perish,' in the second person singular Parasmaipada when without इ, ननंष्ठ (or नेशिथ, § 114, II. 2).

पप्त्, reduplicated base of पत् 'to fall,' in the Veda, in the weak forms (§ 114, II.), पप्तिम.

पप्न्, reduplicated base of पन् Âtm. 'to praise,' likewise in the Veda, पप्ने.

पप्र्, reduplicated base of पॄ 'to fill,' optionally in the weak forms (§ 114, II.) *e.g.* पपरिव or पप्रिव.

पिप्य्, reduplicated base of प्याय् Âtm. 'to be exuberant,' पिप्ये.

फेण्, reduplicated base of फण् 'to go,' optionally in the weak forms (§ 114, II.), फेणिव or पफणिव.

फेल्, reduplicated base of फल् 'to burst,' in the weak forms (§ 114, II.), *e.g.* फेलिव.

बप्स्, reduplicated base of भस् 'to eat,' in the Veda, in the weak forms (§ 114, II.).

बभर्ज् optionally instead of बभ्रज्ज् from भ्रज्ज् 'to fry,' *e.g.* 2nd sing. Par. बभर्ज्जिथ or बभ्रज्जिथ, or without इ, बभर्ष्ठ or बभ्रष्ठ (*cf.* § 102).

बभूव्, reduplicated base of भू 'to become,' 'to be.' It is conjugated as follows:—

बभूव *babhûva*	बभूविव *babhûvivá*	बभूविम *babhûvimá*	बभूवे *babhûvé*	बभूविवहे *babhûviváhe*	बभूविमहे *babhûvimáhe*
बभूविथ *babhûvitha*	बभूवथुस् *babhûváthus*	बभूव *babhûvá*	बभूविषे *babhûvishé*	बभूवाथे *babhûvâthe*	बभूविध्वे *babhûvidhvé* or बभूविढ्वे *babhûviḍhvé*
बभूव *babhûva*	बभूवतुस् *babhûvátus*	बभूवुस् *babhûvús*	बभूवे *babhûvé*	बभूवाते *babhûvâte*	बभूविरे *babhûviré*

बभृ्, reduplicated base of भृ 'to bear,' retains इ only in the third person plural Âtmanepada, बभृव, but बभ्रिरे.

भेज्, reduplicated base of भज् 'to divide,' in the weak forms (§ 114, II.), भेजिव, भेजथुस्.

भ्रेज्, reduplicated base of भ्राज् Âtm. 'to shine,' optionally, 1st sing. भ्रेजे or बभ्राजे.

भ्रेम्, reduplicated base of भ्रम् 'to whirl,' optionally in the weak forms (§ 114, II.), भ्रेमिव or बभ्रमिव.

भ्रेश्, reduplicated base of भ्राश् Âtm. 'to shine,' optionally, भ्रेशे or बभ्राशे.

भ्लेश्, reduplicated base of भ्लाश् Âtm. 'to shine,' optionally.

ममज्ज्, reduplicated base of मज्ज् 'to dive,' in the second person singular Parasmaipada, when without इ, ममङ्क्थ, else ममज्जिथ.

ममा, reduplicated base of मि II. 5, 'to throw,' and मी II. 9, 'to hurt,' in the singular Parasm. ममौ, but 1st dual मिम्यिव.

ममृ, reduplicated base of मृ Âtm. 'to die,' is conjugated in the Parasmaipada, *e.g.* 1st sing. ममर or ममार, etc.

ममार्ज्, see ममृज्.

ममृज्, reduplicated base of मृज् 'to wipe.' In the singular Parasmaipada it must, and in all the other inflexions, when the termination begins with a vowel, it may become मार्ज्, *e.g.* 1st and 3rd sing. ममार्ज, 3rd plur. ममार्जुस् or ममृजुस्. This verb belongs to those which may optionally reject the initial इ of the termination, except in the third person plural Âtmanepada. The 1st dual Par. for instance may be ममृज्व or ममृजिव or ममार्जिव.

मम्न् in the Veda instead of मेन् (§ 114, II. 2) from मन् 'to think,' मम्नाथे.

येज् in the Veda, optionally in the weak forms (§ 114, II.), of यज् 'to sacrifice,' *e.g.* 1st sing. Âtm. येजे (*cf.* इयज्, ईजे).

ररन्ध्, reduplicated base of रध् 'to perish,' before terminations beginning with a vowel, *e.g.* 1st and 3rd person sing. Parasm. ररन्ध, 2nd person ररन्धिथ, but without इ, ररद्ध.

रेज्, reduplicated base of राज् 'to shine,' in the weak forms (§ 114, II.), *e.g.* रेजिव or रराजिव.

रेध्, reduplicated base of राध्, but only when it means 'to hurt,' in the weak forms (§ 114, II.).

लला, reduplicated base of ली 'to adhere,' optionally in the singular Parasmaipada, *e.g.* 3rd person ललौ or लिलाय, but in the Âtm. regularly लिल्ये (Sch. Pâṇini VI. 1, 51; *cf.* Westergaard, Radices).

ववक्, reduplicated base of वङ्क् 'to be crooked,' in the Veda in the weak forms (§ 114, II.), *e.g.* वावक्रे, 3rd plur. Âtm. without इ.

ववृ, reduplicated base of वृ 'to select,' etc., attaches the terminations without इ, except in the second person Par. (but in the Veda also here) and in the third plural Âtm., ववृव, ववरिथ (Ved. ववर्थ) वव्रिरे.

वव्न्, instead of ववन्, from वन् 'to honour,' in the weak forms (§ 114, II.), in the Veda, *e.g.* वव्ने, 1st and 3rd sing. of the Âtmanepada.

विद् 'to know.' If the perfect of this verb is used in the sense of the present (§ 108, p. 91), it rejects the reduplication and the initial इ of the terminations, *e.g.* 1st and 3rd sing. Par. वेद, 2nd sing. वेत्थ, 1st dual Par. विद्व, 1st plur. Par. विद्म. These anomalies are restricted to the Parasmaipada.—When expressing the perfect it is formed regularly, विवेद, etc.

विविच्, reduplicated base of व्यच् 'to surround,' in the weak forms (§ 114, II.), विविचिव (*cf.* विव्यच्).

विविध्, reduplicated base of व्यध् 'to beat,' in the weak forms (§ 114, II.), *cf.* विव्यध्.

विव्यच्, reduplicated base of व्यच् in the sing. Par. (*cf.* विविच्.)

विव्यथ्, reduplicated base of व्यथ्, Âtm. 'to tremble,' 1st sing. विव्यथे.

विव्यध्, reduplicated base of व्यध्, in the sing. Par. (*cf.* विविध्).

विव्यय्, reduplicated base of व्ये 'to cover,' in the singular Parasm. necessarily, in the other forms optionally, *e.g.* 3rd sing. Parasm. विव्याय, 1st dual Par. विव्यिव or विव्ययिव.

वेप्, reduplicated base of वप्, in the Veda optionally in the weak forms (§ 114, II.), *e.g.* वेपे; *cf.* उवप्, ऊप्.

वेम्, reduplicated base of वम् 'to vomit,' likewise.

शशस्, reduplicated base of शस् 'to hurt' (against § 114, II. 2), शशसिव.

शश्र्, reduplicated base of शॄ 'to hurt,' optionally in the weak forms (§ 114, II.), *e.g.* शशरिव or शश्रिव.

शुशू, reduplicated base of श्वि 'to swell,' optionally, *e.g.* 3rd sing. Par. शुशाव or शिश्वाय.

शुश्रु, reduplicated base of श्रु 'to hear,' rejects the initial इ of the terminations, except in the 3rd plur. Âtm., *e.g.* 1st dual Par. शुश्रुव, but शुश्रुविरे.

श्रेथ्, reduplicated base of श्रथ्, and optionally of श्रन्थ् 'to loosen,' in the weak forms (§ 114, II.), *e.g.* श्रेथिव or शश्रन्थिव.

सश्च् in the Veda instead of सेच्, from सच् 'to follow,' *e.g.* सश्चिरे.

ससञ्ज्, reduplicated base of सञ्ज् 'to stick,' optionally in the weak forms (§ 114, II.), *e.g.* ससजिव or ससञ्जिव.

ससूव्, reduplicated base of सू 'to bring forth,' in the Veda, ससूव (*cf.* बभूव).

ससृ, reduplicated base of सृ 'to go,' rejects the initial इ of the terminations, except in the the 3rd plur. Âtm., *e.g.* ससृव.

सस्रज्, reduplicated base of सृज् 'to abandon,' in the second pers. singular Parasm. when without इ, सस्रष्ठ or ससर्जिथ.

सस्वज्, reduplicated base of स्वञ्ज् Âtm. 'to embrace,' optionally, *e.g.* सस्वजे or सस्वञ्जे.

सुषुप्, reduplicated base of स्वप् 'to sleep,' in the weak forms (§ 114, II.). *e.g.* सुषुपिव (*cf.* सुष्वप्).

सुष्वप्, reduplicated base of स्वप् 'to sleep,' in the strong forms (§ 114, I.), *e.g.* 3rd singular Parasm. सुष्वाप.

स्तेन् (?), reduplicated base of स्तन् 'to sound,' optionally in the weak forms (§ 114, II.).

स्तेम् (?), reduplicated base of स्तम् 'to be unconfused,' like the preceding.

क्षेम्, reduplicated base of क्ष्मम् 'to sound,' like the preceding, *e.g.* क्षेमुस् or सक्ष्मुस्, 3rd plur. Par.

स्वेन्, reduplicated base of स्वन् 'to sound,' like the preceding.

Observ. In the Veda the reduplication is sometimes rejected.

§ 119. The reduplicated perfect is restricted to monosyllabic primitive verbs not beginning with ई *í*, ऊ *ú*, ॠ *ṛí*, a diphthong, or इ *i*, उ *u*, ऋ *ṛi* followed by a compound consonant. All other verbs take the periphrastic form.

2. Periphrastic Perfect.

§ 120. According to the preceding paragraph the periphrastic perfect is formed :—

I. From primitive verbs 1. consisting of more than one syllable, *e.g.* चकास् *chakâs*, 'to shine.'

2. Beginning : (*a*) with ई *í*, ऊ *ú*, ॠ *ṛí*, or a diphthong, *e.g.* ईड् *íḍ* 'to praise.'

(*b*) With इ *i*, उ *u*, ऋ *ṛi*, followed immediately by more than one consonant, *e.g.* इन्ध् *indh* 'to kindle.'

II. From all the derivative verbs (§§ 39-62; *cf.* Pâṇini, III. 1, 35).

§ 121. The periphrastic perfect is formed by affixing आम् *ấm* to the verb, *e.g.* चकासाम् *chakâs-ấm*, ईडाम् *íḍ-ấm*, इन्धाम् *indh-ấm*, and by combining with this form the reduplicated perfect of the verbs अस् *as*, 'to be,' भू *bhú*, 'to become,' or कृ *kṛi*, 'to make,' which lose their accents.

When, according to § 65, the verb ought to be conjugated in the Âtmanepada, the reduplicated perfect of कृ *kṛi* follows the Âtmanepada, but अस् *as* and भू *bhú* are always conjugated in the Parasmaipada, *e.g.* ईड् *íḍ*, Âtm., 1st sing. perfect with कृ *kṛi*, ईडां चक्रे *íḍấṁ chakre*, with अस् *as*, or भू *bhú*, ईडामास *íḍấm âsa*, ईडां बभूव *íḍấṁ babhúva*.

§ 122. Before the affix आम् *ấm*, the base undergoes the following modifications :—

1. A final अ *a*, or आ *â*, is rejected, *e.g.* from बोधय *bodhaya*,

causal of बुध् *budh*, 'to understand,' बोधयाम् *bodhayâm*; दरिद्रा *daridrâ*, 'to be poor,' दरिद्राम् *daridrâm*.

2. A final इ *i* or ई *î* is changed to अय् *ay*, उ *u* or ऊ *û* to अव् *av*, ऋ *ṛi* or ॠ *ṛî* to अर् *ar* (guṇa), *e.g.* बोभू *bobhû*, frequentative of भू *bhû*, 'to become,' बोभवाम् *bobhavâm*.

3. Penultimate इ *i*, उ *u*, or ऋ *ṛi*, followed by a simple consonant, are changed to ए *e*, ओ *o*, अर् *ar* (guṇa), *e.g.* वावृत् *vâvṛit*, 'to choose,' वावर्ताम् *vâvartâm*. The last इ *i* of the desiderative preceding ष् remains unchanged, *e.g.* बुबोधिषाम् *bubodhish-âm*; also *i*, *u*, *ṛi*, *ḷi* of frequentatives, followed by a radical consonant.

4. The rule, given § 59, 5, applies also here, *e.g.*, बेभिद्य *bebhidya*, frequentative of भिद् *bhid*, 'to split,' makes बेभिदाम् *bebhidâm*; नमस्य *namasya*, नमस्याम् *namasy-âm* or नमसाम् *namas-âm*.

§ 123. PARADIGM: छादय *chhâdaya* I. 10, of छद् *chhad* 'to shade.'

छादयाम् *chhâdayâm*	आस *âsa*	or बभूव *babhûva*	or चकर *chakara* or चकार *chakâra*		or चक्रे *chakre*
	आसिथ *âsitha*	बभूविथ *babhûvitha*	चकर्थ *chakartha*		चकृषे *chakṛishe*
	आस *âsa*	बभूव *babhûva*	चकार *chakâra*		चक्रे *chakre*
	आसिव *âsiva*	बभूविव *babhûviva*	चकृव *chakṛiva*		चकृवहे *chakṛivahe*
	आसथुस् *âsathus*	बभूवथुस् *babhûvathus*	चक्रथुस् *chakrathus*		चक्राथे *chakrâthe*
	आसतुस् *âsatus*	बभूवतुस् *babhûvatus*	चक्रतुस् *chakratus*		चक्राते *chakrâte*
	आसिम *âsima*	बभूविम *babhûvima*	चकृम *chakṛima*		चकृमहे *chakṛimahe*
	आस *âsa*	बभूव *babhûva*	चक्र *chakra*		चकृढ्वे *chakṛiḍhve*
	आसुस् *âsus*	बभूवुस् *babhûvus*	चक्रुस् *chakrus*		चक्रिरे *chakrire*

§ 124. ALPHABETICAL LIST OF ANOMALOUS FORMS.

अयाम् from अय् 'to go' (against § 119).

आसाम् from आस् Âtm. 'to sit' (likewise).

ऋतीयाम् from ऋत् 'to blame' (*cf.* § 81), which forms also a reduplicated perfect.

ओषाम् from उष् 'to burn' (against § 119, forms also a reduplicated perfect).

कामयाम् from कम् 'to love,' like the preceding.

कासाम् from कास् 'to cough' (against § 119).

गोपायाम् from गुप् 'to protect' (*cf.* § 81), which forms also a reduplicated perfect.

जिह्रयाम् from ह्री 'to be ashamed,' with reduplication (against § 119); forms also a reduplicated perfect.

जुहवाम् from हु 'to sacrifice,' like the preceding.

दयाम् from दय् 'to give' (against § 119).

दीध्याम् from दीधी 'to shine' (against § 122, 2).

धूपायाम् from धूप् 'to fumigate' (*cf.* § 81); forms also a reduplicated perfect.

पणायाम् from पण्, and } 'to praise,' like the preceding.
पनायाम् from पन् }

बिभयाम् from भी 'to fear,' with reduplication; against § 119; forms also a reduplicated perfect.

बिभराम् from भृ 'to bear,' like the preceding.

विच्छायाम् from विच्छ् 'to go' (*cf.* § 81), forms also a reduplicated perfect.

विदाम् from विद् 'to know;' against § 119; forms also a reduplicated perfect.

वेव्याम् from वेवी 'to go;' against § 122, 2.

SIXTH VERBAL FORM: AORIST.

§ 125. The aorist has seven forms. But most verbs are restricted to one, some admit of two, and very few of three.

§ 126. Three of these seven forms are formed by personal terminations, the other four by compounding the verb with the three aorists, or the imperfect and two aorists, of the verb अस् *as* 'to be.' We shall call the latter compound aorists, and the former simple aorists.

§ 127. All the seven forms take the temporal augment according to the rules laid down in § 74, 1. It is rejected when the aorist is used with the negative particle मा *mâ*, or मा स्म *mâ sma*, in the sense of a prohibitive imperative; in the Veda also in many other instances.

THE THREE SIMPLE AORISTS.

FIRST FORM OF THE AORIST.

§ 128. The augmented verb is combined with the terminations of the imperfect (§ 74, 2). Verbs ending in आ *â* or diphthongs, and frequentatives take उस् *us* in the third person plural Parasmaipada, before which final आ *â* and diphthongs are rejected, *e.g.* दा *dâ*, 'to give,' अदा + उस् *ádâ* + *us* = अदुस् *ádus*. Before the other terminations final diphthongs are changed to आ *â*, *e.g.* धे *dhe*, 'to drink,' अधे + म *ádhe* + *ma* = अधाम *ádhâma*. The initial अ *a* of the termination of the first person singular Parasmaipada is dropped after आ *â*, *e.g.* अधा *adhâ* (instead of अधे *adhe*) + अम् *am* becomes अधाम् *ádhâm*.

§ 129. Only twelve verbs and their first frequentatives take this form of the aorist. In the Veda, however, it is used more frequently. The first aorist is conjugated in the Parasmaipada only (but *cf.* § 130). A radical ऋ *ṛi* is changed to अर् *ar*. The second and third persons singular Parasmaipada follow the rules given in § 103, *e.g.* वृज् *vṛij* makes in the 2nd and 3rd persons sing. Par. अवर्क् *ávark*.

§ 130. Nine verbs ending in न् *n* or ण् *ṇ* take this form in the second and third persons singular of the Âtmanepada, before the terminations of which, viz., थास् *thâs* and त *ta*, the nasal is rejected, *e.g.* तन् *tan*, 'to stretch,' अतथास् *á-ta-thâs*, अतत *á-ta-ta*; ऋण् *ṛiṇ*, 'to go,' आर्थास् *âr-thâs*, आर्त *âr-ta*.—सन् *san*, 'to obtain,' lengthens अ *a* at the same time, असाथास् *á-sâ-thâs*, असात *á-sâ-ta*.

§ 131. PARADIGM: दा *dá*, 'to give.'

SINGULAR.	DUAL.	PLURAL.
अदाम् *ádâm*, 'I gave'	अदाव *ádâva*	अदाम *ádâma*
अदास् *ádâs*	अदातम् *ádâtam*	अदात *ádâta*
अदात् *ádât*	अदाताम् *ádâtâm*	अदुस् *ádus*

From स्था *sthâ*, 'to stand,' अस्थाम् *ásthâm*, etc.

SECOND FORM OF THE AORIST.

§ 132. The augmented verb takes the terminations of the imperfect of the first conjugation, or rather of the sixth conjugational class (§ 80, 3), with which, if the augment is rejected, it agrees also in regard to the accent, *e.g.* imperfect of तुद् *tud* without augment तुदम् *tud-ám*, तुदस् *tud-ás*, etc.; aorist 2 of सिच् *sich*, सिचम् *sich-ám*, सिचस् *sich-ás*, etc. (*cf.* my 'Kurze Grammatik,' § 256).

The terminations therefore are:—

Parasmaipada.			Âtmanepada.		
अम् *am*	आव *âva*	आम *âma*	ए *e*	आवहि *âvahi*	आमहि *âmahi*
अस् *as*	अतम् *atam*	अत *ata*	अथास् *athâs*	एथाम् *ethâm*	अध्वम् *adhvam*
अत् *at*	अताम् *atâm*	अन् *an*	अत *ata*	एताम् *etâm*	अन्त *anta*

§ 133. The second form of the aorist is used more frequently than the first (*cf.* my 'Vollständige Grammatik,' § 841).

Verbs containing ऋ *ṛi* change it to अर् *ar*: दृश् *dṛiç*, 'to see,' अदर्शम् *á-darç-am*. A penultimate nasal is rejected: स्कन्द् *skand*, 'to ascend,' अस्कदम् *á-skad-am* (see the list, § 137).

§ 134. PARADIGM: सिच् *sich*, 'to sprinkle.'

असिचम् *ásicham*	असिचाव *ásichâva*	असिचाम *ásichâma*	असिचे *ásiche*	असिचावहि *ásichâvahi*	असिचामहि *ásichâmahi*
असिचस् *ásichas*	असिचतम् *ásichatam*	असिचत *ásichata*	असिचथास् *ásichathâs*	असिचेथाम् *ásichethâm*	असिचध्वम् *ásichadhvam*
असिचत् *ásichat*	असिचताम् *ásichatâm*	असिचन् *ásichan*	असिचत *ásichata*	असिचेताम् *ásichetâm*	असिचन्त *ásichanta*

From लिप् *lip*, 'to anoint,' अलिपम् *álipam*, etc.

THIRD FORM OF THE AORIST.

§ 135. In the third form the base is reduplicated and takes the terminations of the second form and the augment.

The rules for the reduplication of monosyllabic verbs are the same as those given for the reduplicated perfect (§ 111 and especially § 111, I).

A final इ *i* of the base is changed to इय् *iy*, a final उ *u* to उव् *uv*, radical ऋ *ṛi* to अर् *ar*, and final ए *e* is rejected, *e.g.* श्रि *çri*, 'to go,' अशिश्रियम् *a-çi-çriy-am*, अशिश्रियस् *açiçriy-as*, etc.; द्रु *dru*, 'to run,' अदुद्रुवम् *a-du-druv-am*; धे *dhe*, 'to drink,' अदधम् *a-da-dh-am*; कृ *kṛi*, 'to make,' अचकरम् *a-cha-kar-am*.

§ 136. This form is the regular aorist of all the derivative verbs ending in the affix अय *aya*, viz., causals, verbs of the tenth conjugational class, and denominatives in अय *aya*.

But there are some peculiarities regarding the modification of the bases as well as the reduplication.

I. The affix अय *aya* is rejected, तक्षय *taksh-aya*, causal of तक्ष् *taksh*, 'to slice,' अततक्षम् *a-ta-taksh-am*.

II. A long vowel which by the rejection of अय *aya* has become the penultimate, is shortened, and for a penultimate diphthong its second part is substituted, viz., इ *i* for ए *e* and ऐ *ai*, उ *u* for ओ *o* and औ *au*, *e.g.* पाठय *pâṭh-aya*, causal of पठ् *paṭh*, 'to recite,' becomes पठ् *paṭh*; दापय *dâpaya*, causal of दा *dâ*, दप् *dap*; रेपय *re-paya*, causal of री *rî* (§ 60), रिप् *rip*; स्फोरय *sphor-aya*, causal of स्फुर् *sphur*, स्फुर् *sphur*; भावय *bhâv-aya*, causal of भू *bhû*, भव् *bhav*.

There are many exceptions to the latter rule; thus the long vowels and diphthongs of denominatives remain unchanged, मालय *mâl-aya*, from माला *mâlâ*, 'a garland,' becomes माल् *mâl*. For other sporadic instances, as, टीक् *ṭîk*, from टीकय *ṭîk-aya*, causal of टीक् *ṭîk*, 'to go;' नेद् *ned*, from नेदय *ned-aya*, causal of निद् *nid*, 'to blame' and 'to be near;' लोक् *lok*, from लोकय *lok-aya*, causal and tenth conj. cl. of लोक् *lok*, 'to see,' *cf.* my 'Vollständige Grammatik,' § 844.

III. If the verb contains अर् *ar*, आर् *âr*, ईर् *îr*, or अल् *al*, being modifications of ऋ *ṛi*, ॠ *ṛî*, or ऌ *ḷi*, these letters either are left unchanged, or अर् *ar*, आर् *âr*, and ईर् *îr* are changed to ऋ *ṛi*, अल् *al* to ऌ *ḷi*, *e.g.* वर्तय *vart-aya*, causal of वृत् *vṛit*, 'to be occupied,' may form its aorist either from वर्त् *vart* or वृत् *vṛit*; मार्जय *mârjaya*, causal of मृज् *mṛij* (§ 60), either from मार्ज् *mârj* or मृज् *mṛij*; कीर्तय *kîrt-aya*, tenth conj. cl. of कॄत् *kṛît* (§ 61), either from कीर्त् *kîrt* or कृत् *kṛit*; कल्पय *kalpaya*, causal of कॢप् *kḷip*, 'to prosper,' either from कल्प् *kalp* or कॢप् *kḷip*.

IV. The verb modified according to the rules I. II. III. is the base of the reduplication. The reduplication follows the general rules in regard to consonants, medial अ *a*, इ *i*, उ *u*, if they are followed by a compound consonant, and आ *â*, ई *î*, ऊ *û*, ए *e*, ऐ *ai*, ओ *o*, and औ *au* (*cf.* II. and § 46), *e.g.* from तक्षय *takshaya*, अततक्षम् *a-ta-taksh-am*; वर्तय *vartaya*, अववर्तम् *a-va-vart-am* (*cf.* III.); भिक्षय *bhikshaya*, causal of भिक्ष् *bhiksh*, 'to beg,' अबिभिक्षम् *a-bi-bhiksh-am*; मालय *mâlaya*, अममालम् *a-ma-mâl-am*; टीकय *ṭîkaya*, अटिटीकम् *a-ṭi-ṭîk-am*; नेदय *nedaya*, अनिनेदम् *a-ni-ned-am*; लोकय *lokaya*, अलुलोकम् *a-lu-lok-am*.

But there are special rules for the reduplication of अ *a*, इ *i*, and उ *u*, when followed by a single consonant, and of ऋ *ṛi* and ऌ *ḷi*.

1. A medial अ *a*, followed by a single consonant, is represented in the reduplicated syllable by इ *i* when the verb begins with a compound consonant, by ई *î* when the verb begins with a single consonant, *e.g.* क्रमय *kramaya*, causal of क्रम् *kram*, 'to go,' अचिक्रमम् *a-chi-kram-am*; पाठय *pâṭhaya*, causal of पठ् *paṭh*, अपीपठम् *a-pî-paṭh-am*; दापय *dâpaya*, causal of दा *dâ*, अदीदपम् *a-dî-dap-am* (*cf.* II.).

Exceptions. (*a*) The exception 1 to the rule given in § 54, applies also here, *e.g.* च्यावय *chyâvaya*, causal of च्यु *chyu*, makes

अचुच्यवम् *a-chu-chyav-am*, or अचिच्यवम् *a-chi-chyav-am*; other examples see under 2.

(*b*) For some sporadic exceptions, *cf.* my 'Vollständige Grammatik,' §§ 844, 208, 209, 'Kurze Grammatik,' §§ 267-70, *e.g.* सभाजय *sabhâjaya*, 'to honour,' अससभाजम् *a-sa-sabhâi-am*.

2. Medial इ *i* and उ *u*, when followed by a single consonant, are represented in the reduplicated syllable by इ *i* and उ *u* when the verb begins with a compound consonant, by ई *î* and ऊ *û* when the verb begins with a single consonant, *e.g.* क्षेपय *kshepaya*, causal of क्षिप् *kship*, 'to throw,' अचिक्षिपम् *a-chi-kship-am*; क्रोधय *krodhaya*, causal of क्रुध् *krudh*, 'to be angry,' अचुक्रुधम् *a-chu-krudh-am*; but भेदय *bhedaya*, causal of भिद् *bhid*, 'to split,' अबीभिदम् *a-bî-bhid-am*; बोधय *bodhaya*, causal of बुध् *budh*, अबूबुधम् *a-bû-budh-am*.

This rule applies also to उ *u*, when it represents an अ *a*, which is followed by व् *v*, according to Exc. *a*, from 1, *e.g.* (*cf.* § 54, 1) from द्रावय *drâvaya*, अदुद्रवम् *a-du-drav-am* (or अदिद्रवम् *a-di-drav-am*); from नावय *nâvaya*, अनूनवम् *a-nû-nav-am*.

There are some exceptions to this rule, *e.g.* from कुमारय *kumâraya*, denominative of कुमार *kumâra*, 'a youth,' अचुकुमारम् *a-chu-ku-mâr-am*; *cf.* my 'Vollständige Grammatik,' §§ 844, 208, 209.

3. ऋ *ṛi* and ऌ *ḷi*, if preceded or followed by a compound consonant, are represented in the reduplicated syllable by इ *i*, else by ई *î*, *e.g.* स्पर्शय *sparçaya*, causal of स्पृश् *spṛiç*, 'to touch,' when forming its aorist from स्पृश् *spṛiç* (*cf.* III.), makes अपिस्पृशम् *a-pi-spṛiç-am*; तृम्पय *tṛimpaya*, causal of तृम्प् *tṛimp*, 'to satisfy,' अतितृम्पम् *a-ti-tṛimp-am*; but वर्तय *vartaya*, when forming its aorist from वृत् *vṛit* (III.), makes अवीवृतम् *a-vî-vṛit-am*; मार्जय *mârjaya*, causal of मृज् *mṛij*, अमीमृजम् *a-mî-mṛij-am*; कीर्तय *kîrtaya*, tenth conj. class of कॄत् *kṝit*, अचीकृतम् *a-chî-kṛit-am*; कल्पय *kalpaya*, अचीकॢपम् *a-chî-kḷip-am*.

V. Verbs beginning with a vowel or diphthong are reduplicated according to § 54, II., and augmented agreeably to § 74, 1, *e.g.* (*cf.* § 54, II.) from आशय *âçaya*, reduplicated base अशिश् *a-çiç*, with augment and termination आशिशम् *â-çiç-am*; अभ्रय *abhraya*, आबिभ्रम् *â-bibhr-am*; अर्चय *archaya*, आर्चिचम् *âr-chich-am*; इन्धय *indhaya*, ऐन्दिधम् *ain-didh-am*.

§ 137. Alphabetical List of the Most Notable Anomalies in the Three Simple Forms of the Aorist.

अघम्, etc., 2nd form, from घस्, 'to eat,' with syncope for अघसम्.

अख्यम्, etc., 2nd form, from ख्या, 'to speak,' by rejecting the final of the verb.

अग्लुचम्, etc., 2nd form, from ग्लुञ्च्, 'to go.'

अचकथम्, or regularly अचीकथम्, etc., 3rd form, from कथ्, 10th conj. cl., 'to tell.'

अचचह्म्, or regularly अचीचह्म्, etc., 3rd form, from चह्, 10th conj. cl., 'to deceive.'

अचचेष्टम्, or regularly अचिचेष्टम्, etc., 3rd form, from चेष्ट्, 'to struggle.'

अचुदम्, 2nd form (?), *cf.* अबुदम्.

अजगणम्, or regularly अजीगणम्, 3rd form, from गण्, 10th conj. cl., 'to number.'

अजिघ्रिपम्, 3rd form, from घ्रापय, causal of घ्रा, 'to smell.'

अजीहिपम्, Vedic 3rd form, from हापय, causal of हा, 'to leave.'

अजुहावम् or अजूहवम्, 3rd form, from ह्वायय, causal of ह्वे, 'to call' (formed as if the causal was *हावय from हु for ह्वे).

अजूहुरम्, Vedic 3rd form, from ह्वारय, causal of ह्वृ, 'to be crooked.'

अतत्वरम्, 3rd form, from त्वरय, causal of त्वर्, 'to hasten.'

अतस्तरम्, 3rd form, from स्तारय, causal of स्तॄ, 'to spread' (अतिस्तरम्, which would be the regular form, is derived from स्तृ, which is identical with स्तॄ).

अतिष्ठिपम्, 3rd form, from स्थापय, causal of स्था, 'to stand.'

अददरम्, 3rd form, from दारय, causal of दॄ, 'to burst.'

अदिद्युतम्, 3rd form, from द्योतय, causal of द्युत्, 'to shine.'

अध्वसम्, 2nd form, from **ध्वंस्**, 'to fall.'

अनेशम्, 3rd form, from **नश्**, 'to perish' (with syncope for ***अननशम्**, *cf.* § 114, II. 2).

अपप्तम्, 3rd form, from **पत्**, 'to fall' (with syncope for **अपपतम्**).

अपप्रथम्, 3rd form, from **प्रथ्**, 'to spread.'

अपस्पशम्, 3rd form, from **स्पश्**, 'to take.'

अपीप्यम्, 3rd form, from **पायय**, causal of **पा**, 'to drink' (§ 60); with syncope for **अपीपयम्** (which appears actually in the Veda).

अबुदम्, 2nd form, from **बुन्द्** (? or **चुन्द्**, **बुन्ध्**).

अबुधम्, see **अबुदम्**.

अभूवम्, 1st form, from **भू**, 'to become,' which is changed to **भूव्** in the first person singular and in the third person plural Par. (*cf.* § 118, p. 106); the other inflexions are regular, 2nd sing. **अभूस्**, etc.

अभ्रशम्, 2nd form, from **भ्रंश्**, 'to fall.'

अभ्रसम्, 2nd form, from **भ्रंस्**, 'to fall.'

अवोचम्, 3rd form (for ***अववचम्** = **अवउचम्** = **अवोचम्**), from **वच्**, 'to speak.'

अशिषम्, 2nd form, from **शास्**, 'to instruct' (*cf.* § 108 and the accentuation when without augment, **शिषम्**).

अशूशवम्, or regularly **अशिश्वयम्**, 3rd form, from **श्वायय**, causal of **श्वि**, 'to swell,' 'to go.'

अश्रमम्, 2nd form, from **श्रम्**, 'to be careless.'

अश्वम्, 2nd form, from **श्वि**, 'to swell.'

असस्मरम्, 3rd form, from **स्मारय**, causal of **स्मृ**, 'to recollect.'

असिष्वपम्, Vedic } 3rd form, from **स्वापय**, causal of **स्वप्**, 'to sleep.'
असूषुपम्, common }

अस्कदम्, 2nd form, from **स्कन्द्**, 'to ascend.'

अस्तभम्, 2nd form, from **स्तम्भ्**, 'to stop.'

अस्यदम्, 2nd form, from **स्यन्द्**, 'to ooze,' only in the Parasm.

अस्रमम्, 2nd form, from **स्रम्**, 'to be careless.'

अस्रशम्, 2nd form, from **स्रंश्**, } 'to fall.'
अस्रसम्, 2nd form, from **स्रंस्**, }

अस्रहम्, 2nd form, from **स्रंह्**, 'to trust.'

अह्वम्, 2nd form, from ह्वे, 'to call.'

आन्दधम्, 3rd form, from अन्धय, 10th conj. cl. of अन्ध्, 'to be blind.'

आस्थम्, 2nd (? or third, for primitive *á-sas-am*) form, from अस्, 'to throw.'

औननम्, 3rd form, from ऊनय, 10th conj. cl. of ऊन्, 'to diminish.'

और्णुनुवम्, 3rd form, from ऊर्णावय, causal of ऊर्णु, 'to cover.'

THE FOUR COMPOUND AORISTS.

§ 138. The imperfect and the two aorists of अस् *as*, by which the four last aorists are formed (§ 126), reject their initial आ *á* (*cf.* § 139 sqq.).

FOURTH AND FIFTH FORMS OF THE AORIST.

§ 139. In both forms the augmented verb is compounded with the inflexions of the imperfect of अस् *as* (§ 108, p. 84), which reject their initial आ *á*, viz., सम् *sam*, सीस् *sís*, etc.; the third person plural substitutes सुस् *sus* for सन् *san*. In the fourth aorist these forms are attached immediately to the base, in the fifth form इ *i* is inserted before them. When इ *i* is inserted the initial स् *s* of the terminations becomes ष् *sh*, after which त् *t* and थ् *th* are changed to ट् *ṭ* and ठ् *ṭh* (§ 17). In the second and third persons singular of the Parasmaipada the initial स् *s* is rejected after the inserted इ *i*, and the latter combines with the ई *í* of the termination to ई *í*, *इसीस् *isís* = ईस् *ís*, *इसीत् *isít* = ईत् *ít*. The terminations therefore are :—

Parasmaipada.

In the fourth form.			In the fifth form.		
सम् *sam*	स्व *sva*	स्म *sma*	इषम् *isham*	इष्व *ishva*	इष्म *ishma*
सीस् *sís*	स्तम् *stam*	स्त *sta*	ईस् *ís*	इष्टम् *ishṭam*	इष्ट *ishṭa*
सीत् *sít*	स्ताम् *stám*	सुस् *sus*	ईत् *ít*	इष्टाम् *ishṭám*	इषुस् *ishus*

Âtmanepada.

In the fourth form.

सि *si*	स्वहि *svahi*	स्महि *smahi*
स्थास् *sthâs*	साथाम् *sâthâm*	ध्वम् *dhvam* (ढ्वम् *ḍhvam*, see Obs. 3)
स्त *sta*	साताम् *sâtâm*	सत *sata*

In the fifth form.

इषि *ishi*	इष्वहि *ishvahi*	इष्महि *ishmahi*
इष्ठास् *ishṭhâs*	इषाथाम् *ishâthâm*	इध्वम् *idhvam* (इढ्वम् *iḍhvam*, see Obs. 3)
इष्ट *ishṭa*	इषाताम् *ishâtâm*	इषत *ishata*

Obs. 1. ग्रह् *grah*, 'to take,' inserts before all terminations, and the verbs ending in ॠ *ṛî* may insert in the Âtmanepada, ई *î* instead of इ *i*, *e.g.* 1st sing. Par. अग्रहीषम् *agrah-îsham*, Âtm. अग्रहीषि *agrah-îshi*, and from स्तॄ *stṛî*, 'to spread,' 1st sing. Âtm. अस्तरिषि *astar-ishi* or अस्तरीषि *astar-îshi*.

Obs. 2. In the fourth form the terminations beginning with स् *s*, स्त् *st*, or स्थ् *sth* undergo the changes prescribed in § 17, *e.g.* अकार् *akâr* + स्तम् *stam* becomes अकार्ष्टम् *akâr-shṭam*, from कृ *kṛi*, 'to make.'

Obs. 3. The termination of the second pers. plur. Âtman. of the fourth aorist ध्वम् *dhvam*, if preceded by ड् *ḍ*, or any vowel or diphthong, except अ *a* or आ *â*, is changed to ढ्वम् *ḍhvam*, *e.g.* अकृ *akṛi* + ध्वम् *dhvam* makes अकृढ्वम् *akṛi-ḍhvam*. In the fifth aorist the termination इध्वम् *idhvam* or, according to Obs. 1, ईध्वम् *îdhvam*, if preceded by य् *y*, व् *v*, र् *r*, ल् *l*, or ह् *h* (*cf.* § 116, II.), optionally becomes इढ्वम् *iḍhvam*, or ईढ्वम् *îḍhvam*, *e.g.* अलविध्वम् *alavidhvam*, or अलविढ्वम् *alaviḍhvam*, from लू *lû*, 'to cut.'

§ 140. Verbs ending in इ *i*, ई *î*, उ *u*, and ऋ *ṛi* generally take the fourth aorist; also some with final consonants, enumerated in my 'Kurze Grammatik,' § 283. Those ending in आ *â*, ए *e*, ऐ *ai*, and ओ *o* take it in the Âtmanepada, optionally (viz., the fourth or the fifth form) also those which end in ॠ *ṛî*.

All the other verbs, especially those ending in ऊ *ú*, ॠ *ṛí*, or consonants, generally use the fifth form.

But there are many exceptions on either side; thus the verbs with final ऋ *ṛi*, which is preceded by a compound consonant, admit in the Âtmanepada of the fifth form as well as of the fourth.

§ 141. In the Parasmaipada of the fourth form a medial अ *a* of the base is lengthened, इ *i* and ई *í* are changed to ऐ *ai*, उ *u* to औ *au*, ऋ *ṛi* to आर् *âr*,[1] *e.g.* पच् *pach*, 'to cook,' अपाक्षम् *a-pâk-sham* (*cf.* § 145 and § 17), क्षिप् *kship* अक्षैप्सम् *a-kshaip-sam*, नी *ní* अनैषम् *a-nai-sham* (§ 17), तुद् *tud* अतौत्सम् *a-taut-sam*, कृ *kṛi* अकार्षम् *a-kâr-sham* (§ 17).

In the Âtmanepada of the fourth form final इ *i* and ई *í* are changed to ए *e*, उ *u* to ओ *o*, ॠ *ṛí* to ईर् *ír*, and, when preceded by labials or व् *v*, to ऊर् *úr*; final ए *e*, ऐ *ai*, and ओ *o* to आ *â*, *e.g.* नी *ní* अनेषि *a-ne-shi* (§ 17), स्तॄ *stṛí* अस्तीर्षि *a-stír-shi*, त्रै *trai*, 'to protect,' अत्रासि *a-trâ-si*.

In the Parasmaipada of the fifth form final उ *u* and ऊ *ú* of the base become आव् *âv*, final ॠ *ṛí* becomes आर् *âr*, *e.g.* क्षु *kshu*, 'to sneeze' (an exception from § 140), अक्षाविषम् *a-kshâv-isham*, लू *lú*, 'to cut,' अलाविषम् *a-lâv-isham*, कॄ *kṛí*, 'to throw,' अकारिषम् *a-kâr-isham*. An अ *a* followed by a single radical consonant must be lengthened in some instances; sometimes this change is optional, whilst in a third class of verbs it must remain unchanged, *e.g.* ज्वल् *jval*, 'to blaze,' अज्वालिषम् *a-jvâl-isham*, कण् *kaṇ*, 'to sound,' अकाणिषम् *a-kâṇ-isham*, or अकणिषम् *a-kaṇ-isham*, and स्यम् *syam*, 'to sound,' अस्यमिषम् *a-syam-isham*.

In the Âtmanepada of the fifth form a final इ *i* and ई *í* become अय् *ay*, final उ *u* and ऊ *ú* become अव् *av*, and final ऋ *ṛi* and ॠ *ṛí* become अर् *ar*, *e.g.* डी *ḍí*, 'to fly,' अडयिषि *a-ḍay-ishi*; लू *lú*, अलविषि *a-lav-ishi*; कॄ *kṛí*, अकरिषि *a-kar-ishi*.

[1] *Vṛiddhi*, p. 38, n.

In the Parasmaipada and Âtmanepada of the fifth form इ *i*, उ *u*, and ऋ *ṛi*, followed by a single radical consonant, are changed, इ *i* to ए *e*, उ *u* to ओ *o*, and ऋ *ṛi* to अर् *ar* (Guṇa), *e.g.* बुध् *budh*, 'to understand,' अबोधिषम् *a-bodh-isham*, अबोधिषि *a-bodh-ishi*. A final अ *a* is rejected, *e.g.* लोलूय *loḷûya*, second frequentative of लू *lû*, अलोलूयिषि *a-lolûy-ishi*.

The rules laid down in § 56, I. 2, 3, apply also here, *e.g.* from बेभिद्य *bebhidya* अबेभिद्दिषि *a-bebhid-ishi*.

Exc. There are many exceptions from the rules given in this paragraph. Particularly in a class of verbs, enumerated in my 'Kurze Gramm.' (§ 117, Exc. 1, *b*, *cf.* § 279), which belong to the sixth conjug. class and contain a medial or final *u*, this vowel is only changed if final and long; then it becomes *uv*, *e.g.* कुच् *kuch*, 'to contract,' forms अकुचिषम् *a-kuch-isham*, गु *gu*, 'to void excrement,' अगुषम् *a-gu-sham*, but गू *gû*, अगुविषम् *a-guv-isham*. Others will be given in the list § 148. The inserted इ *i* of the desideratives and the radical vowel of the derivative verbs ending originally in य *ya* which must or may be rejected (§ 56, I. 2, 3), are left unchanged, *e.g.* बुबोधिष *bubodhisha*, अबुबोधिषिषम् *a-bubodhish-isham*, बेभिद्य *bebhidya*, second frequentative of भिद् *bhid*, अबेभिद्दिषि *a-bebhid-ishi*.

§ 142. PARADIGM OF THE FOURTH FORM: नी *nî*, 'to lead.'

Parasmaipada.			Âtmanepada.		
अनैषम् *ánaisham*	अनैष्व *ánaishva*	अनैष्म *ánaishma*	अनेषि *áneshi*	अनेष्वहि *áneshvahi*	अनेष्महि *áneshmahi*
अनैषीस् *ánaishîs*	अनैष्टम् *ánaishṭam*	अनैष्ट *ánaishṭa*	अनेष्ठास् *áneshṭhâs*	अनेषाथाम् *áneshâthâm*	अनेढ्वम् *áneḍhvam*
अनैषीत् *ánaishît*	अनैष्टाम् *ánaishṭâm*	अनैषुस् *ánaishus*	अनेष्ट *áneshṭa*	अनेषाताम् *áneshâtâm*	अनेषत *áneshata*

From जि *ji*, 'to overpower,' अजैषम् *ájaisham*, अजेषि *ájeshi*.

§ 143. PARADIGMS OF THE FIFTH FORM: लू *lû*, 'to cut,' बुध् *budh*, 'to understand.'

Parasmaipada.			Âtmanepada.		
अलाविषम् *álâvisham*	अलाविष्व *álâvishva*	अलाविष्म *álâvishma*	अलविषि *álavishi*	अलविष्वहि *álavishvahi*	अलविष्महि *álavishmahi*
अलावीस् *álâvîs*	अलाविष्टम् *álâvishṭam*	अलाविष्ट *álâvishṭa*	अलविष्ठास् *álavishṭhâs*	अलविषाथाम् *álavishâthâm*	अलविध्वम् *álavidhvam* or अलविढ्वम् *álaviḍhvam*
अलावीत् *álâvît*	अलाविष्टाम् *álâvishṭâm*	अलाविषुस् *álâvishus*	अलविष्ट *álavishṭa*	अलविषाताम् *álavishâtâm*	अलविषत *álavishata*
अबोधिषम् *ábodhisham*	अबोधिष्व *ábodhishva*	अबोधिष्म *ábodhishma*	अबोधिषि *ábodhishi*	अबोधिष्वहि *ábodhishvahi*	अबोधिष्महि *ábodhishmahi*
अबोधीस् *ábodhîs*	अबोधिष्टम् *ábodhishṭam*	अबोधिष्ट *ábodhishṭa*	अबोधिष्ठास् *ábodhishṭhâs*	अबोधिषाथाम् *ábodhishâthâm*	अबोधिध्वम् *ábodhidhvam*
अबोधीत् *ábodhît*	अबोधिष्टाम् *ábodhishṭâm*	अबोधिषुस् *ábodhishus*	अबोधिष्ट *ábodhishṭa*	अबोधिषाताम् *ábodhishâtâm*	अबोधिषत *ábodhishata*

From वद् *vad*, 'to speak,' अवादिषम् *avâdisham*, अवदिषि *avadishi*, etc.

§ 144. The terminations of the fourth form beginning with स्त *st* or स्थ *sth*, when preceded by a short vowel or a consonant, except a nasal or र् *r*, reject their स *s*, *e.g.* अकृ + स्थास् *akṛi* + *sthâs*, 2nd sing. Âtm. of कृ *kṛi*, becomes अकृथास् *akṛithâs*, अक्षैप + स्तम् *akshaip* + *stam*, 3rd dual Parasm. of क्षिप् *kship*, अक्षैप्तम् *akshaiptam*.

§ 145. The few verbs ending in consonants, which use the fourth form (enumerated in my 'Kurze Grammatik,' § 283), in attaching the terminations follow the rules laid down in §§ 96-99 and 102, *e.g.* according to § 96, 1 and 3, साध् *sâdh* makes in the first person singular Parasm. असात्सम् *asât-sam*, according to §§ 144 and 96, 3 in the third pers. dual असाद्धाम् *asâd-dhâm*; according to § 96, 4, बुध् *budh*, in the first person singular Âtm. अभुत्सि *abhut-si*, in the second pers. plural अभुद्ध्वम् *abhud-dhvam*; according to § 97, 1, पच् *pach*, in the first pers. singular Parasm. अपाक्षम् *apâk-sham*; दह् *dah*, अधाक्षम् *adhâk-sham*; according to § 97, 2, मन् *man*, in the first pers. singular Âtm. अमंसि *amaṁ-si*; according to

§ 98, 1, त्यज् *tyaj*, in the second pers. dual Parasm. (*cf.* § 144) अत्याक्तम् *atyâk-tam*; according to § 98, 2, प्रछ् *prachh*, अप्राष्टम् *aprâsh-ṭam*; according to § 98, 3, माह् *mâh*, 'to measure,' in the second pers. dual अमाढम् *amâḍham* (§ 144), but, according to the exception, दह् *dah*, अदाग्धम् *adâgdham*; according to § 99, 1, पच् *pach*, in the second pers. plural Âtm. अपग्ध्वम् *apag-dhvam*; according to § 99, 2, प्रछ् *prachh*, अप्रड्ढ्वम् *aprad-ḍhvam*; according to § 99, 3 माह् *mâh*, अमाढ्वम् *amâḍhvam*; दह् *dah*, अधग्ध्वम *adhag-dhvam;* according to § 102, नह् *nah*, in the first person singular Parasm. अनात्सम् *anât-sam*, in the second person dual अनाद्धम् *anâd-dham*, in the second pers. sing. Âtm. अनद्धास् *anad-dhâs;* वह् *vah*, in the second pers. dual Par. अवोढम् *avoḍham*, in the singular Âtm. अवोढास् *avoḍhâs*, but in the first pers. sing. Par. अवाक्षम् *avâk-sham*, Âtm. अवक्षि *avak-shi*.—A final स् *s* before स् *s* and त् *t* is changed to त् *t*, before ध् *dh* to द् *d*, *e.g.* वस् *vas*, 'to dwell,' 1st sing. Par. अवात्सम् *avât-sam*, 2nd dual अवात्तम् *avât-tam* (*cf.* § 144), 2nd plur. Âtm. अवद्ध्वम् *avad-dhvam*.

SIXTH FORM OF THE AORIST.

§ 146. In the sixth form the augmented base is compounded with the third aorist of अस् *as*, which, according to § 136, V., and § 17, would be आसिषम् *âsisham*. The initial आ *â* is rejected in accordance with § 138, and in the second and third persons singular Parasmaipada, as well as in the other persons, it is inflected after the analogy of the imperfect of अस् *as* (*cf.* my 'Kurze Grammatik,' §§ 287 and 270, Obs.).

This form is restricted to the Parasmaipada and to verbs ending in आ *â*, ए *e*, ऐ *ai*, ओ *o*, and some others.

Final diphthongs of the base are changed to आ *â*, and a final म् *m* becomes Anusvâra ं, *e.g.* दै *dai*, 'to purify,' अदासिषम् *adâsisham*; यम् *yam*, 'to restrain,' अयंसिषम् *ayaṁ-sisham*.

The terminations are:—

सिषम् *sisham*	सिष्व *sishva*	सिष्म *sishma*
सीस् *sîs*	सिष्टम् *sishṭam*	सिष्ट *sishṭa*
सीत् *sît*	सिष्टाम् *sishṭâm*	सिषुस् *sishus*

PARADIGM: या *yá*, 'to go.'

अयासिषम् *áyâsisham*	अयासिष्व *áyâsishva*	अयासिष्म *áyâsishma*
अयासीस् *áyâsîs*	अयासिष्टम् *áyâsishṭam*	अयासिष्ट *áyâsishṭa*
अयासीत् *áyâsît*	अयासिष्टाम् *áyâsishṭâm*	अयासिषुस् *áyâsishus*

From ज्ञा *jñá*, 'to know,' अज्ञासिषम् *ajñâsisham*, etc.

SEVENTH FORM OF THE AORIST.

§ 147. The augmented verb is compounded with the second aorist of the verb अस् *as*, *e.g.* आसम् *âsam*, आसस् *âsas*, etc. (*cf.* § 132), the initial आ *â* of which is rejected in accordance with § 138. The conjugation of (आ)सम् (*â*)*sam* has some irregularities, for which *cf.* my 'Kurze Grammatik,' § 289.

This form is only used by some verbs ending in श् *ç*, ष् *sh*, and ह् *h*, which are changed before the initial स् *s* to क् *k* (*cf.* § 97, 1), after which the स् *s* in its turn becomes ष् *sh* (§ 17), *e.g.* दिश् *diç*, 'to show,' अदिक्षम् *adik-sham*.

If a verb ending in ह् *h* begins with ग् *g*, द् *d*, or ब् *b*, these letters are changed to the corresponding aspirate (*cf.* § 97, 1), *e.g.* गुह् *guh*, अघुक्षम् *aghuk-sham*.

The terminations are:—

Parasmaipada.			Âtmanepada.		
सम् *sam*	साव *sâva*	साम *sâma*	सि *si*	सावहि *sâvahi*	सामहि *sâmahi*
सस् *sas*	सतम् *satam*	सत *sata*	सथास् *sathâs*	साथाम् *sâthâm*	सध्वम् *sadhvam*
सत् *sat*	सताम् *satâm*	सन् *san*	सत *sata*	साताम् *sâtâm*	सन्त *santa*

PARADIGM: दिश् *diç*, 'to show.'

अदिक्षम् *ádiksham*	अदिक्षाव *ádikshâva*	अदिक्षाम *ádikshâma*	अदिक्षि *ádikshi*	अदिक्षावहि *ádikshâvahi*	अदिक्षामहि *ádikshâmahi*
अदिक्षस् *ádikshas*	अदिक्षतम् *ádikshatam*	अदिक्षत *ádikshata*	अदिक्षथास् *ádikshathâs*	अदिक्षाथाम् *ádikshâthâm*	अदिक्षध्वम् *ádikshadhvam*
अदिक्षत् *ádikshat*	अदिक्षताम् *ádikshatâm*	अदिक्षन् *ádikshan*	अदिक्षत *ádikshata*	अदिक्षाताम् *ádikshâtâm*	अदिक्षन्त *ádikshanta.*

From दुह् *duh*, 'to milk,' अधुक्षम् *adhuksham*, अधुक्षि *adhukshi*, etc.

§ 148. ALPHABETICAL LIST OF SOME NOTABLE ANOMALIES IN THE FOUR COMPOUND FORMS OF THE AORIST.

अकुविषि, 1st sing. Âtm., etc., 5th form, from कू, 'to cry' (against § 141).

अकुषि, 1st sing. Âtm., 4th form, from कु, 'to cry' (against § 141).

अक्राक्षम्, 1st sing. Par., etc., अक्राष्टम्, 2nd dual, etc. (also regularly अकार्क्षम्, अकार्ष्टम्), 4th form, from कृष्, 'to draw,' which optionally changes आर् to रा.

अगसि, 1st sing. Âtm., अगथास्, 2nd sing., etc., 4th form, from गम्, 'to go,' (also regularly अगंसि, अगंस्थास्, etc.).

(अधि) अगीषि, 1st sing. Âtm., etc., 4th form, from गा, 'to go,' but only when the verb is combined with the preposition अधि, and signifies 'to read.'

अगुविषम्, 1st sing. Par., 5th form, from गू }
अगुषम्, 1st sing. Par., 4th form, from गु } 'to void excrement.'

अगुह्वहि, *cf.* the following.

अगूहिषम्, etc., 5th form, from गुह्, 'to cover.' This verb also takes the seventh form अघुक्षम्, etc., and in the second and third pers. sing., the first pers. dual, and the second pers. plural Âtmanepada also the first form, अगूढास्, अगूढ, अगुह्वहि, अघूढ्वम्, or अघुक्षथास्, अघुक्षत, etc.

अग्रहीषम्, etc., 5th form, from ग्रह्, 'to take' (*cf.* § 139, Obs. 1).

अचासिषम्, etc., 6th form, from चाय्, 'to worship.'

अजागरिषम्, 5th form, from जागृ, 'to wake.'

अदरिद्रिषम्, 5th form, from दरिद्रा, 'to be in distress.'

अदासि, 4th form Âtm., from दी, 'to go to ruin.'

अदिषि, 1st sing. Âtm., etc., 4th form, from दा, 'to give,' दे 'to protect,' and दो, 'to cut,' which change their final to इ in the Âtmanepada.

अदिह्वहि, 1st dual Âtm., from दिह्, 'to smear.' This verb takes generally the 7th form, अधिक्षम्, etc., but, like गुह् (*cf.* अगूहिषम्), in the second and third persons sing., the first pers. dual, and the second pers. plural of the Âtmanepada also the first form, अदिग्धास्, अदिग्ध, अदिह्वहि, अधिग्ध्वम् or अधिक्षथास्, etc.

अदीधिषि, 1st sing. Âtm., 5th form, from दीधी, 'to shine.'

अदुह्वहि, 1st dual Âtm., from दुह्, to milk.' This verb, like दिह्, takes generally the 7th form, अधुक्षम्, etc., and in the 2nd and 3rd sing., 1st dual, and 2nd plur. Âtm. also the first form, अदुग्धास् or अधुक्षथास्, etc.

अद्राक्षम्, 1st sing. Par., 4th form, from दृश्, 'to see,' which makes रा instead of आर्.

अधिषि, 1st sing. Âtm., etc., 4th form, from धा, 'to hold,' and धे 'to drink,' which change their finals to इ in the Âtmanepada.

अधुविषम्, etc., and regularly अधाविषम्, etc., 5th form, from धू, 'to shake.'

अध्रुषम्, and regularly अध्रौषम्, 4th form, from ध्रु, 'to stand firm.'

अनङ्क्षि, etc., अनंष्ठास्, etc., 4th form Âtm., from नश्, 'to perish,' which inserts a nasal before its last radical.

अनुविषम् and regularly अनाविषम्, 5th form, from नू and नु, 'to praise.'

अपादि, 3rd sing. Âtm. (properly 3rd sing. of the passive voice, § 166), from पद्, 'to go;' the 1st and 2nd sing., 1st dual, etc., are regular, अपत्सि, 4th form, etc.

अप्यासिषम्, 6th form Parasm., अप्यासि, 4th form Âtm., from प्याय्, 'to be exuberant.'

अबोधि, like अपादि, 3rd sing. Âtm. (properly of the passive voice), from बुध्, I. 4, 'to awake;' 1st and 2nd sing., 1st dual, etc., are regular, अभुत्सि, etc.

अभार्चम्, etc., अभार्ष्टम्, etc., or regularly अभ्राचम्, अभ्राष्टम्; अभर्चि, or regularly अभ्रचि, etc., 4th form, from भ्रज्ज्, 'to fry,' which may optionally change र and रा to अर् and आर्.

अमाङ्क्ष्म्, etc., अमाङ्क्ष्म्, etc., 4th form, from मज्ज्, 'to dive,' which rejects the second ज् and inserts a nasal after the radical vowel.

अमार्जिषम्, 5th form, from मृज्, 'to wipe.'

अमासिषम्, 6th form Parasm., and अमासि, 4th form Âtm., from मि, 'to throw,' or मी, 'to hurt.'

अम्राचम्, etc., अम्राष्टम्, or regularly अमार्चम्, अमार्ष्टम्, 4th form from मृश्, 'to touch,' which may change आर् to रा.

अलासिषम् 6th form Par., and अलासि, 4th form Âtm., or regularly अलैषम्, अलेषि, 4th form, from ली, 'to adhere' (Sch. Pâṇini, VI., 1, 51; *cf.* Westergaard, Radices).

अलिक्षहि, from लिह्, 'to lick.' This verb, like दुह्, takes the 7th form, अलिक्षम्, etc., and in 2nd and 3rd sing., 1st dual, and 2nd plur. Âtm. also the first form, *e.g.* अलीढास् or अलिक्षथास्, etc.

अवरीषि or अवरिषि, etc., 5th form Âtm., from वृ, 'to select.'

अविजिषम्, 5th form, from विज्, 'to tremble.'

अवेविषि, 5th form Âtm., from वेवी, 'to go.'

अश्वयिषम्, 5th form, from श्वि, 'to swell.'

अस्थिषि, 4th form Âtm., from स्था, 'to stand,' which changes its final to इ in the Âtmanepada.

अस्प्राचम्, etc., or regularly अस्पार्चम्, etc., 4th form, from स्पृश्, 'to touch,' which may change आर् to रा.

अस्फासिषम्, 6th form Par., from स्फाय्, 'to swell.'

अस्राचम्, 4th form, from सृज्, 'to abandon,' which changes आर् to रा.

अहसि, अहथास्, etc., 4th form Âtm., from हन्, 'to kill,' which rejects its final.

और्णुनुविषम्, or regularly और्णुनाविषम्, 5th form Parasmaipada, और्णुनुविषि, or regularly और्णुनविषि, 5th form Âtm., from ऊर्णु 'to cover.'

17

THE FOUR LAST VERBAL FORMS.

§ 149. The seventh verbal form is the *first* or *periphrastic future.*

The third persons singular, dual, and plural are expressed by the nominatives singular, dual, and plural of the masculine gender of a noun ending in तृ *tṛi* and implying agency (Nomen agentis). The nominative of the singular ends in ता *tâ*, the nominative of the dual in तारौ *târau*, and the nominative of the plural in तारस् *târas* (*cf.* § 233).

In the first and second persons singular, dual, and plural ता *tâ* is compounded with the corresponding persons of the present of the verb अस् *as*, 'to be' (*cf.* 108, p. 83).

The terminations therefore are:—

Parasmaipada.			Âtmanepada.		
ता॑स्मि	ता॑स्वस्	ता॑स्मस्	ता॑हे	ता॑स्वहे	ता॑स्महे
tấsmi	*tấsvas*	*tấsmas*	*tấhe*	*tấsvahe*	*tấsmahe*
ता॑सि	ता॑स्थस्.	ता॑स्थ	ता॑से	ता॑साथे	ता॑ध्वे
tấsi	*tấsthas*	*tấstha*	*tấse*	*tấsâthe*	*tấdhve*
ता	ता॑रौ	ता॑रस्	ता	ता॑रौ	ता॑रस्
tấ	*tấrau*	*tấras*	*tấ*	*tấrau*	*tấras*

§ 150. The eighth verbal form is the *second future*, formed by compounding the verb with the present of the verb अस् *as*, 'to be,' which follows the analogy of the fourth conjugational class (§ 71, 2 and § 80, 2), but with rejection of its initial अ *a* (*cf.* § 108, p. 83). The terminations of this future therefore are:—

Parasmaipada.			Âtmanepada.		
स्या॑मि	स्या॑वस्	स्या॑मस्	स्ये॑	स्या॑वहे	स्या॑महे
syấmi	*syấvas*	*syấmas*	*syé*	*syấvahe*	*syấmahe*
स्य॑सि	स्य॑थस्	स्य॑थ	स्य॑से	स्ये॑थे	स्य॑ध्वे
syási	*syáthas*	*syátha*	*syáse*	*syéthe*	*syádhve*
स्य॑ति	स्य॑तस्	स्य॑न्ति	स्य॑ते	स्ये॑ते	स्य॑न्ते
syáti	*syátas*	*syánti*	*syáte*	*syéte*	*syánte*

§ 151. The ninth verbal form is the *conditional*, properly the imperfect of the future, and formed from the second future quite like the imperfect in the fourth conjugational class from its present. It takes the augment (§ 74, 1) and substitutes the terminations of the imperfect (§ 74, 2) for those of the present, *e.g.* second future of पच् *pach*, in 1st sing. Par. पक्ष्यामि *pak-shyámi*, in 2nd पक्ष्यसि *pak-shyási*, etc., conditional 1st sing. Par. अपक्ष्यम् *á-pak-shyam*, 2nd अपक्ष्यस् *á-pak-shyas*, etc. (*cf.* the paradigms in § 159, with § 80, 2).

§ 152. The tenth and last verbal form is the *precative*, which affixes to the crude form the following terminations:—

Parasmaipada.

यासम् *yásam*	यास्व *yásva*	यास्म *yásma*
यास् *yás*	यास्तम् *yástam*	यास्त *yásta*
यात् *yát*	यास्ताम् *yástâm*	यासुस् *yásus*

Âtmanepada.

सीय *síyá*	सीवहि *síváhi*	सीमहि *símáhi*
सीष्ठास् *síshṭhás*	सीयास्थाम् *síyásthâm*	सीध्वम् *sídhvám* (सीढ्वम् *síḍhvám*, *cf.* § 153)
सीष्ट *síshṭá*	सीयास्ताम् *síyástâm*	सीरन् *sírán*

§ 153. The initial स् *s* of the terminations of the second future and of the Âtmanepada of the precative undergoes the changes prescribed in § 17.

The termination of the second person plural Âtmanepada of the precative, सीध्वम् *sídhvam*, follows the analogy of the corresponding termination of the fourth and fifth aorist (§ 139, Obs. 3). After any vowel or diphthong, except आ *á* and इ *i*, it must, and after यि *yi*, रि *ri*, लि *li*, वि *vi*, हि *hi* it may be changed to सीढ्वम् *síḍhvam*, *e.g.* 4th aorist अनेढ्वम् *aneḍhvam*, precative नेषीढ्वम् *neshíḍhvam*, 5th aorist अलविध्वम् *alavidhvam*, or अलविढ्वम् *ala-*

viḍhvam, precative लविषीध्वम् *lavishídhvam*, or लविषीढ्वम् *lavishíḍhvam*.

§ 154. Primitive verbs ending in आ *á*, इ *i*, ई *í*, उ *u*, ऋ *ṛi*, ए *e*, ऐ *ai*, ओ *o* attach the terminations of the first and second future and of the Âtmanepada of the precative immediately to the base. Primitive verbs ending in ऊ *ú*, ॠ *ṛí*, or a consonant, and all derivative verbs (§§ 39-62) insert इ *i*, those with the final ॠ *ṛí* may interpose इ *i* or ई *í*, except in the precative, where the इ *i* is absolute, *e.g.* from दा *dá*, 'to give,' 1st sing. of the first future Par. दातास्मि *dá-tásmi*; from जि *ji*, 'to conquer,' जेतास्मि *je-tásmi* (§ 156); from म्लै *mlai*, म्लातास्मि *mlá-tásmi* (§ 155); but from भू *bhú*, 'to become,' भवितास्मि *bhav-i-tásmi* (§ 156); from जॄ *jṛí*, 'to grow old,' जरितास्मि *jar-i-tásmi*, or जरीतास्मि *jar-í-tásmi* (§ 156); from पत् *pat*, 'to fall,' पतितास्मि *pat-i-tásmi*; likewise in the second future दास्यामि *dá-syámi*, जेष्यामि *je-shyámi*, म्लास्यामि *mlá-syámi*, भविष्यामि *bhav-i-shyámi*, जरिष्यामि *jar-i-shyámi*, or जरीष्यामि *jar-í-shyámi*, पतिष्यामि *pat-i-shyámi*.

Exc. 1. Verbs ending in ऋ *ṛi* insert इ *i* before the terminations of the second future, *e.g.* कृ *kṛi*, करिष्यामि *kar-i-shyámi*.

Exc. 2. After the final ऋ *ṛi* which is preceded by a compound consonant, इ *i* may optionally be prefixed to the terminations of the Âtmanepada of the precative, *e.g.* ध्वृ *dhvṛi*, 'to bend,' ध्वरिषीय *dhvar-i-shíyá*, or ध्वृषीय *dhvṛi-shíyá*. Verbs ending in ॠ *ṛí* may optionally omit the इ *i* and change ॠ *ṛí* to ईर् *ír*, or ऊर् *úr*, if it is preceded by labials or व् *v*, *e.g.* स्तॄ *stṛí*, either स्तरिषीय *star-i-shíyá* or स्तीर्षीय *stír-shíyá*; पॄ *pṛí*, either परिषीय *par-i-shíyá* or पूर्षीय *púr-shíyá*.

For other exceptions, especially the verbs with final consonants which do not take इ *i*, see my 'Kurze Grammatik,' § 293, and my 'Vollständige Grammatik,' §§ 155, 156.

§ 155. Final ए *e*, ऐ *ai*, and ओ *o* are changed to आ *á*, *e.g.* धे *dhe*, 'to drink,' 1st sing. of the first future Par. धातास्मि *dhá-tásmi*, म्लै *mlai*, म्लातास्मि *mlá-tásmi*, शो *ço*, 'to sharpen,' शातास्मि *çá-tásmi*.

The derivative verbs ending in अ *a* reject their final before इ *i*, and the rules given in § 56, 3 apply also to these forms, *e.g.* बोधय *bodhaya*, causal of बुध् *budh*, in the first future बोधयितास्मि *bodhay-i-tásmi*, बेभिद्य *bebhidya*, frequentative of भिद् *bhid*, 1st sing. of the first future Âtm. बेभिदिताहे *bebhid-i-táhe*, but from the denominative नमस्य *namasya* either नमस्यितास्मि *namasy-i-tásmi*, or नमसितास्मि *namas-i-tásmi*.

§ 156. In the first and second future and the Âtmanepada of the precative final इ *i* and ई *í* are changed to ए *e*, or, if इ *i* is inserted, to अय् *ay*, final उ *u* to ओ *o*, or, if इ *i* is inserted, to अव् *av*, final ऊ *ú* to अव् *av*, final ऋ *ṛi* and ॠ *ṛí* to अर् *ar* (guṇa), *e.g.* जि *ji*, जेतास्मि *je-tásmi*, जेष्यामि *je-shyámi*, जेषीय *je-shíyá*, but from श्वि *çvi*, 'to swell,' which takes इ *i*, श्वयितास्मि *çvay-i-tásmi*; स्तु *stu*, 'to praise,' स्तोतास्मि *sto-tásmi*, etc.; but क्षु *kshu*, क्षवितास्मि *kshav-i-tásmi*; भू *bhú*, भवितास्मि *bhav-i-tásmi*; कृ *kṛi*, कर्तास्मि *kar-tásmi*, करिष्यामि *kar-i-shyámi* (*cf.* § 154, Exc. 1 and § 156, Exc. 2); कॄ *kṛí*, करितास्मि *kar-i-tásmi*, or करीतास्मि *kar-í-tásmi* (*cf.* § 154 and 156, Exc. 2).

Penultimate इ *i*, उ *u*, and ऋ *ṛi*, followed by a single consonant, become ए *e*, ओ *o*, and अर् *ar* (guṇa); ॠ *ṛí* is changed to ईर् *ír*, *e.g.* क्ष्विद् *kshvid*, 'to sound inarticulately,' क्ष्वेदितास्मि *kshved-i-tásmi*, क्ष्वेदिष्यामि *kshved-i-shyámi*, क्ष्वेदिषीय *kshved-i-shíyá*; बुध् *budh*, बोधितास्मि *bodh-i-tásmi*; पृच् *pṛich*, 'to mix,' पर्चितास्मि *parch-i-tásmi*; स्तॄह् *stṛíh*, 'to hurt,' स्तीर्हितास्मि *stírh-i-tásmi*.

Exc. 1. The exception to § 141 holds good also here, *e.g.*

कुचितास्मि *kuch-i-tā́smi*, गुतास्मि *gu-tā́smi*, गुवितास्मि *guv-i-tā́smi*, बुबोधिषितास्मि *bubodhish-i-tā́smi*, बेभिदिताहे *bebhid-i-tā́he*.

Exc. 2. In the Âtmanepada of the precative, when इ *i* is not inserted, final ऋ *ṛi* and penultimate इ *i*, उ *u*, ऋ *ṛi* are left unchanged, and ॠ *ṛí*, when preceded by labials or व् *v*, is changed to ऊर् *úr*, or, if preceded by other consonants to ईर् *ír*, *e.g.* कृ *kṛi*, कृषीय *kṛi-shīyá*; क्षिप् *kship*, 'to throw,' क्षिप्सीय *kship-sīyá*; पॄ *pṛí*, 'to fill,' पूर्षीय *púr-shīyá* (or परिषीय *par-i-shīyá*); कॄ *kṛí*, कीर्षीय *kír-shīyá* (or करिषीय *kar-i-shīyá*).

§ 157. The small number of verbs with final consonants which affix the terminations immediately (§ 154, Exc. 2), follow:

1. Before the initial त् *t* of the first future the rules given in § 95, 3, *e.g.* गम् *gam*, गन्तास्मि *gan-tā́smi*; § 96, 3 *e.g.* भिद् *bhid*, भेत्तास्मि *bhet-tā́smi*; क्रुध् *krud*, क्रोद्धास्मि *krod-dhā́smi*; § 98, 1, युज् *yuj*, योक्तास्मि *yok-tā́smi*; § 98, 2, प्रछ् *prachh*, प्रष्टास्मि *prash-ṭā́smi*; § 98, 3, लिह् *lih*, लेढास्मि *leḍhā́smi*; but दुह् *duh*, दोग्धास्मि *dog-dhā́smi*; § 102, द्रुह् *druh*, द्रोढास्मि *droḍhā́smi*, or द्रोग्धास्मि *drog-dhā́smi* (also with inserted इ *i*, द्रोहितास्मि *droh-i-tā́smi*); नह् *nah*, नद्धास्मि *nad-dhā́smi*; भ्रज्ज् *bhrajj*, भ्रष्टास्मि *bhrash-ṭā́smi*; वह् *vah*, वोढास्मि *voḍhā́smi*.

2. Before the initial स् *s* of the second future and the Âtmanepada of the precative the rules given in § 96, 3, *e.g.* भिद् *bhid*, भेत्स्यामि *bhet-syā́mi*, भित्सीय *bhit-sīyá*; § 96, 4, बुध् *budh*, I. 4, Âtm. भोत्स्ये *bhot-syé*, भुत्सीय *bhut-sīyá*; § 97, 1, युज् *yuj*, योक्ष्यामि *yok-shyā́mi*, युक्षीय *yuk-shīyá*; लिह् *lih*, लेक्ष्यामि *lek-shyā́mi*, लिक्षीय *lik-shīyá*; दुह् *duh*, धोक्ष्यामि *dhok-shyā́mi* धुक्षीय *dhuk-shīyá*; § 97, 2, मन् *man*, I., 4, Âtm. मंस्ये *mam̃-syé*, मंसीय *mam̃-sīyá*.—A final स् *s* becomes त् *t*, *e.g.* वस् *vas*, 'to dwell,' वत्स्यामि *vat-syā́mi*, वत्सीय *vat-sīyá*.

§ 158. In the Parasmaipada of the precative final इ *i* and उ *u* of the verb are lengthened, final ऋ *ṛi* becomes रि *ri*, and, when preceded by a compound consonant, अर् *ar*; ॠ *ṛî* becomes ईर् *îr*, and when preceded by labials or व् *v*, ऊर् *ûr*; final ऐ *ai* and ओ *o* are generally changed to आ *â*. In some verbs however these diphthongs as well as आ *â*, must or may be changed to ए *e* (*cf.* my 'Kurze Grammatik,' § 316, Bem.), *e.g.* श्रि *çri*, श्रीयासम् *çrî-yâsam*; स्तु *stu*, 'to praise,' स्तूयासम् *stû-yâsam*; कृ *kṛi*, क्रियासम् *kri-yâsam*; स्मृ *smṛi*, 'to recollect,' स्मर्यासम् *smar-yâsam*; स्तॄ *stṛî*, स्तीर्यासम् *stîr-yâsam*; पॄ *pṛî*, पूर्यासम् *pûr-yâsam*; दै *dai*, 'to purify,' दायासम् *dâ-yâsam*; but दा *dâ*, 'to give,' दे *de*, 'to protect,' and दो *do*, 'to cut,' make देयासम् *de-yâsam*; ध्यै *dhyai*, 'to think,' optionally ध्यायासम् *dhyâ-yâsam* or ध्येयासम् *dhye-yâsam*.

इ *i* and उ *u*, when preceding a radical र् *r* or व् *v*, are lengthened (*cf.* § 18), *e.g.* कुर् *kur*, 'to sound,' कूर्यासम् *kûr-yâsam*; दिव् *div*, दीव्यासम् *dîv-yâsam*.

Some verbs, enumerated in my 'Vollständige Grammatik,' § 154, 2, 2, reject their penultimate nasal, *e.g.* दंश् *daṁç*, 'to bite,' दश्यासम् *daç-yâsam*.

The verbs ending in अय *aya*, viz. the causals, the verbs of the tenth conjugational class, and denominatives in अय *aya*, reject these two syllables, *e.g.* बोधय *bodh-aya*, बोध्यासम् *bodh-yâsam*.

A final अ *a* is rejected, *e.g.* बुबोधिष *bubodhisha*, desiderative of बुध् *budh*, बुबोधिष्यासम् *bubodhish-yâsam*; the denominatives derived by the affix य *ya* reject it, when preceded by a consonant, *e.g.* नमस्य *namasya*, नमस्यासम् *namas-yâsam*.

§ 159. **Paradigms**: नी *ní*, 'to lead,' and क्लिद् *klid*, 'to be moist;' the second may optionally insert इ *i*.

FIRST FUTURE.

	Parasmaipada.			Âtmanepada.		
	नेतास्मि *netā́smi* 'I shall lead'	नेतास्वस् *netā́svas*	नेतास्मस् *netā́smas*	नेताहे *netā́he* 'I shall lead'	नेतास्वहे *netā́svahe*	नेतास्महे *netā́smahe*
	नेतासि *netā́si*	नेतास्थस् *netā́sthas*	नेतास्थ *netā́stha*	नेतासे *netā́se*	नेतासाथे *netā́sāthe*	नेताध्वे *netā́dhve*
	नेता *netā́*	नेतारौ *netā́rau*	नेतारस् *netā́ras*	नेता *netā́*	नेतारौ *netā́rau*	नेतारस् *netā́ras*
1.	क्लेदितास्मि or *kleditā́smi* क्लेत्तास्मि *klettā́smi*	क्लेदितास्वस् or क्लेत्तास्वस्	क्लेदितास्मस् or क्लेत्तास्मस्	क्लेदिताहे or *kleditā́he* क्लेत्ताहे *klettā́he*	क्लेदितास्वहे or क्लेत्तास्वहे	क्लेदितास्महे or क्लेत्तास्महे
2.	क्लेदितासि or क्लेत्तासि	क्लेदितास्थस् or क्लेत्तास्थस्	क्लेदितास्थ or क्लेत्तास्थ	क्लेदितासे or क्लेत्तासे	क्लेदितासाथे or क्लेत्तासाथे	क्लेदिताध्वे or क्लेत्ताध्वे
3.	क्लेदिता or क्लेत्ता	क्लेदितारौ or क्लेत्तारौ	क्लेदितारस् or क्लेत्तारस्	क्लेदिता or क्लेत्ता	क्लेदितारौ or क्लेत्तारौ	क्लेदितारस् or क्लेत्तारस्

SECOND FUTURE.

Parasmaipada.			Âtmanepada.		
नेष्यामि *neshyā́mi* 'I shall lead'	नेष्यावस् *neshyā́vas*	नेष्यामस् *neshyā́mas*	नेष्ये *neshyé* 'I shall lead'	नेष्यावहे *neshyā́vahe*	नेष्यामहे *neshyā́mahe*
नेष्यसि *neshyási*	नेष्यथस् *neshyáthas*	नेष्यथ *neshyátha*	नेष्यसे *neshyáse*	नेष्येथे *neshyéthe*	नेष्यध्वे *neshyádhve*
नेष्यति *neshyáti*	नेष्यतस् *neshyátas*	नेष्यन्ति *neshyánti*	नेष्यते *neshyáte*	नेष्येते *neshyéte*	नेष्यन्ते *neshyánte*

SECOND FUTURE.

	Parasmaipada.			Âtmanepada.		
1.	क्लेदिष्यामि or *klēdishyā́mi* क्लेत्स्यामि *klētsyā́mi*	क्लेदिष्यावस् or क्लेत्स्यावस्	क्लेदिष्यामस् or क्लेत्स्यामस्	क्लेदिष्ये or *klēdishyé* क्लेत्स्ये *klētsyé*	क्लेदिष्यावहे or क्लेत्स्यावहे	क्लेदिष्यामहे or क्लेत्स्यामहे
2.	क्लेदिष्यसि or क्लेत्स्यसि	क्लेदिष्यथस् or क्लेत्स्यथस्	क्लेदिष्यथ or क्लेत्स्यथ	क्लेदिष्यसे or क्लेत्स्यसे	क्लेदिष्येथे or क्लेत्स्येथे	क्लेदिष्यध्वे or क्लेत्स्यध्वे
3.	क्लेदिष्यति or क्लेत्स्यति	क्लेदिष्यतस् or क्लेत्स्यतस्	क्लेदिष्यन्ति or क्लेत्स्यन्ति	क्लेदिष्यते or क्लेत्स्यते	क्लेदिष्येते or क्लेत्स्येते	क्लेदिष्यन्ते or क्लेत्स्यन्ते

CONDITIONAL.

	अनेष्यम् *áneshyam* 'I should lead'	अनेष्याव *áneshyâva*	अनेष्याम *áneshyâma*	अनेष्ये *áneshye* 'I should lead'	अनेष्यावहि *áneshyâvahi*	अनेष्यामहि *áneshyâmahi*
	अनेष्यस् *áneshyas*	अनेष्यतम् *áneshyatam*	अनेष्यत *áneshyata*	अनेष्यथास् *áneshyathâs*	अनेष्येथाम् *áneshyethâm*	अनेष्यध्वम् *áneshyadhvam*
	अनेष्यत् *áneshyat*	अनेष्यताम् *áneshyatâm*	अनेष्यन् *áneshyan*	अनेष्यत *áneshyata*	अनेष्येताम् *áneshyetâm*	अनेष्यन्त *áneshyanta*
1.	अक्लेदिष्यम् or *ákledishyam* अक्लेत्स्यम् *ákletsyam*	अक्लेदिष्याव or अक्लेत्स्याव	अक्लेदिष्याम or अक्लेत्स्याम	अक्लेदिष्ये or *ákledishye* अक्लेत्स्ये *ákletsye*	अक्लेदिष्यावहि or अक्लेत्स्यावहि	अक्लेदिष्यामहि or अक्लेत्स्यामहि
2.	अक्लेदिष्यस् or अक्लेत्स्यस्	अक्लेदिष्यतम् or अक्लेत्स्यतम्	अक्लेदिष्यत or अक्लेत्स्यत	अक्लेदिष्यथास् or अक्लेत्स्यथास्	अक्लेदिष्येथाम् or अक्लेत्स्येथाम्	अक्लेदिष्यध्वम् or अक्लेत्स्यध्वम्
3.	अक्लेदिष्यत् or अक्लेत्स्यत्	अक्लेदिष्यताम् or अक्लेत्स्यताम्	अक्लेदिष्यन् अक्लेत्स्यन्	अक्लेदिष्यत or अक्लेत्स्यत	अक्लेदिष्येताम् or अक्लेत्स्येताम्	अक्लेदिष्यन्त or अक्लेत्स्यन्त

PRECATIVE.

Parasmaipada.			Âtmanepada.		
नीयासम् *nīyāsam* 'Pray I may lead'	नीयास्व *nīyāsva*	नीयास्म *nīyāsma*	नेषीय *neshīyá* 'Pray I may lead'	नेषीवहि *neshīváhi*	नेषीमहि *neshīmáhi*
नीयास् *nīyās*	नीयास्तम् *nīyāstam*	नीयास्त *nīyāsta*	नेषीष्ठास् *neshīshṭhās*	नेषीयास्थाम् *neshīyāsthâm*	नेषीढ्वम् *neshīḍhvám*
नीयात् *nīyāt*	नीयास्ताम् *nīyāstâm*	नीयासुस् *nīyāsus*	नेषीष्ट *neshīshṭá*	नेषीयास्ताम् *neshīyāstâm*	नेषीरन् *neshīrán*
क्लिद्यासम् *klidyāsam*	क्लिद्यास्व	क्लिद्यास्म	क्लेदिषीय or *kledishīyá* क्लित्सीय *klitsīyá*	क्लेदिषीवहि or क्लित्सीवहि	क्लेदिषीमहि or क्लित्सीमहि
क्लिद्यास्	क्लिद्यास्तम्	क्लिद्यास्त	क्लेदिषीष्ठास् or क्लित्सीष्ठास्	क्लेदिषीयास्थाम् or क्लित्सीयास्थाम्	क्लेदिषीध्वम् or क्लित्सीध्वम्
क्लिद्यात्	क्लिद्यास्ताम्	क्लिद्यासुस्	क्लेदिषीष्ट or क्लित्सीष्ट	क्लेदिषीयास्ताम् or क्लित्सीयास्ताम्	क्लेदिषीरन् or क्लित्सीरन्

In the same way are inflected the forms mentioned in §§ 154-58.

§ 160. Alphabetical List of the Anomalies in the Four last Verbal Forms (Future I. and II., Conditional, and Precative).

अर्यासम्, precative Parasmaipada, from ऋ, 'to go.'

इज्यासम्, ,, ,, ,, यज्, 'to sacrifice.'

इयासम्, ,, ,, ,, इ 'to go,' but only when preceded by a preposition, else regularly ईयासम्.

उच्यासम्, precative Parasmaipada, from वच्, 'to speak.'

उद्यासम्, ,, ,, ,, वद्, 'to speak.'

उप्यासम्, ,, ,, ,, वप्, 'to sow.'

उश्यासम्, ,, ,, ,, वश्, 'to wish.'

उष्यासम्, ,, ,, ,, वस्, 'to dwell.'

उह्यासम्, ,, ,, ,, वह्, 'to bear,' and, when preceded by prepositions, also from ऊह्, 'to reason.'

ऊयासम्, precative Parasmaipada, from वे, 'to weave.'

ऊर्णुवितास्मि or ऊर्णवितास्मि, etc., fut. I.; ऊर्णुविष्यामि or ऊर्णविष्यामि, fut. II.; और्णुविष्यम् or और्णविष्यम्, conditional; ऊर्णुविषीय or ऊर्णविषीय, Âtmanepada of the precative, from ऊर्णु 'to cover.'

ऋतीयिताहे or अर्तिताहे, future I.; ऋतीयिष्ये or अर्तिष्ये, fut. II.; आर्तीयिष्ये or आर्तिष्ये, conditional; ऋतीयिषीय or अर्तिषीय, precative, from ऋत् Âtm. 'to blame.'

कामयिताहे or कमिताहे, future I.; कामयिष्ये or कमिष्ये, future II.; अकामयिष्ये or अकमिष्ये, conditional; कामयिषीय or कमिषीय, precative, from कम् Âtm. 'to love.'

कुताहे, कुष्ये, अकुष्ये, कुषीय, from कु Âtm. 'to cry' (contrary to § 156).

कुविताहे, कुविष्ये, अकुविष्ये, कुविषीय, from कू Âtm. 'to cry' (contrary to § 156).

क्रष्टास्मि, or regularly कर्ष्टास्मि, क्रक्ष्यामि or कर्क्ष्यामि, अक्रक्ष्यम् or अकर्क्ष्यम्, from कृष्, 'to draw' (*cf.* § 148), with र optionally instead of अर् (§ 156).

क्षवितास्मि, क्षविष्यामि, अक्षविष्यम्, क्षविषीय, from क्षु, 'to sneeze' (contrary to § 154).

क्ष्णवितास्मि, क्ष्णविष्यामि, अक्ष्णविष्यम्, क्ष्णविषीय, from क्ष्णु, 'to sharpen' (contrary to § 154).

खायासम्, or regularly खन्यासम्, precative Parasmaipada, from खन्, 'to dig.'

गसीय, or regularly गंसीय, precative Âtman., from गम्, 'to go.'

गुतास्मि, गुष्यामि, अगुष्यम्, गुषीय, from गु
गुवितास्मि, गुविष्यामि, अगुविष्यम्, गुविषीय, from गू } 'to void excrement' (contrary to § 156).

गूहितास्मि, गूहिष्यामि, अगूहिष्यम्, गूहिषीय (but without इ regularly गोढास्मि, घोक्ष्यामि, अघोक्ष्यम्, घुक्षीय), from गुह्, 'to hide.'

गृह्यासम्, precative Parasmaipada, from ग्रह्, 'to take,' *cf.* ग्रहीतास्मि.

गेयासम्, precative Parasmaipada, from गै, 'to sing' (*cf.* § 158).

गोपायितास्मि or गोपितास्मि or गोप्तास्मि, future I.; गोपायिष्यामि or गोपिष्यामि or गोप्स्यामि, future II.; अगोपायिष्यम् or अगोपिष्यम् or अगोप्स्यम्, conditional; गोपाय्यासम् or गुप्यासम्, precative Parasm.; गोपायिषीय or गोपिषीय or गुप्सीय, precative Âtm., from गुप्, 'to protect.'

ग्रहीतास्मि, ग्रहीष्यामि, अग्रहीष्यम्, ग्रहीषीय, from ग्रह्, 'to take,' *cf.* गृह्यासम्.

चातास्मि, चास्यामि, अचास्यम्, चासीय, from चाय्, 'to worship.'

जायासम्, or regularly जन्यासम्, precative Parasm., from जन्, 'to bring forth.'

जीयासम्, precative Parasm., from ज्या, 'to become old,' and from ज्यो, 'to restrain.'

डयिताहे, डयिष्ये, अडयिष्ये, डयिषीय, from डी, Âtm. 'to fly' (contrary to § 154).

दरिद्रितास्मि, दरिद्रिष्यामि, अदरिद्रिष्यम्, दरिद्र्यासम्, दरिद्रिषीय, from दरिद्रा, 'to be in distress' (contrary to § 154).

दाताहे, दास्ये, अदास्ये, दासीय, from दी Âtm. 'to go to ruin' (of course also from दा, दे, दो).

दीधिताहे, दीधिष्ये, अदीधिष्ये, दीधिषीय, from दीधी, Âtman., 'to shine.'

देयासम्, precative Parasm., from दा, 'to give,' दे, 'to protect,' and दो, 'to cut.'

द्रष्टास्मि, द्रक्ष्यामि, अद्रक्ष्यम्, from दृश्, 'to see,' with र instead of of अर् (§ 156).

धुवितास्मि and regularly धवितास्मि, धुविष्यामि and regularly धविष्यामि, अधुविष्यम् or अधविष्यम्, धुविषीय or धविषीय, from धू, 'to shake.'

धूपायितास्मि or धूपितास्मि, धूपायिष्यामि or धूपिष्यामि, अधूपायिष्यम् or अधूपिष्यम्, धूपाय्यासम् or धूप्यासम्, धूपायिषीय or धूपिषीय, from धूप्, 'to fumigate.'

धेयासम्, precative Parasm., from धा, 'to hold,' and धे, 'to drink.'

ध्रुतास्मि or regularly ध्रोतास्मि, ध्रुष्यामि or ध्रोष्यामि, अध्रुष्यम् or अध्रोष्यम्, ध्रुषीय or ध्रोषीय, from ध्रु, 'to stand firm.'

नंष्टास्मि, नङ्क्ष्यामि, अनङ्क्ष्यम्, नङ्क्षीय, from नश्, 'to perish.'

नवितास्मि, नविष्यामि, अनविष्यम्, नविषीय, from नु 'to praise' (contrary to § 154).

नुवितास्मि, नुविष्यामि, अनुविष्यम्, नुविषीय, from नू, 'to praise' (contrary to § 156).

पणायितास्मि or पणितास्मि (? according to other grammarians Âtmanepada only पणायिताहे or पणिताहे), पणायिष्यामि or पणिष्यामि (? पणायिष्ये or पणिष्ये only), पणाय्यासम् or पण्यासम् (?), पणायिषीय or पणिषीय, from पण्, 'to praise.'

पनायितास्मि or पनितास्मि (? according to other grammarians Âtmanepada only, etc., quite as the preceding, only with न् instead of ण्), from पन्, 'to praise.'

पृच्छ्यासम्, precative Parasmaipada, from प्रच्छ्, 'to ask.'

पेयासम्, precative Parasmaipada, from पा, 'to drink.'

प्याताहे, प्यास्ये, अप्यास्ये, प्यासीय, from प्याय् Âtm., 'to be exuberant.'

भर्ष्टास्मि, or regularly भ्रष्टास्मि, भर्क्ष्यामि or भ्रक्ष्यामि, अभर्क्ष्यम् or अभ्रक्ष्यम्, भर्क्षीय or भ्रक्षीय, from भ्रज्ज्, 'to fry.'

मङ्क्तास्मि, मङ्क्ष्यामि, अमङ्क्ष्यम्, मङ्क्षीय, from मज्ज्, 'to dive.'

मातास्मि, मास्यामि, अमास्यम्, मासीय, from मि, 'to throw,' मी, 'to hurt' (and of course also from मा, 'to measure,' and मे, 'to barter').

मार्ष्टास्मि or मार्जितास्मि, मार्क्ष्यामि or मार्जिष्यामि, अमार्क्ष्यम् or अमार्जिष्यम्, मार्जिषीय (or regularly मृक्षीय), from मृज्, 'to wipe.'

मेयासम्, precative Parasmaipada, from मा, 'to measure,' and मे, 'to barter.'

म्रष्टास्मि or regularly मर्ष्टास्मि, म्रक्ष्यामि or मर्क्ष्यामि, अम्रक्ष्यम् or अमर्क्ष्यम्, from मृश्, 'to touch,' with र optionally instead of अर्.

यवितास्मि, यविष्यामि, अयविष्यम्, यविषीय, from यु, 'to join' (contrary to § 154).

रवितास्मि, रविष्यामि, अरविष्यम्, रविषीय, from रु, 'to sound' (contrary to § 154).

लातास्मि, लाताहे, or regularly लेतास्मि, लेताहे, लास्यामि, लास्ये, or लेष्यामि, लेष्ये, अलास्यम्, अलास्ये or अलेष्यम्, अलेष्ये, लासीय or लेषीय, from ली, 'to adhere;' but लीयासम् regularly (Sch. Pâṇini, VI. 1, 51; *cf.* Westergaard, Radices).

वरितास्मि or वरीतास्मि, वरिष्यामि or वरीष्यामि, अवरिष्यम् or अवरीष्यम्, वरिषीय, from वृ, 'to select.'

विच्यासम्, precative Parasmaipada from व्यच्, 'to deceive.'

विच्छायितास्मि or विच्छितास्मि, विच्छायिष्यामि or विच्छिष्यामि, अविच्छायिष्यम् or अविच्छिष्यम्, विच्छायिषीय or विच्छिषीय, from विछ्, 'to go.'

विजितास्मि, विजिष्यामि, अविजिष्यम्, विजिषीय, from विज्, 'to tremble.'

विध्यासम्, precative Parasmaipada, from व्यध्, 'to pierce.'

वीयासम्, precative Parasmaipada, from व्ये, 'to cover.'

वृश्च्यासम्, precative Parasmaipada, from व्रश्च्, 'to tear.'

वेविताहे, वेविष्ये, अवेविष्ये, वेविषीय, from वेवी Âtm. 'to go.'

वोढास्मि, future I., from वह्, 'to bear.'

शयिताहे, शयिष्ये, अशयिष्ये, शयिषीय, from शी, Âtm., 'to lie down' (contrary to § 154).

शिष्यासम्, precative Parasmaipada, from शास्, 'to instruct.'

शूयासम्, precative Parasmaipada, from श्वि, 'to swell.'

श्रयितास्मि, श्रयिष्यामि, अश्रयिष्यम्, श्रयिषीय, from श्रि, 'to go' (contrary to § 154).

सायासम्, or regularly सन्यासम्, precative Parasmaipada, from सन्, 'to obtain.'

सुप्यासम्, precative Parasmaipada, from स्वप्, 'to sleep.'

सेयासम्, precative Parasmaipada, from शै, 'to waste,' and सो, 'to destroy.'

सोढास्मि, future I., from सह्, 'to bear.'

स्थेयासम्, precative Parasmaipada, from स्था, 'to stand.'

स्रवितास्मि, स्रविष्यामि, अस्रविष्यम्, स्रविषीय, from स्रु, 'to flow' (contrary to § 154).

स्प्रष्टास्मि, or regularly स्पर्ष्टास्मि, स्प्रक्ष्यामि or स्पर्क्ष्यामि, अस्प्रक्ष्यम् or अस्पर्क्ष्यम्, from स्पृश्, 'to touch.'

स्फाताहे, स्फास्से, अस्फास्ये, स्फासीय, from स्फाय्, 'to swell.'

स्रप्तास्मि, or regularly सर्प्तास्मि, स्रप्स्यामि or सर्प्स्यामि, अस्रप्स्यम् or असर्प्स्यम्, from सृप्, 'to go.'

स्रष्टास्मि, स्रक्ष्यामि, अस्रक्ष्यम्, from सृज्, 'to abandon.'

हूयासम्, precative Parasmaipada, from ह्वे, 'to call.'

हेयासम्, precative Parasmaipada, from हा, 'to leave.'

II. Passive Voice.

I. THE FIRST FOUR VERBAL FORMS OF THE PASSIVE VOICE.

§ 161. The first four verbal forms of the passive are formed:—

1. By affixing य *yá* to the verb, *e.g.* दृश् *dṛiç*, 'to see,' दृश्य *dṛiçyá*, 'to be seen.'

2. By conjugating this base in the Âtmanepada according to the analogy of the Âtmanepada of the fourth conjugational class (§ 80, 2), from which it only differs in regard to the accent.

Paradigm.

PRESENT.			IMPERFECT.		
दृश्ये *dṛiçyé* 'I am seen'	दृश्यावहे *dṛiçyấvahe*	दृश्यामहे *dṛiçyấmahe*	अदृश्ये *ádṛiçye* 'I was seen'	अदृश्यावहि *ádṛiçyâvahi*	अदृश्यामहि *ádṛiçyâmahi*
दृश्यसे *dṛiçyáse*	दृश्येथे *dṛiçyéthe*	दृश्यध्वे *dṛiçyádhve*	अदृश्यथास् *ádṛiçyathâs*	अदृश्येथाम् *ádṛiçyethâm*	अदृश्यध्वम् *ádṛiçyadhvam*
दृश्यते *dṛiçyáte*	दृश्येते *dṛiçyéte*	दृश्यन्ते *dṛiçyánte*	अदृश्यत *ádṛiçyata*	अदृश्येताम् *ádṛiçyetâm*	अदृश्यन्त *ádṛiçyanta*

IMPERATIVE.			POTENTIAL.		
दृश्यै *dṛiçyái* 'May I be seen'	दृश्यावहै *dṛiçyấvahai*	दृश्यामहै *dṛiçyấmahai*	दृश्येय *dṛiçyéya* 'I may be seen'	दृश्येवहि *dṛiçyévahi*	दृश्येमहि *dṛiçyémahi*
दृश्यस्व *dṛiçyásva*	दृश्येथाम् *dṛiçyéthâm*	दृश्यध्वम् *dṛiçyádhvam*	दृश्येथास् *dṛiçyéthâs*	दृश्येयाथाम् *dṛiçyéyâthâm*	दृश्येध्वम् *dṛiçyédhvam*
दृश्यताम् *dṛiçyátâm*	दृश्येताम् *dṛiçyétâm*	दृश्यन्ताम् *dṛiçyántâm*	दृश्येत *dṛiçyéta*	दृश्येयाताम् *dṛiçyéyâtâm*	दृश्येरन् *dṛiçyéran*

§ 162. The final letters of the verb undergo the same changes before the affix य *ya*, as before the य *ya* of the terminations of the precative Parasmaipada, except that final आ *á*, ए *e*, ऐ *ai*, and ओ *o* in the passive voice are changed only to आ *á*, never to ए *e*; *e.g.* (*cf.* § 158) श्रीये *çríyé*, स्तूये *stúyé*, क्रियें *kriyé*, स्मर्ये *smaryé*, स्तीर्ये *stíryé*, पूर्ये *púryé*, दाये *dáyé*, from दै *dai*, 'to purify;' ध्याये *dhyáyé*, from ध्यै *dhyai*; कूर्ये *kúryé*, दीव्ये *dívyé*, दश्ये *daçyé*, बोध्ये *bodhyé*, बुबोधिष्ये *bubodhishyé*; add from लोलूय *lolúya*, second frequentative of लू *lú*, 'to cut,' लोलूय्ये *lolúyyé*, नमस्ये *namasyé*, and in the same way from बेभिद्य *bebhidya*, second frequentative of भिद् *bhid*, बेभिद्ये *bebhidyé*.

§ 163. List of Anomalies in the First Four Verbal Forms of the Passive Voice (*cf.* the corresponding anomalous precatives Parasmaipada in § 160).

अर्ये from ऋ, 'to go.'
इज्ये from यज्, 'to sacrifice.'
उच्ये from वच्, 'to speak.'
उद्ये from वद्, 'to speak.'
उप्ये from वप्, 'to sow.'
उश्ये from वश्, 'to desire.'

उष्ये from वस्, 'to dwell.'

उह्ये from वह्, 'to bear,' and, when preceded by prepositions, also from ऊह्, 'to reason.'

ऊये from वे, 'to weave.'

ऋतीय्ये or ऋत्ये from ऋत् 'to blame.'

काम्ये or कम्ये from कम्, 'to love.'

खाये or खन्ये from खन्, 'to dig.'

गृह्ये from ग्रह्, 'to take.'

गीये from गै, 'to sing.'

गोपाय्ये or गुप्ये from गुप् 'to protect.'

जाये or जन्ये from जन्, 'to bring forth.'

जीये from ज्या, 'to become old,' and ज्यो, 'to restrain.'

दरिद्र्ये from दरिद्रा, 'to be poor.'

दीध्ये from दीधी, 'to shine.'

दीये from दा, 'to give,' दे, 'to protect,' and दो, 'to cut.'

धीये from धा, 'to hold,' and धे, 'to drink.'

धूपाय्ये or धूप्ये from धूप्, 'to fumigate.'

पणाय्ये or पण्ये from पण् } 'to
पनाय्ये or पन्ये from पन् } praise.'

पीये from पा, 'to drink.'

पृच्छ्ये from प्रछ्, 'to ask.'

भृज्ज्ये from भ्रज्ज्, 'to fry.'

मीये from मा, 'to measure,' and मे, 'to barter.'

विच्ये from व्यच्, 'to deceive.'

विच्छाय्ये or विच्छ्ये from विछ् 'to go.'

विध्ये from व्यध्, 'to pierce.'

वीये from व्ये, 'to cover.'

वृश्च्ये from व्रश्च्, 'to tear.'

वेव्ये from वेवी, 'to go.'

शय्ये from शी, 'to lie.'

शिष्ये from शास्, 'to instruct.'

शूये from श्वि, 'to swell.'

साये or सन्ये from सन्, 'to obtain.'

सीये from सै, 'to waste,' and सो 'to destroy.'

सुप्ये from स्वप्, 'to sleep.'

स्थीये from स्था, 'to stand.'

हीये from हा, 'to leave.'

हूये from ह्वे, 'to call.'

II. THE LAST SIX VERBAL FORMS OF THE PASSIVE VOICE.

§ 164. The last six verbal forms of the passive are mostly identical with the corresponding forms of the Âtmanepada. Thus in the reduplicated perfect of the passive दा makes ददे, शिश्रिये, क्री चिक्रिये, etc., *cf.* § 117; वच् ऊचे, *cf.* § 118; in the periphrastic perfect छद् makes छादयां चक्रे (*cf.* § 123).

In the aorist सिच् makes असिचे (§ 134), श्रि अशिश्रिये (§ 135), पाठय, when reflective (Exc. 1 to § 166), अपीपठे (§ 136, IV., 1), नी अनेषि (§ 142), लू अलविषि (§ 143), दिश् अदिशि (§ 147).

In the first future नी makes नेताहे, छिद् छेदिताहे or छेत्ताहे; in the second future नेष्ये, छेदिष्ये or छेत्स्ये; in the conditional अनेष्ये, अच्छेदिष्ये or अच्छेत्स्ये; in the precative नेषीय, छेदिषीय or छित्सीय (§ 159).

There are, however, some slight differences between the passive and the Âtmanepada, which will be pointed out in the following paragraphs.

§ 165. In the periphrastic perfect of the passive भू *bhû* and अस् *as*, as well as कृ (§§ 123, 164), take the terminations of the Âtmanepada.

PARADIGM.

छादयां *chhâdayâm*	चक्रे *chakre*	or आसे *âse*	or बभूवे *babhûve*
	चकृषे *chakṛishe*	आसिषे *âsishe*	बभूविषे *babhûvishe*
	चक्रे *chakre*	आसे *âse*	बभूवे *babhûve*
	चकृवहे *chakṛivahe*	आसिवहे *âsivahe*	बभूविवहे *babhûvivahe*
	चक्राथे *chakrâthe*	आसाथे *âsâthe*	बभूवाथे *babhûvâthe*
	चक्राते *chakrâte*	आसाते *âsâte*	बभूवाते *babhûvâte*
	चकृमहे *chakṛimahe*	आसिमहे *âsimahe*	बभूविमहे *babhûvimahe*
	चकृढ्वे *chakṛiḍhve*	आसिध्वे *âsidhve*	बभूविध्वे or बभूविढ्वे *babhûvidhve babhûviḍhve*
	चक्रिरे *chakrire*	आसिरे *âsire*	बभूविरे *babhûvire*

§ 166. The third person singular of the aorist is formed by affixing to the augmented verb the termination इ, before which the final and penultimate letters of the base undergo the following changes:

1. Final ए *e*, ऐ *ai*, and ओ *o*, are changed to आ *â*, after which as well as after an original final आ *â*, य् *y* is inserted, *e.g.* दा *dâ*, 'to give,' दे *de*, 'to protect,' दै *dai*, 'to purify,' and दो *do*, 'to cut,' make अदायि *á-dâ-y-i*.

2. A final इ *i*, or ई *í*, is changed to आय् *ây*, *e.g.* जि *ji*, 'to conquer,' अजायि *á-jây-i*; नी *ní*, 'to lead,' अनायि *á-nây-i*.

3. A final उ *u*, or ऊ *ú*, is changed to आव् *âv*, *e.g.* नु *nu*, or नू *nú*, 'to praise,' अनावि *á-nâv-i*.

4. Final ऋ *ṛi* and ॠ *ṛí* become आर् *âr*, *e.g.* कृ *kṛi*, 'to make,' कॄ *kṛí* 'to throw,' अकारि *á-kâr-i*.

5. A penultimate अ *a* followed by a single consonant is lengthened, *e.g.* पत् *pat*, 'to fall,' अपाति *a-pât-i*. There are many exceptions to this rule, especially all the verbs ending in अम् retain the short vowel, *e.g.* क्लम्, 'to be sad,' अक्लमि.

6. Penultimate इ *i*, उ *u*, and ऋ *ṛi*, followed by a single consonant, are changed to ए *e*, ओ *o*, and अर् *ar* (guṇa), *e.g.* छिद् *chhid*, 'to cut,' अच्छेदि *a-chchhed-i*; तुद् *tud*, 'to strike,' अतोदि *a-tod-i*; दृश् *dṛiç*, 'to see,' अदर्शि *a-darç-i*.

This rule does not apply to the last इ of the desiderative, nor to the इ, उ, or ऋ of verbs ending in the affix य preceded by a consonant (*cf.* 8).

7. Penultimate ॠ *ṛí* becomes ईर् *ír*, *e.g.*, स्तॄह् *stṛíh*, अस्तीर्हि *a-stírh-i*.

8. Final अ *a* is rejected, *e.g.* बुबोधिष *bubodhisha*, desiderative of बुध् *budh*, अबुबोधिषि *a-bubodhish-i*; लोलूय *lolúya*, second frequentative of लू *lú*, अलोलूयि *a-lolúy-i*. Second frequentatives and denominatives formed by the affix य which have a consonant immediately before this affix, follow the rule given in § 56, 3, *e.g.* वेभिद्य अवेभिदि, नमस्य अनमस्यि or अनमसि.

9. Derivative verbs ending in अय *aya*, *i.e.*, the causals, verbs of the tenth conjugational class, and denominatives in अय, reject this affix, *e.g.* बोधय *bodhaya* अबोधि *a-bodh-i*, दापय अदापि *a-dâp-i*.

In the causals derived from causals, which do not lengthen a medial अ (§ 59), this अ may be lengthened optionally *e.g.* क्षमय, causal of क्षमय, causal of क्षम्, अक्षमि or अक्षामि (*cf.* 5).

The Paradigm of the passive aorist of नी therefore is:—

अनेषि *áneshi*, 'I was lead'	अनेष्वहि *áneshvahi*, etc., as § 142 Âtman.	अनेष्महि
अनेष्ठास् *áneshṭhâs*	अनेषाथाम्	अनेढ्वम्
अनायि *ánâyi*	अनेषाताम्	अनेषत

Exceptions to § 166:—

1. The derivative verbs ending in अय (§ 166, 9), except when used as reflective passives, take the Âtmanepada of the fifth form of the aorist and may subjoin its terminations either to their full form or after having rejected अय, *e.g.* भावय, causal of भू, 'to become,' in the 1st sing. अभावयिषि *á-bhâvay-ishi* or अभाविषि *á-bhâv-ishi*; in the 2nd अभावयिष्ठास् or अभाविष्ठास्; but in the 3rd, according to § 166, 9, अभावि only, in the 1st dual अभावयिष्वहि or अभाविष्वहि, etc.

A medial अ of causals derived from causals which do not lengthen it, may optionally be lengthened in all the inflexions of this aorist as in the third person singular (*cf.* § 166, 9), *e.g.* from क्षमय, causal of क्षमय, in the 1st sing. अक्षमयिषि, or अक्षमिषि, or अक्षामयिषि, or अक्षामिषि.

2. Many verbs, when used as reflective passives, take in the third person singular the termination of the Âtmanepada instead of that of the passive (*cf.* my V. G. § 879), *e.g.* श्रि, 'to go,' अशिश्रियत (*cf.* § 164), not अश्रायि, but in the sense of a real passive only अश्रायि.

3. Alphabetical List of some Anomalies.

अकमिषि or अकामिषि or अकामयिषि, 1st person singular (fifth form of the aorist), अकामि, 3rd person singular of कम्, 'to love,' when real passive, but अचकमे, 1st sing. (third form of the aorist), अचकमत, 3rd sing., when reflective (*cf.* Except. 1).

अकान्दि or regularly अकन्दि, third person singular of कन्दय, causal of कन्द्, 'to call.'

अक्रमि from क्रम्, 'to go.'

अक्रान्दि or regularly अक्रन्दि, from क्रन्दय, causal of क्रन्द् 'to call.'

अक्लमि from क्लम्, 'to be sad.'

अक्लान्दि or regularly अक्लन्दि from क्लन्दय, causal of क्लन्द्, 'to call.'

अक्षपि or अक्षापि from क्षपय, causal of क्षै, 'to decrease,' (§ 60).

अक्षमि from क्षम्, 'to bear.'

अक्षाञ्जि or अक्षञ्जि from क्षञ्जय, causal of क्षञ्ज्, 'to give,' 'to go.'

अख्यासि (fourth form of the aorist), but, when reflective, अख्ये (second form of the aorist), from ख्या, 'to speak.'

अगूहि, third person singular, from गुह् 'to cover.'

अगोपायि or अगोपि from गुप्, 'to protect.'

अग्लपि or अग्लापि from ग्लापय or ग्लपय, causal of ग्लै, 'to become exhausted' (§ 60).

अघानि from हन्, 'to kill.'

अचमि, but, when preceded by the preposition आ, अचामि, from चम्, 'to eat.'

अच्छमि from छम्, 'to eat.'

अजनि from जन्, 'to bring forth.'

अजमि from जम्, 'to eat.'

अजम्भि from जभ्, 'to yawn.'

अजरि or अजारि from जरय, causal of जॄ, 'to become old' (§ 60).

अज्ञपि or अज्ञापि from ज्ञपय or ज्ञापय, causal of ज्ञा, 'to know' (§ 60).

अझमि from झम्, 'to eat.'

अतमि from तम्,' 'to become breathless.'

अदमि from दम्, 'to tame.'

अदरि or अदारि from दरय, causal of दॄ 'to burst' (§ 60).

अदाघि or अदघि from दघय, causal of दघ्, 'to go.'

अद्रमि from द्रम्, 'to run.'

अद्रोषि (1st sing. of the fourth form of the aorist), but, when reflective, अदुद्रुवे (third form of the aorist), from द्रु, 'to run.'

अधूपायि or अधूपि, third singular from धूप्, 'to fumigate.'

अनरि or अनारि from नरय, causal of नॄ, 'to lead.'

अपणायि or अपाणि from पण् } 'to praise.'
अपनायि or अपानि from पन् }

अभाञ्जि or अभञ्जि from भञ्ज्, 'to break.'

अमार्जि from मृज्, 'to wipe.'

अयामि or अयमि from यमय, causal of यम्, 'to restrain.'

अरन्धि from रध्, 'to hurt.'

अरम्भि from रभ्, 'to desire vehemently.'

अराञ्जि or अरञ्जि from रञ्ज्, 'to colour.'

अलम्भि from लभ्, 'to obtain.'

अविच्छायि or अविच्छि from विछ्, 'to go.'

अशमि or, when signifying 'to observe,' अशामि, from शम्, 'to cease.'

अश्रपि or अश्रापि from श्रापय or श्रपय, causal of श्रा, श्रै 'to cook' (§ 60).

अश्रयिषि (first pers. sing. of the fifth form of the aorist), but, when reflective, अशिश्रियें (third form), from श्रि, 'to go.'

अश्वयिषि and, when reflective, अशिश्वियें, from श्वि, 'to swell.'

असमि, third singular, from सम् } 'to be unconfused.'
अस्तमि from स्तम् }

अस्नपि or अस्नापि from स्नापय or स्नपय, causal of स्ना, 'to bathe' (§ 60).

अस्मरि or अस्मारि from स्मरय, causal of स्मृ, 'to recollect' (§ 60).

अस्वमि from स्वम्, 'to sound.'

अस्रोषि (1st sing. of the fourth form of the aorist), but, when reflective, असुस्रुवे (third form) from स्रु, 'to flow.'

अहिडि and } or regularly अहेडि, third person singular, from
अहीडि } हेड् 'to surround.'

आर्तीयि or आर्ति from ऋत्, 'to blame.'

4. All verbs ending in vowels or diphthongs, and the verbs हन्, 'to kill,' दृश्, 'to see,' and ग्रह्, 'to take,' may in the aorist, the first and second future, the conditional, and the precative either use the forms which are prescribed in §§ 164-166, *e.g.* from दा, aorist अदिषि, अदिथास्, अदायि, अदिष्वहि, etc. (§§ 148 and 144), fut. I. दाताहे, etc.; fut. II. दास्ये, etc.; condit. अदास्ये, etc.; precat. दासीय, etc., or derive new ones from the base of the third person singular of the aorist, which remains after having rejected the augment and the termination, *e.g.* (*cf.* § 166) from दाय् (3rd sing. अदायि *a-dây-i*), जाय् (from जि), नाय् (from नी), नाव् (from नु and नू), कार् (from कृ and कॄ), घान् (3rd sing. अघानि, § 166, Exc. 3, from हन्), दर्श् (3rd sing. अदर्शि, § 166, 6), ग्राह् (3rd sing. अग्राहि, § 166, 5).

To this base are subjoined in the first and second persons singular and in the dual and plural of the aorist the terminations of the Âtmanepada of the fifth aorist, and in the last four verbal forms those of the Âtmanepada, with prefixed इ, *e.g.* aorist अदायिषि *a-dây-ishi*, अदायिष्ठास्, अदायि, अदायिष्वहि, etc.

अजायिषि, अजायिष्ठास्, अजायि, अजायिष्वहि, etc.

अनायिषि, etc., अनाविषि, अकारिषि, अघानिषि, अदर्शिषि, अग्राहिषि.

In the first future दायिताहे, जायिताहे, ग्राहिताहे, etc.

In the second future दायिष्ये, जायिष्ये, ग्राहिष्ये, etc.

In the conditional अदायिष्ये, अजायिष्ये, अग्राहिष्ये, etc.

In the precative दायिषीय, जायिषीय, ग्राहिषीय, etc.

§ 167. When the passive is reflective, and in the Veda also in other instances, the Âtmanepada of the active voice is often used instead of the special forms of the passive, *e.g.* in the verbs which signify 'to adorn,' 'he adorns himself' (properly 'he is adorned by himself') भूषते, Âtmanep. of भूष्, 'to adorn' (*cf.* my V.G. §§ 873, 875, 879).

SECTION III. OTHER VERBAL DERIVATIVES.

PARTICIPLES.

§ 168. The participles of the present and of the second future Parasmaipada are formed from the corresponding third persons of the plural, which reject the final न्, *e.g.*

	3rd plur. of the present.	participle of the present.
(*cf.* § 80)	बोधन्ति *bódhanti* 'they know'	बोधन्त् *bódhant* 'knowing'
	नह्यन्ति *náhyanti*	नह्यन्त् *náhyant*
	तुदन्ति *tudánti*	तुदन्त् *tudánt*
	बोधयन्ति *bodháyanti*	बोधयन्त् *bodháyant*
	बुबोधिषन्ति *búbodhishanti*	बुबोधिषन्त् *búbodhishant*
	नमस्यन्ति *namasyánti*	नमस्यन्त् *namasyánt*
	पितरन्ति *pitáranti*	पितरन्त् *pitárant*
(*cf.* § 85)	चिन्वन्ति *chinvánti*	चिन्वन्त् *chinvánt*
	आप्नुवन्ति *âpnuvánti*	आप्नुवन्त् *âpnuvánt*
	तन्वन्ति *tanvánti*	तन्वन्त् *tanvánt*
	युनन्ति *yunánti*	युनन्त् *yunánt*
(*cf.* § 104)	लिहन्ति *lihánti*	लिहन्त् *lihánt*
(*cf.* § 105)	पिप्रति *píprati*	पिप्रत् *píprat*
(*cf.* § 106)	बोभुवति *bóbhuvati*	बोभुवत् *bóbhuvat*

	3rd plur. of the present.	participle of the present.
(*cf.* § 107)	युञ्जन्ति *yuñjánti*	युञ्जन्त् *yuñjánt*
(*cf.* § 108)	यन्ति *yánti*	यन्त् *yánt* from इ, 'to go'
	ददति *dádati*	ददत् *dádat* from दा, 'to give'

	3rd plur. of the second future.	participle of the second future.
(*cf.* § 159)	नेष्यन्ति 'they will lead' *neshyánti*	नेष्यन्त् 'what will lead' *neshyánt*
	क्लेदिष्यन्ति or क्लेत्स्यन्ति	क्लेदिष्यन्त् क्लेत्स्यन्त्

§ 169. The participle of the reduplicated perfect Parasmaipada is formed from the corresponding third person, which rejects the termination उस् *us*, *e.g.* from रुरुद् *rurud* (third person plural रुरुदुस् *rurud-us*), and subjoins a termination which appears in the declension in the shape of वत् *vat*, वन् *van*, वान् *vân*, वांस् *vâṁs*, वस् *vas*, and उस् *us*, or rather, in accordance with § 17, उष् *ush*, *e.g.* रुरुद्वत् *rurud-vát*, रुरुद्वन्, रुरुद्वान्, रुरुद्वांस्, रुरुद्वस् (only in the Veda), रुरुदुस् or rather रुरुदुष् (*cf.* § 221, V.) 'having wept.'

The last form differs from the third person plural Parasmaipada merely in the substitution of ष् *sh* for स् *s*, *e.g.* (*cf.* § 117) 3rd plur. Par. ददुस् *dadús*, participle ददुष् *dadúsh*, 3rd plur. शिश्युस्, participle शिश्युष्, 3rd plur. चिक्रियुस्, participle चिक्रियुष्, etc.

Before the other five forms (which begin with व् *v*), य् *y*, इय् *iy*, उव् *uv*, ऊव् *ûv*, and र् *r*, preceding the termination of the third person plural Parasmaipada and deduced from इ *i*, ई *î*, उ *u*, ऊ *û*, or ऋ *ṛi*, are changed to their original elements, *e.g.* (*cf.* § 117), 3rd plur. शिश्युस् *çiçy-us*, from श्रि *çi*, participle शिशिवत् *çiçi-vat*, शिशिवन्, शिशिवान्, शिशिवांस्, शिशिवस्; चिक्रियुस् from क्री, participle चिक्रीवत्, etc.; दुद्रुवुस् from द्रु, participle दुद्रुवत्, etc.; लुलुवुस्

from लू, लुलूवत्, etc.; बभूवुस् (§ 118) from भू, बभूवत्, etc.; दध्रुस् from धृ, दधृवत्, etc. Final ऋ *ṛí* of a verb is changed to ईर् *ír*, and after labials and व् *v*, to ऊर् *úr*.

Verbs whose third person plural Parasmaipada consists only of two syllables, attach the terminations beginning with व् *v*, by an auxiliary इ, *e.g.* दधुस्, *dadh-ús*, 3rd plur. of धा *dhâ*, participle दधिवत् *dadh-i-vát*, etc.; तेनुस् *ten-ús* (§ 117, 7), तेनिवत् *ten-i-vát*, etc.; ईजुस् (§ 118, ईज्) ईजिवत्, etc.

Anomalous forms are जगन्वत् *jaganvat* (and regularly जग्मिवत्), from गम्, 'to go,' जघन्वत् *jaghanvat* (and regularly जघ्निवत्) from हन्, 'to strike,' दाश्वत्, °वन्, etc., from दाश्, 'to worship,' मीढ्वत्, etc., from मिह्, 'to sprinkle,' साह्वत्, etc., from सह्, etc., 'to bear,' etc.

The participle of the periphrastic perfect is formed by combining the participles of the reduplicated perfect of अस्, भू, or कृ with the form ending in the affix आम्, *e.g.* (*cf.* § 123) छादयामासिवत् (°वन्, °वान्, °वांस्, °वस्, °उष्), or छादयां चकृवत्, etc., or छादयां बभूवत्, etc., 'having covered.'

§ 170. The participles of the present Âtmanepada in the first conjugation (§§ 71-81), of the present of the passive voice, and of the second future of the Âtmanepada and of the passive voice are formed by the affix मान *mâna*, which is attached to that form of the corresponding third persons plural, which is left after the final न्ते *nte* has been rejected, *e.g.*

	3rd plur. present Âtm.	participle.
(*cf.* § 80)	बोधन्ते *bódhante* 'they know'	बोधमान *bódhamâna* 'knowing'
	नह्यन्ते *náhyante*	नह्यमान *náhyamâna*
	तुदन्ते *tudánte*	तुदमान *tudámâna*
	बोधयन्ते *bodháyante*	बोधयमान *bodháyamâna*

	3rd plur. present Âtm.	participle.
	बुबोधिषन्ते *búbodhishante*	बुबोधिषमाण (*cf.* § 16) *búbodhishamâṇa*
	नमस्यन्ते *namasyánte*	नमस्यमान *namasyámâna*
	पितरन्ते *pitárante*	पितरमाण *pitáramâṇa*
	3rd plur. of the present of the passive.	**participle.**
(*cf.* § 161)	दृश्यन्ते *dṛiçyánte* 'they are seen'	दृश्यमान *dṛiçyámâna* 'being seen'
(*cf.* § 162)	श्रीयन्ते *çrîyánte*	श्रीयमाण (§ 16) *çrîyámâṇa*
	स्तूयन्ते *stûyánte*	स्तूयमान *stûyámâna*
	क्रियन्ते *kriyánte*	क्रियमाण (§ 16) *kriyámâṇa*
	3rd plur. of the second future, Âtm. and passive.	**participle.**
(*cf.* §§ 159 and 164)	नेष्यन्ते *neshyánte* 'they will lead,' or 'they will be led'	नेष्यमाण (§ 16) *neshyámâṇa* 'what will lead,' or 'will be led.'
	क्लेदिष्यन्ते or क्लेत्स्यन्ते	क्लेदिष्यमाण (§ 16) or क्लेत्स्यमान
	3rd plur. of the second future of the passive voice alone.	**participle.**
(*cf.* § 166 Ex.4, p.151)	नायिष्यन्ते *nâyishyánte* 'they will be led'	नायिष्यमाण (§ 16) *nâyishyámâṇa* 'what will be led'
	दायिष्यन्ते	दायिष्यमाण (§ 16)

§ 171. The participles of the present Âtmanepada in the second conjugation (§§ 82-109) and of the reduplicated perfect Âtmanepada are formed by the affix आन *ânâ*, or without accent आन *âna*.

In the present it is attached to the third person plural after having rejected the final अते *ate*, in the perfect to the third person plural after having cut off the final इरे *ire*, *e.g.*

	3rd plur. present.	participle.
(*cf.* § 85)	चिन्वते *chinváte* 'they arrange'	चिन्वान *chinvâná* 'arranging'
	आप्नुवते *âpnuváte*	आप्नुवान *âpnuvâná*
	तन्वते *tanváte*	तन्वान *tanvâná*
	युनते *yunáte*	युनान *yunâná*
(*cf.* § 104)	लिहते *liháte*	लिहान *lihâná*
(*cf.* § 105)	पिप्रते *píprate*	पिप्राण *piprâṇa*
(*cf.* § 107)	युञ्जते *yuñjáte*	युञ्जान *yuñjâná*
(*cf.* § 108)	दद्ते *dádate*	ददान *dádâna*

	3rd plur. of the reduplicated perfect.	participle.
(*cf.* § 117)	ददिरे *dadiré* 'they have given'	ददान *dadâná* 'having given'
	शिश्यिरे *çiçyiré*	शिश्यान *çiçyâná*
	चिक्रियिरे *chikriyiré*	चिक्रियाण (§ 16) *chikriyâṇá*
	दुदुविरे *duduviré*	दुदुवान *duduvâná*
	लुलुविरे *luluviré*	लुलुवान *luluvâná*
	दध्रिरे *dadhriré*	दध्राण *dadhrâṇá*

Exception. The participle of the present of the verb आस्, II. 2, Âtm., 'to sit,' is आसीन *âs-îná*, 'sitting' (in the Veda also regularly आसान).

§ 172. There is another participle of the perfect of the active voice in general, which is formed by subjoining the affix वन्त् *vant*, to the participle of the perfect of the passive voice (§ 173), *e.g.* भुक्त *bhuktá*, 'eaten,' भुक्तवन्त् *bhuktá-vant*, 'having eaten.'

§ 173. The participle of the perfect of the passive voice is formed by affixing to the verb त *tá*, or sometimes न *ná*, *e.g.* जि *ji*, 'to conquer,' जित *ji-tá*, 'conquered;' लू *lú*, 'to cut,' लून *lú-ná*.

I. त *tá* 1. is attached immediately to the primitive verbs ending in vowels (except ॠ, *cf.* II.), or diphthongs, and also to many of those which end in consonants.

Final ऐ *ai* is mostly changed to आ *â*, *e.g.* दै *dai*, 'to purify,' दात *dâ-tá*. Final ए *e* and ओ *o*, and sometimes also ऐ *ai* and आ *â* are changed to ई *í* (by the influence of the accent on the following syllable), *e.g.* धे *dhe*, 'to drink,' धीत *dhí-tá*; पा *pâ*, 'to drink,' पीत *pí-tá*; in some instances to इ *i*, *e.g.* स्था *sthâ*, 'to stand,' स्थित *sthi-tá*; मे 'to barter,' मित (see the alphabetical list of anomalies in IV.).

Other final vowels are generally left unchanged, *e.g.* पा *pâ*, 'to protect,' पात *pâ-tá*; नी, 'to lead,' नीत; स्तु, 'to praise,' स्तुत; भू, 'to become,' भूत; कृ, 'to make,' कृत.

Verbs ending in म् when attaching त immediately follow the rule given in § 95, 3, and lengthen a penultimate अ, *e.g.* क्लम्, 'to be sad,' क्लान्त.

Those ending in other consonants undergo the changes prescribed in §§ 96, 3; 98, 1-3, the exception, and § 102. Thus, according to § 96, 3, मद्, 'to get drunk,' makes मत्त; सिध्, 'to become perfect,' सिद्ध; लुभ्, 'to covet,' लुब्ध; according to § 98, 1, पृच्, 'to mix,' makes पृक्त; युज्, 'to join,' युक्त; according to § 98, 2, तक्ष्, 'to pare,' makes तष्ट; स्पृश्, 'to touch,' स्पृष्ट; according to § 98, 3, and the exception, लिह्, 'to lick,' makes लीढ; दुह् 'to milk,' दुग्ध; according to § 102, मृज्, 'to clean,' makes मृष्ट; मुह्, 'to be foolish,' मूढ or मुग्ध.

As the acute falls on the affix, the base is often weakened, *i.e.* य is often changed to इ, व to उ, र to ऋ, and a penultimate nasal rejected, *e.g.* यज्, 'to sacrifice,' makes इष्ट (*cf.* § 102); वच्, 'to speak,' उक्त; प्रच्छ्, 'to ask,' पृष्ट; दंश्, 'to bite,' दष्ट (*cf.* the anomalies in IV.).

2. Most primitive verbs ending in consonants and all the derivative verbs insert इ between the base and the affix. In some instances a penultimate इ, उ, and ऋ is changed to ए, ओ, and अर् *i.e.* guṇa (*cf.* my K. G. § 374, Bem. 2, V. G. § 895, 9).

The derivative verbs formed with अय reject this affix, *e.g.* बोधय, causal of बुध्, बोधित; others ending in अ reject this vowel, *e.g.* लोलूय, second frequentative of लू, 'to cut,' लोलूयित; those ending in य preceded by a consonant follow the rule given in § 56, 3, *e.g.* बेभिद्य, second frequentative of भिद्, बेभिदित; नमस्य, denominative, नमस्यित or नमसित.

II. न *ná* is affixed instead of त *tá*:—

1. To verbs ending in ॠ, which, when preceded by labials or व्, is changed to ऊर्; when preceded by other consonants, to ईर्, *e.g.* वॄ, 'to choose,' वूर्ण (*cf.* § 16); स्तॄ, 'to stretch,' स्तीर्ण.

2. To many verbs which begin with a compound consonant, containing य्, र्, ल्, or व्, and terminate in आ, ए, ऐ, or ओ. The final diphthongs must be changed to आ, *e.g.* ग्लै, 'to become exhausted,' ग्लान.

3. To some verbs ending in द् which then becomes न्, *e.g.* छिद्, 'to cut,' छिन्न.

4. In some sporadic instances (*cf.* IV.).

III. Some verbs which cannot form a participle of this kind substitute an adjective for it, *e.g.* शुष्, 'to dry,' makes शुष्क; पच्, 'to cook,' पक्व (*cf.* IV.).

IV. Alphabetical List of the Most Remarkable Anomalies.

Participle.	Verb.	Participle.	Verb.
अक्त	अञ्च् 'to go' and अञ्ज् 'to anoint.'	ऽअर्ण, only with prepositions.	अर्द् 'to go.'
अक्न	अञ्च् 'to go.'		
अवित	अम्ब् 'to sound.'	आन्त	अन् 'to breathe.'

Participle.	Verb.	Participle.	Verb.
इद्ध	इन्ध् 'to kindle.'	क्षाम (*cf.* III.)	क्षै 'to decrease.'
इष्ट	यज् 'to sacrifice' and इष् 'to wish.'	क्षित	क्षिण् 'to injure' and क्षि 'to destroy.'
उक्त	वच् 'to speak.'	क्षीण	क्षि 'to destroy.'
उत	वे 'to weave.'	क्षीव 'intoxicated' (*cf.* III.)	क्षीव् 'to spit.'
उत्त	उन्द् 'to be wet.'	क्षुण्ण	क्षुद् 'to grind.'
उदित	वद् 'to speak.'	क्ष्मात	क्ष्माय् 'to shake.'
उन्न	उन्द् 'to be wet.'	क्ष्यूत	क्षिव् and क्षीव् 'to spit.'
उप्त	वप् 'to sow.'	क्ष्विड्ड	क्ष्विड् } 'to sound inarticulately'
उभित	उभ् 'to fill.'	क्ष्विण्ण	क्ष्विद् } and 'to be unctuous'
उशित	वश् 'to wish.'	खात	खन् 'to dig.'
उषित	वस् 'to dwell.'	ख्यात	ख्या 'to speak.'
ऊढ	वह् 'to bear.'	गत	गम् 'to go.'
ऊत	ऊय् 'to weave' and अव् 'to protect.'	गीत	गै 'to sing.'
ऊर्ण	उर्व् 'to injure.'	गुफित	गुम्फ् 'to tie.'
ऋत	ऋण् and ऋ 'to go.'	गून	गु and गू 'to void excrement.'
ऋफित	ऋम्फ् 'to injure.'	गूर्ण	गुर्, गूर्, and गुर्व् 'to make an effort'
कपित, only in certain significations.	कम्प् 'to tremble.'	गृहीत	ग्रह् 'to take.'
कान्त	कन् 'to shine' and कम् 'to love.'	ग्रथित	ग्रन्थ् 'to tie.'
कुक्त	कुञ्च् 'to be crooked' and कुज् 'to steal.'	ग्लुक्त	ग्लुञ्च् 'to go' and ग्लुच् 'to rob.'
कुथित	कुन्थ् II. 9, 'to afflict.'	घृत	घृण् 'to shine,' and घृ 'to shine,' and 'to sprinkle.'
कृश (*cf.* III.)	कृश् 'to become thin.'	चक्त	चञ्च् 'to hop.'
क्नूत	क्नूय् 'to stink.'		
क्रुक्त	क्रुञ्च् 'to be crooked.'		
क्षत	क्षण् 'to hurt.'		

Participle.	Verb.	Participle.	Verb.
चित	चाय् 'to worship' and चि 'to arrange.'	तृपित तृफित	तृम्प् तृम्फ् } 'to be satisfied.'
चुक्त	चुच्य् 'to express juice.'	°त्त, *cf.* दत्त	
चुन्न	चुन्द् 'to perceive.'	त्राण त्रात	त्रै 'to protect.'
छात and छित	छो 'to cut.'	त्रुपित त्रुफित	त्रुम्प् त्रुम्फ् } 'to hurt.'
छृण्ण	छृद् 'to shine.'	त्वक्त	त्वञ्च् 'to go.'
जग्ध	घस् 'to eat.'	थूर्ण	थुर्व् 'to hurt.'
जात	जन् 'to produce' and जै 'to wane.'	दत्त	दा 'to give' and दे 'to protect.'
जीत	ज्यो 'to restrain.'		
जीन	ज्या 'to become old.'		
जूत	जु 'to hurry,' in the Veda.		
जूर्ण	जुर्व् 'to hurt,' जॄ 'to grow old,' and ज्वर् 'to be feverish.'		
डीन (डीत)	डी 'to fly.'	दब्ध	दम्भ् 'to hurt.'
तक्त	तञ्च् and तञ्ज् 'to contract.'	दरिद्रित	दरिद्रा 'to be in distress.'
तत	तन् 'to stretch.'	दष्ट	दंश् 'to bite.'
तुपित	तुम्प् 'to hurt.'	दित	दो 'to tie.'
तुफित	तुम्फ् 'to hurt.'	दीन	दी 'to go to ruin.'
तूर्त	तुर्व् 'to overcome' in the Veda.	दून	दु 'to suffer pain.'
		दूर्ण	दुर्व् 'to hurt.'
तूर्ण	तुर्व् 'to hurt,' and त्वर् 'to hurry.'	दृढ	दृंह् 'to fasten.'
		दृफित	दृम्फ् 'to hurt.'
तृढ	तृंह् and तृह् 'to hurt.'	द्यूत and द्यून	दिव् 'to play.'
तृण्ण	तृद् 'to hurt.'	धित	धा 'to hold,' in the Veda.
तृत	तृण् 'to eat.'		

After prepositions, ending in vowels, the syllable द may be rejected and then a preceding इ or उ must be lengthened, *e.g.* प्रदत्त or प्रत्त, निदत्त or नीत्त, सुदत्त or सूत्त.

Participle.	Verb.
धीत	धे 'to drink,' and ध्यै 'to think,' in the Veda.
धूर्ण	धुर्व् and धूर् 'to hurt'
धौत	धाव् 'to cleanse.'
ध्यात	ध्यै 'to think.'
ध्वस्त	ध्वंस् 'to fall.'
नग्न 'naked'	नज् 'to be ashamed.'
नत	नम् 'to bow to.'
नद्ध	नह् 'to tie.'
नुत्त and नुन्न	नुद् 'to push on.'
पक्व (*cf.* III.)	पच् 'to cook.'
पीत	पा 'to drink.'
पीन	प्याय् 'to be exuberant.'
पूत	पूय् 'to stink' and पू 'to purify.'
पूर्ण, पूर्त	पूर्, पॄ 'to fill.'
पृष्ट	प्रछ् 'to ask.'
प्यान	पी and प्याय् 'to be exuberant.'
प्रीण (प्रीत)	प्री 'to love.'
प्रौढ	प्र ऽ वह्, *cf.* ऊढ.
प्लीन	प्ली 'to go.'
फाण्ट	फण् 'to go.'
फुल्त and फुल्ल	फल् 'to bear fruit.'
बद्ध	बन्ध् 'to bind.'
बुधित, बुन्न	बुन्ध्, बुन्द् 'to perceive.'

Participle.	Verb.
ब्लीन s. व्लीन.	
भग्न	भञ्ज् 'to break.'
भर्ण	भर्व् 'to injure.'
भुग्न	भुज् 'to bend.'
भृष्ट	भ्रज्ज् 'to fry' and भृंश् 'to fall.'
भ्रष्ट	भ्रंश् 'to fall.'
भ्रीण	भ्री 'to fear.'
मक्त	मञ्च् 'to hold.'
मग्न	मज्ज् 'to dive.'
मचित	मञ्च् 'to hold.'
मत	मन् 'to think.'
मत्त	मद् 'to get drunk.'
मथित	मन्थ् 'to churn.'
मित	मा 'to measure' and मे 'to barter.'
मीन	मी 'to hurt.'
मुक्त	मुञ्च् 'to deceive' and मुच् 'to let loose.'
मूत	मव् and मू 'to bind.'
मूर्ण	मुर्व् 'to tie' and मॄ 'to kill.'
मूर्त	मुर्छ् 'to be faint.'
मृष्ट	मृज् 'to wipe.' मृश् 'to touch,' and मृष् 'to endure patiently.'
म्रुक्त	म्रुञ्च् and म्रुच् 'to go.'
म्लिष्ट	म्लेछ् 'to speak barbarously.'
म्लुक्त	म्लुञ्च् and म्लुच् 'to set.'

Participle.	Verb.
यत	यम् 'to restrain.'
रक्त	रञ्ज् 'to colour.'
रत	रम् 'to rest.'
रिफित	रिम्फ् 'to hurt.'
रुग्ण	रुज् 'to break.'
लगित	लङ्ग् 'to go limpingly.'
लग्न	लग् 'to adhere' and लज् or लज्ज् 'to be ashamed.'
(उद्ऽ) लाघ (cf. III.)	लाघ् 'to be able' or 'equal to.'
लीन	ली 'to adhere.'
लुक्त	लुञ्च् 'to pull out.'
लून	लू 'to cut.'
वक्त	वञ्च् 'to go.'
वत	वन् 'to ask.'
वान	वै 'to become dry.'
विग्न	विज् 'to tremble.'
विचित	व्यच् 'to deceive.'
वित्त, विन्न	विद् 'to gain,' 'to find.'
वीत	व्ये 'to surround.'
वृक्ण	व्रश्च् 'to tear.'
वृत	वृण् 'to eat' and वृ 'to select.'
व्रीण	व्री 'to choose.'
व्लीन (or ब्लीन)	व्ली (or ब्ली) 'to select,' etc.
शयित	शी 'to lie down.'
शस्त	शंस् 'to praise' and शस् 'to hurt.'

Participle.	Verb.
शात	(श्रै 'to cook') and शो 'to sharpen.'
शित	शो and शि 'to sharpen.'
शिष्ट	शास् 'to instruct' and शिष् 'to leave.'
शीत, शीन	श्यै 'to curdle' cf. श्यान.
शुक्त	शुच्य् 'to express juice' and शुच् 'to be pure.'
शुधित	शुन्ध् 'to purify.'
शुभित	शुम्भ् 'to shine.'
शुष्क (cf. III.)	शुष् 'to become dry.'
शून	श्वि 'to swell.'
शृत	श्रा and श्रै 'to cook' cf. श्राण.
श्यान	श्यै 'to curdle.'
श्रथित	श्रन्थ् 'to tie.'
श्रब्ध	श्रम्भ् 'to be careless.'
श्राण	श्रा and श्रै 'to cook.'
ऽषाढ	सह् 'to bear,' in the Veda.
ष्ठ्यूत	ष्ठिव् and ष्ठीव् 'to spit.'
सक्त	सञ्ज् 'to adhere to,' 'to go.'
सचित	सश्च् 'to go.'

Participle.	Verb.	Participle.	Verb.
सत्त in the Veda, सन्न commonly (conform to II.3)	सद् 'to sit.'	स्फीत	स्फाय् 'to swell.'
		स्फूर्ग्ण	स्फुर्ज् 'to thunder.'
		स्फूर्ण	स्फुर्छ् 'to expand.'
		स्यन्न	स्यन्द् 'to ooze.'
		स्यूत	सिव् 'to sew.'
सात	सन् 'to obtain.'	स्रस्त	स्रंस् 'to fall.'
सित	सो 'to destroy' and सि 'to bind.'	स्रिब्ध	स्रिभ् 'to kill.'
		स्रुत	स्रिव् 'to go.'
सिन (सित)	सि 'to bind.'	स्वक्त	स्वज् 'to embrace.'
सिब्ध	सिभ् 'to kill.'	ऽ स्वान्त	स्वन् 'to sound.'
सीत	सै 'to waste.'	स्वूर्ण	स्वुर्छ् 'to expand.'
सुप्त	स्वप् 'to sleep.'		स्वृ 'to injure.'
सृब्ध	सृभ् 'to kill.'	हत	हन् 'to kill.'
सोढ	सह् 'to bear.'	हान	हा 'to go.'
स्कन्न	स्कन्द् 'to ascend.'	हित	धा 'to hold.'
स्कब्ध	स्कभ् 'to make firm.'	हीन	हा 'to leave.'
स्कुब्ध	स्कुभ् 'to make firm.'	हूत	ह्वे 'to call.'
स्तब्ध	स्तभ् 'to make firm.'	ह्वर्ण	हुर्छ् 'to be crooked.'
(प्र ऽ) स्तीत, स्तीम	स्त्यै 'to be collected.'	ह्रीण (ह्रीत)	ह्री 'to be ashamed.'
		ह्रुत	ह्वृ 'to be crooked' in the Veda.
स्तुब्ध	स्तुभ् 'to make firm.'		
स्थित	स्था 'to stand.'	ह्लन्न	ह्लाद् 'to be glad.'

§ 174. The participle of the future of the passive voice is formed by affixing to the verb तव्यं *távya* (or तव्यं *tavyà*), अनीयं *anī́ya*, य *yá*, also with independent svarita *yà*, and without accent *ya* (or त्य *tya*), or एलिमं *elíma*.

These forms have nearly the same signification as the Latin participles in *ndus*, like *amandus*, and imply that the action, which the verb expresses must be done, or is ordered, caused, allowed, deserves to be done.

I. The verbs in taking तव्य *tavya*, follow the rules prescribed in §§ 154, 155, 156 and Exc. 1, § 157, 1, *e.g.*

According to § 154 दातव्यं *dá-távya* (or दातव्यं *dá-tavyà*), 'to be given,' what may or ought to be given,' जेतव्य from जि, स्नातव्य from स्ना, भवितव्य from भू, जरितव्य or जरीतव्य from जॄ, पतितव्य from पत्.

According to § 155 ध्रातव्य from ध्रो, बोधयितव्य from बोधय, causal of बुध्, बेभिद्तिव्य from बेभिद्य, second frequentative of भिद्, नमस्यितव्य or नमसितव्य, from नमस्य, denominative.

According to § 156 जेतव्य from जि, श्वयितव्य from श्वि, स्तोतव्य from स्तु, चवितव्य from चु, भवितव्य from भू, कर्तव्य from कृ, करितव्य or करीतव्य from कॄ, क्ष्वेदितव्य from क्ष्विद्, बोधितव्य from बुध्, पर्चितव्य from पृच्.

According to § 156, Exc. 1 कुचितव्य from कुच्, गुवितव्य from गू, बुबोधिषितव्य, बेभिद्तिव्य.

According to § 157, 1, गन्तव्य from गम्, भेत्तव्य from भिद्, क्रोद्धव्य from क्रुध्, योक्तव्य from युज्, प्रष्टव्य from प्रछ्, लेढव्य from लिह्, दोग्धव्य from दुह्, द्रोढव्य or द्रोग्धव्य from द्रुह् (also द्रोहितव्य), नद्धव्य from नह्, भ्रष्टव्य from भ्रज्ज्, वोढव्य from वह्.

II. Before अनीयं *aníya* and य *ya*:—

1. Final अ of the verb is rejected, *e.g.* लोलूय *lolúya*, second frequentative of लू *lú*, लोलूयनीयं *lolúy-aníya*, लोलूय्यं *lolúy-yà*. The derivative verbs ending in the affix य preceded by a consonant follow before अनीय the rule given in § 56, 3, *e.g.* बेभिद्य, second frequentative of भिद्, बेभिद्नीयं, नमस्य, denominative, नमस्यनीयं or नमसनीयं; before the affix य they reject their final य, *e.g.* बेभिद्यं, नमस्यं. The verbs ending in derivative अय reject this affix, *e.g.* बोधय, causal of बुध्, बोधनीयं, बोध्यं.

2. Before अनीय final ए, ऐ, and ओ are changed to आ and the initial अ of the affix is rejected, *e.g.* धे 'to drink,' धानीय. Before य, these diphthongs as well as final आ are changed to ए, *e.g.* दा, 'to give;' दे, 'to protect;' and दो, 'to cut,' make देयं.

3. Final इ and ई are changed before अनीय to अय्, and before य to ए, *e.g.* चि 'to arrange,' चयनीयं, चेयं, नी नयनीयं, नेयं.

Exception. Two verbs ending in इ take त्य instead of य and leave the vowel unchanged, viz. इ, 'to go,' इत्यं and जि 'to conquer,' जित्यं (but also regularly जेयं), two others ending in इ and one in ई change their finals before the affix य to अय्, *e.g.* क्री 'to buy,' क्रय्यं.

4. Final उ and ऊ are changed to अव्, *e.g.* च्यु 'to move,' च्यवनीयं, च्यव्यं. But when the participle implies 'absolute necessity,' they are changed before य to आव्, *e.g.* भू भाव्यं.

Some verbs ending in उ take त्य instead of य and leave the vowel unchanged, *e.g.* स्तु 'to praise,' स्तुत्यं.

5. Final ऋ and ॠ are changed before अनीय to अर्, before य to आर्, *e.g.* कृ, 'to make,' and कॄ, 'to throw,' करणीयं (§ 16), कार्यं.

Some verbs ending in ऋ take त्य instead of य, before which the vowel remains unchanged, *e.g.* वृ 'to screen,' etc. वृत्यं.

6. इ and उ, followed by a single radical consonant, are changed to ए and ओ (guṇa), *e.g.* छिद्, 'to split,' छेदनीयं, छेद्यं, बुध् बोधनीयं, बोध्यं; ऋ followed by one radical consonant before अनीय, and very rarely before य (*cf.* the anomalies in 8, *e.g.* वर्ष्यं *varshya*) becomes अर् (guṇa), *e.g.* तृप्, 'to be satisfied,' तर्पणीयं (§ 16), but तृप्यं.

Exception to the rules 3-6. The verbs noticed in the Exception to § 141 leave their vowels unchanged, *e.g.* कुचनीयं, बुबोधिषणीयं (§ 16), बेभिद्नीयं, कुच्यं, बुबोधिष्यं, बेभिद्यं. But final *u* before अनीय is changed to *uv*, *e.g.* गुवनीय from गु or गू (against 4).

7. When the affix य is attached,

(*a*) A radical अ, followed by a single radical consonant, except a labial, is lengthened, *e.g.* पद् 'to go,' पाद्यं; but शप् 'to execrate,' शप्यं.

(*b*) The final च् and ज् of those verbs which attach the termination of the participle of the perfect of the passive voice immediately, are changed to क् and ग्, *e.g.* पच् 'to cook' (forming as participle of the perfect passive पक्व, § 173, IV.) makes पाक्यं, युज्

(participle of the perfect passive युक्त) योग्य. But the consonant is left unchanged when the participle implies 'absolute necessity,' *e.g.* पाच्य.

8. Alphabetical List of the most Notable Anomalies of the Participles formed by तव्य, अनीय, य, त्य.

Participle.	Verb.
अर्च्य 'to be praised, revered'	अर्च् 'to praise.'
इत्य	इ 'to go.'
ऽउद्य	वद् 'to speak,' in compounds.
ऊर्णुवितव्य or ऊर्णवितव्य	ऊर्णु 'to cover.'
ऋतीयितव्य or अर्तितव्य ऋतीयनीय or अर्तनीय ऋतीय्य or ऋत्य	ऋत् 'to blame.'
कामयितव्य or कमितव्य कामनीय or कमनीय काम्य	कम् 'to love.'
कुत्य कूय	कु कू } 'to cry.'
कृत्य and regularly कार्य	कृ 'to make.'
क्रष्टव्य and regularly कर्ष्टव्य	कृष् 'to draw.'
क्षवितव्य	क्षु 'to sneeze.'
क्ष्णवितव्य	क्ष्णु 'to sharpen.'
खेय	खन् 'to dig.'
गद्य (after prepositions regularly गाद्य)	गद् 'to speak.'
गुत्य गूय	गु गू } 'to void excrement.'
गूहितव्य or गोढव्य गूहनीय गुह्य or regularly गोह्य	गुह् 'to cover.'
गृह्य (Vedic, commonly, according to the rule, ग्राह्य)	ग्रह् 'to take.'

Participle.	Verb.
गोपायितव्य or गोपितव्य गोपायनीय or गोपनीय गोपाय्य or गोप्य	गुप् 'to protect.'
चत्य	चत् 'to abscond.'
चर्त्य	चृत् 'to connect.'
चर्य (but after prepositions regularly चार्य)	चर् 'to go.'
चातव्य	चाय् 'to worship.'
(उप ऽ) चाय्य	चि 'to arrange.'
जन्य and जान्य	जन् 'to bring forth.'
जित्य and जेय	जि 'to conquer.'
जुष्य	जुष् 'to be pleased.'
डयितव्य	डी 'to fly.'
तक्य	तक् 'to endure.'
त्याज्य	त्यज् 'to abandon.'
त्राप्य	त्रप् 'to be ashamed.'
दरिद्रितव्य दरिद्र्य	दरिद्रा 'to be in distress.'
दातव्य दानीय	दी 'to go to ruin,' of course also from दा, दे, दो.
दाभ्य or regularly दम्भ्य	दम्भ् 'to hurt.'
दीधितव्य दीध्यनीय दीध्य	दीधी 'to shine.'
दुह्य or regularly दोह्य	दुह् 'to milk.'
दृत्य	दृ 'to respect.'
द्रष्टव्य	दृश् 'to see.'
धूपायितव्य or धूपितव्य धूपायनीय or धूपनीय धूपाय्य or धूप्य	धूप् 'to fumigate.'

Participle.	Verb.
धूय	धू 'to shake.'
ध्रुत्य	ध्रु 'to stand firm.'
नंष्टव्य	नश् 'to perish.'
(उद्ऽ) नीय	नी 'to lead.'
नुत्य नूय	नु नू } 'to praise.'
पणायितव्य or पणितव्य पणायनीय or पणनीय पणाय्य or पण्य	पण् 'to praise.'
पनायितव्य or पनितव्य पनायनीय or पननीय पनाय्य or पन्य	पन् 'to praise.'
प्यातव्य	प्याय् 'to be exuberant.'
भज्य and regularly भाग्य	भज् 'to divide.'
भर्ष्टव्य or भ्रष्टव्य भर्ज्जनीय or भ्रज्जनीय भर्ज्ज्य or भ्रज्ज्य	भ्रज्ज् 'to fry.'
भृत्य and regularly भार्य	भृ 'to bear.'
भोज्य when the verb signifies 'to eat,' otherwise regularly भोग्य	भुज् 'to eat,' 'to enjoy.'
मङ्क्तव्य	मज्ज् 'to dive.'
मद्य (but with prepositions regularly माद्य)	मद् 'to get drunk.'
मातव्य मानीय	मी 'to hurt,' of course also from मा 'to measure,' and मे 'to barter.'
मार्ग्य and मृज्य मार्ष्टव्य and मार्जितव्य मार्जनीय	मृज् 'to wipe.'
म्रष्टव्य or मर्ष्टव्य	मृश् 'to touch.'
यज्य (Vedic, and याज्य)	यज् 'to sacrifice.'

Participle.	Verb.
यत्य	यत् 'to endeavour.'
यवितव्य	यु 'to bind.'
याज्य *cf.* यज्य.	
याव्य after the preposition आ	यु 'to bind.'
युग्य	युज् 'to join.'
योज्य after the prepositions नि and प्र	युज् 'to join.'
राप्य	रप् 'to sound.'
लम्भ्य and regularly लभ्य	लभ् 'to obtain.'
लातव्य, लानीय and regularly लेतव्य, लयनीय	ली 'to adhere.'
लाप्य	लप् 'to speak.'
वद्य (*cf.* उद्य)	वद् 'to speak.'
वरितव्य or वरीतव्य	वृ 'to select,' etc.
वर्ष्य or वृष्य	वृष् 'to rain.'
वाच्य	वच् 'to speak.'
विच्छायितव्य or विच्छितव्य, विच्छायनीय or विच्छनीय, विच्छाय्य or विच्छ्य	विच्छ् 'to go.'
वृत्य or वार्य	वृ 'to select,' etc.
वोढव्य	वह् 'to bear.'
शक्य	शक् 'to be able.'
शयितव्य	शी 'to lie down.'
शस्य and शंस्य	शंस् 'to praise.'
शिष्य	शास् 'to instruct.'
श्रयितव्य	श्रि 'to go.'
सह्य	सह् 'to endure.'
ऽसाव्य after the preposition आ	सु 'to beget.'
सृज्य, but सर्ग्य after the prepositions अव and सम्	सृज् 'to abandon.'
सोढव्य	सह् 'to endure.'
स्प्रष्टव्य or स्पर्ष्टव्य	स्पृश् 'to touch.'
स्फातव्य	स्फाय् 'to swell.'

Participle.	Verb.
सप्तव्य or सर्प्तव्य	सृप् 'to go.'
स्रवितव्य	स्रु 'to flow.'
स्रष्टव्य	सृज् 'to abandon.'

ABSOLUTIVES FORMED BY त्वा *tvā́*, य *ya* (त्य *tya*), AND अम् *am*.

§ 175. These forms generally denote that the action which the verb expresses has been done, and that some other action follows it. Thus in the sentence 'having eaten he sleeps,' the words 'having eaten' are expressed by the absolutive.

§ 176. The verbs without a preposition, or words treated like prepositions, (§§ 189, 190), affix in the absolutive त्वा *tvā́*; those which are compounded with prepositions, etc., य *ya*, or when they end in a short vowel, त्य *tya*, *e.g.* भू *bhū́* makes भूत्वा *bhū́-tvā́*, जि *ji* जित्वा *ji-tvā́*, प्र + भू प्रभूय *pra-bhū́-ya*, सम् + जि संजित्य, *sañ-ji-tya*.

§ 177. The affix त्वा is subjoined immediately to nearly all the primitive verbs ending in vowels or diphthongs, *e.g.* ज्ञा 'to know,' ज्ञात्वा, जि जित्वा, नी नीत्वा, यु युत्वा, भू भूत्वा, कृ कृत्वा.

Final ऋ becomes ईर्, and after labials and व्, ऊर्, *e.g.* तॄ, 'to cross,' तीर्त्वा; पॄ, 'to fill,' पूर्त्वा.

Final diphthongs are changed to आ, *e.g.* दै 'to purify,' दात्वा.

Further, त्वा is immediately subjoined also to many primitive verbs ending in consonants (*cf.* my V.G. § 914, I. and Ausnahme and Bemerkung), and the finals of such verbs undergo the same changes as before the affix of the participle of the perfect in the passive त (§ 173, I. 1), *e.g.* क्रम् क्रान्त्वा, मद् मत्त्वा, सिध् सिद्ध्वा, लभ् 'to obtain,' लब्ध्वा; पच् 'to cook,' पक्त्वा; युज् युक्त्वा, तच् तक्त्वा, सृप् सृप्त्वा, लिह् लीढ्वा, दुह् दुग्ध्वा, मृज् मृष्ट्वा, मुह् मूढ्वा, or मुग्ध्वा. Final इव् is changed to यू, *e.g.* दिव् 'to play,' द्यूत्वा.

The greater number of the primitive verbs with final consonants and some of those which end in इ, ई, ऊ, or ॠ, and all the derivative verbs, insert इ, *e.g.* पत् पतित्वा.

When इ is inserted :—

1. Final इ and ई are changed to अय्, ऊ to अव्, ॠ to अर् (guṇa), *e.g.* पू, 'to purify,' पवित्वा (or without इ, पूत्वा).

2. Penultimate ऋ is changed to अर्, *e.g.* पृच्, 'to mix,' पर्चित्वा.

3. The verbs ending in इव् change इ to ए, *e.g.* दिव् देवित्वा (or द्यूत्वा, as observed before).

4. Other verbs with penultimate इ or उ may optionally change them to ए and ओ (guṇa), *e.g.* लिख्, 'to write,' लेखित्वा, or लिखित्वा, द्युत्, 'to sparkle,' द्योतित्वा, or द्युतित्वा. When इ and उ at the same time are the initial letters of the verb, they must be changed to ए and ओ, *e.g.* इष्, 'to wish,' एषित्वा (also without इ, इष्ट्वा). The verbs noticed in the exception to § 141 leave their इ and उ unchanged, *e.g.* कुचित्वा, *cf.* 5.

5. Final अ is rejected, *e.g.* लोलूय लोलूयित्वा, बुबोधिष बुबोधिषित्वा, बोधय बोधयित्वा, and the rule given in § 56, 3 applies also here, *e.g.* बेभिद्य, second frequentative of भिद्, makes बेभिद्त्वा, नमस्य, denominative, नमस्यित्वा, or नमसित्वा.

6. The anomalous changes which some verbs undergo before the affix त्वा, are similar to those which occur in the perfect participle of the passive voice (§ 173, IV.). In fact, when the termination is attached immediately, this absolutive may be formed from many anomalous verbs by simply substituting त्वा for त or न of the perfect participle. Thus यज् makes in the perfect participle इष्ट, in the absolutive इष्ट्वा ; वे उत, उत्वा ; तॄ तीर्ण, तीर्त्वा ; दा दत्त, दत्त्वा ; पा, 'to drink,' पीत, पीत्वा ; धा हित, हित्वा ; हन् हत, हत्वा.

This analogy however does not extend to the verbs with penultimate nasal. The rejection of the nasal is optional in the absolutive, *e.g.* अञ्ज् in the perfect participle अक्त, but in the absolutive अङ्क्त्वा or अक्त्वा.

In the verbs मज्ज् 'to dive,' and नश् 'to perish,' a nasal is optionally inserted before the last letter, *e.g.* मक्त्वा, or मङ्क्त्वा, नष्ट्वा, or नंष्ट्वा.

मृज् forms मार्जित्वा or मृष्ट्वा, रध् रन्धित्वा.

Observation. In the Veda the affixes त्वायं *tvâya*, त्वी *tvî*, त्वानंम् *tvânam*, and त्वीनंम् *tvînam*, sometimes are substituted for त्वा, *e.g.* गम् गन्त्वायं, पा 'to drink,' पीत्वी, पीत्वानंम्, यज् इष्ट्वीनंम्.

§ 178. Before the affix य (§ 176) a radical ऋ is changed to ईर् and, when preceded by labials or व्, to ऊर्. Final ए, ऐ, and ओ are changed to आ. Final अ and the affix अय of the causals, verbs of the tenth conjugational class, and denominatives in अय are rejected, likewise the affix य of the second frequentative and of denominatives when preceded by a consonant, *e.g.*

प्र + तॄ	makes	प्रतीर्य
प्र + पॄ	„	प्रपूर्य
प्र + दे	„	प्रदाय
प्र + ग्लै	„	प्रग्लाय
प्र + लोलूय, second frequentative of लू,	„	प्रलोलूय्य
प्र + बोधय, causal of बुध्	„	प्रबोध्य
प्र + बेभिद्य, second frequentative of भिद्,	„	प्रबेभिद्य
प्र + नमस्य, denominative, ...	„	प्रनमस्य.

Radical इ and उ, when followed by radical र् or व्, are lengthened, *e.g.* प्र + दिव् प्रदीव्य.

Exc. Derivative verbs ending in the affix अय, viz. causals, verbs of the tenth conjugational class, and denominatives in अय reject only the final अ, when अय is preceded by a single consonant with अ before it, *e.g*, प्र + कथय (tenth conjug. cl.) प्रकथय्य.

§ 179. ALPHABETICAL LIST OF ANOMALOUS FORMS.

Observation. The sign ꣱ indicates that the following forms can be used only when the verb is compounded with a preposition:—

Absolutive.	Verb.
ऽआपय्य (also regularly ऽआप्य)	आपय causal of आप् 'to reach.'
ऽइज्य	यज् 'to sacrifice.'
ऽउच्य	वच् 'to speak.'
ऽउद्य	वद् 'to speak.'
ऽउप्य	वप् 'to sow.'
ऽउश्य	वश् 'to desire.'
ऽउष्य	वस् 'to dwell.'
ऽऋतीय्य or ऽऋत्य	ऋत् 'to blame.'
ऽऋत्य	ऋण् and ऋ 'to go.'
ऽक्षत्य	क्षण् 'to wound.'
ऽक्षित्य	क्षिण् 'to hurt.'
ऽक्षीय	क्षि 'to destroy.'
ऽखाय (or खन्य)	खन् 'to dig.'
ऽगत्य (or गम्य)	गम् 'to go.'
ऽगृह्य	ग्रह् 'to seize.'
ऽगोपाय्य (or गुप्य)	गुप् 'to protect.'
ऽघृत्य	घृण् 'to shine,' and घृ 'to shine' and 'sprinkle.'
ऽजागर्य	जागृ 'to wake.'
ऽजाय (or जन्य)	जन् 'to bring forth.'
ऽतत्य	तन् 'to stretch.'
ऽतृत्य	तृण् 'to eat.'
ऽदाय	दी 'to go to ruin.'
ऽधूपाय्य (धूप्य)	धूप् 'to fumigate.'
ऽनत्य (or नम्य)	नम् 'to bow to.'
ऽपणाय्य (or पण्य)	पण् 'to praise.'
ऽपनाय्य (or पन्य)	पन् 'to praise.'
ऽपृच्छ्य	प्रछ् 'to ask.'
ऽप्लूय, in the Veda	प्लु 'to swim.'
ऽभृज्ज्य	भ्रज्ज् 'to fry.'
ऽमत्य	मन् 'to think.'

Absolutive.	Verb.
ऽ माय	मि 'to throw,' and मी 'to hurt' (of course also from मा 'to measure,' and मे 'to barter').
ऽ मित्य (or माय)	मे 'to barter.'
ऽ यत्य	यम् 'to restrain.'
ऽ यूय, in the Veda.	यु 'to bind.'
ऽ रत्य	रम् 'to rest.'
ऽ लम्भ्य, only after the preposition आ and sometimes after उप, otherwise regularly लभ्य . . .	लभ् 'to obtain.'
ऽ लाय (or लीय)	ली 'to adhere.'
ऽ वत्य	वन् 'to desire.'
ऽ विच्य	व्यच् 'to deceive.'
ऽ विच्छाय्य (or विछ्य)	विछ् 'to go.'
ऽ विध्य	व्यध् 'to pierce.'
ऽ वीय, optionally after the prepositions परि and सम्; otherwise regularly व्याय	व्ये 'to surround.'
ऽ वृश्च्य	व्रश्च् 'to tear.'
ऽ वृत्य	वृण् 'to eat' and वृ 'to select,' etc.
ऽ शय्य	शी 'to lie down.'
ऽ शिष्य	शास् 'to teach.'
ऽ शूय	श्वि 'to swell.'
ऽ साय (or सन्य)	सन् 'to obtain.'
ऽ सुप्य	स्वप् 'to sleep.'
ऽ हत्य	हन् 'to kill.'
ऽ हूय	ह्वे 'to call.'

The verbs which are enumerated in my V.G. § 154, 2, 2, reject their penultimate nasal, *e.g.* स्तम्भ् 'to stop,' विष्टभ्य (*cf.* § 17).

§ 180. Before the affix अम् *am* the verb undergoes the same changes as before the termination इ *i* of the third person singular of the passive aorist (*cf.* § 166). Thus दा 'to give,' दे 'to protect,' दै 'to purify,' and दो 'to cut,' make in the third person singular of the passive aorist अदायि, in the absolutive दायम्, जि अजायि, जायम्, नु अनावि, नावम्, कृ and कॄ अकारि, कारम्, पत् अपाति, पातम्, छिद् अच्छेदि, छेदम्, तुद् अतोदि, तोदम्, दृश् अदर्शि, दर्शम्. For some exceptions see my V.G. § 916.

Generally this absolutive is repeated, whereupon the second word rejects its accent and is compounded with the first. The compound then signifies 'having performed repeatedly the action which the verb implies,' *e.g.* चायंचायम्, from चि 'to arrange, collect,' 'having arranged or collected repeatedly.'

INFINITIVE.

§ 181. The infinitive is formed by attaching to the verb the affix तुम् *tum*, before which the verb undergoes the same modifications as before the affix of the first active future, तास्मि, etc.

Thus according to § 154 दा makes दातुम् *dā́-tum*, जि जेतुम्, ग्लै ग्लातुम्, भू भवितुम्, जॄ जरितुम् or जरीतुम्, पत् पतितुम्. According to § 155 ग्लौ ग्लातुम्, बोधय बोधयितुम्, बेभिद्य बेभिदितुम्, नमस्य, denominative, नमस्यितुम् or नमसितुम्.

According to § 156 जि makes जेतुम्, but श्वि श्वयितुम्, स्तु स्तोतुम्, but क्षु क्षवितुम्, भू भवितुम्, कृ कर्तुम्, कॄ करितुम् or करीतुम्, क्लिद् क्लेदितुम्, बुध् बोधितुम्, पृच् पर्चितुम्. According to Exc. 1 कुच् कुचितुम्, बुबोधिष बुबोधिषितुम्, बेभिद्य बेभिदितुम्.

According to § 157, 1, गम् makes गन्तुम्, भिद् भेत्तुम्, क्रुध् क्रोद्धुम्, युज् योक्तुम्, प्रछ् प्रष्टुम्, लिह् लेढुम्, दुह् दोग्धुम्, द्रुह् द्रोढुम् or द्रोग्धुम् (also with inserted इ, द्रोहितुम्), नह् नद्धुम्, भ्रज्ज् भ्रष्टुम्, वह् वोढुम्.

The anomalies are similar to those which occur in the first future, *cf.* § 160, *e.g.* ऊर्णुवितुम् or ऊर्णवितुम् in analogy with the first future Parasm. ऊर्णुवितास्मि or ऊर्णवितास्मि, ऋतीयितुम् or अर्तितुम्, etc.

§ 182. Further, the dative singular of any primitive abstract noun may be used in the sense of the infinitive, *e.g.* इष्टये dative of इष्टि 'the wish,' properly 'to the wish,' in the sense of 'to wish.'

§ 183. In the Veda infinitives are formed also by the affixes :—

तवे *tave, e.g.* कर्तवे from कृ 'to make.'

तोस् *tos, e.g.* स्थातोस् from स्था 'to stand.'

तवै *tavái, e.g.* पातवै *pātavái*, from पा, 'to drink.'

अम् *am, e.g.* आरुहम् from रुह् 'to mount,' with the preposition आ.

ए *é, e.g.* दृशे from दृश् 'to see.'

अस् *as, e.g.* विलिखस् from लिख् 'to write,' with the preposition वि.

ऐ *ái, e.g.* प्रख्यै from ख्या 'to speak,' with the preposition प्र.

स्यै *syai, e.g.* रोहिष्यै from रुह् 'to mount.'

से *se, e.g.* वक्षे from वह् 'to bear.'

असे *ase, e.g.* चयसे from चि 'to arrange.'

अध्यै *adhyai*, or with accent on the penultimate *ádhyai, e.g.* यजध्यै from यज् 'to sacrifice;' दुहध्यै from दुह् 'to milk.'

cf. my V.G. § 919.

TABLE OF CONJUGATION.

	Active.		Passive.
	Parasmaipada.	Âtmanepada.	
	PRESENT.		
S. 1.	*bódhâmi*, I know	*bódhe*, I know	*budhyé*, I am known
2.	*bódhasi*, thou knowest	*bódhase*, thou knowest	*budhyáse*, thou art known
3.	*bódhati*, he knows	*bódhate*	*budhyáte*, he is known
D. 1.	*bódhâvas*, we two know	*bódhâvahe*	*budhyấvahe*, we two are known
2.	*bódhathas*, you two know	*bódhethe*	*budhyéthe*, you two are known
3.	*bódhatas*, they two know	*bódhete*	*budhyéte*, they two are known
P. 1.	*bódhâmas*, we know	*bódhâmahe*	*budhyấmahe*, we are known
2.	*bódhatha*, you know	*bódhadhve*	*budhyádhve*, you are known
3.	*bódhanti*, they know	*bódhante*	*budhyánte*, they are known
	PRESENT PARTICIPLE.		
	bódhant, knowing	*bódhamâna*, knowing	*budhyámâna*, being known
	IMPERFECT.		
S. 1.	*ábodham*, I knew	*ábodhe*, I knew	*ábudhye*, I was known
2.	*ábodhas*	*ábodhathâs*	*ábudhyathâs*
3.	*ábodhat*	*ábodhata*	*ábudhyata*
D. 1.	*ábodhâva*	*ábodhâvahi*	*ábudhyâvahi*
2.	*ábodhatam*	*ábodhethâm*	*ábudhyethâm*
3.	*ábodhatâm*	*ábodhetâm*	*ábudhyetâm*
P. 1.	*ábodhâma*	*ábodhâmahi*	*ábudhyâmahi*
2.	*ábodhata*	*ábodhadhvam*	*ábudhyadhvam*
3.	*ábodhan*	*ábodhanta*	*ábudhyanta*
	POTENTIAL.		
S. 1.	*bódheyam*, I may, or I might know	*bódheya*, I may know	*budhyéya*, I may be known
2.	*bódhes*	*bódhethâs*	*budhyéthâs*
3.	*bódhet*	*bódheta*	*budhyéta*
D. 1.	*bódheva*	*bódhevahi*	*budhyévahi*
2.	*bódhetam*	*bódheyâthâm*	*budhyéyâthâm*
3.	*bódhetâm*	*bódheyâtâm*	*budhyéyâtâm*
P. 1.	*bódhema*	*bódhemahi*	*budhyémahi*
2.	*bódheta*	*bódhedhvam*	*budhyédhvam*
3.	*bódheyus*	*bódheran*	*budhyéran*

	Active.		Passive.
	Parasmaipada.	Âtmanepada.	
	IMPERATIVE.		
S. 1.	*bódhâni*, may I know	*bódhai*, may I know	*budhyái*, may I be known
2.	*bódha* or *bódhatât*	*bódhasva*	*budhyásva*
3.	*bódhatu* or *bódhatât*	*bódhatâm*	*budhyátâm*
D. 1.	*bódhâva*	*bódhâvahai*	*budhyấvahai*
2.	*bódhatam*	*bódhethâm*	*budhyéthâm*
3.	*bódhatâm*	*bódhetâm*	*budhyétâm*
P. 1.	*bódhâma*	*bódhâmahai*	*budhyấmahai*
2.	*bódhata* or *bódhatât*	*bódhadhvam*	*budhyádhvam*
3.	*bódhantu*	*bódhantâm*	*budhyántâm*
	PERFECT.		
S. 1.	*bubódha*, I have known	*bubudhé*, I have known	*bubudhé*, I have been known, etc., like the Âtmanepada
2.	*bubodhitha*	*bubudhishé*	
3.	*bubódha*	*bubudhé*	
D. 1.	*bubudhivá*	*bubudhiváhe*	
2.	*bubudháthus*	*bubudhấthe*	
3.	*bubudhátus*	*bubudhấte*	
P. 1.	*bubudhimá*	*bubudhimáhe*	
2.	*bubudhá*	*bubudhidhvé*	
3.	*bubudhús*	*bubudhiré*	

PARTICIPLE OF THE PERFECT.

Parasmaipada	Âtmanepada	Passive
bubudhvát, etc., *cf.* §§ 169, and 221 V., having known	*bubudhâná*, having known	*budhitá*, known

budhitávant, having known

	Active.		Passive.
	Parasmaipada.	Âtmanepada.	

AORIST OF THE SECOND FORM.

S. 1.	*ábudham,* I had known	*ábudhe,* I had known	*ábudhe,* I had been known
2.	*ábudhas*	*ábudhathâs*	*ábudhathâs*
3.	*ábudhat*	*ábudhata*	*ábodhi*
D. 1.	*ábudhâva*	*ábudhâvahi*	*ábudhâvahi,* etc., like the Âtmanepada
2.	*ábudhatam*	*ábudhethâm*	
3.	*ábudhatâm*	*ábudhetâm*	
P. 1.	*ábudhâma*	*ábudhâmahi*	
2.	*ábudhata*	*ábudhadhvam*	
3.	*ábudhan*	*ábudhanta*	

AORIST OF THE FIFTH FORM.

S. 1.	*ábodhisham,* I had known	*ábodhishi,* I had known	*ábodhishi,* I had been known
2.	*ábodhîs*	*ábodhishṭhâs*	*ábodhishṭhâs*
3.	*ábodhît*	*ábodhishṭa*	*ábodhi*
D. 1.	*ábodhishva*	*ábodhishvahi*	*ábodhishvahi,* etc., like the Âtmanepada
2.	*ábodhishṭam*	*ábodhishâthâm*	
3.	*ábodhishṭâm*	*ábodhishâtâm*	
P. 1.	*ábodhishma*	*ábodhishmahi*	
2.	*ábodhishṭa*	*ábodhidhvam*	
3.	*ábodhishus*	*ábodhishata*	

FUTURE I.

S. 1.	*bodhitásmi,* I shall know	*bodhitáhe,* I shall know	*bodhitáhe,* I shall be known, etc., like the Âtmanepada
2.	*bodhitási*	*bodhitáse*	
3.	*bodhitá*	*bodhitá*	
D. 1.	*bodhitásvas*	*bodhitásvahe*	
2.	*bodhitásthas*	*bodhitásâthe*	
3.	*bodhitárau*	*bodhitárau*	
P. 1.	*bodhitásmas*	*bodhitásmahe*	
2.	*bodhitástha*	*bodhitádhve*	
3.	*bodhitáras*	*bodhitáras*	

	Active. Parasmaipada.	Active. Âtmanepada.	Passive.
	FUTURE II.		
S. 1.	*bodhishyā́mi*, I shall [know	*bodhishyé*, I shall [know	*bodhishyé*, I shall be known, etc., like the Âtmanepada
2.	*bodhishyási*	*bodhishyáse*	
3.	*bodhishyáti*	*bodhishyáte*	
D. 1.	*bodhishyā́vas*	*bodhishyā́vahe*	
2.	*bodhishyáthas*	*bodhishyéthe*	
3.	*bodhishyátas*	*bodhishyéte*	
P. 1.	*bodhishyā́mas*	*bodhishyā́mahe*	
2.	*bodhishyátha*	*bodhishyádhve*	
3.	*bodhishyánti*	*bodhishyánte*	

PARTICIPLE OF THE FUTURE.

Parasmaipada	Âtmanepada	Passive
bodhishyánt, what will know	*bodhishyámâṇa*, what will know	*bódhya*, or *bodhanī́ya*, or *bodhitávya*, what is or ought to be known

CONDITIONAL.

	Parasmaipada	Âtmanepada	Passive
S. 1.	*ábodhishyam*, I should know	*ábodhishye*, I should know	*ábodhishye*, I should be known, etc., like the Âtmanepada
2.	*ábodhishyas*	*ábodhishyathâs*	
3.	*ábodhishyat*	*ábodhishyata*	
D. 1.	*ábodhishyâva*	*ábodhishyâvahi*	
2.	*ábodhishyatam*	*ábodhishyethâm*	
3.	*ábodhishyatâm*	*ábodhishyetâm*	
P. 1.	*ábodhishyâma*	*ábodhishyâmahi*	
2.	*ábodhishyata*	*ábodhishyadhvam*	
3.	*ábodhishyan*	*ábodhishyanta*	

PRECATIVE.

	Parasmaipada	Âtmanepada	Passive
S. 1.	*budhyā́sam*, I pray, I may know	*bodhishī́yá*, I pray, I may know	*bodhishī́yá*, I pray, I may be known, etc., like the Âtmanepada
2.	*budhyā́s*	*bodhishī́shṭhā́s*	
3.	*budhyā́t*	*bodhishī́shṭá*	
D. 1.	*budhyā́sva*	*bodhishī́váhi*	
2.	*budhyā́stum*	*bodhishī́yā́sthâm*	
3.	*budhyā́stâm*	*bodhishī́yā́stâm*	
P. 1.	*budhyā́sma*	*bodhishī́máhi*	
2.	*budhyā́sta*	*bodhishī́dhvám*	
3.	*budhyā́sus*	*bodhishī́rán*	

ABSOLUTIVE.

budhitvā́, or *bodhitvā́*, having known and having been known

INFINITIVE.

bódhitum, to know

FREQUENTATIVE.

	First Form.		Second Form.	
	Active.	Passive.	Active.	Passive.
	PRESENT.			
S. 1.	*bóbodhmi,* I know repeatedly or *bóbudhî́mi*	*bobudhyé,* I am known repeatedly	*bobudhyé,* I know repeatedly	*bobudhyé,* I am known repeatedly, etc., like the Passive of the first form
2.	*bóbhotsi* or *bóbudhî́shi*	*bobudhyáse*	*bobudhyáse*	
3.	*bóboddhi* or *bóbudhî́ti*	*bobudhyáte*	*bobudhyáte*	
D. 1.	*bobudhvás*	*bobudhyấvahe*	*bobudhyấvahe*	
2.	*bobuddhás*	*bobudhyéthe*	*bobudhyéthe*	
3.	*bobuddhás*	*bobudhyéte*	*bobudhyéte*	
P. 1.	*bobudhmás*	*bobudhyấmahe*	*bobudhyấmahe*	
2.	*bobuddhá*	*bobudhyádhve*	*bobudhyádhve*	
3.	*bóbudhati*	*bobudhyánte*	*bobudhyánte*	
	PRESENT PARTICIPLE.			
	bóbudhat, knowing repeatedly	*bobudhyámâna,* being known repeatedly	*bobudhyámâna,* knowing repeatedly	*bobudhyámâna,* being known repeatedly
	IMPERFECT.			
S. 1.	*ábobudham,* I knew repeatedly	*ábobudhye,* I was known repeatedly	*ábobudhye,* I knew repeatedly	*ábobudhye,* I was known repeatedly, etc., like the Passive of the first form
2.	*ábobhot* or *ábobudhî́s*	*ábobudhyathâs*	*ábobudhyathâs*	
3.	*ábobhot* or *ábobudhî́t*	*ábobudhyata*	*ábobudhyata*	
D. 1.	*ábobudhva*	*ábobudhyâvahi*	*ábobudhyâvahi*	
2.	*ábobuddham*	*ábobudhyethâm*	*ábobudhyethâm*	
3.	*ábobuddhâm*	*ábobudhyetâm*	*ábobudhyetâm*	
P. 1.	*ábobudhma*	*ábobudhyâmahi*	*ábobudhyâmahi*	
2.	*ábobuddha*	*ábobudhyadhvam*	*ábobudhyadhvam*	
3.	*ábobudhus*	*ábobudhyanta*	*ábobudhyanta*	

	First Form.		Second Form.	
	Active.	Passive.	Active.	Passive.
	POTENTIAL.			
S. 1.	*bobudhyā́m*, I may know repeatedly	*bobudhyéya*, I may be known repeatedly	*bobudhyéya*, I may know repeatedly	*bobudhyéya*, I may be known repeatedly, etc., like the Passive of the first form
2.	*bobudhyā́s*	*bobudhyéthâs*	*bobudhyéthâs*	
3.	*bobudhyā́t*	*bobudhyéta*	*bobudhyéta*	
D. 1.	*bobudhyā́va*	*bobudhyévahi*	*bobudhyévahi*	
2.	*bobudhyā́tam*	*bobudhyéyâthâm*	*bobudhyéyâthâm*	
3.	*bobudhyā́tâm*	*bobudhyéyâtâm*	*bobudhyéyâtâm*	
P. 1.	*bobudhyā́ma*	*bobudhyémahi*	*bobudhyémahi*	
2.	*bobudhyā́ta*	*bobudhyédhvam*	*bobudhyédhvam*	
3.	*bobudhyús*	*bobudhyéran*	*bobudhyéran*	
	IMPERATIVE.			
S. 1.	*bóbudhâni*, may I know repeatedly	*bobudhyái*, may I be known repeatedly	*bobudhyái*, may I know repeatedly	*bobudhyái*, may I be known repeatedly, etc., like the Passive of the first form
2.	*bobuddhí* or *bobuddhā́t*	*bobudhyásva*	*bobudhyásva*	
3.	*bóboddhu* or *bóbudhîtu* or *bobuddhā́t*	*bobudhyátâm*	*bobudhyátâm*	
D. 1.	*bóbudhâva*	*bobudhyā́vahai*	*bobudhyā́vahai*	
2.	*bobuddhám*	*bobudhyéthâm*	*bobudhyéthâm*	
3.	*bobuddhā́m*	*bobudhyétâm*	*bobudhyétâm*	
P. 1.	*bóbudhâma*	*bobudhyā́mahai*	*bobudhyā́mahai*	
2.	*bobuddhá* or *bobuddhā́t*	*bobudhyádvam*	*bobudhyádhvam*	
3.	*bóbudhatu*	*bobudhyántâm*	*bobudhyántâm*	

PERFECT.

First Form. Active.

S. 1.	*bobudhâm̃*	*chakara* or *chakâra*, or *âsa*, or *babhûva*, I have known repeatedly
2.		*chakartha, âsitha, babhûvitha*
3.		*chakâra, âsa, babhûva*
D. 1.		*chakṛiva, âsiva, babhûviva*
2.		*chakrathus, âsathus, babhûvathus*
3.		*chakratus, âsatus, babhûvatus*
P. 1.		*chakṛima, âsima, babhûvima*
2.		*chakra, âsa, babhûva*
3.		*chakrus, âsus, babhûvus*

First Form. Passive.

S. 1.	*bobudhâm̃*	*chakre, âse, babhûve*, I have been known repeatedly
2.		*chakṛishe, âsishe, babhûvishe*
3.		*chakre, âse, babhûve*
D. 1.		*chakṛivahe, âsivahe, babhûvivahe*
2.		*chakrâthe, âsâthe, babhûvâthe*
3.		*chakrâte, âsâte, babhûvâte*
P. 1.		*chakṛimahe, âsimahe, babhûvimahe*
2.		*chakṛiḍhve, âsidhve, babhûvidhve* or *babhûviḍhve*
3.		*chakrire, âsire, babhûvire*

Second Form. Active.

S. 1.	*bobudhâm̃*	*chakre, âsa, babhûva*, I have known repeatedly
2.		*chakṛishe, âsitha, babhûvitha*
3.		*chakre, âsa, babhûva*
D. 1.		*chakṛivahe, âsiva, babhûviva*
2.		*chakrâthe, âsathus, babhûvathus*
3.		*chakrâte, âsatus, babhûvatus*
P. 1.		*chakṛimahe, âsima, babhûvima*
2.		*chakṛiḍhve, âsa, babhûva*
3.		*chakrire, âsus, babhûvus*

Passive like the Passive of the first form.

PARTICIPLE OF THE PERFECT.

Active.	Passive.	Active.	Passive.
bobudhâm̃chakṛivat, âsivat, babhûvat, etc., (*cf.* § 169), having known repeatedly	*bobudhitá*, being known repeatedly	*bobudhâm̃chakrâṇa* or *âsivat* or *babhûvat*, etc. (*cf.* § 169), having known repeatedly	*bobudhitá*, being known repeatedly
bobudhitávant, having known repeatedly		*bobudhitávant*, having known repeatedly	

	First Form. Active.	First Form. Passive.	Second Form. Active.
		AORIST.	
S. 1.	*ábobudhisham*, I had known repeatedly	*ábobudhishi*, I had been known repeatedly	*ábobudhishi*, I had known repeatedly
2.	*ábobudhîs*	*ábobudhishṭhâs*	*ábobudhishṭhâs*
3.	*ábobudhît*	*ábobudhi*	*ábobudhishṭa*
D. 1.	*ábobudhishva*	*ábobudhishvahi*	*ábobudhishvahi*
2.	*ábobudhishṭam*	*ábobudhishâthâm*	*ábobudhishâthâm*
3.	*ábobudhishṭâm*	*ábobudhishâtâm*	*ábobudhishâtâm*
P. 1.	*ábobudhishma*	*ábobudhishmahi*	*ábobudhishmahi*
2.	*ábobudhishṭa*	*ábobudhidhvam*	*ábobudhidhvam*
3.	*ábobudhishus*	*ábobudhishata*	*ábobudhishata*
			[Passive like the Passive of the first form.
		FUTURE I.	
S. 1.	*bobudhitấsmi*, I shall know repeatedly	*bobudhitấhe*, I shall be known repeatedly	*bobudhitấhe*, I shall know repeatedly
2.	*bobudhitấsi*	*bobudhitấse*	*bobudhitấse*
3.	*bobudhitấ*	*bobudhitấ*	*bobudhitấ*
D. 1.	*bobudhitấsvas*	*bobudhitấsvahe*	*bobudhitấsvahe*
2.	*bobudhitấsthas*	*bobudhitấsâthe*	*bobudhitấsâthe*
3.	*bobudhitấrau*	*bobudhitấrau*	*bobudhitấrau*
P. 1.	*bobudhitấsmas*	*bobudhitấsmahe*	*bobudhitấsmahe*
2.	*bobudhitấstha*	*bobudhitấdhve*	*bobudhitấdhve*
3.	*bobudhitấras*	*bobudhitấras*	*bobudhitấras*
			[Passive like the Passive of the first form.
		FUTURE II.	
S. 1.	*bobudhishyấmi*, I shall know repeatedly	*bobudhishyé*, I shall be known repeatedly	*bobudhishyé*, I shall know repeatedly
2.	*bobudhishyási*	*bobudhishyáse*	*bobudhishyáse*
3.	*bobudhishyáti*	*bobudhishyáte*	*bobudhishyáte*
D. 1.	*bobudhishyấvas*	*bobudhishyấvahe*	*bobudhishyấvahe*
2.	*bobudhishyáthas*	*bobudhishyéthe*	*bobudhishyéthe*
3.	*bobudhishyátas*	*bobudhishyéte*	*bobudhishyéte*
P. 1.	*bobudhishyấmas*	*bobudhishyấmahe*	*bobudhishyấmahe*
2.	*bobudhishyátha*	*bobudhishyádhve*	*bobudhishyádhve*
3.	*bobudhishyánti*	*bobudhishyánte*	*bobudhishyánte*
			[Passive like the Passive of the first form.

Active.	First Form.	Passive.
	PARTICIPLE OF THE FUTURE.	
bobudhishyánt, what will know repeatedly		*bobudhyà*, or *bobudhaníya*, or *bobudhitávya*, what is or ought to be known repeatedly

Active.	Second Form.	Passive.
bobudhishyámâṇa, what will know repeatedly		*bobudhyà*, *bobudhaníya*, *bobudhitávya*, what is or ought to be known repeatedly

	First Form. Active.	Passive.	Second Form. Active.
		CONDITIONAL.	
S. 1.	*ábobudhishyam*, I should know repeatedly	*ábobudhishye*, I should be known repeatedly	*ábobudhishye*, I should know repeatedly
2.	*ábobudhishyas*	*ábobudhishyathâs*	*ábobudhishyathâs*
3.	*ábobudhishyat*	*ábobudhishyata*	*ábobudhishyata*
D. 1.	*ábobudhishyâva*	*ábobudhishyâvahi*	*ábobudhishyâvahi*
2.	*ábobudhishyatam*	*ábobudhishyethâm*	*ábobudhishyethâm*
3.	*ábobudhishyatâm*	*ábobudhishyetâm*	*ábobudhishyetâm*
P. 1.	*ábobudhishyâma*	*ábobudhishyâmahi*	*ábobudhishyâmahi*
2.	*ábobudhishyata*	*ábobudhishyadhvam*	*ábobudhishyadhvam*
3.	*ábobudhishyan*	*ábobudhishyanta*	*ábobudhishyanta*
			[Passive like the Passive of the first form.
		PRECATIVE.	
S. 1.	*bobudhyā́sam*, I pray, I may know repeatedly	*bobudhishī́yá*, I pray, I may be known repeatedly	*bobudhishī́yá*, I pray I may know repeatedly
2.	*bobudhyā́s*	*bobudhishī́shṭhā́s*	*bobudhishī́shṭhā́s*
3.	*bobudhyā́t*	*bobudhishī́shṭá*	*bobudhishī́shṭá*
D. 1.	*bobudhyā́sva*	*bobudhishī́váhi*	*bobudhishī́váhi*
2.	*bobudhyā́stam*	*bobudhishī́yā́sthâm*	*bobudhishī́yā́sthâm*
3.	*bobudhyā́stâm*	*bobudhishī́yā́stâm*	*bobudhishī́yā́stâm*
P. 1.	*bobudhyā́sma*	*bobudhishī́máhi*	*bobudhishī́máhi*
2.	*bobudhyā́sta*	*bobudhishī́dhvám*	*bobudhishī́dhvám*
3.	*bobudhyā́sus*	*bobudhishī́rán*	*bobudhishī́rán*
			[Passive like the Passive of the first form.

ABSOLUTIVE.

bobudhitvā́, having known repeatedly, or having been known repeatedly

INFINITIVE. ACTIVE.

bóbudhitum, to know repeatedly

DESIDERATIVE.

	Active.		Passive.
	Parasmaipada.	Âtmanepada.	
	PRESENT.		
S. 1.	*búbodhishâmi,* I wish to know	*búbodhishe,* I wish to know	*bubodhishyé,* I am wished to know
2.	*búbodhishasi*	*búbodhishase*	*bubodhishyáse*
3.	*búbodhishati*	*búbodhishate*	*bubodhishyáte*
D. 1.	*búbodhishâvas*	*búbodhishâvahe*	*bubodhishyấvahe*
2.	*búbodhishathas*	*búbodhishethe*	*bubodhishyéthe*
3.	*búbodhishatas*	*búbodhishete*	*bubodhishyéte*
P. 1.	*búbodhishâmas*	*búbodhishâmahe*	*bubodhishyấmahe*
2.	*búbodhishatha*	*búbodhishadhve*	*bubodhishyádhve*
3.	*búbodhishanti*	*búbodhishante*	*bubodhishyánte*
	PARTICIPLE OF THE PRESENT.		
	búbodhishant, wishing to know	*búbodhishamâṇa,* wishing to know	*bubodhishyámâṇa,* being wished to know
	IMPERFECT.		
S. 1.	*ábubodhisham,* I wished to know	*ábubodhishe,* I wished to know	*ábubodhishye,* I was wished to know
2.	*ábubodhishas*	*ábubodhishathâs*	*ábubodhishyathâs*
3.	*ábubodhishat*	*ábubodhishata*	*ábubodhishyata*
D. 1.	*ábubodhishâva*	*ábubodhishâvahi*	*ábubodhishyâvahi*
2.	*ábubodhishatam*	*ábubodhishethâm*	*ábubodhishyethâm*
3.	*ábubodhishatâm*	*ábubodhishetâm*	*ábubodhishyetâm*
P. 1.	*ábubodhishâma*	*ábubodhishâmahi*	*ábubodhishyâmahi*
2.	*ábubodhishata*	*ábubodhishadhvam*	*ábubodhishyadhvam*
3.	*ábubodhishan*	*ábubodhishanta*	*ábubodhishyanta*

	Active.		Passive.
	Parasmaipada.	Âtmanepada.	

POTENTIAL.

S. 1.	*búbodhisheyam*, I may wish to know	*búbodhisheya*, I may wish to know	*bubodhishyéya*, I may be wished to know
2.	*búbodhishes*	*búbodhishethâs*	*bubodhishyéthâs*
3.	*búbodhishet*	*búbodhisheta*	*bubodhishyéta*
D. 1.	*búbodhisheva*	*búbodhishevahi*	*bubodhishyévahi*
2.	*búbodhishetam*	*búbodhisheyâthâm*	*bubodhishyéyâthâm*
3.	*búbodhishetâm*	*búbodhisheyâtâm*	*bubodhishyéyâtâm*
P. 1.	*búbodhishema*	*búbodhishemahi*	*bubodhishyémahi*
2.	*búbodhisheta*	*búbodhishedhvam*	*bubodhishyédhvam*
3.	*búbodhisheyus*	*búbodhisheran*	*bubodhishyéran*

IMPERATIVE.

S. 1.	*búbodhishâṇi*, may I wish to know	*búbodhishai*, may I wish to know	*bubodhishyaí*, I may be wished to know
2.	*búbodhisha* or *búbodhishatât*	*búbodhishasvà*	*bubodhishyásva*
3.	*búbodhishatu* or *búbodhishatât*	*búbodhishatâm*	*bubodhishyátâm*
D. 1.	*búbodhishâva*	*búbodhishâvahai*	*bubodhishyấvahai*
2.	*búbodhishatam*	*búbodhishethâm*	*bubodhishyéthâm*
3.	*búbodhishatâm*	*búbodhishetâm*	*bubodhishyétâm*
P. 1.	*búbodhishâma*	*búbodhishâmahai*	*bubodhishyấmahai*
2.	*búbodhishata* or *búbodhishatât*	*búbodhishadhvam*	*bubodhishyádhvam*
3.	*búbodhishantu*	*búbodhishantâm*	*bubodhishyántâm*

PERFECT.

Parasmaipada. Active.

S. 1. *bubodhishâm̃* *chakara* or *chakâra, âsa, babhûva,* I have wished to know
2. *chakartha, âsitha, babhûvitha*
3. *chakâra, âsa, babhûva*
D. 1. *chakṛiva, âsiva, babhûviva*
2. *chakrathus, âsathus, babhûvathus*
3. *chakratus, âsatus, babhûvatus*
P. 1. *chakṛima, âsima, babhûvima*
2. *chakra, âsa, babhûva*
3. *chakrus, âsus, babhûvus*

Âtmanepada. Active.

S. 1. *bubodhishâm̃* *chakre, âsa, babhûva,* I have wished to know
2. *chakṛishe, âsitha, babhûvitha*
3. *chakre, âsa, babhûva*
D. 1. *chakṛivahe, âsiva, babhûviva*
2. *chakrâthe, âsathus, babhûvathus*
3. *chakrâte, âsatus, babhûvatus*
P. 1. *chakṛimahe, âsima, babhûvima*
2. *chakṛiḍhve, âsa, babhûva*
3. *chakrire, âsus, babhûvus*

Passive.

S. 1. *bubodhishâm̃* *chakre, âse, babhûve,* I have been wished to know
2. *chakṛishe, âsishe, babhûvishe*
3. *chakre, âse, babhûve*
D. 1. *chakṛivahe, âsivahe, babhûvivahe*
2. *chakrâthe, âsâthe, babhûvâthe*
3. *chakrâte, âsâte, babhûvâte*
P. 1. *chakṛimahe, âsimahe, babhûvimahe*
2. *chakṛiḍhve, âsidhve, babhûvidhve,* or *babhûviḍhve*
3. *chakrire, âsire, babhûvire*

PARTICIPLE OF THE PERFECT.

Parasmaipada. Active.	Âtmanepada. Active.	Passive.
bubodhishâm̃ chakṛivat, âsivat, or *babhûvat,* etc. (*cf.* § 169), having wished to know	*bubodhishâm̃ chakrâṇa, âsivat* or *babhûvat,* having wished to know	*bubodhishitá,* being wished to know

Active in general.

bubodhishitávant, having wished to know

	Active. Parasmaipada.	Active. Âtmanepada.	Passive.
	AORIST.		
S. 1.	*ábubodhishisham*, I had wished to know	*ábubodhishishi*, I had wished to know	*ábubodhishishi*, I had been wished to know
2.	*ábubodhishî́s*	*ábubodhishishṭhâs*	*ábubodhishishṭhâs*
3.	*ábubodhishî́t*	*ábubodhishishṭa*	*ábubodhishi*
D. 1.	*ábubodhishishva*	*ábubodhishishvahi*	*ábubodhishishvahi*
2.	*ábubodhishishṭam*	*ábubodhishishâthâm*	etc., like the Âtmanepada
3.	*ábubodhishishṭâm*	*ábubodhishishâtâm*	
P. 1.	*ábubodhishishma*	*ábubodhishishmahi*	
2.	*ábubodhishishṭa*	*ábubodhishidhvam*	
3.	*ábubodhishishus*	*ábubodhishishata*	
	FUTURE I.		
S. 1.	*bubodhishitấsmi*, I shall wish to know	*bubodhishitấhe*, I shall wish to know	*bubodhishitấhe*, I shall be wished to know, etc., like the Âtmanepada
2.	*bubodhishitấsi*	*bubodhishitấse*	
3.	*bubodhishitấ*	*bubodhishitấ*	
D. 1.	*bubodhishitấsvas*	*bubodhishitấsvahe*	
2.	*bubodhishitấsthas*	*bubodhishitấsâthe*	
3.	*bubodhishitấrau*	*bubodhishitấrau*	
P. 1.	*bubodhishitấsmas*	*bubodhishitấsmahe*	
2.	*bubodhishitấstha*	*bubodhishitấdhve*	
3.	*bubodhishitấras*	*bubodhishitấras*	
	FUTURE II.		
S. 1.	*bubodhishishyấmi*, I shall wish to know	*bubodhishishyé*, I shall wish to know	*bubodhishishyé*, I shall be wished to know, etc., like the Âtmanepada
2.	*bubodhishishyási*	*bubodhishishyáse*	
3.	*bubodhishishyáti*	*bubodhishishyáte*	
D. 1.	*bubodhishishyấvas*	*bubodhishishyấvahe*	
2.	*bubodhishishyáthas*	*bubodhishishyéthe*	
3.	*bubodhishishyátas*	*bubodhishishyéte*	
P. 1.	*bubodhishishyấmas*	*bubodhishishyấmahe*	
2.	*bubodhishishyátha*	*bubodhishishyádhve*	
3.	*bubodhishishyánti*	*bubodhishishyánte*	
	PARTICIPLE OF THE FUTURE.		
	bubodhishishyánt, what will wish to know.	*bubodhishishyámâṇa*, what will wish to know	*bubodhishyà*, *bubodhishaṇî́ya*, *bubodhishitávya*, what is or ought to be wished to know

	Active. Parasmaipada.	Active. Âtmanepada.	Passive.
	CONDITIONAL.		
S. 1.	*ábubodhishishyam,* I should wish to know	*ábubodhishishye,* I should wish to know	*ábubodhishishye,* I should be wished to know, etc., like the Âtmanepada
2.	*ábubodhishishyas*	*ábubodhishishyathâs*	
3.	*ábubodhishishyat*	*ábubodhishishyata*	
D. 1.	*ábubodhishishyâva*	*ábubodhishishyâvahi*	
2.	*ábubodhishishyatam*	*ábubodhishishyethâm*	
3.	*ábubodhishishyatâm*	*ábubodhishishyetâm*	
P. 1.	*ábubodhishishyâma*	*ábubodhishishyâmahi*	
2.	*ábubodhishishyata*	*ábubodhishishyadhvam*	
3.	*ábubodhishishyan*	*ábubodhishishyanta*	
	PRECATIVE.		
S. 1.	*bubodhishyā́sam,* I pray, I may wish to know	*bubodhishishī́yá,* I pray I may wish to know	*bubodhishishī́yá,* I pray I may be wished to know, etc., like the Âtmanepada
2.	*bubodhishyā́s*	*bubodhishishī́shṭhā́s*	
3.	*bubodhishyā́t*	*bubodhishishī́shṭá*	
D. 1.	*bubodhishyā́sva*	*bubodhishishī́váhi*	
2.	*bubodhishyā́stam*	*bubodhishishī́yā́sthâm*	
3.	*bubodhishyā́stâm*	*bubodhishishī́yā́stâm*	
P. 1.	*bubodhishyā́sma*	*bubodhishishī́máhi*	
2.	*bubodhishyā́sta*	*bubodhishishī́dhvám*	
2.	*bubodhishyā́sus*	*bubodhishishī́rán*	

ABSOLUTIVE.

bubodhishitvā́, having wished to know, or having been wished to know

INFINITIVE. ACTIVE.

búbodhishitum, to wish to know

CAUSAL.

	Active. Parasmaipada.	Active. Âtmanepada.	Passive.

PRESENT.

S. 1.	*bodháyâmi,* I cause to know	*bodháye,* I cause to know	*bodhyé,* I am caused to know
2.	*bodháyasi*	*bodháyase*	*bodhyáse*
3.	*bodháyati*	*bodháyate*	*bodhyáte*
D. 1.	*bodháyâvas*	*bodháyâvahe*	*bodhyấvahe*
2.	*bodháyathas*	*bodháyethe*	*bodhyéthe*
3.	*bodháyatas*	*bodháyete*	*bodhyéte*
P. 1.	*bodháyâmas*	*bodháyâmahe*	*bodhyấmahe*
2.	*bodháyatha*	*bodháyadhve*	*bodhyádhve*
3.	*bodháyanti*	*bodháyante*	*bodhyánte*

PARTICIPLE OF THE PRESENT.

bodháyant, causing to know	*bodháyamâna,* causing to know	*bodhyámâna,* being caused to know

IMPERFECT.

S. 1.	*ábodhayam,* I caused to know	*ábodhaye,* I caused to know	*ábodhye,* I was caused to know
2.	*ábodhayas*	*ábodhayathâs*	*ábodhyathâs*
3.	*ábodhayat*	*ábodhayata*	*ábodhyata*
D. 1.	*ábodhayâva*	*ábodhayâvahi*	*ábodhyâvahi*
2.	*ábodhayatam*	*ábodhayethâm*	*ábodhyethâm*
3.	*ábodhayatâm*	*ábodhayetâm*	*ábodhyetâm*
P. 1.	*ábodhayâma*	*ábodhayâmahi*	*ábodhyâmahi*
2.	*ábodhayata*	*ábodhayadhvam*	*ábodhyadhvam*
3.	*ábodhayan*	*ábodhayanta*	*ábodhyanta*

	Active. Parasmaipada.	Active. Âtmanepada.	Passive.
	POTENTIAL.		
S. 1.	*bodháyeyam*, I may cause to know	*bodháyeya*, I may cause to know	*bodhyéya*, I may be caused to know
2.	*bodháyes*	*bodháyethâs*	*bodhyéthâs*
2.	*bodháyet*	*bodháyeta*	*bodhyéta*
D. 1.	*bodháyeva*	*bodháyevahi*	*bodhyévahi*
2.	*bodháyetam*	*bodháyeyâthâm*	*bodhyéyâthâm*
3.	*bodháyetâm*	*bodháyeyâtâm*	*bodhyéyâtâm*
P. 1.	*bodháyema*	*bodháyemahi*	*bodhyémahi*
2.	*bodháyeta*	*bodháyedhvam*	*bodhyédhvam*
3.	*bodháyeyus*	*bodháyeran*	*bodhyéran*
	IMPERATIVE.		
S. 1.	*bodháyâni*, may I cause to know	*bodháyai*, may I cause to know	*bodhyaí*, may I be caused to know
2.	*bodháya* or *bodháyatât*	*bodháyasva*	*bodhyásva*
3.	*bodháyatu* or *bodháyatât*	*bodháyatâm*	*bodhyátâm*
D. 1.	*bodháyâva*	*bodháyâvahai*	*bodhyấvahai*
2.	*bodháyatam*	*bodháyethâm*	*bodhyéthâm*
3.	*bodháyatâm*	*bodháyetâm*	*bodhyétâm*
P. 1.	*bodháyâma*	*bodháyâmahai*	*bodhyấmahai*
2.	*bodháyata* or *bodháyatât*	*bodháyadhvam*	*bodhyádhvam*
3.	*bodháyantu*	*bodháyantâm*	*bodhyántâm*

ACTIVE. PERFECT.

Parasmaipada.

S. 1.		*chakara* or *chakâra*, *âsa*, *babhûva*, I have caused [to know
2.		*chakartha*, *âsitha*, *babhûvitha*
3.		*chakâra*, *âsa*, *babhûva*
D. 1.		*chakṛiva*, *âsiva*, *babhûviva*
2.	*bodhayâm̃*	*chakrathus*, *âsathus*, *babhûvathus*
3.		*chakratus*, *âsatus*, *babhûvatus*
P. 1.		*chakṛima*, *âsima*, *babhûvima*
2.		*chakra*, *âsa*, *babhûva*
3.		*chakrus*, *âsus*, *babhûvus*

Âtmanepada.

S. 1.		*chakre*, *âsa*, *babhûva*, I have caused to know
2.		*chakṛishe*, *âsitha*, *babhûvitha*
3.		*chakre*, *âsa*, *babhûva*
D. 1.		*chakṛivahe*, *âsiva*, *babhûviva*
2.	*bodhayâm̃*	*chakrâthe*, *âsathus*, *babhûvathus*
3.		*chakrâte*, *âsatus*, *babhûvatus*
P. 1.		*chakṛimahe*, *âsima*, *babhûvima*
2.		*chakṛiḍhve*, *âsa*, *babhûva*
3.		*chakrire*, *âsus*, *babhûvus*

Passive.

S. 1.		*chakre*, *âse*, *babhûve*, I have been caused to [know
2.		*chakṛishe*, *âsishe*, *babhûvishe*
3.		*chakre*, *âse*, *babhûve*
D. 1.		*chakṛivahe*, *âsivahe*, *babhûvivahe*
2.	*bodhayâm̃*	*chakrâthe*, *âsathe*, *babhûvâthe*
3.		*chakrâte*, *âsâte*, *babhûvâte*
P. 1.		*chakṛimahe*, *âsimahe*, *babhûvimahe*
2.		*chakṛiḍhve*, *âsidhve*, *babhûvidhve* or *babhûviḍhve*
3.		*chakrire*, *âsire*, *babhûvire*

PARTICIPLE OF THE PERFECT.

Parasmaipada.	Âtmanepada.	Passive.
bodhayâm̃chakṛivat, *âsivat* or *babhûvat*, etc., (*cf.* § 169) having caused to know	*bodhayâm̃chakrâṇa*, *âsivat*, or *babhûvat*, having caused to know	*bodhitá*, caused to know

Active.

bodhitâvant, having caused to know

	Active. Parasmaipada.	Active. Âtmanepada.	Passive.	
	AORIST.			
S. 1.	*ábûbudham*, I had caused to know	*ábûbudhe*, I had caused to know	*ábodhayishi*	or *ábodhishi*, I have been caused to know
2.	*ábûbudhas*	*ábûbudhathâs*	*ábodhayishṭhâs*	*ábodhishṭhâs*
3.	*ábûbudhat*	*ábûbudhata*	*ábodhi*	
D. 1.	*ábûbudhâva*	*ábûbudhâvahi*	*ábodhayishvahi*	*ábodhishvahi*
2.	*ábûbudhatam*	*ábûbudhethâm*	*ábodhayishâthâm*	*ábodhishâthâm*
3.	*ábûbudhatâm*	*ábûbudhetâm*	*ábodhayishâtâm*	*ábodhishâtâm*
P. 1.	*ábûbudhâma*	*ábûbudhâmahi*	*ábodhayishmahi*	*ábodhishmahi*
2.	*ábûbudhata*	*ábûbudhadhvam*	*ábodhayidhvam* or *ábodhayiḍhvam*	*ábodhidhvam*
3.	*ábûbudhan*	*ábûbudhanta*	*ábodhayishata*	*ábodhishata*
	FUTURE I.			
S. 1.	*bodhayitấsmi*, I shall cause to know	*bodhayitấhe*, I shall cause to know	*bodhayitấhe*, etc., like the Âtmanepada	or *bodhitấhe*, I shall be caused to know
2.	*bodhayitấsi*	*bodhayitấse*		*bodhitấse*
3.	*bodhayitấ*	*bodhayitấ*		*bodhitấ*
D. 1.	*bodhayitấsvas*	*bodhayitấsvahe*		*bodhitấsvahe*
2.	*bodhayitấsthas*	*bodhayitấsâthe*		*bodhitấsâthe*
3.	*bodhayitấrau*	*bodhayitấrau*		*bodhitấrau*
P. 1.	*bodhayitấsmas*	*bodhayitấsmahe*		*bodhitấsmahe*
2.	*bodhayitấstha*	*bodhayitấdhve*		*bodhitấdhve*
3.	*bodhayitấras*	*bodhayitấras*		*bodhitấras*
	FUTURE II.			
S. 1.	*bodhayishyấmi*, I shall cause to know	*bodhayishyé*, I shall cause to know	*bodhayishyé*, etc., like the Âtmanepada	or *bodhishyé*, I shall be caused to know
2.	*bodhayishyási*	*bodhayishyáse*		*bodhishyáse*
3.	*bodhayishyáti*	*bodhayishyáte*		*bodhishyáte*
D. 1.	*bodhayishyấvas*	*bodhayishyấvahe*		*bodhishyấvahe*
2.	*bodhayishyáthas*	*bodhayishyéthe*		*bodhishyéthe*
3.	*bodhayishyátas*	*bodhayishyéte*		*bodhishyéte*
P. 1.	*bodhayishyấmas*	*bodhayishyấmahe*		*bodhishyấmahe*
2.	*bodhayishyátha*	*bodhayishyádhve*		*bodhishyádhve*
3.	*bodhayishyánti*	*bodhayishyánte*		*bodhishyánte*
	PARTICIPLE OF THE FUTURE.			
	bodhayishyánt, what will cause to know	*bodhayishyámâṇa*, what will cause to know	*bódhya*, *bodhanī́ya*, and *bodhayitávya*, what is or ought to be caused to know	

	Active.		Passive.	
	Parasmaipada.	Âtmanepada.		

CONDITIONAL.

	Parasmaipada	Âtmanepada	Passive	
S. 1.	*ábodhayishyam*, I should cause to know	*ábodhayishye*, I should cause to know	*ábodhayishye*, etc., like the Âtmanepada	or *ábodhishye*, I should be caused to know
2.	*ábodhayishyas*	*ábodhayishyathâs*		*ábodhishyathâs*
3.	*ábodhayishyat*	*ábodhayishyata*		*ábodhishyata*
D. 1.	*ábodhayishyâva*	*ábodhayishyâvahi*		*ábodhishyâvahi*
2.	*ábodhayishyatam*	*ábodhayishyethâm*		*ábodhishyethâm*
3.	*ábodhayishyatâm*	*ábodhayishyetâm*		*ábodhishyetâm*
P. 1.	*ábodhayishyâma*	*ábodhayishyâmahi*		*ábodhishyâmahi*
2.	*ábodhayishyata*	*ábodhayishyadhvam*		*ábodhishyadhvam*
3.	*ábodhayishyan*	*ábodhayishyanta*		*ábodhishyanta*

PRECATIVE.

	Parasmaipada	Âtmanepada	Passive	
S. 1.	*bodhyā́sam*, I pray, I may cause to know	*bodhayishī́yá*, I pray, I may cause to know	*bodhayishī́yá*, etc., like the Âtmanepada	or *bodhishī́yá*, I pray, I may be caused to know
2.	*bodhyā́s*	*bodhayishī́shṭhā́s*		*bodhishī́shṭhā́s*
3.	*bodhyā́t*	*bodhayishī́shṭá*		*bodhishī́shṭá*
D. 1.	*bodhyā́sva*	*bodhayishī́váhi*		*bodhishī́váhi*
2.	*bodhyā́stam*	*bodhayishī́yā́sthâm*		*bodhishī́yā́sthâm*
3.	*bodhyā́stâm*	*bodhayishī́yā́stâm*		*bodhishī́yā́stâm*
P. 1.	*bodhyā́sma*	*bodhayishī́máhi*		*bodhishī́máhi*
2.	*bodhyā́sta*	*bodhayishī́dhvám* or *bodhayishī́ḍhvám*		*bodhishī́dhvám*
3.	*bodhyā́sus*	*bodhayishī́rán*		*bodhishī́rán*

ABSOLUTIVE.

bodhayitvā́, having caused to know, or having been caused to know

INFINITIVE. ACTIVE.

bódhayitum, to cause to know.

APPENDIX.

SOME VERBAL FORMS OF THE VEDA.

§ 184. The potential and imperative, which in ordinary Sanskrit are connected only with the present, in the Vedas are formed also from the stems of the perfect and aorist, *e.g.* potential of the perfect बभूयाम्, imperative बभूतु (*cf.* my V.G., § 837); potential of the first form of the aorist भूयाम्, of the second aorist रुहेयम्, from रुह् 'to ascend;' of the third aorist शूशुयाम, from श्वि 'to swell;' of the sixth aorist प्यासिषीमहि, from the verb प्याय् 'to be exuberant;' of the seventh aorist तरुषेम, from the verb तॄ 'to cross' (*cf.* my V.G. § 861); imperative of the first aorist श्रोतु from श्रु 'to hear;' of the third aorist वोचतु from वच् 'to speak,' पूपुरन्तु from पॄ 'to fill;' of the fourth aorist स्तोषाणि from स्तु 'to praise,' श्रोषन्तु from श्रु 'to hear;' of the fifth aorist सनिषन्तु from सन् 'to obtain;' of the seventh aorist धुक्षस्व from दुह् 'to milk' (*cf. ib.* § 862).

The potential of the second future धक्ष्येत् from दह् 'to burn,' occurs in Epic poetry, and even in the Panchatantra वक्ष्येत् from वच् 'to speak.'

In the Veda infinitives may be formed from the stems of the perfect, aorist, and second future, *e.g.* वावृधध्यै, जेषे, रोहिष्ये, from the verbs वृध् 'to increase,' जि 'to conquer,' and रुह् 'to mount' (*cf.* my V.G. § 919).

Likewise some participles of the aorist occur, *e.g.* of the first aorist स्थान्त् from स्था 'to stand,' गमन्त् from गम् 'to go;' of the second aorist वृधन्त् from वृध्; of the third aorist पीप्यान (from पायय, causal of पा 'to drink,' *cf.* § 137, अपीप्यम्); of the fourth or seventh aorist हासमान from हा; of the fifth aorist सनिषन्त् from सन्; of the seventh aorist कृक्षमाण from कृष् (*cf.* my V.G. pp. 410, 411, n. 2).

§ 185. Further, the Vedas have a special mood which corresponds to the Greek subjunctive. It is formed :—

1. By inserting अ (or आ before व् and म्) before the personal terminations, which combines with a preceding अ or आ to आ, *e.g.* present indicative हन्ति *han-ti,* subjunctive हनति *han-a-ti,* indic. बोधति *bodha-ti,* subjunctive बोधाति *bodhâ-ti,* for *bodha-a-ti.*

2. By changing optionally the final ए of the terminations to ऐ *ai, e.g.* pres. indic. यजते *yajate,* subj. यजातै *yajâtai.*

3. By using in the second conjugation generally the strong form (*cf.* §§ 82, 83), *e.g.* pres. indic. धुक्षे (for *duh + se*), subj. दोहसे *doh-a-se* (§ 83, II. A. 1), indic. युङ्क्ते (for *yuñj + te*), subj. युनजते *yunaj-a-te* (§ 83, II. A. 4).

4. In the imperfect and the aorist the augment is rejected, *e.g.* imperf. indic. अभरत् *abharat,* subj. भरात् *bharât* (for *bhara-a-t*), indic. अगच्छन् *agachchhan,* subj. गच्छान् *gachchhân,* अजङ्गन् *ajangan* (frequentative of गम्, for अजंगम् + त् *ajangam + t*), subj. जङ्गमत् *jangam-a-t,* first aorist indic. अभूत् *abhût,* subj. भुवत् *bhuv-a-t* (*cf.* § 115, 3), third aorist indic. अववर्तत्, subj. ववर्तात् (for *vavarta-a-t*), fifth aorist indic. आवीत् *âvît* (contracted from आविषीत् *âvishît,* § 139, which stands for original आविष् + त् *âv-ish + t,* without the insertion of the auxiliary ई), subj. अविषत् *avish-a-t.*

5. Further, the subjunctive of the aorist has often the personal terminations of the present (*cf.* the Greek subjunctive), *e.g.* third aorist indic. अवोचत् *avochat,* subj. वोचति *vochati* (*cf.* my V.G. § 860).

A subjunctive of the perfect is formed from वृध् and irregularly from पृच्, viz. वावृधन्ते, पपृचासि (*cf.* my V.G. § 837, and Rig-Veda I. 141, 11).

§ 186. Lastly, the Vedas show also a past-perfect, formed from the perfect by substituting instead of its personal terminations those of the imperfect, and sometimes by adding the temporal augment, *e.g.* from the third pers. plural of the perfect Âtm. पेचिरे, past-perfect अपेचिरन् (Atharva-Veda V. 18, 11), from the verb पच् 'to cook;' third pers. sing. perfect Par. आनर्ष, past-perfect आनर्षत् (Taittir. Âr. 2, 9, Nirukt. II. 11), from the verb ऋष्; from the second pers. sing. perf. Âtm. सुषुपिषे, past-perf. सुषुप्थास् (Pâraskara in Z.D.M.G. [Journal of the German Oriental Society] VII. 533, 37).

PRIMITIVE NOUNS.

§ 187. A great number of nouns, substantives as well as adjectives, are derived immediately from the crude form of the verb. These nouns are called primitive nouns. The affixes, by which they are formed, have been treated of and enumerated in alphabetical order in my V.G. §§ 250-425.

The crude form of the verb sometimes is left unchanged, *e.g.* वृज् + अन *vṛij + ana* makes वृजन *vṛijana*; sometimes it undergoes changes analogous to those which occur in the conjugational forms. Final इ *i* and ई *î* become ए *e* before consonants, and इय् *iy*, अय् *ay*, and आय् *ây* before vowels, *e.g.* नी + तृ *nî + tṛi*, नेतृ *netṛi*; भी + अस *bhî + asa*, भियस *bhiyasa*; जि + अ *ji + a*, जय *jaya*; नी + अक *nî + aka*, नायक *nâyaka*. Final उ *u* and ऊ *û* in the same way become ओ *o*, उव् *uv*, अव् *av*, and आव् *âv*; final ऋ *ṛi* and ॠ *ṛî* become अर् *ar*, आर् *âr*, and र् *r*, and ॠ *ṛî* besides इर् *ir*, ईर् *îr*, उर् *ur*, and ऊर् *ûr*; final ए *e*, ऐ *ai*, and ओ *o*, become आ *â*, after which as well as after an original आ *â*, य् *y* is often inserted, *e.g.* दा *dâ*, or दो *do* + अ *a*, make दाय *dâ-y-a*. Penultimate इ *i* followed by a single radical consonant is often changed to ए *e*, उ *u* to ओ *o*, ऋ *ṛi* to अर् *ar* (guṇa), *e.g.* बुध् + अक *budh + aka*, makes बोधक *bodhaka*; वृध् *vṛidh*, वर्धक *vardhaka*. Penultimate अ *a* before a single radical consonant is often lengthened, *e.g.* ज्वल् + अ *jval + a*, makes ज्वाल *jvâl-a*.

On the other hand, many verbs, as in the conjugational derivations, are weakened by changing य *ya* to इ *i*, व *va* to उ *u*, र *ra* to ऋ *ṛi*, and by rejecting final or penultimate nasals, *e.g.* वच् + थ

makes उक्थ, प्रछ् + आ *prachh* + *á*, पृच्छा *pṛichchhá*; गम् + ति *gam* + *ti*, गति *gati*; स्रंस् + ति *sraṁs* + *ti*, स्रस्ति *srasti*.

Many verbs insert the vowel इ *i* before the affixes which begin with a consonant, except य् *y*, व् *v*, nasals, or स् *s*. When the affixes are subjoined immediately to the base, the final consonants of the verbs and the initial of the affixes are modified in general according to the rules given in §§ 94-102. For further details see my V.G. § 54 sqq. and § 363 sqq.

SECTION IV. COMBINATION AND COMPOSITION OF VERBAL DERIVATIVES WITH PREPOSITIONS AND SIMILAR WORDS.

§ 188. All the verbal forms and derivatives which are formed according to the rules laid down in §§ 64-187, may be combined and compounded with the prepositions and similar words, which will be specified in §§ 189 and 190.

A single preposition or similar word preceding a present, imperfect, imperative, potential, reduplicated perfect, aorist, second future, conditional, or precative, in general is not compounded with the verbal form, *e.g.* प भ॑वति. But in some exceptional cases, for instance when the verb stands in an accessory sentence commencing with a relative pronoun, and when preceded by more than one preposition or similar word in the Veda (Sch. Pâṇini, II. 1, 4), these tenses are compounded with the preceding preposition or prepositions or similar words, *e.g.* यः प्रभ॑वति *yáḥ* (relative pronoun) *prabhávati*, समुद्भ॑वति *samúdbhavati* (where *sam* and *ud* are prepositions).

The periphrastic perfect, the first future, the participles, and all the other verbal derivatives must be compounded with the preceding prepositions or similar words, *e.g.* periphrastic perfect प्रभवयाम् (आस, etc.) *prabhavayấm* (*ása*), first future प्रभवितास्मि *prabhavitấsmi*, etc., participle present प्रभ॑वन्त् *prabhávant*, participle of the passive perfect प्रभू॑त *prábhúta*, a primitive noun (§ 187), *e.g.* प्रभू॑ति *prábhúti*.

§ 189. The prepositions which may be combined or compounded with the verbal forms and derivatives, are:—

अति, 'beyond.'	दुस्, 'ill.'
अधि, 'above,' 'over.'	नि, 'into,' 'downwards.'
अनु, 'after.'	निस्, 'out,' 'without.'
अप, 'off.'	परा, 'away,' 'back.'
अपि, 'upon.'	परि, 'around.'
अभि, 'towards.'	प्र, 'before.'
अव, 'down.'	प्रति, (opposite) 'to,' 'back.'
आ, 'near to.'	वि, 'apart.'
उद्, 'up.'	सम्, 'together.'
उप, 'below.'	सु, 'well.'

As prepositions अदस्, 'thus,' अन्तर्, 'between,' अस्तम्, 'down,' तिरस्, 'across,' 'under,' श्रत्, 'belief,' अच्छ, 'to,' and some others (*cf.* my V.G. § 241) are prefixed to some verbs.

Observ. 1. The verbs स्था, 'to stand,' स्तम्भ् 'to stop,' and in the Veda स्कन्द्, 'to ascend,' reject their स्, when preceded immediately by the preposition उद्, *e.g.* उत्थास्यति, second future (although not compounded, § 188), उत्थातृ (compounded with the primitive noun स्थातृ), but उदस्थात्, first aorist.

2. The prepositions प्र, परा, and परि, when prefixed to the verb अय्, 'to go,' change their र् to ल्, *e.g.* प्लायति, पलायति. In निस् (निः), which, according to § 28, must change its final : (for the original स्) to र्, the change to ल् is optional, निरय *nir-aya* or निलय *nil-ay-a*, a primitive noun.

3. The prepositions अधि, अपि, and अव sometimes reject the initial, *e.g.* पिधान (for *apidhâna*), a primitive noun, प्रवेरित *pra-va* (for *ava*) *-îrita*, 'thrown' (Lass. Anth. Sansc. ed. Gildemeister, p. 115).

4. The verbs कृ, 'to make,' कॄ, 'to throw,' and तुम्प्, 'to hurt,' when preceded by the prepositions अप, उप, परि, प्रति, or सम्,

generally insert स्, which, in analogy with § 17, must become ष् after परि and प्रति, e.g. संस्करोति, परिष्करोति.

5. Before some nouns the finals of the prepositions are lengthened, e.g. अति ऽ सार becomes अतीसार (cf. my V.G. p. 142.)

§ 190. The verbs अस्, 'to be,' भू, 'to become' and 'to be,' and कृ, 'to make,' may be combined or compounded after the rules given in § 188:

I. With every noun, e.g. वधू, 'a wife,' वधू करोति, 'he makes somebody a wife' (not compounded), यो (pronoun relative) वधूकरोति (compounded) वधूकृत (compounded).

A final अ or आ of the prefixed noun is changed to ई, final इ and उ are lengthened, and final ऋ is changed to री, e.g. शुक्ल, 'white,' शुक्ली भू; शुचि, 'pure,' शुची भू; मृदु, 'soft,' मृदू भू; मातृ, 'mother,' मात्री भू.

All other nouns are modified according to the phonetic rules given in §§ 19-36; if ending in consonants, they take the form which they have before the termination of the locative plur., e.g. न्यञ्च् loc. plur. न्यक्षु *nyak-shu*, makes न्यक्कृ *nyak kṛi*, 'to insult.' If this form ends in a vowel the preceding rule is applied, for instance, भस्मन् loc. plur. भस्मसु *bhasma-su* changes the final *a* to *ī*, and makes भस्मी कृ, 'to reduce to ashes' (cf. § 193, 2).

II. With some words imitating sounds, e.g. पटत्, 'the sound of a flapping elephant's ear.' These words are repeated and आ is substituted for the final अत्, e.g. पटत्पटा करोति, पटत्पटाकृत.

III. With other words, some of which are used with कृ only (cf. my V.G. §§ 244, 245).

CHAPTER II.—THE NOUN.

SECTION I. CRUDE FORMS OF THE NOUNS.

§ 191. The nouns are either derived immediately from verbs (primitive nouns, § 187), or from nouns (secondary nouns, §§ 193, 194); they are simple, or compound; they differ in gender, being masculines, feminines, or neuters.

§ 192. I. For the PRIMITIVE NOUNS see § 187.

II. SECONDARY NOUNS.

§ 193. The secondary nouns are derived from primitive, secondary, or compound nouns of the three genders by means of many affixes. The secondary affixes have been enumerated and their application has been shown in my V.G. §§ 426-617.

1. They are subjoined immediately to nouns ending in vowels. Before affixes which begin with a vowel, diphthong, or य् *y*, final अ *a*, आ *á*, इ *i*, and ई *í* are rejected, *e.g.* अङ्कुर + इत makes अङ्कुरित. Final उ and ऊ are changed to अव्, *e.g.* ऋतु + य ऋतव्य. Final ऋ is changed to र्, *e.g.* पितृ + य पित्र्य. Final ऐ to आय्, ओ to अव्, and औ to आव्.

2. Nouns ending in consonants generally attach the secondary affix to the form which they have before the termination of the locative of the plural, *e.g.* राजन् 'king,' of which the plural locative is राजसु, makes with the secondary affix त्व, राजत्व 'the condition of a king, sovereignty.' For the phonetic changes of final and initial consonants see §§ 19 and 25-36. Final र् or स् of a crude form must be treated as if they were Visarga (:) and changed according to §§ 25-28.

Exceptions:—

1. Nouns ending in अञ्च् and the participles of the reduplicated perfect Parasmaipada substitute before affixes beginning with vowels, diphthongs, or य्, the form which they have before the termination of the instrumental of the singular, *e.g.* प्राञ्च् + ईन = प्राचीन (instrum. sing. प्राचा *prâch-â*), प्रत्यञ्च् + ईन = प्रतीचीन (instrum. sing. प्रतीचा *pratîch-â*).

2. मद्, before surd letters (§ 12) मत्, is substituted for the singular of the pronoun of the first person; अस्मद्, before surd letters अस्मत्, for the dual and plural; त्वद्, before surd letters त्वत्, for the singular of the pronoun of the second person; युष्मद्, before surd letters युष्मत्, for the dual and plural; *e.g.* with ईय, मदीय 'mine,' अस्मदीय 'our' (dual and plural, 'of two and more'), त्वदीय 'thine,' युष्मदीय 'your' (dual and plural).

3. Final त् and स् are left unchanged (contrary to § 33 and § 28, Exc.) before the secondary affixes वन्त्, विन्, and वल्, *e.g.* विद्युत् + वन्त् विद्युत्वन्त्, तेजस् + विन् तेजस्विन्.—Final इस् and उस् change their स् to ष् before the affixes मन्त्, *e.g.* ज्योतिस् + मन्त् = ज्योतिष्मन्त्.

4. The change of final क्, ट्, त्, and प् to the homogeneous nasal before secondary affixes beginning with a nasal, is already mentioned (§ 33), *e.g.* त्वच् with the affix मय becomes त्वङ्मय (for त्वक् + मय, the locative plural being *tvak-shu*, *cf.* § 193, 2).

§ 194. In the greatest part of the secondary nouns the vowel of the first syllable is changed, viz., अ *a* to आ *â*; इ *i*, ई *î*, and ए *e* to ऐ *ai*; उ *u*, ऊ *û*, and ओ *o* to औ *au*; ऋ *ṛi* to आर् *âr* (Vṛiddhi, *cf.* p. 38, note) *e.g.* शिव + अ becomes शैव (*cf.* § 193, 1), पृथिवी + अ पार्थिव (*cf.* § 193, 1).

If the first syllable contains a य् or व्, deduced from an original इ, ई, उ or ऊ, य् is changed to ऐय्, and व् to औव्, *e.g.* व्यसन (from वि ऽ असन, according to § 22), with secondary अ, makes वैयसन, स्वश्व (from सु ऽ अश्व, § 22) सौवश्व.

Some other words follow this analogy, though their य् and व्

are of different origin, *e.g.* द्वार 'the door,' with secondary इक becomes दौवारिक.

Some compound nouns change in this manner the first vowel of their second member, others the first syllables of both members. For these and other irregularities *cf.* my V.G. § 588.

III. Compound Words.

§ 195. The compound words may be divided into two general categories. The first comprises derivatives from verbs, which are combined with prepositions or nouns signifying the object of the action, or restricting or determining in any other manner the action or condition which the verb expresses, *e.g.* प्रभु 'strong,' from the verb भू 'to be,' with the preposition प्र 'before,' शत्रुघ्न 'a slayer of enemies,' from शत्रु 'enemy,' and हन् 'to kill, to slay.' Most of the nominal forms which are used as second members in this class of compounds, do not occur separately, thus neither भु nor घ्न exist as simple words.

§ 196. The second class comprises the compounds, the elements of which, with very few exceptions, occur also as simple words, and retain in their composition, or originally retained, the signification which they have when used singly, *e.g.* देव 'god' + पुत्र 'son,' देवपुत्र 'a son of a god.'

The words forming compounds of this category are either nouns, viz., substantives, adjectives, participles, numerals, pronouns, or indeclinables, viz., prepositions, absolutives, infinitives, particles, and sometimes even verbal forms.

These compounds, except those of the copulative or Dvandva-class (§ 197), which may comprise two, three, and more component parts, consist of two members, each of which again may comprise two members. Thus अनेकयजमानप्रदत्तसूक्ष्मवस्त्रविक्रयवशात् is a compound belonging to the second species of the second class, the Tatpurusha *κατ' ἐξοχήν* (§ 204), the first member of which comprises the words from अनेक up to विक्रय,

and the second member of which is वशात् 'by way of.' The first member is also a compound of the same species, having as its first part the words from अनेक up to वस्त्र, and as its second विक्रय, 'the selling' of that which the first member implies. The latter is a compound of the first species of the second class, *i.e.*, a Karmadhâraya compound (§ 201), consisting of अनेकयजमानप्रदत्त and सूक्ष्मवस्त्र. This second member is a compound of the same species, has as its former member सूक्ष्म 'fine,' and as its second वस्त्र 'cloth,' and signifies 'fine clothes.' The first member, अनेकयजमानप्रदत्त, is again a compound of the second species of the second or Tatpurusha-class, consisting of the members अनेकयजमान and प्रदत्त; the latter is the perfect participle of the passive voice of दा with the preposition प्र meaning 'given.' The first member is a compound of the first species of the second class, having as first member अनेक, and as second member यजमान 'an employer of priests for sacrifices,' or 'a sacrificer.' अनेक finally is also a compound of this species formed by the negative अन् and एक 'one,' and signifying 'many.' The whole compound signifies 'by way of selling (of) the fine clothes given (to him) by many sacrificers.'

Almost all nouns, when used as first members of a compound, take the crude form. The nouns ending in consonants take that which they have before the termination of the locative of the plural (*cf.* § 193, 2), *e.g.* राजन् 'king,' compounded with पुत्र 'son,' makes राजपुत्र (locative plural राजसु *râja-su*). The pronouns of the first and second person substitute the forms मद्, अस्मद्, त्वद्, युष्मद्, in the same signification and manner as in § 193, Exc. 2, *e.g.* मत्पुत्र 'my son,' अस्मत्पुत्र 'our son.' For the phonetic changes *cf.* §§ 19-36.

For न 'not,' which can be used as first member only, अन् is substituted before vowels and अ before consonants, *e.g.* ऋत 'right,' अनृत 'not right,' पुत्र 'son,' अपुत्र 'not having a son,' 'childless.'

कु, कद् (particularly before vowels), कव, and का, derived from the interrogative pronoun, are prefixed to nouns in the signification of 'bad,' *e.g.* कुपुत्र, 'a bad son.'

For सह, 'with,' and समान, 'equal,' forming the first part of a compound, स is commonly substituted, *e.g.* सपुत्र, 'being with sons.'

Final vowels of the first member are sometimes lengthened, *e.g.* मणिऽकर्ण makes मणीकर्ण. Sometimes they are shortened.

Some nouns ending in consonants, when used as second members, subjoin अ, *e.g.* अप्, 'water,' ऽअप; ऋच्, 'a verse,' ऽऋच.

This category of compounds comprises three classes.

FIRST CLASS: COPULATIVE COMPOUNDS (called द्वन्द्व).

§ 197. Compounds of this class consist of nouns which, if not compounded, would be copulated by a particle signifying 'and,' *e.g.* 'Bhîshma, Arjuna, and Yudishṭhira,' may form a compound भीष्मार्जुनयुधिष्ठिर.

They take generally the terminations of the dual, if there are two objects; of the plural, if there are more than two, *e.g.* 'Bhîshma and Arjuna,' भीष्मार्जुनौ, nominative dual; 'Bhîshma, Arjuna, and Yudishṭhira,' भीष्मार्जुनयुधिष्ठिरास्, nominative plural; 'the Kshatriyas and the Vaiçyas' (names of two Hindu castes), क्षत्रियवैश्यास्, plur. nom. In this case the compound has the gender of its last part.

But a compound of this class may also become a singular of the neuter gender, *e.g.* पाणि, 'hand,' and पाद, 'foot,' पाणिपादम्, 'hand and foot,' nominative singular.

Observ. 1. Crude forms ending in ऋ, when followed by another crude form ending in ऋ, or by पुत्र, change their final ऋ to आ *e.g.* पितृ, 'father,' before मातृ, 'mother' or पुत्र, पितामातृ, पितापुत्र.

2. Crude forms ending in च्, छ्, ज्, झ्, द्, ष्, or ह्, when forming the last member, and the compound being a neuter singular, subjoin अ, *e.g.* वाक्ऽत्वच् makes वाक्त्वचम्, nominative singular.

Sometimes अ is subjoined also to other final consonants, and even when the compound takes the terminations of the dual or plural.

रात्रि, fem. 'night,' being the last member, substitutes रात्र and the compound becomes masculine, *e.g.* अहर्ऽरात्रि, with irregular change of the final syllable of the first member, makes अहोरात्र, masc. (but also neuter, *cf.* the Sanskrit Dictionary published in St. Petersburgh, *s.v.*), 'day and night.'

SECOND CLASS: DETERMINATIVE COMPOUNDS (called तत्पुरुष).

§ 198. Compounds of this class consist of two members, the first of which restricts or determines the signification of the second.

The compound generally takes the gender of the second part.

§ 199. When the determinative (*i.e.* the first) member is used in the sense of an apposition, expressed by a substantive or adjective or adverb or particle, we shall call the compound an appositional compound; *e.g.* राजर्षि, compounded of राजन्, 'king,' and ऋषि, 'a saint,' signifies 'a saint belonging to the order of the kings;' देवर्षि, compounded of देव, 'a god,' and ऋषि, 'a saint,' signifies 'a saint belonging to the order of the gods;' नीलोत्पल, compounded of नील, 'blue,' and उत्पल, 'lotus,' 'blue lotus;' ईषत्पिङ्गल, 'a little (ईषत्) brown (पिङ्गल),' सुकृत, 'well (सु) done (कृत).'

When the determinative member is used in the sense of a case, governed by the second member, we shall call the compound an inflectional compound, *e.g.* राजपुरुष, compounded of राजन्, 'a king,' and पुरुष, 'a man,' properly 'the king's man,' 'a watchman.'

§ 200. The terminations of some crude forms, when forming the second member, are changed. Thus, सखि, 'a friend,' becomes ऽसख; गो, 'a cow,' by adding अ, ऽगव; नौ, 'a ship,' in the same way ऽनाव; अनस्, 'a cart,' ऽअनस; राजन् rejects its final न् (*cf.* my V.G. § 639).

SPECIAL RULES FOR THE FIRST SPECIES, OR THE APPOSITIONAL COMPOUNDS (called कर्मधारय).

§ 201. When the determinative word signifies 'good' or 'bad,' it is put as the second member (contrary to § 198), *e.g.* भरत, 'one belonging to the family of the Bharatas,' and श्रेष्ठ, 'best,' becomes भरतश्रेष्ठ, 'the best Bharata;' राजन्, 'king,' and अधम, 'meanest,' राजाधम, 'a very mean king.'

Compounds of this species may also consist of words which express actions immediately succeeding one another, *e.g.* स्नातानुलिप्त, 'first bathed (स्नात) and then anointed (अनुलिप्त).'

They are also formed to express comparison, *e.g.* घनश्याम 'as black (श्याम) as a cloud (घन).'

If the comparison of two objects is declared to hold good in every point, and one object is said to be in every respect similar to another, the word denoting the object, with which the other is compared, is placed last, *e.g.* पुरुषव्याघ्र, 'a man (पुरुष) (in every respect similar to) a tiger (व्याघ्र).' We may call this kind of compounds: Compositio Karmadhâraya comparativa.

§ 202. For महन्त्, 'great,' being the first member, is substituted महा, *e.g.* महाराज, 'a great king.'

NUMERAL COMPOUNDS (called द्विगु).

§ 203. The compounds, in which the determinative word is a numeral, form a subdivision of this species. Any numeral, except एक, 'one,' may be its first member. These compounds take in general the terminations of the neuter singular, or of the singular of the feminine in ई, *e.g.* चतुर् 'four,' and युग 'age,' चतुर्युगम्, nominative sing. neuter, 'the four ages,' पञ्चन् 'five,' and तीर्थ 'a place of pilgrimage,' पञ्चतीर्थी nom. sing. fem., 'the five principal places of pilgrimage' (called Prayâga, Naimisha, etc.). Or they are used as adjectives signifying 'having the value, measure, weight, etc., of,' *e.g.* पञ्चन् 'five,' and कपाल 'cup' = पञ्चकपाल (adjective, crude form) 'measured by five cups.'

When the compound becomes a substantive of the neuter gender, or an adjective, final आ, ई, and ऊ of the last component are shortened, *e.g.* द्वि 'two' + खारी 'a measure of grain' = द्विखारि. गो 'cow,' being second member, becomes गु, *e.g.* द्विगु, adj. 'of the value of two cows.'

SPECIAL RULES FOR THE SECOND SPECIES OR INFLECTIONAL COMPOUNDS (called तत्पुरुष κατ' ἐξοχήν).

§ 204. Words in the sense of the genitive case may be compounded with almost any other word as governing member, *e.g.* देवपुत्र, 'a son (पुत्र) of a god (देव).'

Compounds, the first part of which stands in the sense of another case, seldom occur. For the instances, in which words in such relations may be compounded, see my V.G. §§ 652, 653. Thus the first member has the sense of an accusative in ग्रामप्राप्त, 'one who has reached (प्राप्त) a village (ग्राम),' of an instrumental in धान्यार्थ, 'wealth (अर्थ) by grain (धान्य),' of a dative in यूपदारु, 'timber (दारु) for a stake (यूप),' of an ablative in स्वर्गपतित 'fallen (पतित) from heaven (स्वर्ग),' of a locative in स्थालीपक्व, 'boiled (पक्व) in a pot (स्थाली).'

§ 205. This class includes also some compounds, the first member of which governs the second, and is

1. A preposition, *e.g.* अतिराज 'surpassing (अति, properly 'beyond') the king' (*cf.* § 200).

2. A participle, *e.g.* भरद्वसु, 'bringing (भरन्त्, *cf.* § 168; 193, 2) wealth (वसु).'

Compounds of the latter kind are used in the Veda only.

The compounds of both kinds become adjectives, which shorten a final आ, ई, ऊ, of the last component as in § 203.

THIRD CLASS: RELATIVE COMPOUNDS (called बहुव्रीहि).

§ 206. A determinative compound may be used as the attribute of a substantive and consequently become an adjective, *e.g.* the

Karmadhâraya-compound महाबाहु, 'a great (महा, *cf.* § 202) arm (बाहु),' may immediately be used also as the attribute, *e.g.* of a mighty king in the sense of 'great-arm-ed,' 'having a great arm;' पीताम्बर, also a Karmadhâraya, 'a yellow (पीत) cloth (अम्बर),' as the attribute, *e.g.* of Çiva, 'yellow-cloth-ed;' the Tatpurusha-compound स्त्रीप्रमाण, 'authority (प्रमाण) of a wife (स्त्री),' as the attribute, *e.g.* of a doctrine 'wife-witness-ed,' 'a doctrine whose authority is a wife.'

§ 207. The change of a determinative compound to a relative one is generally indicated only by the accent being displaced (for which *cf.* my V.G. §§ 673-677) and the word being changed from a substantive to an adjective, *e.g.* स्त्रीप्रमाण (§ 206), being as Tatpurusha a neuter, becomes as Bahuvrîhi an adjective.

When the latter change take place, the shortening of final आ, ई, and ऊ of the last component and the changing of final गो, 'cow,' to गु takes place as in § 203, *e.g.* दीर्घजङ्घा, fem. Karmadhâraya, 'a long leg,' becomes as Bahuvrîhi दीर्घजङ्घ ('long-legg-ed'), 'having a long leg,' But many words necessarily or optionally add the affix क, which is generally employed for the formation of adjectives. Thus nearly all the compounds ending in ऋ must add it, *e.g.* ख्यातभर्तृ, 'a renowned husband' (Karmadhâraya), as relative compound (Bahuvrîhi) makes ख्यातभर्तृक, 'having a renowned husband.' But सुरूपमाला, 'a beautiful garland' (Karmadhâraya), may become either सुरूपमाल or सुरूपमालक, 'having a beautiful garland.'

Some compounds of this class change the termination of the second members. Thus we have:—

ऽअक्ष instead of अक्षि 'the eye.'	ऽकाकुद् instead of काकुद 'the palate.'
ऽअश्र „ „ अश्रि 'an edge,' 'a corner.'	ऽकुक्ष „ „ कुक्षि 'the belly.'
ऽईर्मन् „ „ ईर्म 'a wound.'	ऽगन्धि „ „ गन्ध 'smell.'
ऽककुद् „ „ ककुद 'a summit.'	ऽचतुर „ „ चतुर् 'four.'
	ऽजम्भन् „ „ जम्भ 'a tooth.'

ऽज्ञु	instead of	जानु 'the knee.'	ऽपद् and ऽपाद्	instead of	पाद 'a foot.'
ऽदन्त्	„	„ दन्त 'a tooth.'			
ऽदिव	„	„ दिवन् 'the day.'	ऽप्रजस्	instead of	प्रजा 'progeny.'
ऽधन्वन्	„	„ धनुस् 'a bow.'	ऽमूर्ध	„	„ मूर्धन् 'the head.'
ऽधर्मन्	„	„ धर्म 'law.'	ऽमेधस्	„	„ मेधा 'understanding.'
ऽनस	„	„ नासिका 'the nose.'	ऽसक्थ	„	„ सक्थि 'the thigh.'
ऽनाभ	„	„ नाभि 'the navel.'	ऽहल	„	„ हलि 'a furrow.'
ऽनेत्र	„	„ नेतृ 'a guide.'	ऽहृद्	„	„ हृदय 'the heart.'

The first member also sometimes takes a form differing from that which it would have when belonging to a determinative compound, *e.g.* 'a fifth consort' (Karmadhâraya) would be पञ्चमभार्या, but 'having a fifth wife' (Bahuvrîhi), पञ्चमीभार्य with the sign of the feminine (§ 261) added to the first member. The feminine termination is subjoined to the first member also in some other instances, *cf.* my V.G. § 667.

For महत्, 'great,' being the first member, is substituted महा, as in § 202.

APPENDIX.

§ 208. In order to express the continual repetition of an action, or the continual recurrence of the same object, the word signifying it is doubled and thus forms a compound, the second part of which loses its accent, *e.g.* प॑चति, 'he cooks,' प॑चतिपचति, 'he cooks continually;' ग्रा॑मः, 'a village,' ग्रा॑मोग्रामः (§ 28, Exc. 1), 'one village after the other.'

प॑र and अ॒न्य, 'another,' are repeated and form compounds in a similar manner, signifying 'one another.' But then the first member is put in the nominative singular masculine (§ 222, 1), *e.g.* प॑रस्पर (at the same time without changing the original स् to Visarga :), अ॒न्यो॑न्य (§ 28, Exc. 1, and § 23). इतर, 'another,' doubles the crude form इतरेतर (§ 21, 1).

The particle इव, 'like,' is compounded with the preceding word, *e.g.* राजा ऽ इव (§ 7) राजेव (§ 21, 1), 'like a king.'

IV. Gender. Formation of Feminines and Neuters.

§ 209. The crude forms ending in अ *a* are of masculine or neuter gender.

Masculines are all, with few exceptions, the primitive abstract nouns formed by the affix अ *a*, *e.g.* जय *jaya*, 'victory,' from जि *ji*, 'to conquer.'

Neuters are the primitive nouns formed by the affix अन *ana*, *e.g.* वचन *vachana*, 'speech,' from वच् *vach*, 'to speak.' Those abstract nouns only, which are derived from verbs formed by the affix अय *aya*, become feminines by lengthening the final अ *a*, *e.g.* भावना *bhâvanâ*, from भावय *bhâvaya*, causal of भू *bhû*.

Neuters are further the collective and abstract nouns formed by secondary अ *a*. Those formed by the secondary affix य *ya* may be of the neuter or feminine gender. In the latter case they take the termination ई *î* (§ 210), before which य *ya*, when preceded by a consonant, is rejected, *e.g.* मैत्र्य *maitrya*, 'friendship,' neut., or मैत्री *maitrî*, fem.

Most crude forms ending in आ *â* are feminines. Very few are substantives of the masculine gender, but some are adjectives of the masculine and feminine gender.

Crude forms of substantives ending in इ *i* are of the masculine and feminine, very few of the neuter gender.

The words in ई *î* are, like those in आ *â*, mostly feminines; very few are substantives of the masculine gender, but some are adjectives of the masculine and feminine gender.

Those in उ *u* mostly are masculines.

Those in ऊ *û* are nearly all feminines; some few masculines.

Substantives in ऋ *ṛi* are mostly masculines, some are feminines, very few neuters.

रै *rai*, 'wealth,' the only substantive in ऐ *ai*, is masculine; द्यो *dyo*, 'heaven,' fem.; गो *go*, 'ox, cow,' masc. and fem.; ग्लौ *glau*, 'moon,' masculine; नौ *nau*, 'ship,' feminine.

The substantives ending in अन् *an* are masculines; those in मन् *man* mostly neuters. Of the latter gender is also the greatest part of those in अस् *as*, इस् *is*, and उस् *us*. The substantives ending in other consonants, the number of which is very small, are mostly feminines; some also masculines or neuters (*cf.* my V.G. § 707 sqq.)

Compound substantives have, with few exceptions, the gender of their last member.

§ 210. Substantives or adjectives of feminine gender, when derived from masculines ending in अ *a*, lengthen this vowel or substitute ई *í* for it, *e.g.* गत *gata*, masc. and neuter, 'gone,' गता, *gatá*, fem., देव *deva*, masc., 'a god,' देवी *deví*, fem., 'a goddess.'

Masculines in इ *i* generally have no special form for the feminine. Some however lengthen their final, *e.g.* सखि *sakhi*, masc., 'a friend,' सखी *sakhí*, fem., 'a female friend.'

Masculines ending in उ *u* likewise modify very seldom their crude form, when becoming feminines, but some may optionally subjoin ई *í*, before which उ *u* is changed to व् *v*, *e.g.* लघु *laghu*, masc. and neut., 'light,' in the fem. either unchanged or लघ्वी *laghví*. Some lengthen their final, *e.g.* पङ्गु *pangu*, masc. and neut., 'lame,' fem. पङ्गू *pangú*.

The affix ई is added also to the remaining crude forms, which are changed when expressing the feminine gender, viz.:—

1. To many of those ending in ऋ *ṛi*, which must be changed to र् *r*, *e.g.* दातृ *dátṛi*, 'one who gives,' fem. दात्री *dátrí*.

2. To the words ending in अञ्च् *anch*, the present and future participles in अन्त् *ant* and अत् *at* (§ 168), the nouns in मन्त् *mant*, वन्त् *vant*, यन्त् *yant*, and न् *n*, the participles of the reduplicated perfect (§ 169) and the second comparative (§ 243).

These words subjoin the affix ई *î* to that form which they have before the termination of the instrumental singular, *e.g.*

प्रत्यञ्च् *pratyañch* 'following,'	instrum. sing. प्रतीचा, *pratîchâ*	fem. प्रतीची *pratîchî*
चिन्वन्त् *chinvant* 'arranging,'	" " चिन्वता, *chinvatâ*	" चिन्वती *chinvatî*
पिप्रत् *piprat* 'filling,'	" " पिप्रता, *pipratâ*	" पिप्रती *pipratî*
अग्निमन्त् *agnimant* 'having fire,'	" " अग्निमता, *agnimatâ*	" अग्निमती *agnimatî*
कियन्त् *kiyant* 'how great,'	" " कियता, *kiyatâ*	" कियती *kiyatî*
राजन् *râjan* 'king,'	" " राज्ञा, *râjñâ*	" राज्ञी *râjñî*
Participle of the reduplicated perfect of रुद् 'having wept' (§ 169),	" " रुरुदुषा, *rurudushâ*	" रुरुदुषी *rurudushî*
यवीयंस् *yavîyaṁs* (comparative of युवन् *yuvan* 'young'),	" " यवीयसा, *yavîyasâ*	" यवीयसी *yavîyasî*

Exceptions :—

1. The present participles of the first conjugation, except those of the sixth conjugational class, retain the penultimate न् *n*, *e.g.* बोधन्त् *bodhant*, fem. बोधन्ती *bodhantî*. The verbs of the sixth conjugational class and those of the second conjugational class ending in आ *â*, and the future participles of the active may optionally retain it, *e.g.* तुदन्त् *tudant* (from तुद् *tud*, I. 6), fem. तुदती *tudatî* or तुदन्ती *tudantî*, यान्त् *yânt* (from या *yâ*, II. 2, 'to go'), fem. याती *yâtî* or यान्ती *yântî*, नेष्यन्त् *neshyant* (from नी *nî*, 'to lead'), fem. नेष्यती *neshyatî* or नेष्यन्ती *neshyantî*.

2. Many words ending in न् change final न् *n* to र् *r*, *e.g.* पीवन् *pîvan*, fem. पीवरी *pîvarî*.

§ 210 *b*. The crude form of the neuter accords with that of the masculine; only, when the masculines end in a long vowel, the vowel is shortened, and a final ए *e*, or ऐ *ai*, becomes इ *i*, a final ओ *o*, or औ *au*, उ *u*, *e.g.* सोमपा *somapâ*, masc. and fem., 'one who drinks the Soma juice,' becomes in the neuter सोमप *somapa*; ग्रामणी *grâmaṇí*, masc. and fem., ग्रामणि *grâmaṇi*, neuter; खलपू *khalapû*, masc. and fem., खलपु *khalapu*, neuter; बहुरै *bahurai*, masc. and fem., बहुरि *bahuri*, neuter; सुद्यो *sudyo*, masc. and fem., सुद्यु *sudyu*, neuter; अतिनौ *atinau*, masc. and fem., अतिनु *atinu*, neuter.

SECTION II. DECLENSION OF NOUNS.

1. SUBSTANTIVES AND ADJECTIVES.

§ 211. There are very few indeclinable substantives, as स्वर् *svar*, 'heaven' (*cf.* my V.G. § 781), also a few which are used in the plural only (*ib.* § 716). All the rest have three numbers, singular, dual, and plural, and in each of them eight cases, nominative, vocative, accusative, instrumental, signifying *by*, and sometimes *with*; dative, *to*; ablative, *from*; genitive, *of*; and locative, *in*.

Some nouns, especially patronymics, form the plural not from the crude form of the singular, but from its etymological base, *e.g.* आत्रेय *âtreya*, patronymic derived from अत्रि *atri*, 'a descendant of Atri,' is used in the singular and dual only, while the cases of the plural are derived from अत्रि *atri*.

The accent is generally that of the crude form, *e.g. mánas*, 'mind,' dat. sing. *mánas-e*. But the vocative has the acute on its first syllable, *e.g. agní*, 'fire,' nom. sing. *agnís*, but voc. *ágne*. Crude forms ending in any letter but अ *a* or आ *â*, and consisting only of one syllable, have generally the accent on the inflectional termination, except in the nominative, vocative, and accusative, *cf. e.g.* § 230.

FIRST CLASS: CRUDE FORMS ENDING IN CONSONANTS.

§ 212. The terminations are:

	SINGULAR m.f.n.	m.f.	n.	DUAL m.f.n.	m.f.	n.	PLURAL m.f.n.	m.f.	n.
N.Voc.	0	—	—	—	N.V. Acc. औ au	ई i	—	N.V. Acc. अस् as	इ i (cf. Obs. I.)
Acc.	—	अम् am	0	—			—		
Instr.	आ â	—	—	Inst. Dat. Abl. भ्याम् bhyâm	—	—	Inst. भिस् bhis	—	—
Dat.	ए e	—	—				Dat. Abl. भ्यस् bhyas	—	—
Abl.	अस् as	—	—						
Gen.				Gen. Loc. ओस् os	—	—	Gen. आम् âm	—	—
Loc.	इ i	—	—				Loc. सु su	—	—

Observ. I. In the plural nominative, vocative, and accusative of the neuter gender a nasal is inserted after the last vowel of the crude form, viz., ङ् *ṅ* before gutturals; ञ् *ń* before palatals; ण् *ṇ* before linguals; न् *n* before dentals, र् *r* and ल् *l*; म् *m* before labials; Anusvâra ं (or ँ) before sibilants and ह् *h*, *e.g.* सर्वशक् *sarvaçak*, plur. nom. voc. acc. सर्वशङ्कि *sarvaça-ṅ-k-i*; असृज् *asṛij*, असृञ्जि *asṛi-ń-j-i*; शकृत् *çakṛit*, शकृन्ति *çakṛi-n-t-i*.

The nasal is not inserted in crude forms:—

1. Which are identical with the crude form of the desiderative after having rejected the final अ *a*, or with the crude form of the frequentative, *e.g.* पिपठिष् *pipaṭhish* (from पिपठिष *pipaṭhisha*, desiderative of पठ् *paṭh*), plural nom. voc. acc. पिपठिषि *pipaṭhish-i*.

2. Which end in a semi-vowel or nasal, *e.g.* बहुपुर् *bahupur*, plur. nom. voc. acc. बहुपुरि *bahupuri*, प्रशाम् *praçâm*, प्रशामि *praçâmi*.

The insertion is optional:—

1. In the present participles which have no न् *n* before their

final त् *t* (§ 168), *e.g.* पिप्रत् *piprat*, plur. nom. voc. acc. पिप्रति *piprat-i* or पिप्रन्ति *pipra-n-ti*.

2. In crude forms with a final compound consonant, the first element of which is र् *r* or ल् *l*, *e.g.* सुवल्ग् *suvalg*, plur. nom. voc. acc. सुवल्गि *suvalg-i* or सुवन्ल्गि *suva-n-lg-i*.

Observ. II. The rule for the change of स् *s* to ष् *sh*, given in § 17, is applicable to the termination of the locative plural.

PARADIGM: सुगण् *sugaṇ*, m.f.n., 'counting well, a good reckoner.'

SINGULAR.

	m.f.n.	m.f.	n.
N.V.	सुगण् *sugaṇ*	—	—
Acc.	—	सुगणम् *sugaṇam*	सुगण् *sugaṇ*
Instr.	सुगणा *sugaṇâ*	—	—
Dat.	सुगणे *sugaṇe*	—	—
Abl. Gen.	सुगणस् *sugaṇas*	—	—
Loc.	सुगणि *sugaṇi*	—	—

DUAL.

	m.f.n.	m.f.	n.
N.V. Acc.	—	सुगणौ *sugaṇau*	सुगणी *sugaṇî*
Instr. Dat. Abl.	सुगण्भ्याम् *sugaṇbhyâm*	—	—
Gen. Loc.	सुगणोस् *sugaṇos*	—	—

PLURAL.

	m.f.n.	m.f.	n.
N.V. Acc.	—	सुगणस् *sugaṇas*	सुगणि *sugaṇi*
Instr.	सुगण्भिस् *sugaṇbhis*	—	—
Dat. Abl.	सुगण्भ्यस् *sugaṇbhyas*	—	—
Gen.	सुगणाम् *sugaṇâm*	—	—
Loc.	सुगण्सु *sugaṇsu*	—	—

This paradigm suffices also for crude forms ending in ल् *l, e.g.* सुज्वल् *sujval,* adj. 'blazing beautifully.'

§ 213. Crude forms ending in other simple or compound consonants undergo various euphonic changes in the singular nominative and vocative masc., fem., and neuter; the singular accusative neuter; the instrumental, dative, and ablative of the dual and plural; and the locative of the plural.

I. In the singular nominative and vocative masc., fem., and neuter, the singular accusative neuter, and the plural locative:—

Final ख् *kh,* ग् *g,* घ् *gh,* च् *ch,* ज् *j,* and झ् *jh* are changed to क् *k.*

Final ठ् *ṭh,* ड् *ḍ,* ढ् *ḍh,* छ् *chh,* श् *ç,* ष् *sh,* क्ष् *ksh,* and ह् *h* to ट् *ṭ.*

Final थ् *th,* द् *d,* and ध् *dh* to त् *t.*

Final फ् *ph,* ब् *b,* and भ् *bh,* to प् *p.*

Final म् *m* to न् *n.*

Final ण् *ṇ,* र् *r,* and ल् *l* are left unchanged. But in the nominative and vocative masc., fem., and neuter, and in the accusative neuter र् *r,* according to § 13, is changed to Visarga (:).

For the change of final न् *n, cf.* § 221, III., IV., for that of a final स् *s, cf.* § 215.

II. In the instrumental, dative, and ablative dual and plural, the terminations of which begin with भ् *bh*:—

Final क् *k,* ख् *kh,* घ् *gh,* च् *ch,* ज् *j,* and झ् *jh* are changed to ग् *g.*

Final ट् *ṭ,* ठ् *ṭh,* ढ् *ḍh,* छ् *chh,* श् *ç,* ष् *sh,* क्ष् *ksh,* and ह् *h* to ड् *ḍ.*

Final त् *t,* थ् *th,* and ध् *dh* to द् *d.*

Final प् *p,* फ् *ph,* and भ् *bh* to ब् *b.*

Final म् *m* to न् *n,* as in I.

Final ण् *ṇ,* र् *r,* and ल् *l* are left unchanged, and for न् *n* and स् *s, cf.* § 221, III., IV., and § 215.

Except. to I. and II. ह् *h* terminating a syllable which begins with द् *d,* and the noun उष्णिह् *ushṇih,* 'a kind of metre,' is changed in the singular nominative and vocative masc., fem., and neuter, in the sing. accusative neuter, and in the locative plural to क् *k,* before भ् *bh* to ग् *g.*

Observ. to I. and II.:—

1. If the last syllable of the crude form ends in घ् *gh*, ढ् *ḍh*, ध् *dh*, भ् *bh*, or ह् *h*, and begins with ग् *g*, ड् *ḍ*, द् *d*, or ब् *b*, the latter are changed to घ् *gh*, ढ् *ḍh*, ध् *dh*, and भ् *bh*, *e.g.* कामदुह् *kâma-duh*, nom. and voc. कामधुक् *kâma-dhuk*, *cf.* p. 221.

2. इ् *i* and उ *u*, when preceding a final radical र् *r* or स् *s*, are lengthened, *e.g.* गिर् *gir*, fem., 'speech,' nom. and voc. sing. गीर् *gîr* (गीः *gîḥ*), instr., dat., abl. dual गीर्भ्याम् *gîr-bhyâm*, instr., plur., गीर्भिस् *gîr-bhis*, dat. and abl. plur. गीर्भ्यस् *gîr-bhyas*, loc. plur. गीर्षु *gîr-shu* (*cf.* § 17); पुर् *pur*, fem., 'town,' पूर् *pûr* (पूः *pûḥ*), पूर्भ्याम् *pûr-bhyâm*.

III. Crude forms ending in compound consonants, except क्ष् *ksh*, for which see I. and II., undergo the following changes:—

1. If the compound consonant consists of two letters, the first element of which is र् *r* and the second a guttural, palatal, lingual, dental or labial, except a nasal, the rules given in I. and II. must be applied also here, *e.g.* ऊर्ज् *ûrj*, fem., 'strength,' nom. voc. sing. ऊर्क् *ûrk*, instr. dat. abl. sing. ऊर्ग्भ्याम् *ûrg-bhyâm*, loc. plur. ऊर्क्षु *ûrk-shu* (*cf.* § 17).

2. If the compound consists of two other letters, or of three letters, the first of which is र् *r*, the last element is rejected. If it consists of three letters, the first of which is any other consonant than र् *r*, the two last must be dropped. The remaining final or finals are modified according to the rules given in I. II., and III., 1, *e.g.* सुवल्ग् *suvalg*, nom. voc. sing. masc., fem., and neuter, and acc. sing. neuter सुवल् *suval*, instr. dat. abl. dual सुवल्भ्याम् *suval-bhyâm*, loc. plur. सुवल्षु *suval-shu* (§ 17); चिकीर्ष् *chikîrsh* (for original चिकीर्स् *chikîrs*, from the desiderative चिकीर्ष *chikîrsha*, for original चिकीर्स *chikîr-sa*, § 53), nom. voc. sing. m.f.n. and acc. sing. n. चिकीर् *chikîr* (चिकीः *chikîḥ*), instr. dat. abl. dual चिकीर्भ्याम् *chikîr-bhyâm*, loc. plur. चिकीर्षु *chikîr-shu*; सिस्यन्त्स् *sisyants*, nom. voc. sing. m.f.n. and acc. sing. n. सिस्यन्

sisyan, instr. dat. abl. dual सिस्यन्भ्याम् *sisyan-bhyâm*, loc. plur. सिस्यन्सु *sisyan-su*; सुव्रश्च् *suvraçch*, nom. voc. sing. m.f.n. and acc. sing. n. सुव्रट् *suvraṭ*, instr. dat. abl. dual सुव्रड्भ्याम् *suvraḍ-bhyâm*, loc. plur. सुव्रट्सु *suvraṭ-su*.

If the remaining consonant is Anusvâra, it is changed to न्, *e.g.* सुहिंस् *suhiṁs*, nom. voc. sing. m.f.n. and acc. sing. n. सुहिन् *suhin*, instr. dat. abl. dual सुहिन्भ्याम् *suhin-bhyâm*, loc. plur. सुहिन्सु *suhin-su*.

IV. When the termination of the locative plural सु is preceded by ण्, ट् is optionally inserted, when preceded by ट् or न्, त्, *e.g.* from सुगण्, सुगण्सु or सुगण्ट्सु, from श्वलिह्, श्वलिट्सु or श्वलिट्त्सु, from सुहिंस्, सुहिन्सु or सुहिन्त्सु.

§ 214. Examples for the Rules in the preceding Paragraph.

सर्वशक् *sarvaçak*, nom. voc. sing. m.f.n. and acc. sing. n. सर्वशक् *sarvaçak*, instr. dat. abl. dual सर्वशग्भ्याम् *sarvaçag-bhyâm*, instr. pl. °ग्भिस् *°g-bhis*, dat. abl. pl. °ग्भ्यस् *°g-bhyas*, loc. plur. सर्वशक्षु *sarvaçak-shu*. The other cases follow the analogy of the paradigm in § 212, sing. instr. सर्वशका *sarvaçak-â*, etc., nom. acc. voc. plur. neuter सर्वशङ्कि *sarvaçaṅk-i* (§ 212, Obs. 1).

सुलिख् *sulikh*, nom. voc. sing. m.f.n. and acc. sing. n. सुलिक् *sulik*, instr. dat. abl. dual सुलिग्भ्याम् *sulig-bhyâm*, loc. plur. सुलिक्षु *sulik-shu*, instr. sing. सुलिखा *sulikh-â*, etc., nom. voc. acc. plur. neuter सुलिङ्खि *suliṅkh-i*.

गजमृग् *gajamṛig*, गजमृक् *gajamṛik*, गजमृग्भ्याम् *gajamṛig-bhyâm*, गजमृक्षु *gajamṛik-shu*, गजमृगा *gajamṛig-â*, गजमृङ्गि *gajamṛiṅg-i*.

वाच् *vâch*, fem. 'speech,' वाक् *vâk*, वाग्भ्याम् *vâg-bhyâm*, वाक्षु *vâk-shu*, वाचा *vâch-â*. सुवाच् *suvâch*, adj. 'well speaking,' nom. voc. acc. plur. neuter सुवाञ्चि *suvâñch-i*.

ऋत्विज् *ṛitvij*, masc. 'a priest,' ऋत्विक् *ṛitvik*, ऋत्विग्भ्याम् *ṛitvig-bhyâm*, ऋत्विक्षु *ṛitvik-shu*, ऋत्विजा *ṛitvij-â*.

प्राछ् *prâchh*, masc. 'an inquirer,' प्राट् *prâṭ*, प्राड्भ्याम् *prâḍ-bhyâm*, प्राट्सु *prâṭsu* or प्राट्त्सु, प्राछा *prâchh-â*.

विश् *viç*, masc. 'a man of the third caste,' विट् *viṭ*, विड्भ्याम् *viḍ-bhyâm*, विट्सु *viṭ-su* or विट्त्सु, विशा *viç-â*.

अभ्रंलिह् *abhraṁlih*, अभ्रंलिट् *abhraṁliṭ*, अभ्रंलिड्भ्याम् *°liḍ-bhyâm*, अभ्रंलिट्सु *°liṭ-su* or °लिट्त्सु *°liṭ-tsu*, अभ्रंलिहा *abhraṁlih-â*.

कामदुह् *kâmaduh* (§ 213, Obs. 1), nom. voc. sing. m.f.n. and acc. sing. n. कामधुक् *kâmadhuk*, instr. dat. abl. dual कामधुग्भ्याम् *°dhug-bhyâm*, loc. plur. कामधुक्षु *°dhuk-shu*, instr. sing. कामदुहा *kâmaduh-â*.

वेदबुध् *vedabudh*, nom. voc. sing. m.f.n. and acc. sing. n. वेदभुत् *vedabhut*, instr. dat. abl. dual वेदभुद्भ्याम् *°bhud-bhyâm*, loc. plur. वेदभुत्सु *°bhut-su*, instr. sing. वेदबुधा *vedabudh-â*.

सुलभ् *sulabh*, सुलप् *sulap*, सुलब्भ्याम् *sulab-bhyâm*, सुलप्सु *sulap-su*, सुलभा *sulabh-â*.

प्रशाम् *praçâm*, nom. voc. sing. m.f.n. and acc. sing. n. प्रशान् *praçân*, instr. dat. abl. dual प्रशान्भ्याम् *praçân-bhyâm*, loc. plur. प्रशान्सु *praçân-su* or प्रशान्त्सु, instr. sing. प्रशामा *praçâm-â*.

Cf. the examples in II. Obs. 2, III. and IV.

Exceptions:—

1. Nouns derived without affix from the verbs भ्राज् *bhrâj*, 'to shine,' मृज् *mṛij*, 'to clean,' यज् *yaj*, 'to sacrifice' (except ऋत्विज् *ṛitvij*, compounded from ऋतु ऽ इज् for यज्), राज् *râj*, 'to shine,' सृज् *sṛij*, 'to abandon,' भ्रज्ज् *bhrajj*, 'to fry,' and the noun परिव्राज् *parivrâj*, 'a mendicant devotee,' change their final in the nominative and vocative singular m.f.n., accusative sing. neuter, and the locative plural to ट् *ṭ*, and before the terminations beginning with भ् *bh* to ड् *ḍ*, *e.g.* अमार्ज् *amârj*, sing. nom. voc. m.f.n. and acc. n. अमार्ट् *amârṭ*, instr. dat. abl. dual अमार्ड्भ्याम् *amârḍ-bhyâm*, loc. plur. अमार्ट्सु *amârṭ-su*, instr. sing. अमार्जा *amârj-â*, but from ऋत्विज् regularly nom. voc. sing. ऋत्विक्, etc. (*cf.* supra).

2. Those derived without affix from दिश् *diç*, 'to show,' दृश् *dṛiç*, 'to see,' मृश् *mṛiç* and स्पृश् *spṛiç*, 'to touch,' and धृष् *dhṛish*,

'to dare,' change their final to क् *k*, and before भ् *bh* to ग् *g*. The same changes are optional in the derivatives from नश् *naç*, 'to perish;' *e.g.* दिश् *diç*, fem. 'region,' nom. voc. sing. दिक् *dik*, instr. dat. abl. dual दिग्भ्याम् *dig-bhyâm*, loc. plur. दिक्षु *dik-shu*, instr. sing. दिशा *diç-â*; दधृष् *dadhṛish*, 'impudent,' दधृक् *dadhṛik*, दधृग्भ्याम् *dadhṛig-bhyâm*, दधृक्षु *dadhṛik-shu*, दधृषा *dadhṛish-â*, but नश् *naç*, nom. voc. sing. m.f.n. and acc. n. नक् *nak* or नट् *naṭ*, etc.

3. Nouns derived from desideratives, terminating in ष *sha*, by rejecting their final अ *a*, *e.g.* पिपठिष् *pipaṭhish* from पिपठिष *pipaṭhisha*, desiderative of पठ् *paṭh*, 'to recite,' and the noun सजुष् *sajush*, 'companion,' follow the rules for the change of a final स् *s* (§ 219), *i.e.* they change their final in the nom. voc. sing. m.f.n., and acc. n. to स् *s* (Visarga :), in the loc. plur. they may leave it unchanged or change it also to Visarga, in the instr. dat. abl. dual and plur. they change it to र् *r*; in all these cases the penultimate इ *i* and उ *u* is lengthened according to § 213, II. Obs. 2, *e.g.* nom. voc. sing. m.f.n. and acc. n. पिपठीस् *pipaṭhîs* (पिपठीः °*ṭhîḥ*), सजूस् *sajûs* (सजूः °*jûḥ*), instr. dat. abl. dual पिपठीर्भ्याम् *pipaṭhîr-bhyâm*, सजूर्भ्याम् *sajûr-bhyâm*, loc. plur. पिपठीष्षु *pipaṭhîsh-shu* or पिपठीःषु °*ṭhîḥ-shu*, सजूष्षु *sajûsh-shu* or सजूःषु *sajûḥ-shu*.

4. Those derived without affix from the verbs द्रुह् *druh*, 'to injure,' मुह् *muh*, 'to be perplexed,' स्निह् *snih*, 'to love,' स्नुह् *snuh*, 'to vomit,' may optionally change their final to ट् *ṭ* or क् *k*, and before भ् *bh* to ड् *ḍ* or ग् *g*, *e.g.* nom. voc. sing. m.f.n. and acc. sing. n. ऽध्रुक् -*dhruk* or ऽध्रुट् -*dhruṭ*, ऽध्रुग्भ्याम् -*dhrug-bhyâm* or ऽध्रुड्भ्याम् -*dhruḍ-bhyâm*, ऽध्रुक्षु -*dhruk-shu* or ऽध्रुट्सु -*dhruṭ-su*, instr. sing. ऽद्रुहा -*druh-â*.

5. Those from the verb नह् *nah*, 'to tie,' change the ह् *h* to त् *t*, and before भ् *bh* to द् *d*, *e.g.* उपानह् *upânah*, fem. 'a shoe,' nom. voc. sing. उपानत् °*nat*, instr. dat. abl. dual उपानद्भ्याम् °*nad-bhyâm*, loc. plur. उपानत्सु °*nat-su*, instr. sing. उपानहा *upânah-â*.

CRUDE FORMS ENDING IN स् *s*.

§ 215. The termination of the locative plural, सु *su*, is changed to षु *shu*, when subjoined to इस् *is*, उस् *us*, or ओस् *os*, and the final स् *s* is changed either to ष् *sh* or to Visarga (:), *e.g.* ज्योतिस् *jyotis*, neut. 'light,' ज्योतिष्षु *jyotish-shu* or ज्योतिःषु *°tiḥ-shu*, चक्षुस् *chakshus*, neut. 'the eye,' चक्षुष्षु *chakshush-shu* or चक्षुःषु *°shuḥ-shu*, दोस् *dos*, m.n. 'the arm,' दोष्षु *dosh-shu* or दोःषु *doḥ-shu*.

The nouns ending in अस् *as* or आस् *âs* either change their final to Visarga (:), or leave it unchanged, *e.g.* मनस् *manas*, neut. 'the mind,' मनःसु *manaḥ-su* or मनस्सु *manas-su*.

§ 216. Crude forms ending in affixal अस् *as* lengthen the penultimate अ *a* in the nominative singular of the masculine and feminine genders, *e.g.* सुमनस् *sumanas* (= सु ऽ मनस् *su-manas*, where the latter word is derived from मन् *man*, 'to think,' by the affix अस् *as*) adj., 'well disposed,' nom. sing. m.f. सुमनास् *sumanâs* (सुमनाः *°nâḥ*, § 13), but पिण्डग्रस् *piṇḍa-gras* (पिण्ड ऽ ग्रस्, where the अस् *as* is radical), adj., 'eating a mouthful,' nom. sing. m.f. पिण्डग्रस् *piṇḍagras* (पिण्डग्रः *°graḥ*).

§ 217. Before the terminations of the instrumental, dative, and ablative dual and plural, beginning with भ् *bh*, final अस् *as* becomes ओ *o*, final आस् *âs* drops the स् *s*, and in final इस् *is*, उस् *us*, and ओस् *os*, the स् *s* is changed to र् *r*, *e.g.* मनस् *manas*, instr. dat. abl. dual मनोभ्याम् *mano-bhyâm*; चकास् *chakâs*, adj. (*cf.* § 28 with Exc. 1, 2), 'resplendent,' चकाभ्याम् *chakâ-bhyâm*; ज्योतिस् *jyotis*, ज्योतिर्भ्याम् *jyotir-bhyâm*; चक्षुस् *chakshus*, चक्षुर्भ्याम् *chakshur-bhyâm*; दोस् *dos*, दोर्भ्याम् *dor-bhyâm*.

§ 218. Those nouns, the final स् *s* of which belongs to an affix, lengthen the vowels preceding the Anusvâra ं, which must be inserted in the nominative, vocative, and accusative plural of the neuter, according to § 212, Obs. 1, and those which end in affixal इस् *is*, उस् *us*, or ओस् *os*, change the स् *s*, when followed by vowels, to ष् *sh*, *e.g.* मनस् *manas*, neut., nom. voc. acc. plur. मनांसि *ma-*

nâm̃s-i ; ज्योतिस् *jyotis*, ज्योतींषि *jyotîm̃sh-i*, instr. sing. ज्योतिषा *jyotish-â* ; चक्षुस् *chakshus*, चक्षूंषि *chakshûm̃sh-i*, चक्षुषा *chakshush-â*. But from सुतुस् *sutus*, adj., 'well sounding,' where the final उस् *us* is radical, सुतुंसि *sutum̃s-i*, सुतुसा *sutus-â*, without lengthening the vowel or changing the स् *s*.

Observation. आशिस् *âçis*, fem., 'blessing,' also changes its final स् *s*, though it be radical (from the verb शास् *çâs*), before vowels to ष् *sh*, *e.g.* instr. sing. आशिषा *âçish-â*.

§ 219. Crude forms ending in radical इस् *is* or उस् *us* lengthen the penultimate इ *i* and उ *u* in the singular nominative and vocative m.f.n and accusative n., the instrumental, dative, and ablative dual and plural, and the locative plural, *e.g.* from सुतुस् *sutus* (§ 218), sing. nom. voc. m.f.n. and acc. n. सुतूस् *sutûs* (सुतूः *°tûḥ*), instr. dat. abl. dual सुतूर्भ्याम् *sutûr-bhyâm*, loc. plur. सुतूष्षु *sutûsh-shu* or सुतूःषु *sutûḥ-shu*.

Paradigms : मनस् *mánas*, neut. 'mind,' सुमनस् *sumánas*, adj. 'well disposed,' ज्योतिस् *jyótis*, neut. 'light,' चक्षुस् *chákshus*, neut. 'the eye,' all with affixal स् *s*, and पिण्डग्रस् *piṇḍagras*, adj., सुतुस् *sutus*, adj., with radical स् *s*.

	SINGULAR.	DUAL.	PLURAL.
N.V.A.	मनस् *mánas*	मनसी *mánas-î*	मनांसि *mánâm̃s-i*
Instr.	मनसा *mánas-â*	Instr. Dat. Abl. मनोभ्याम् *máno-bhyâm*	मनोभिस् *máno-bhis*
Dat.	मनसे *mánas-e*		Dat. Abl. मनोभ्यस् *máno-bhyas*
Abl. Gen.	मनसस् *mánas-as*	Gen. Loc. मनसोस् *mánas-os*	Gen. मनसाम् *mánas-âm*
Loc.	मनसि *mánas-i*		Loc. मनस्सु or मनःसु *mánas-su mánaḥ-su*

In the same way are declined पयस् *páyas*, n. 'milk,' यशस् *yáças*, n. 'glory.'

	SINGULAR. m.f.n.	m.f.	n.		DUAL. m.f.n.	m.f.	n.
N.	—	सुमनास् *sumánâs*	सुमनस् *sumánas*	N.	—	सुमनसौ *sumanas-au*	सुमनसी *sumanas-î*
V.	सुमनस् *súmanas*	—	—	V.	—	सुमनसौ *sumanas-au*	सुमनसी *sumanas-î*
Acc.	—	सुमनसम् *sumánas-am*	सुमनस् *sumánas*	A.	—	सुमनसौ *sumanas-au*	सुमनसी *sumanas-î*
I.	सुमनसा *sumánas-â*	—	—	I.D.Abl.	सुमनोभ्याम् *sumáno-bhyâm*	—	—
D.	सुमनसे *sumánas-e*	—	—	I.D.Abl.	सुमनोभ्याम् *sumáno-bhyâm*	—	—
Abl. G.	सुमनसस् *sumánas-as*	—	—	I.D.Abl. / G.L.	सुमनोभ्याम् / सुमनसोस् *sumánas-os*	—	—
L.	सुमनसि *sumánas-i*	—	—	G.L.	सुमनसोस् *sumánas-os*	—	—

PLURAL.

	m.f.n.	m.f.	n.
N.	—	सुमनसस् *sumanas-as*	सुमनांसि *sumanâṁs-i*
V.	—	सुमनसस् *sumanas-as*	सुमनांसि *sumanâṁs-i*
Acc.	—	सुमनसस् *sumanas-as*	सुमनांसि *sumanâṁs-i*
I.	सुमनोभिस् *sumáno-bhis*	—	—
D. Abl.	सुमनोभ्यस् *sumáno-bhyas*	—	—
G.	सुमनसाम् *sumánas-âm*	—	—
L.	सुमनस्सु (or सुमनःसु) *sumánas-su* *sumánaḥ-su*	—	—

	SINGULAR.	DUAL.	PLURAL.
N.V.A.	ज्योतिस् *iyótis*	ज्योतिषी *jyótish-î*	ज्योतींषि *jyótiṁsh-i*
I.	ज्योतिषा *jyótish-â*	I.D.Abl. ज्योतिर्भ्याम् *jyótir-bhyâm*	ज्योतिर्भिस् *jyótir-bhis*
D.	ज्योतिषे *jyótish-e*	I.D.Abl. ज्योतिर्भ्याम् *jyótir-bhyâm*	D.Abl. ज्योतिर्भ्यस् *jyótir-bhyas*
Abl. G.	ज्योतिषस् *jyótish-as*	G.L. ज्योतिषोस् *jyótish-os*	G. ज्योतिषाम् *jyótish-âm*
L.	ज्योतिषि *jyótish-i*	G.L. ज्योतिषोस् *jyótish-os*	L. ज्योतिष्षु (°तिःषु) *jyótish-shu* (°*tiḥ-shu*)

हविस् *havis*, n. 'oblation.'

	SINGULAR.		DUAL.		PLURAL.
N.V.A.	चक्षुस् *chákshus*		चक्षुषी *chákshush-î*		चक्षूंषि *chákshûṁsh-i*
I.	चक्षुषा *chákshush-â*	I.D.Abl.	चक्षुर्भ्याम् *chákshur-bhyâm*	I.	चक्षुर्भिस् *chákshur-bhis*
D.	चक्षुषे *chákshush-e*			D. Abl.	चक्षुर्भ्यस् *chákshur-bhyas*
Abl. G.	चक्षुषस् *chákshush-as*			G.	चक्षुषाम् *chákshush-âm*
L.	चक्षुषि *chákshush-i*	G. L.	चक्षुषोस् *chákshush-os*	L.	चक्षुष्षु (°क्षुःषु) *chákshush-shu (°kshuḥ-shu)*

आयुस् *âyus*, n. 'life.'

	SINGULAR. m.f.n.	m.f.	n.		DUAL. m.f.n.	m.f.	n.
N.V.	पिण्डग्रस्	—	—	N.V. Acc.	—	पिण्डग्रसौ	पिण्डग्रसी
Acc.	—	पिण्डग्रसम्	पिण्डग्रस्				
I.	पिण्डग्रसा	—	—	I.D. Abl.	पिण्डग्रोभ्याम्	—	—
D.	पिण्डग्रसे	—	—				
Abl. G.	पिण्डग्रसस्	—	—				
L.	पिण्डग्रसि	—	—	G. L.	पिण्डग्रसोस्	—	—

PLURAL.

	m.f.n.	m.f.	n.
N.V. Acc.	—	पिण्डग्रसस्	पिण्डग्रंसि
I.	पिण्डग्रोभिस्	—	—
D. Abl.	पिण्डग्रोभ्यस्	—	—
G.	पिण्डग्रसाम्	—	—
L.	पिण्डग्रस्सु (°ग्रःसु)	—	—

	SINGULAR. m.f.n.	m.f.	n.		DUAL. m.f.n.	m.f.	n.
N.V.	सुतूस्	—	—	N.V. Acc.	—	सुतुसौ	सुतुसी
Acc.	—	सुतुसम्	सुतूस्				
I.	सुतुसा	—	—	I.D. Abl.	सुतूर्भ्याम्	—	—
D.	सुतुसे	—	—				
Abl. G.	सुतुसस्	—	—				
L.	सुतुसि	—	—	G. L.	सुतुसोस्	—	—

PLURAL.

	m.f.n.	m.f.	n.
N.V. Acc.	—	सुतुसस्	सुतुंसि
I.	सुतूर्भिस्	—	—
D. Abl.	सुतूर्भ्यस्	—	—
G.	सुतुसाम्	—	—
L.	सुतूष्षु (°तूःषु)	—	—

CRUDE FORMS WITH STRONG AND WEAK BASES INCLUDING THE CRUDE FORMS ENDING IN न्.

§ 220. There are some nouns which have a strong and a weak form. The terminations of the nominative, vocative, and accusative of the singular and dual, of the nominative and vocative of the plural in the masculine and feminine, and of the nominative, vocative, and accusative plural of the neuter are subjoined to the former, those of the other cases to the latter. Some have even three, a strong, a weak, and a weakest form. Then the application of the strong form remains unchanged, the weak form is used in the singular nominative, vocative, and accusative of the neuter, the plural locative, and before the terminations beginning with भ् *bh*; the weakest in the remaining cases.

§ 221. Nouns with strong and weak, or strong, weak, and weakest forms are:—

I. Those ending in अञ्च् *añch*, e.g. प्राञ्च् *prâñch* (*i.e. pra-añch*), adj. 'being before,' प्रत्यञ्च् *pratyañch* (*prati-añch*), 'being behind.' The full form is used in the strong cases only; in the rest the nasal is rejected, and those which have य् *y* or व् *v* before it make a weakest form, by changing य *ya* to ई *î* and व *va* to ऊ *û*. Thus प्राञ्च् *prâñch* forms all cases, except the strong ones, from प्राच् *prâch*, but प्रत्यञ्च् *pratyañch* and विष्वञ्च् *vishvañch* (*vishu-añch*), 'going everywhere,' have as weak forms प्रत्यच् *pratyach*,

विष्वच् *vishvach,* and as weakest forms प्रतीच् *pratîch,* विषूच् *vishûch.*

In the singular nominative and vocative of the masculine gender ङ् is substituted for the two finals.

PARADIGMS: प्राञ्च् *prâńch,* प्रत्यञ्च् *pratyańch* (*cf.* § 213, I., II.).

Observ. The feminine, according to § 209, is formed by adding ई *î,* and follows the paradigm देवी *devî* in § 230.

SINGULAR.

	m.n.	m.	n.
N.V.	—	प्राङ् *prâń*	प्राक् *prâk* (N.V., Acc.)
Acc.	—	प्राञ्चम् *prâńch-am*	
I.	प्राचा *prâch-â*	—	—
D.	प्राचे *prâch-e*	—	—
Abl., G.	प्राचस् *prâch-as*	—	—
Loc.	प्राचि *prâch-i*	—	—

DUAL.

	m.n.	m.	n.
N.V., Acc.	—	प्राञ्चौ *prâńch-au*	प्राची *prâch-î*
I.D., Abl.	प्राग्भ्याम् *prâg-bhyâm*	—	—
G., L.	प्राचोस् *prâch-os*	—	—

PLURAL.

	m.n.	m.	n.
N.V.	—	प्राञ्चस् *prâńch-as*	प्राञ्चि *prâńch-i* (N.V., Acc.)
Acc.	—	प्राचस् *prâch-as*	
I.	प्राग्भिस् *prâg-bhis*	—	—
D., Abl.	प्राग्भ्यस् *prâg-bhyas*	—	—
G.	प्राचाम् *prâch-âm*	—	—
L.	प्राक्षु *prâk-shu*	—	—

अवाञ्च् *avâńch,* adj., 'downward,' weak form अवाच् *avâch.*

SINGULAR.

	m.n.	m.	n.
N.V.	—	प्रत्यङ् *pratyań*	प्रत्यक् *pratyak* (N.V. Acc.)
Acc.	—	प्रत्यञ्चम् *pratyańch-am*	
I.	प्रतीचा *pratich-â*	—	—
D.	प्रतीचे *pratich-e*	—	—
Abl. G.	प्रतीचस् *pratich-as*	—	—
L.	प्रतीचि *pratich-i*	—	—

DUAL.

	m.n.	m.	n.
N.V. Acc.	—	प्रत्यञ्चौ *pratyańch-au*	प्रतीची *pratich-î*
I.D. Abl.	प्रत्यग्भ्याम् *pratyag-bhyâm*	—	—
G. L.	प्रतीचोस् *pratich-os*	—	—

PLURAL.

	m.n.	m.	n.
N.V.	—	प्रत्यञ्चस् *pratyańch-as*	प्रत्यञ्चि *pratyańch-i* (N.V. Acc.)
Acc.	—	प्रतीचस् *pratich-as*	
I.	प्रत्यग्भिस् *pratyag-bhis*	—	—
D. Abl.	प्रत्यग्भ्यस् *pratyag-bhyas*	—	—
G.	प्रतीचाम् *pratich-âm*	—	—
L.	प्रत्यक्षु *pratyak-shu*	—	—

सम्यञ्च् *samyańch*, adj., 'right,' weak form सम्यच् *samyach*, weakest form समीच् *samích*.

Exc. उदञ्च् (*ud-ańch*), 'being upwards,' weak form उदच् *udach*, weakest form उदीच् *udích*. तिर्यञ्च् *tiryańch*, 'moving tortuously,' weak form तिर्यच् *tiryach*, weakest form तिरश्च् *tiraçch*, *e.g.* singular instrumental उदीचा *udích-â*, तिरश्चा *tiraçch-â*.

II. To this class belong also the crude forms ending in न्त् *nt*, which drop the न् *n* in all the weak cases.

Exc. 1. The nasal is not rejected in the dual nominative, vocative, and accusative neuter of the participles of the first conjugation, except the sixth conjugational class. In this class, in the verbs ending in आ *â* of the second conjugational class, and in the future participles, the nasal is optionally rejected, *e.g.* बोधन्त् *bódhant,* participle of the present of बुध् *budh,* I. 1, nominative, vocative, and accusative dual neuter बोधन्ती *bódhant-î*; तुदन्त् *tudant,* present participle of तुद् *tud,* I. 6, तुदन्ती *tudant-î* or तुदती *tudat-î*; यान्त् *yânt,* the same of या *yâ,* II. 2, यान्ती *yânt-î* or याती *yât-î*; नेष्यन्त् *neshyant,* future participle of नी *nî,* नेष्यन्ती *neshyant-î* or नेष्यती *neshyat-î* (*cf.* § 210).

Exc. 2. The adjective महन्त् *mahánt,* 'great,' lengthens the अ *a* before the nasal in all strong cases, except the singular vocative of the masculine, *e.g.* acc. singular masc. महान्तम् *mahânt-am.* The same change takes place in the singular nominative of the masc. of the nouns ending in मन्त् *mant,* वन्त् *vant,* and यन्त् *yant.*

Observ. 1. In the singular nominative and vocative of the masculine the final त् *t* is dropped.

Observ. 2. The feminine, according to § 210, is formed by adding ई *î* and follows the paradigm देवी *devî* in § 230.

PARADIGM (*cf.* § 213, II.).

युनन्त् *yunánt,* present participle of यु (§ 168).

	SINGULAR.				DUAL.		
	m.n.	m.	n.		m.n.	m.	n.
N.V.	—	युनन् *yunan*[1]	युनत् *yunat*[1] (N.V. Acc.)	N.V. Acc.	—	युनन्तौ *yunant-au*[2]	युनती *yunat-î*[2]
Acc.	—	युनन्तम् *yunánt-am*					
I.	युनता *yunat-ấ*	—	—	I.D. Abl.	युनद्भ्याम् *yunád-bhyâm*	—	—
D.	युनते *yunat-é*	—	—				
Abl. G.	युनतस् *yunat-ás*	—	—	G. L.	युनतोस् *yunat-ós*	—	—
L.	युनति *yunat-í*	—	—				

[1] Nom. *yunán*; Nom. and Acc. *yunát*; Voc. *yúnan, yúnat.*
Nom. and Acc. *yunántau, yunatî́,* Voc. *yúnantau, yúnatî.*

PLURAL.

N.V.	—	युनन्तस् yunant-as[1]	युनन्ति yunant-i[1]
Acc.	—	युनतस् yunat-ás	
I.	युनद्भिस् yundd-bhis	—	—
D. Abl.	युनद्भ्यस् yundd-bhyas	—	—
G.	युनताम् yunat-ā́m	—	—
L.	युनत्सु yundt-su	—	—

Similarly बोधन्त् *bódhant*, *e.g.* singular nominative and vocative of the masculine बोधन् *bódhan*, of the neuter बोधत् *bódhat*, but in the dual nominative, vocative, and accusative of the neuter बोधन्ती *bódhant-ī*. तुदन्त् *tudánt*, nominative and vocative singular of the masculine तुदन् *tudan*, of the neuter तुदत् *tudat*, but in the nominative, vocative, and accusative dual of the neuter तुदन्ती *tudant-ī* or तुदती *tudat-ī*.

महन्त् *mahánt*, nominative singular of the masculine महान् *mahā́n*, vocative महन् *máhan*, accusative महान्तम् *mahā́nt-am*; but in the nominative, vocative, and accusative singular of the neuter महत् *mahat*, singular instrumental of the masculine and neuter महता *mahat-ā́*, etc., in the nominative, vocative, and accusative dual of the masculine महान्तौ *mahânt-au*, and in the nominative and vocative plural of the masculine महान्तस् *mahânt-as*, in the nominative, vocative, and accusative plural of the neuter महान्ति *mahânt-i*.

अग्निमन्त् *agnimant*, adj., 'one who maintains a sacrificial fire,' in the singular nominative of the masculine अग्निमान् *agnimán*,

[1] Nom. *yundntas;* Nom. and Acc. *yundnti*; Voc. *yúnantas, yúnanti.*

but in the vocative अग्निमन् *agniman*, in the nominative, accusative, and vocative of the neuter अग्निमत् *agnimat*, in the instrumental अग्निमता *agnimat-â*, etc., regularly; पयस्वन्त् *payasvant*, adj., 'having milk,' पयस्वान् *payasvân*, पयस्वन् *payasvan*, पयस्वत् *payasvat*, पयस्वता *payasvatâ*; कियन्त् *kiyant*, adj., 'how great,' कियान् *kiyân*, कियन् *kiyan*, कियत् *kiyat*, कियता *kiyatâ*.

III. Further belong to this class the crude forms ending in अन् *an*.

These lengthen the अ *a* in the strong cases, except the vocative sing. masc. and fem.; in the weak cases they reject the final न् *n*; in the weakest cases they reject अ *a*, whereupon न् *n*, when following a palatal, is changed to ञ् *ñ*, when following a lingual, to ण् *ṇ*, *e.g.* राजन् *râjan*, 'a king,' strong form राजान् *râjân*, weak form राज *râja*, weakest form राज्ञ् *râjñ*; तक्षन् *takshan*, 'a carpenter,' strong form तक्षान् *takshân*, weak form तक्ष *taksha*, weakest form तक्ष्ण् *takshṇ*.

The final न् *n* is dropped in the nominative singular of the masculine and neuter, and in the accusative singular of the neuter, optionally also in the vocative singular of the neuter.

Exc. 1. Nouns ending in the affixes मन् *man* or वन् *van*, preceded by a consonant, have no weakest form, *e.g.* वर्मन् *varman*, n. 'armour,' singular instrum. वर्मणा *varmaṇ-â* (§ 16); यज्वन् *yajvan*, m. 'sacrificer,' यज्वना *yajvan-â*.

Exc. 2. The rejection of अ *a* is optional in the locative singular of all genders and in the nominative, vocative, accusative dual of the neuter, *e.g.* मूर्धन् *mûrdhan*, masc. 'the head,' locative मूर्ध्नि *mûrdhn-i* or मूर्धनि *mûrdhan-i*; नामन् *nâman*, neut. 'the name,' loc. sing. नाम्नि *nâmn-i* or नामनि *nâman-i*, nom. voc. acc. dual नाम्नी *nâmn-î* or नामनी *nâman-î*.

PARADIGMS: राजन् *râjan*, masc., 'a king;' नामन् *nâman*, neut., 'the name.'

	SINGULAR.	DUAL.	PLURAL.
N.	राजा *râjâ*	N.V. Acc. राजानौ *râjân-au*	N. V. राजानस् *râjân-as*
V.	राजन् *râjan*		
Acc.	राजानम् *râjân-am*		Acc. राज्ञस् *râjñ-as*
I.	राज्ञा *râjñ-â*	I.D. Abl. राजभ्याम् *râja-bhyâm*	I. राजभिस् *râja-bhis*
D.	राज्ञे *râjñ-e*		D. Abl. राजभ्यस् *râja-bhyas*
Abl. G.	राज्ञस् *râjñ-as*	G. L. राज्ञोस् *râjñ-os*	G. राज्ञाम् *râjñ-âm*
L.	राज्ञि *râjñ-i* or राजनि *râjan-i*		L. राजसु *râja-su*

	SINGULAR.	DUAL.	PLURAL.
N.	नाम *nâma*	N.V. Acc. नाम्नी *nâmn-î* or नामनी *nâman-î*	N.V. Acc. नामानि *nâmân-i*
V.	नामन् *nâman* or नाम *nâma*		
Acc.	नाम *nâma*		
I.	नाम्ना *nâmn-â*	I.D. Abl. नामभ्याम् *nâma-bhyâm*	I. नामभिस् *nâma-bhis*
D.	नाम्ने *nâmn-e*		D. Abl. नामभ्यस् *nâma-bhyas*
Abl. G.	नाम्नस् *nâmn-as*	G. L. नाम्नोस् *nâmn-os*	G. नाम्नाम् *nâmn-âm*
L.	नाम्नि *nâmn-i* or नामनि *nâman-i*		L. नामसु *nâma-su*

IV. Fourthly belong to this class the crude forms ending in इन् *in.* These have a strong form in the singular nominative of the masculine and in the nominative, vocative, and accusative plural of the neuter only, in which the इ *i* is lengthened. In the singular nominative of the masculine and of the neuter, also in the accusative singular of the neuter, and before the terminations beginning with a consonant, the न् *n* is rejected, optionally also in the vocative singular of the neuter.

Obs. The feminine is formed by adding ई *í* (§ 210) and follows the paradigm देवी *deví* in § 230.

PARADIGM: धनिन् *dhanín*, adj., 'wealthy.'

SINGULAR.

	m.n.	m.	n.
N.	—	धनी *dhaní*	धनि *dhani*
V.	—	धनिन् *dhánin*	धनिन् *dhánin* or धनि *dháni*
Acc.	—	धनिनम् *dhanin-am*	धनि *dhani*
I.	धनिना *dhanin-á*	—	—
D.	धनिने *dhanin-e*	—	—
Abl. G.	धनिनस् *dhanin-as*	—	—
L.	धनिनि *dhanin-i*	—	—

DUAL.

	m.n.	m.	n.
N.V. Acc.	—	धनिनौ *dhanin-au*[1]	धनिनी *dhanin-í*
I.D. Abl.	धनिभ्याम् *dhani-bhyám*	—	—
G. L.	धनिनोस् *dhanin-os*	—	—

PLURAL.

	m.n.	m.	n.
N.V.Acc.	—	धनिनस् *dhanin-as*[2]	धनीनि *dhanín-i*[2]
Instr.	धनिभिस् *dhani-bhis*	—	—
D.Abl.	धनिभ्यस् *dhani-bhyas*	—	—
Gen.	धनिनाम् *dhanin-ám*	—	—
Loc.	धनिषु *dhani-shu*	—	—

In the same way is declined यशस्विन् *yaçasvin*, adj. 'glorious.'

[1] Nom. and Acc. *dhaninau, dhanini;* Voc. *dháninau, dhánini.*

[2] Nom. and Acc. *dhaninas, dhaníni;* Voc. *dháninas, dhánini.*

V. Fifthly belong to this class the participles of the reduplicated perfect. The affix is वंस् *vaṁs* in the vocative singular of the masculine, वांस् *vâṁs* in the other strong cases. But in the nominative and vocative singular of the masculine the final स् *s* is rejected and Anusvâra (ं) changed to न् *n*.

In the weak cases the affix is वत् *vat*, and in the weakest उष् *ush*.

In the feminine ई *î* is added, according to § 210, and its declension follows the paradigm देवी *deví* in § 230.

PARADIGM: Participle of the reduplicated perfect of रुद् *rud*, 'to cry' (§ 169).

	SINGULAR. m.n.	m.	n.		DUAL. m.n.	m.	n.
N.	—	रुरुद्वान् *rurudvân*					
V.	—	रुरुद्वन् *rúrudvan*	रुरुद्वत् *rurudvat*[1] (N.V.Acc.)	N.V. Acc.	—	रुरुद्वांसौ *rurudvâṁs-au*[2]	रुरुदुषी *rurudush-î*[2]
Acc.	—	रुरुद्वांसम् *rurudvâṁs-am*					
I.	रुरुदुषा *rurudúsh-â*	—	—				
D.	रुरुदुषे *rurudúsh-e*	—	—	I.D. Abl.	रुरुद्वद्भ्याम् *rurudvád-bhyâm*	—	—
Abl. G.	रुरुदुषस् *rurudúsh-as*	—	—				
L.	रुरुदुषि *rurudúsh-i*	—	—	G. L.	रुरुदुषोस् *rurudúsh-os*	—	—

[1] Nom. and Acc. *rurudvát*; Voc. *rúrudvat*.

[2] Nom. and Acc. *rurudvấṁsau, rurudúshî*; Voc. *rúrudvâṁsau, rúrudushî*.

PLURAL.

	m.n.	m.	n.
N.V.	—	रुरुद्वांसस् *rurudváṁs-as*[1]	रुरुद्वांसि *rurudváṁs-i*[1]
Acc.	—	रुरुदुषस् *rurudúsh-as*	(same)
Instr.	रुरुद्वद्भिस् *rurudvád-bhis*	—	—
D. Abl.	रुरुद्वद्भ्यस् *rurudvád-bhyas*	—	—
Gen.	रुरुदुषाम् *rurudúsh-âm*	—	—
Loc.	रुरुद्वत्सु *rurudvát-su*	—	—

Look for examples to § 169.

VI. Finally belong to this class the second forms of the comparative (§ 243). Its affix is in the vocative singular of the masculine ईयंस् *íyaṁs*, in the other strong cases ईयांस् *íyâṁs*, in the weak cases ईयस् *íyas*. The final स् *s* is rejected in the nominative and vocative singular of the masculine and the Anusvâra (–̇) changed to न् *n*. The paradigm will be given in § 243.

SECOND CLASS: CRUDE FORMS ENDING IN VOWELS OR DIPHTHONGS.

§ 222. The terminations of the cases differ from those given in § 212 in the following instances:—

1. The nominative singular of the masculine and feminine terminates in स् *s*, except in the feminines ending in आ *â* and those in ई *î* consisting of more than one syllable, *e.g.* गत *gata*, 'gone,' masc. nom. गतस् *gata-s*; but गता *gatâ*, fem., नदी *nadî*, fem., nom. also गता *gatâ*, नदी *nadî*.

2. In the accusative singular the crude forms subjoin म् *m* only, except the monosyllabic feminines ending in ई *î* and ऊ *û*,

[1] Nom. *rurudváṁsas;* Nom. and Acc. *rurudváṁsi*; Voc. *rúrudvâṁsas, rúrudvâṁsi.*

and those which end in diphthongs, *e.g.* गत *gata*, acc. गतम् *gata-m*; but भी *bhí*, fem., भियम् *bhiy-am* (*cf.* § 230, *b*).

3. The feminines ending in vowels affix in the dative singular ऐ *ai*, in the ablative and genitive singular आस् *ás*, and in the singular locative आम् *âm*. The feminines in इ *i* and उ *u*, and the monosyllables in ई *í* and ऊ *ú* may also take the affixes given in § 212, *e.g.* from गता *gatá*, fem., गतायै *gatá-y-ai*, गतायास् *gatá-y-âs*, गतायाम् *gatá-y-âm* (*cf.* § 223); from भी *bhí*, fem., भियै *bhiy-ai* or भिये *bhiy-e*, भियास् *bhiy-âs* or भियस् *bhiy-as*, भियाम् *bhiy-âm* or भियि *bhiy-i*.

4. In the accusative plural the masculines ending in vowels take न् *n*, and the feminines, except the monosyllables in ई *í* and ऊ *ú*, take स् *s*, before which a short vowel is lengthened, *e.g.* गत *gata*, masc., plur. acc. गतान् *gatâ-n*; मति *mati*, 'mind,' fem., मतीस् *matí-s*; पितृ *pitṛi*, masc., 'father,' पितॄन् *pitṛí-n*; मातृ *mâtṛi*, fem., 'mother,' मातॄस् *mâtṛí-s*.

§ 223. Some of the terminations beginning with vowels are combined with the finals of the crude forms by crasis. Before some, in order to avoid hiatus, य *y* or न् *n* is inserted. Before the न् *n* which is inserted in the nominative, vocative, and accusative plural of the neuter, and in the genitive plural of the three genders, a short vowel is lengthened, *e.g.* गत *gata*, neut., nom. voc. acc. plur. गतानि *gatâ-n-i*, gen. plur. of all the three genders गतानाम् *gatâ-n-âm*.

§ 224. Special rules will be given in the observations at the head of the paradigms.

CRUDE FORMS ENDING IN अ, MASCULINES AND NEUTERS.

§ 225. 1. The neuters affix म् *m* in the nominative and accusative singular, *e.g.* गत *gata*, neut., गतम् *gata-m*.

2. The termination of the instrumental singular in the mas-

culine and neuter is एन *ena*, before which the final अ *a* of the base is dropped, *e.g.* गत *gata*, गतेन *gatena*.

3. The termination of the singular dative is आय *áya*, गताय *gatá-y-a*.

4. The ablative and genitive singular have different terminations; the ablative has अत् *at*, the अ *a* of which combines with the final अ *a* of the base to आ *á*; the genitive has स्य *sya*, *e.g.* गतात् *gatát*, गतस्य *gata-sya*.

5. The termination of the locative singular इ *i* coalesces with the final अ *a* of the base to ए *e*, गते *gate*.

6. Likewise the ई *í* of the nominative, vocative, and accusative dual of the neuter, गते *gate*.

7. Before the termination औ *au* of the nominative, vocative, and accusative dual of the masculine the final अ *a* of the base is dropped, गतौ *gatau*.

8. Before the termination of the instrumental, dative, and ablative dual, भ्याम् *bhyám*, the final अ *a* of the base is lengthened, गताभ्याम् *gatá-bhyám*.

9. Before the termination of the genitive and locative dual, ओस् *os*, य् *y* is inserted, गतयोस् *gata-y-os*.

10. The initial अ *a* of the termination of the nominative and vocative plural of the masculine combines with the final अ *a* of the base to आ *á*, गतास् *gatás*.

11. The instrumental plural has, instead of the final अ *a* and the termination भिस् *bhis*, the termination ऐस् *ais*, गतैस् *gatais*.

12. Before the terminations of the dative and ablative plural, भ्यस् *bhyas*, and the locative, सु *su*, the final अ *a* of the base is changed to ए *e*, गतेभ्यस् *gate-bhyas*, गतेषु *gate-shu*.

PARADIGM: कान्त *kántá*, m.n. 'dear.' The feminine is, according to § 210, कान्ता *kántá*, the declension of which will be given in the following paragraph.

SINGULAR.

	m.n.	m.	n.
N.	—	कान्तस् *kấntá-s*	कान्तम् *kấntá-m*
V.	कान्त *kấnta*	—	—
Acc.	कान्तम् *kấntá-m*	—	—
I.	कान्तेन *kấnté-n-a*	—	—
D.	कान्ताय *kấntấ-y-a*	—	—
Abl.	कान्तात् *kấntất*	—	—
G.	कान्तस्य *kấntá-sya*	—	—
L.	कान्ते *kấnté*	—	—

DUAL.

	m.n.	m.	n.
N.V. Acc.	—	कान्तौ *kântau*[1]	कान्ते *kânte*[1]
I.D. Abl.	कान्ताभ्याम् *kấntấ-bhyâm*	—	—
G. L.	कान्तयोस् *kấntá-y-os*	—	—

PLURAL.

	m.n.	m.	n.
N.V.	—	कान्तास् *kântâs*[2]	कान्तानि *kântâ-n-i*[2] (N.V. Acc.)
Acc.	—	कान्तान् *kấntấn*	
Instr.	कान्तैस् *kấntáis*	—	—
D. Abl.	कान्तेभ्यस् *kấnté-bhyas*	—	—
Gen.	कान्तानाम् *kấntấ-n-âm*[3]	—	—
Loc.	कान्तेषु *kấnté-shu*	—	—

Look for examples to § 173, IV.; decline also अश्व *açva*, m. 'a horse,' भय *bhaya*, n. 'fear.'

[1] Nom. and Acc. *kântáu, kânté*; Voc. *kấntau, kấnte.*

[2] Nom. *kântấs*; Nom. and Acc. *kântấni*; Voc. *kấntâs, kấntâni.*

[3] Or *kântânấm.*

CRUDE FORMS ENDING IN आ.

1. FEMININES.

§ 226. 1. In the vocative singular the final आ *â* is changed to ए *e, e.g.* गता *gatâ*, voc. गते *gate.*

2. The instrumental singular inserts य् *y*, before which the final आ *â* is made short, गतया *gata-y-â.*

3. य् *y* is inserted also in the dative, ablative, genitive, and locative singular, *e.g.* गतायै *gatâ-y-ai* (*cf.* § 223).

4. The nominative, vocative, and accusative dual have ए *e* instead of the final आ *â* and the termination, गते *gate.*

5. The genitive and locative dual have the same form as in the masculine, गतयोस् *gata-y-os.*

6. In the nominative plural the final आ *â* combines with the initial अ *a* of the termination अस् *as* to आ *â*, गतास् *gatâs.*

PARADIGM: कान्ता (*cf.* the paradigm of the preceding paragraph).

	SINGULAR.	DUAL.	PLURAL.
N.	कान्ता *kântâ*	N.V. Acc. कान्ते *kânte*[1]	N.V. Acc. कान्तास् *kântâs*[2]
V.	कान्ते *kânte*		
Acc.	कान्ताम् *kântâ-m*		
I.	कान्तया *kânta-y-â*	I.D. Abl. कान्ताभ्याम् *kântâ-bhyâm*	I. कान्ताभिस् *kântâ-bhis*
D.	कान्तायै *kântâ-y-ai*		D. Abl. कान्ताभ्यस् *kântâ-bhyas*
Abl. G.	कान्तायास् *kântâ-y-âs*	G. L. कान्तयोस् *kânta-y-os*	G. कान्तानाम् *kântâ-n-âm*
L.	कान्तायाम् *kântâ-y-âm*		L. कान्तासु *kântâ-su*

अश्वा *açvâ*, f. 'a mare.'

[1] Nom. and Acc. *kânté;* Voc. *kânte.* [2] Nom. and Acc. *kântâs;* Voc. *kântâs.*

2. Substantives of the Masculine Gender and Adjectives of the Masculine and Feminine Genders.

§ 227. These affix स् *s* in the nominative and vocative singular, *e.g.* हाहा *hâhâ*, masc., 'a Gandharva,' and अतिहाहा *atihâhâ*, adj. m.f., 'surpassing a Gandharva,' nom. voc. हाहास् *hâhâ-s*, अतिहाहास् *atihâhâ-s*.

The remaining cases, except the accusative plural, are formed by the terminations given in § 212, which drop the initial अ *a* or आ *â*; initial इ *i* combines with the final आ *â* of the base to ए *e*, initial ए *e* to ऐ *ai*, initial ओ *o* and औ *au* to औ *au* (*cf.* § 21). In the accusative plural of the masculine न् *n* is subjoined.

PARADIGM: अतिहाहा, adj.

	SINGULAR. m.f.		DUAL. m.f.
N.V.	अतिहाहास्	N.V. Acc.	अतिहाहौ
Acc.	अतिहाहाम्		
I.	अतिहाहा	I.D. Abl.	अतिहाहाभ्याम्
D.	अतिहाहै		
Abl. G.	अतिहाहास्	G. L.	अतिहाहौस्
L.	अतिहाहे		

PLURAL.

	m.f.	m.	f.
N.V.	अतिहाहास्	—	—
Acc.	—	अतिहाहान्	अतिहाहास्
I.	अतिहाहाभिस्	—	—
D.Abl.	अतिहाहाभ्यस्	—	—
G.	अतिहाहाम्	—	—
L.	अतिहाहासु	—	—

§ 228. The declension of adjectives derived from verbs without affix, *e.g.* विश्वपा, 'all-ruling,' from पा, 'to protect,' differs from the preceding paradigm:—

1. In rejecting the final of the noun before all terminations beginning with vowels, except the accusative singular and the nominative and vocative plural, *e.g.* in the dative singular विश्वपे.

2. In forming the plural accusative according to § 212.

PARADIGM: विश्वपा, masc. fem.

	SINGULAR.	DUAL.		PLURAL.
N.V.	विश्वपास्	N.V. Acc.	विश्वपौ	N.V. विश्वपास्
Acc.	विश्वपाम्			Acc. विश्वपस्
I.	विश्वपा	I.D. Abl.	विश्वपाभ्याम्	I. विश्वपाभिस्
D.	विश्वपे			D. Abl. विश्वपाभ्यस्
Abl. G.	विश्वपस्			G. विश्वपाम्
L.	विश्वपि	G. L.	विश्वपोस्	L. विश्वपासु

Observ. to §§ 227, 228. The neuter of the adjectives ending in आ, according to § 210 *b*, shortens the final and follows the paradigm in § 225.

CRUDE FORMS ENDING IN इ *i* AND उ *u* OF THE MASCULINE, FEMININE, AND NEUTER GENDERS.

§ 229. 1. In the vocative singular the masculines and feminines change the final इ *i* to ए *e*, उ *u* to ओ *o*, *e.g.* कवि *kavi*, 'a poet,' कवे *kave*. In the neuter this change is optional, *e.g.* वारि *vâri*, 'water,' वारे *vâre* or वारि *vâri*.

2. In the instrumental singular the masculines and neuters insert न् *n*, कविना *kavi-n-â*.

3. In the dative singular the masculines change the final इ *i* to अय् *ay*, उ to अव् *av*, कवये *kavay-e*.

4. In the ablative and genitive singular the masculines change the final इ *i* to ए *e*, उ *u* to ओ *o*, and drop the initial अ *a* of the termination, *e.g.* कवेस् *kave-s*.

5. In the locative singular औ *au* is substituted for the final of the noun and the inflectional termination, कवौ *kavau*.

6. The feminines may follow the rules given for the masculines in 3, 4, and 5, or those given in § 222, 3. In the latter case final इ *i* becomes य् *y*, final उ *u* व् *v*, *e.g.* from मति *mati* in the dative singular either मतये *matay-e*, according to 3, or मत्यै *maty-ai*, according to § 222, 3.

7. In the nominative, vocative, and accusative dual the masculines and feminines lengthen their final without adding any termination, *e.g.* कवी *kaví*.

8. In the nominative and vocative plural the masculines and feminines change their final इ *i* to अय् *ay*, उ *u* to अव् *av*, *e.g.* कवयस् *kavay-as*.

9. In the instrumental singular of the feminines and genitive and locative dual of the masculines and feminines final इ *i* is changed to य् *y*, उ *u* to व् *v*, मत्या *maty-á*, कव्योस् *kavy-os*.

10. The neuters insert न् *n* (in accordance with § 16, ण *ṇ*) before the terminations beginning with a vowel, *e.g.* dative singular वारिणे *vári-ṇ-e*.

11. When a noun in इ *i* or उ *u*, whether substantive or adjective, is used in the neuter gender in the same sense in which it is employed in the masculine, it may optionally be declined like a masculine, except the nominative, vocative, and accusative, *e.g.* शुचि *çuchi*, adj., 'pure,' in the dative singular of the neuter either शुचिने *çuchi-n-e* (10), or शुचये *çuchay-e* (3).

Paradigms: अग्नि *agní*, masc., 'fire,' मति *máti*, fem., 'mind,' वारि *vấri*, neut., 'water,' मधु *mádhu*, neut., 'honey,' गुरु *gurú*, adj. m.f.n., 'heavy.'

	SINGULAR.		DUAL.		PLURAL.
N.	अग्निस् *agní-s*	N.V. Acc.	अग्नी *agnî*[1]	N.V.	अग्नयस् *agnay-as*[2]
V.	अग्ने *ágne*				
Acc.	अग्निम् *agní-m*			Acc.	अग्नीन् *agnî́-n*
I.	अग्निना *agní-n-â*	I.D. Abl.	अग्निभ्याम् *agní-bhyâm*	I.	अग्निभिस् *agní-bhis*
D.	अग्नये *agnáy-e*			D. Abl.	अग्निभ्यस् *agní-bhyas*
Abl. G.	अग्नेस् *agné-s*	G. L.	अग्न्योस् *agny-ós*	G.	अग्नीनाम् *agnî́-n-âm*[3]
L.	अग्नौ *agnáu*			L.	अग्निषु *agní-shu*

कवि *kavi*, m., 'a poet.'

	SINGULAR.		DUAL.		PLURAL.
N.	मतिस् *máti-s*	N.V. Acc.	मती *mátî*	N.V.	मतयस् *mátay-as*
V.	मते *máte*				
Acc.	मतिम् *máti-m*			Acc.	मतीस् *mátî-s*
I.	मत्या *máty-â*	I.D. Abl.	मतिभ्याम् *máti-bhyâm*	I.	मतिभिस् *máti-bhis*
D.	मतये or मत्यै *mátay-e* *máty-ai*			D. Abl.	मतिभ्यस् *máti-bhyas*
Abl. G.	मतेस् or मत्यास् *máte-s* *máty-âs*	G. L.	मत्योस् *máty-os*	G.	मतीनाम् *mátî-n-âm*
L.	मतौ or मत्याम् *mátau* *máty-âm*			L.	मतिषु *máti-shu*

भूति *bhûti*, f., 'state of being.'

[1] Nom. and Acc. *agnî́*; Voc. *ágnî*.
[2] Nom. *agnáyas*; Voc. *ágnayas*.
[3] Or *agninā́m*.

	SINGULAR.	DUAL.	PLURAL.
N.	वारि *vâri*	N.V. Acc. वारिणी *vâri-ṇ-î*	N.V. Acc. वारीणि *vârî-ṇ-i*
V.	वारि or वारे *vâri* *vâre*		
Acc.	वारि *vâri*		
I.	वारिणा *vâri-ṇ-â*	I.D. Abl. वारिभ्याम् *vâri-bhyâm*	I. वारिभिस् *vâri-bhis*
D.	वारिणे *vâri-ṇ-e*		D. Abl. वारिभ्यस् *vâri-bhyas*
Abl. G.	वारिणस् *vâri-ṇ-as*	G. L. वारिणोस् *vâri-ṇ-os*	G. वारीणाम् *vârî-ṇ-âm*
L.	वारिणि *vâri-ṇ-i*		L. वारिषु *vâri-shu*

	SINGULAR.	DUAL.	PLURAL.
N.	मधु *madhu*	N.V. Acc. मधुनी *madhu-n-î*	N.V. Acc. मधूनि *madhû-n-i*
V.	मधु or मधो *madhu* *madho*		
Acc.	मधु *madhu*		
I.	मधुना *madhu-n-â*	I.D. Abl. मधुभ्याम् *madhu-bhyâm*	I. मधुभिस् *madhu-bhis*
D.	मधुने *madhu-n-e*		D. Abl. मधुभ्यस् *madhu-bhyas*
Abl. G.	मधुनस् *madhu-n-as*	G. L. मधुनोस् *madhu-n-os*	G. मधूनाम् *madhû-n-âm*
L.	मधुनि *madhu-n-i*		L. मधुषु *madhu-shu*

त्रपु *trapu*, n. 'tin' (observe § 16).

SINGULAR.

	m.f.n.	m.f.	m.n.	f.	n.
N.	—	गुरुस् *gurú-s*	—	—	गुरु *gurú*
V.	गुरो *gúro*	—	—	—	or गुरु *gúru*
Acc.	—	गुरुम् *gurú-m*	—	—	गुरु *gurú*
I.	—	—	गुरुणा *gurú-ṇ-â*	गुर्वा *gurv-ấ*	—
D.	गुरवे *guráv-e*	—	—	or गुर्वै *gurv-ái*	or गुरुणे *gurú-ṇ-e*
Abl. G.	गुरोस् *guró-s*	—	—	or गुर्वास् *gurv-ấs*	or गुरुणस् *gurú-ṇ-as*
L.	गुरौ *guráu*	—	—	or गुर्वाम् *gurv-ấm*	or गुरुणि *gurú-ṇ-i*

DUAL.

	m.f.n.	m.f.	n.
N.V. Acc.	—	गुरू *gurû*[1]	गुरुणी *guru-ṇ-î*[1]
I.D. Abl.	गुरुभ्याम् *gurú-bhyâm*	—	—
G. L.	गुर्वोस् *gurv-ós*	—	or गुरुणोस् *gurú-ṇ-os*

PLURAL.

	m.f.n.	m.f.	m.	f.	n.
N.V.	—	गुरवस् *gurav-as*[2]	—	—	गुरूणि *gurû-ṇ-i*[2] (N.V. Acc.)
Acc.	—	—	गुरून् *gurû́-n*	गुरूस् *gurû́-s*	
Instr.	गुरुभिस् *gurú-bhis*	—	—	—	—
D. Abl.	गुरुभ्यस् *gurú-bhyas*	—	—	—	—
Gen.	गुरूणाम् *gurû́-ṇ-âm*[3]	—	—	—	—
Loc.	गुरुषु *gurú-shu*	—	—	—	—

लघु *laghu*, adj., 'light.'

Obs. गुरु and लघु, according to § 210, may form also the feminines गुर्वी *gurv-î*, लघ्वी *laghvî*, which follow the paradigm देवी *devî*, in § 230.

[1] Nom. and Acc. *gurû́, gurúṇî;* Voc. *gúrû, gúruṇî.*

[2] Nom. *gurávas;* Nom. and Acc. *gurû́ṇi;* Voc. *gúravas, gúrûṇi.*

[3] Or *gurúṇấm.*

CRUDE FORMS ENDING IN ई ī AND ऊ ū.

1. Feminines.

§ 230. (*a.*) Those consisting of more than one syllable:—

1. Shorten their final in the vocative singular.

2. Change their final ई *ī* to य् *y*, ऊ *u* to व् *v*, before the terminations beginning with a vowel.

(*b.*) The monosyllabic forms:—

1. Use the nominative singular also as vocative.

2. Optionally insert न् *n* in the plural genitive (§ 223).

3. Change ई *ī* to इय् *iy* and ऊ *ū* to उव् *uv* before the terminations beginning with a vowel.

PARADIGMS: देवी *devī́*, 'a goddess,' वधू *vadhū́*, 'a wife,' श्री *çrī́*, n. p. of a goddess, भ्रू *bhrū́*, 'the brow.'

	SINGULAR.		DUAL.		PLURAL.
N.	देवी *devī́*	N.V. Acc.	देव्यौ *devy-au*[1]	N. V.	देव्यस् *devy-as*[2]
V.	देवि *dévi*			A.	देवीस् *devī́-s*
Acc.	देवीम् *devī́-m*			I.	देवीभिस् *devī́-bhis*
I.	देव्या *devy-ā́*	I.D. Abl.	देवीभ्याम् *devī́-bhyâm*	D. A.	देवीभ्यस् *devī́-bhyas*
D.	देव्यै *devy-âi*				
Abl. G.	देव्यास् *devy-ā́s*	G. L.	देव्योस् *devy-ós*	G.	देवीनाम् *devī́-n-âm*
L.	देव्याम् *devy-ā́m*			L.	देवीषु *devī́-shu*

नदी *nadī́*, f. 'river.'

[1] In the Nom. and Acc. *devyâu*; in the Voc. *dévyau.*

[2] In the Nom. *devyâs*; in the Voc. *dévyas.*

	SINGULAR.	DUAL.	PLURAL.
N.	वधूस् *vadhū́-s*	N.V. Acc. वध्वौ *vadhv-au*[1]	N. V. वध्वस् *vadhv-as*[2]
V.	वधु *vádhu*		
Acc.	वधूम् *vadhū́-m*		A. वधूस् *vadhū́-s*
I.	वध्वा *vadhv-ā́*	I.D. Abl. वधूभ्याम् *vadhū́-bhyâm*	I. वधूभिस् *vadhū́-bhis*
D.	वध्वै *vadhv-ái*		D. A. वधूभ्यस् *vadhū́-bhyas*
Abl. G.	वध्वास् *vadhv-ā́s*	G. L. वध्वोस् *vadhv-ós*	G. वधूनाम् *vadhū́-n-âm*
L.	वध्वाम् *vadhv-ā́m*		L. वधूषु *vadhū́-shu*

	SINGULAR.	DUAL.	PLURAL.
N.V.	श्रीस् *çrī́-s*	N.V. Acc. श्रियौ *çríy-au*	N.V. Acc. श्रियस् *çríy-as*
Acc.	श्रियम् *çríy-am*		
I.	श्रिया *çriy-ā́*		I. श्रीभिस् *çrī-bhís*
D.	श्रिये or श्रियै *çriy-é* *çriy-ái*	I.D. Abl. श्रीभ्याम् *çrī-bhyā́m*	D. Abl. श्रीभ्यस् *çrī-bhyás*
Abl. G.	श्रियस् or श्रियास् *çriy-ás* *çriy-ā́s*		G. श्रियाम् or श्रीणाम् *çriy-ā́m* *çrī-ṇ-ā́m*
L.	श्रियि or श्रियाम् *çriy-í* *çriy-ā́m*	G. L. श्रियोस् *çriy-ós*	L. श्रीषु *çrī-shú*

धी *dhī́*, f. 'understanding.'

[1] In the Nom. and Acc. *vadhvaú*; in the Voc. *vádhvau*.

[2] In the Nom. *vadhvàs*; in the Voc. *vádhvas*.

	SINGULAR.	DUAL.	PLURAL.
N.V.	भ्रूस् *bhrú-s*	N.V. Acc. भ्रुवौ *bhruv-au*	N.V. Acc. भ्रुवस् *bhruv-as*
Acc.	भ्रुवम् *bhruv-am*		
I.	भ्रुवा *bhruv-á*	I.D. Abl. भ्रूभ्याम् *bhrú-bhyám*	I. भ्रूभिस् *bhrú-bhis*
D.	भ्रुवे or भ्रुवै *bhruv-é bhruv-ai*		D. Abl. भ्रूभ्यस् *bhrú-bhyas*
Abl. G.	भ्रुवस् or भ्रुवास् *bhruv-as bhruv-ás*	G. L. भ्रुवोस् *bhruv-os*	G. भ्रुवाम् or भ्रूणाम् *bhruv-ám bhrú-ṇ-ám*
L.	भ्रुवि or भ्रुवाम् *bhruv-i bhruv-ám*		L. भ्रूषु *bhrú-shu*

भू *bhú*, f. 'earth.'

2. Masculine Substantives and Nouns Declinable in Masculine and Feminine Genders.

§ 231. I. When derived from a verb without affix and

1. When monosyllabic, *e.g.* लू *lú* (from लू *lú*, 'to cut'), 'a male or female reaper,' they follow the analogy of the two last paradigms, except in the dative, ablative, genitive, and locative singular, and the genitive plural, where they have the first form only, *e.g.* लुवे *luv-e*, not लुवै *luv-ai*, लुवस् *luv-as*, etc.

2. When forming the second member of a compound, *e.g.* जलपी *jala-pí*, 'drinking-water,' they take the terminations prescribed in 1, and change the final ई *í* and ऊ *ú* of the crude form to य् *y* and व् *v* before vowels, *e.g.* sing. acc. जलप्यम् *jalapy-am*, instr. जलप्या *jalapy-á*, etc.; but, when the finals are preceded by a compound consonant, they are changed to इय् *iy* and उव् *uv*, as in 1, *e.g.* यवक्री *yava-krí*, 'buying grain,' sing. acc. यवक्रियम् *yavakriy-am*, instr. यवक्रिया *yavakriy-á*.

II. Polysyllabic non-compound masculines take the terminations prescribed in § 212 and follow the rules given in § 222,

1, 2, and 4, but use the singular nominative also as vocative. The feminines differ from the masculines only in the accusative plural, *e.g.* पपी *papí*, masc., 'the sun,' nom. and voc. sing. पपीस् *papí-s*, acc. पपीम् *papí-m*, plur. acc. पपीन् *papí-n*. आरू *árú*, m.f., 'tawny,' plur. acc. masc. आरून् *árú-n*, fem. आरूस् *árú-s*. The finals ई *í* and ऊ *ú* become य् *y* and व् *v* before the terminations beginning with a vowel, except in the locative singular of the nouns in ई *í*, where ई *í* + इ *i* makes ई *í*, *e.g.* पपी *papí*, sing. instr. पप्या *papy-á*, loc. पपी *papí*.

III. The compound adjectives, the second member of which is a monosyllabic feminine ending in ई *í* or ऊ *ú*, as प्रधी *pradhí* (from धी *dhí*, fem., 'understanding'), may optionally be declined in the feminine like देवी *deví* and वधू *vadhú* in the vocative, dative, ablative, genitive, and locative singular, and in the genitive plural, or follow the declension of the masculine, with which they accord in all the other cases.

The masculine is declined according to rule II., except in the locative singular, where final ई *í* is changed to य् *y*, and in the accusative plural, where अस् *as* is affixed. *E.g.* sing. voc. masc. and fem. प्रधीस् *pradhí-s*, or fem. प्रधि *pradhi*; dative masc. and fem. प्रध्ये *pradhy-e*, or fem. प्रध्यै *pradhy-ai*; abl. and gen. masc. and fem. प्रध्यस् *pradhy-as*, or fem. प्रध्यास् *pradhy-ás*; loc. masc. and fem. प्रध्यि *pradhy-i*, or fem. प्रध्याम् *pradhy-ám*; gen. plur. masc. and fem. प्रध्याम् *pradhy-ám*, or fem. प्रधीनाम् *pradhí-n-ám*. But sing. acc. masc. and fem. प्रध्यम् *pradhy-am*, instr. प्रध्या *pradhy-á*; nom. voc. and acc. plur. masc. and fem. प्रध्यस् *pradhy-as*.

IV. Compound adjectives having as a second member a polysyllabic feminine in ई *í* or ऊ *ú*, *e.g.* अतिचमू *atichamú* (चमू *chamú*, fem., 'an army'), follow the declension of देवी *deví* and वधू *vadhú* in the masculine as well as in the feminine. The accusative plural in the masculine, however, terminates in न् *n*, *e.g.* vocative singular masc. and fem. अतिचमु *atichamu*, dative अतिचम्वै *ati-*

chamv-ai, but plural accusative masc. अतिचमून् *atichamû-n* (fem. अतिचमूस् *atichamû-s*).

§ 232. In the neuter the adjectives in ई *î* and ऊ *û* shorten their finals according to § 210 *b*, and are declined like the neuter nouns in इ *i* and उ *u* (§ 229). But in all cases, except the three first of the three numbers, they may substitute the inflexions of the masculine, *e.g.* अतिचमु *atichamu*, neuter of अतिचमू *atichamû* (§ 231, IV.), in the singular dative अतिचमुने *atichamu-n-e* or अतिचम्वै *atichamv-ai*.

CRUDE FORMS ENDING IN ऋ *ṛi*, MASCULINE, FEMININE, AND NEUTER.

§ 233. 1. The nominative singular of the masculines and feminines substitutes आ *â* for the final and the termination, *e.g.* पितृ *pitṛí*, 'father,' nom. पिता *pitấ*, मातृ *mâtṛí*, 'mother,' माता *mâtấ*.

2. In the vocative singular the final is changed to अर् *ar*. In the neuter this change is optional.

3. The termination of the accusative singular in the masculine and feminine is अम् *am*.

4. In the accusative singular, nominative, vocative, accusative dual, and nominative and vocative plural of the masculine and feminine the final ऋ *ṛi* is changed to आर् *âr*.

Exc. जामातृ *jâmâtṛi*, masc., 'a son-in-law;' दुहितृ *duhitṛi*, fem., 'a daughter;' देवृ *devṛi*, masc., 'a brother-in-law;' ननन्दृ *nanandṛi* or ननान्दृ *nanândṛi*, fem., 'a husband's sister;' नृ *nṛi*, masc., 'a man;' पितृ *pitṛi*, masc., 'father;' भ्रातृ *bhrâtṛi*, masc., 'brother;' मातृ *mâtṛi*, fem., 'mother;' यातृ *yâtṛi*, fem., 'the wife of the husband's brother;' यामातृ *yâmâtṛi* = जामातृ *jâmâtṛi*; शंस्तृ *çam̃stṛi*, masc., 'one who praises;' and सव्येष्टृ *savyeshṭhṛi*, masc., 'a charioteer,' change the final ऋ *ṛi* to अर् *ar*.

5. In the ablative and genitive singular of the masculine and feminine उर् *ur* is substituted for the final and the termination, पितुर् *pitur*.

6. In the locative singular of the masculine and feminine the final is changed to अर् *ar*.

7. In the dative and instrumental singular and in the genitive and locative dual the final ऋ *ṛi* is changed to र् *r*.

8. The neuter, according to § 16, inserts ण् before the terminations which begin with vowels. But when the neuter has a corresponding masculine, which is different only by the gender, it may optionally take the forms of the latter, except in the nominative, vocative, and accusative (*cf.* § 229, 11, and § 232).

PARADIGMS: दातृ *dâtṛí*, m.n. 'a giver,' स्वसृ *svásṛi*, fem. 'a sister.'

	SINGULAR m.n.	m.	n.
N.	—	दाता *dâtấ*	दातृ *dâtṛi*
V.	दातर् *dấtar*	—	or दातृ *dấtṛi*
Acc.	—	दातारम् *dâtấr-am*	दातृ *dâtṛí*
I.	दात्रा *dâtr-ấ*	—	or दातृणा *dâtṛi-ṇ-â*
D.	दात्रे *dâtr-é*	—	or दातृणे *dâtṛi-ṇ-e*
Abl. G.	दातुर् *dâtúr*	—	or दातृणस् *dâtṛi-ṇ-as*
L.	दातरि *dâtár-i*	—	or दातृणि *dâtṛi-ṇ-i*

	DUAL m.n.	m.	n.
N.V. Acc.	—	दातारौ *dâtâr-au*[1]	दातृणी *dâtṛi-ṇ-î*[1]
I.D. Abl.	दातृभ्याम् *dâtṛi-bhyâm*	—	—
G. L.	दात्रोस् *dâtr-ós*	—	or दातृणोस् *dâtṛi-ṇ-os*

[1] In the Nom. and Acc. *dâtấrau, dâtṛiṇî*; in the Voc. *dấtârau, dấtṛiṇî*.

PLURAL.

	m.n.	m.	n.
N.V.	—	दातारस् *dâtâras*[1]	दातॄणि *dâtṛî-ṇ-i*[2] (N.V. Acc.)
Acc.	—	दातॄन् *dâtṛî-n*	
Instr.	दातृभिस् *dâtṛi-bhis*	—	—
D.Abl.	दातृभ्यस् *dâtṛi-bhyas*	—	—
Gen.	दातॄणाम् *dâtṛî-ṇ-âm*	—	—
Loc.	दातृषु *dâtṛi-shu*	—	—

Like the masculine is declined नप्तृ *naptṛi*, m. 'grandson.'

	SINGULAR.		DUAL.		PLURAL.
N.	स्वसा *svásâ*	N.V. Acc.	स्वसारौ *svásâr-au*	N.V.	स्वसारस् *svásâr-as*
V.	स्वसर् *svásar*				
Acc.	स्वसारम् *svásâr-am*			Acc.	स्वसॄस् *svásṛî-s*
I.	स्वस्रा *svásr-â*	I.D. Abl.	स्वसृभ्याम् *svásṛi-bhyâm*	I.	स्वसृभिस् *svásṛi-bhis*
D.	स्वस्रे *svásr-e*			D. Abl.	स्वसृभ्यस् *svásṛi-bhyas*
Abl. G.	स्वसुर् *svásur*	G. L.	स्वस्रोस् *svásr-os*	G.	स्वसॄणाम् *svásṛî-ṇ-âm*
L.	स्वसरि *svásar-i*			L.	स्वसृषु *svásṛi-shu*

[1] In the Nom. *dâtấras*; in the Voc. *dấtâras*.

[2] In the Nom. and Acc. *dâtṛ́îṇi*; in the Voc. *dấtṛiṇi*.

PARADIGM OF THE EXCEPTION TO 4: पितृ *pitṛí*, masc.

	SINGULAR.	DUAL.	PLURAL.
N.	पिता *pitā́*	N.V. Acc. पितरौ *pitar-au*[1]	N.V. पितरस् *pitar-as*[2]
V.	पितर् *pitar*		
Acc.	पितरम् *pitár-am*		Acc. पितॄन् *pitṝ́-n*
I.	पित्रा *pitr-ā́*	I.D. Abl. पितृभ्याम् *pitṛí-bhyâm*	I. पितृभिस् *pitṛí-bhis*
D.	पित्रे *pitr-é*		D. Abl. पितृभ्यस् *pitṛí-bhyas*
Abl. G.	पितुर् *pitúr*	G. L. पित्रोस् *pitr-ós*	G. पितॄणाम् *pitṝ́-ṇ-âm*[3]
L.	पितरि *pitár-i*		L. पितृषु *pitṛí-shu*

In the same way is declined भ्रातृ *bhrâtṛi*, m. 'brother;' also मातृ *mâtṛi*, f. 'mother,' except in the acc. plur. which has final *s* instead of *n*, मातॄस् *mâtṝ́s*.

CRUDE FORMS ENDING IN ऐ, ओ AND औ, MASCULINE AND FEMININE.

§ 234. I. The nominative singular is used also as a vocative.

II. Before the terminations beginning with a vowel final ऐ *ai* is changed to आय् *ây*, ओ *o* to अव् *av*, and औ *au* to आव् *âv*.

Except. Final ओ *o*, 1. becomes आ *â* before the terminations of the accusative singular and plural, which reject their initial अ *a*; 2. is left unchanged before the termination of the ablative and genitive singular which drops its initial अ *a*; 3. becomes आव् *âv* in the nominative, vocative, accusative, dual, and nominative and vocative plural; 4. becomes औ *au* in the nominative and vocative singular.

[1] In the Nom. and Acc. *pitárau;* in the Voc. *pitarau.*

[2] In the Nom. *pitáras*; in the Voc. *pitaras.*

[3] Or *pitṛiṇā́m.*

III. Final ऐ *ai* before the terminations beginning with स् *s* (nominative and vocative singular, locative plural) and भ् *bh* (instrumental, dative, ablative dual and plural) is changed to आ *â*.

PARADIGMS: रै *rai*, m. 'wealth,' गो *go*, m.f. 'ox, cow,' नौ *nau*, fem. 'a ship.'

	SINGULAR.		DUAL.		PLURAL.
N.V.	रास् *rā́-s*	N.V. Acc.	रायौ *rā́y-au*	N.V. Acc.	रायस् *rā́y-as*
Acc.	रायम् *rā́y-am*				
I.	राया *rây-ā́*			I.	राभिस् *râ-bhís*
D.	राये *rây-é*	I.D. Abl.	राभ्याम् *râ-bhyā́m*	Dat. Abl.	राभ्यस् *râ-bhyás*
Abl. G.	रायस् *rây-ás*			G.	रायाम् *rây-ā́m*
		G. L.	रायोस् *rây-ós*		
L.	रायि *rây-í*			L.	रासु *râ-sú*

	SINGULAR.		DUAL.		PLURAL.
N.V.	गौस् *gáu-s*	N.V. Acc.	गावौ *gā́v-au*	N.V.	गावस् *gā́v-as*
Acc.	गाम् *gā́m*			Acc.	गास् *gā́-s*
I.	गवा *gav-ấ*			I.	गोभिस् *gó-bhis*
D.	गवे *gav-é*	I.D. Abl.	गोभ्याम् *gó-bhyâm*	D. Abl.	गोभ्यस् *gó-bhyas*
Abl. G.	गोस् *gós*			G.	गवाम् *gav-ấm*
		G. L.	गवोस् *gav-ós*		
L.	गवि *gav-í*			L.	गोषु *gó-shu*

	SINGULAR.	DUAL.	PLURAL.
N.V.	नौस् *nâu-s*	N.V. Acc. नावौ *nâv-au*	N.V. Acc. नावस् *nâv-as*
Acc.	नावम् *nâv-am*		
I.	नावा *nâv-â*	I. D. Abl. नौभ्याम् *nau-bhyâm*	I. नौभिस् *nau-bhis*
D.	नावे *nâv-é*		D. Abl. नौभ्यस् *nau-bhyás*
Abl. G.	नावस् *nâv-ás*	G. L. नावोस् *nâv-ós*	G. नावाम् *nâv-âm*
L.	नावि *nâv-i*		L. नौषु *nau-shú*

The rule in § 232 applies also here, *e.g.* the neuter अतिनु *atinu* (§ 210 *b*) of the masc. and fem. अतिनौ *atinau* makes in the singular dative अतिनुने *atinu-n-e*, or like the dative of the masculine अतिनावे *atinâv-e*.

§ 235. A Synopsis of all the Terminations of Nouns.

Observ. Those which contain a part of the crude form, are distinguished by an asterisk.

SINGULAR.

	m.f.n.	m.f.	m.n.	f.n.	m.	f.	n.
N.	*क् *ट् *त् *प् *ण् *न् *ल् *: (for र् and स्)	:(स्) *आः (आस्)	. . .	. .	*अन् *आन्	*आ *ई	*अ *इ *उ *ऋ *म्
V.	The same and *ए *ओ	. . .	*अ	*इ *उ	. . .	. . .	*इ *उ *ऋ
Acc.	म्	*अम्	. . .	. .	. . .	. . .	*इ *उ *ऋ *क् *ट् *त् *प् *ण् *ल् *: (for *र् and *स्)
I.	आ	. . .	ना णा *एन *एण	. . .	. . .	*अया	. . . .
D.	ए	. . .	*आय	. . .	. . .	ऐ *आयै	ने णे
Abl. G.	अस् स् *एस् *ओस् *उः (for उर्)	. . .	Abl. *आत् G. स्य	. . .	. . .	आस् *आयाः	नस् णस्
L.	इ *औ	. . .	. . .	. . .	. . .	आम् *आयाम्	नि णि

DUAL.

	m.f.n.	m.f.	m.n.	f.n.	m.	f.	n.
N.V.Acc.	. .	°औ °ई °ऊ	. .	°ए	. . .	. . .	ई
I.D.Abl.	भ्याम्	. . .	. .	. .	. . .	. . .	. . .
G.L.	ओस्	. . .	. .	. .	. . .	. . .	नोस् योस्

PLURAL.

	m.f.n.	m.f.	m.n.	f.n.	m.	f.	n.
N.V.	. . .	अस् °आस् °अयस् °अवस्	. .	. .	. . .	. . .	इ °आनि °ईनि °ऊनि °ॠणि and insertion of a nasal.
Acc.	. . .	अस् स्	. .	. .	°आन् °ईन् °ऊन् °ॠन्	°आस् °ईस् °ऊस् °ॠस्	Like the nominative and vocative.
I.	भिस्	. . .	°ऐस्	. .	. . .	. . .	. . .
D.Abl.	भ्यस्	. . .	°एभ्यस्	. .	. . .	. . .	. . .
G.	आम् °आनाम् °ईनाम् °ऊनाम् °ॠणाम्	. . .	. .	. .	. . .	. . .	. . .
L.	सु (षु)	. . .	°एषु	. .	. . .	. . .	. . .

APPENDIX.

SOME VEDIC ANOMALIES IN THE DECLENSION OF NOUNS.

§ 236. Though the Vedic declension of nouns presents a great number of variations, the regular forms are more frequent.

§ 237. *Singular: nominative.* Some feminines ending in आ or ई take the termination स्.

Vocative. Some feminines ending in आ shorten the final. The masculines ending in मन्त् have मस्, and those in वन्त् and वन्, and the participle of the reduplicated perfect Parasmaipada have वस्, *e.g.* भानुमन्त्, भानुमस्.

Accusative. Some nouns ending in ई, उ, or ऊ, take अम्, before which ई is changed to य्, and उ or ऊ to व्.—Sometimes न् is inserted in order to avoid the hiatus.—महान्तम् from महन्त्

'great' is contracted into महाम्; पन्थानम् from पथिन्, 'path,' into पन्थाम् (see § 239, No. 24).

Instrumental. Nouns ending in अ have एना (instead of एन), or combine the termination immediately with the final अ of the crude form to आ, *e.g.* सख्या, particularly in those ending in त्वन, कवित्वना. The feminines in आ do not insert य्, धारा instead of धारया. Masculines and even neuters in इ and उ do not insert न्, but change इ to य् and उ to व्, *e.g.* क्रतु masc., क्रत्वा; मधु neut., मध्वा; or उ to अव्, बाहु masc., बाहवा; or उव्, घृतस्नुवा. The termination sometimes combines with a preceding य् to ई, with a preceding व् to ऊ, *e.g.* मती instead of मत्या, from मति. य् is inserted after अ and उ, स्वप्नया, साधुया, and उय् changed to विय्, दार्विया (from दारु). When य् is inserted, final अ of the base is rejected, विश्व्या from विश्व. या appears as termination also in नावया from नौ, and even in त्मन्या (from आत्मन्, *cf.* § 239, No. 17).—प्रथिना, महिना, भूना, instead of प्रथिम्ना, etc., from प्रथिमन्, etc., reject the म् of the crude form, and शमिता for शमित्रा, from शमितृ, the र्.

Dative. Forms in ये are changed to ई, ऊती for ऊत्ये from ऊति; final ऋ of the crude form is changed to अर्, नरे from नृ.

Ablative and *genitive.* ज्मा shortens its final and makes ज्मयास्. Nouns in इ and उ, even neuters, take the termination अस् and change इ to य्, उ to व्, *e.g.* पश्वस्, वस्वस् (वसु neut.). Some neuters in उ change their final to ओ, मधोस्.—सोभरि and तिरश्ची, although masc., take the termination of the fem. आस्; on the other hand feminines in ई and ऊ take अस्.—विद्यु takes the real termination of the ablative अत्, विद्योत्.

Locative. The termination इ may be lengthened.—Nouns ending in अ or आ have sometimes आ instead of final ए or आयाम्, मध्या (for मध्ये), गुहा (for गुहायाम्); those in आ occur also with ए, देवते instead of देवतायाम्. Those in उ take the regular termination and change उ to अव्, सूनवि from सूनु.—आ occurs instead of final औ, नाभा from नाभि.—Those in ऊ have the regular termination, तन्वि from तनू.—Final याम् and वाम् drop the म् and are changed to ई and ऊ, गौरी, तनू.—Nouns ending in अन् may reject the termination, e.g. चर्मन् for चर्मणि.—यादृश् takes the termination मिन् (cf. the locative of the pronouns, § 247).

Dual: nominative, vocative, and *accusative.* आ, or even अ, is substituted for final औ, असुर.—य् is inserted after अ and ऊ, before which अ is rejected and ऊ changed to व्, मयूरशेप्या (instead of °शेपौ), चम्व्यौ (instead of चम्वौ from चमू).—भूमा occurs instead of भूमी from भूमि.—Nouns in ई and ऊ reject the termination, चरन्ती (for चरन्त्यौ), also अनर्वन्.

Genitive and *locative.* पस्त्योस् occurs instead of पस्त्ययोस्.

Plural: nominative and *vocative.* Nouns ending in अ and आ double the termination, देवासस्. आर्यास् is contracted to आरीस्. Final उ is changed to उव्, अग्रुवस्; to आव्, अध्रिगावस् (cf. § 234, II., Exc.).—Nouns ending in ई and ऊ make ईस् and अयस् instead of यस्, and ऊस् and अवस् instead of वस्, उर्वीस् from उर्वी, पत्नयस् from पत्नी.—भक्तिवन्त् forms भक्तिवांसस् (cf. § 221, V.).—The neuters frequently drop their final नि (णि), वृषा instead of वृषाणि, and shorten the preceding vowel, कर्म instead of कर्माणि, अस्थूरि for अस्थूरीणि, पुरु for पुरूणि. Nouns ending in अन्त् lengthen the अ, सान्ति, घृतवान्ति (cf. § 221. II. Exc. 2).

Accusative. Nouns ending in ई (consisting of more than one syllable, § 230, a.) and उ take the termination अस्, before which ई is changed to य्, उ to व् or उव्; on the other hand न् occurs instead of अस्, मयोभून् from मयोभू. In Epic Poetry अस् is affixed to nouns ending in ऋ, which is then changed to अर्, पितरस्.

Instrumental. Nouns in अ have °एभिस् instead of ऐस् (cf. § 225, 11). नद्री forms नद्यैस्.

Dative and *ablative.* नारी and सेनानी occur with shortened ई.

Genitive. The affix is added immediately to some nouns, चरथाम्. The final ऋ may become र् or अर्, स्वस्राम् from स्वसृ,

नराम् from नृ. When न् is inserted, it may be left unchanged, धातॄणाम्. न् is inserted irregularly in ग्रामणीनाम्.

Locative. The termination is doubled in पृत्सुषु; विश् makes विचु instead of विक्षु. वन्, रन्, दम् change their final to Anusvâra ं, वंसु, etc.

§ 238. 1. In the Veda the distinction between the strong and weak cases (§ 220) is less regularly observed than in the later Sanskrit. Thus the termination of the accusative is attached to the weak form in अर्वावतम् instead of अर्वावन्तम्, and that of the nominative plural even to the weakest in तस्थुषस् instead of तस्थिवांसस्. In the nouns ending in षन् the use of the strong form is absolute in the nominative singular only; in all the other strong cases it is optional, *e.g.* तचन् sing. nom. तचा, accus. तचणम् or तचाणम्. On the other hand दावने occurs instead of दाव्ने. The nouns ending in अस् lengthen the penultimate also in other cases than the singular nominative, *e.g.* in the nom. voc. acc. dual उषासा, gen. plur. उषासाम्, from उषस्. Sometimes they reject अस्, *e.g.* उषाम्, or drop their final स् and are declined like nouns ending in अ, *e.g.* अङ्गिरास्, nom. plur. of अङ्गिर, for अङ्गिरस्. Nouns ending in अम् sometimes have a strong form like those in अन्, *e.g.* चम्, nom. voc. acc. dual चामा, nom. plur. चामस्, nom. sing. चास् (for *चम्स्), accus. sing. चाम् (for *चामम्).

2. The inflectional terminations are sometimes rejected, particularly, as already noticed, in the locative singular, but also in other cases, especially when the noun is conjoined with another inflected noun, *cf.* Rig-veda I. 26, 2; 64, 5, Atharva-veda IV. 22, 3.

3. *Cf.* § 239.

§ 239. Alphabetical List of Anomalous Nouns.

1. अक्का, अल्ला, and अम्बा, fem. 'mother,' shorten their final in the vocative singular.

2. अक्षि n. 'the eye,' अस्थि n. 'a bone,' दधि n. 'curdled milk,' सक्थि n. 'the thigh,' derive the weakest cases from (§ 220) अक्षन्, अस्थन्, दधन्, and सक्थन् (*cf.* § 221, III.), *e.g.*

	SINGULAR.		DUAL.		PLURAL.
N.V.A.	अक्षि	N.V. Acc.	अक्षणी or अक्ष्णी	N.V. Acc.	अक्षीणि
Instr.	अक्ष्णा	I.D. Abl.	अक्षिभ्याम्	I.	अक्षिभिस्
Dat.	अक्ष्णे			D. Abl.	अक्षिभ्यस्
Abl. Gen.	अक्ष्णस्	G. L.	अक्ष्णोस्	G.	अक्ष्णाम्
Loc.	अक्षणि or अक्ष्णि			L.	अक्षिषु

In the Veda the forms ending in अन् are also used as the bases of other cases, *e.g.* अक्षभिस्, and the nom. voc. acc. dual of अक्षि is अक्षी, the instr. dat. abl. अक्षीभ्याम्, the gen. loc. अक्ष्योस्, etc.

3. मघवन्त् and भगवन्त् make in the vocative sing. मघोस्, भगोस् (*os* for original *avas*, *cf.* § 237, *vocative*).

4. अनडुह् masc. 'ox,' singular nominative अनड्वान्, voc. अनड्वन्, acc. अनड्वाहम्, instr. अनडुहा, dat. ०हे, abl. gen. ०हस्, loc. ०हि; dual nom. voc. acc. अनड्वाहौ, instr. dat. abl. अनडुद्भ्याम्, gen. loc. अनडुहोस्; plural nom. voc. अनड्वाहस्, acc. अनडुहस्, instr. अनडुद्भिस्, dat. abl. अनडुद्भ्यस्, gen. अनडुहाम्, loc. अनडुत्सु.

5. अनर्वन्, see अर्वन्.

6. अनेहस् m. 'time,' उशनस् m. a proper name, पुरुदंशस् m. 'a name of Indra,' and in the Veda धन्वासहस् m. 'an archer,' reject in the nominative singular the final स् and lengthen the penultimate अ, *e.g.* अनेहा.

7. अप् fem. 'water,' lengthens the अ in the strong cases (§ 220), in the nom. voc. acc. plur. of the neuter, when compound, optionally; *e.g.* nom. voc. plur. आपस्; before the terminations beginning with भ् it has द् instead of प्, *e.g.* अद्भिस्. When not compound it is generally used in the plural only.

8. अम्बा, see No. 1.

9. अर्यमन् m. a proper name, पूषन् m. do. and the nouns

ending in हन्, 'killing,' do not lengthen their penultimate अ in the strong cases (§ 221, III.), except in the nominative singular masc. and in the nom. voc. acc. plur. neuter, *e.g.* acc. sing. अर्यमणम्, वृत्रहणम्, nom. sing. m. वृत्रहा (*cf.* 57 and 85).

10. अर्वन् m. 'a horse,' uses this crude form only in the nominative and vocative singular (*cf.* § 221, III.), and when compounded; in the other cases it substitutes अर्वन्त्, which follows § 221, II., *e.g.* sing. nom. अर्वा, voc. अर्वन्, acc. अर्वन्तम्, instr. अर्वता. In the Veda अर्वन् is also used in the acc. sing.

The bases ऋहन्न् and ऋहन्त् m. 'one who praises,' विवस्वन् and विवस्वन्त् m. a proper name, are substituted for each other in a similar manner.

11. अज्ञा, see अक्का.

12. अवयाज् 'part of a sacrifice,' and पुरोडाश् m. 'an oblation,' make in the nom. and voc. sing. अवयास्, पुरोडास्; before the terminations beginning with भ् and in the locative plural they substitute अवयस्, पुरोडस्, and उक्थशास् m. 'one who praises,' in the same way उक्थशस्, *e.g.* अवयोभिस् (*cf.* § 217), अवयस्सु or अवयःसु (§ 215), in the other cases regularly, *e.g.* instr. sing. अवयाजा.

13. The feminines अवी 'a woman in her menses,' तन्त्री 'a lute,' तरी 'a ship,' लक्ष्मी a proper name, स्तरी 'smoke,' and in the Veda also some others, take स् in the nominative singular, *e.g.* अवीस्.

14. असृज् n. 'blood,' आस्य n. 'the face,' उदक n. 'water,' दन्त m. 'a tooth,' दोस् m.n. 'an arm,' नासिका f. 'the nose,' निशा f. 'the night,' पाद m. 'a foot,' पृतना f. 'an army,' मांस n. 'meat,' मास m. 'the month,' यकृत् n. 'the liver,' यूष m.n. 'soup,' शकृत् n. 'excrement,' शिरस् n. 'the head,' सानु n. 'the top,' and हृदय n. 'the heart,' may substitute in all cases, except in the nom. voc. acc. sing. and dual masc., fem., and neut., nom. voc. plur. masc. and fem., and nom. voc. acc. plur. of the neut., the following corresponding crude forms, viz., असन्, आसन्, उदन्, दत् (properly दन्त्), दोषन्, नस्, निश्, पद्, पृत्, मांस्, मास् (*cf.* No. 22), यकन्, यूषन्, शकन्,

शीर्षन्, स्नु, and हृद्, *e.g.* sing. nom. voc. acc. असृक् only, but instr. असृजा or अस्ना, dual nom. voc. acc. only असृजी, but instr. dat. abl. असृग्भ्याम् or असभ्याम्, plur. nom. voc. acc. असृञ्जि, instr. असृग्भिस् or असभिस्.

15. अस्थन्, see अस्थि in No. 2.

16. अहन् n. 'the day,' derives the nom. voc. acc. sing., loc. plur., and the cases, the terminations of which begin with भ्, from अहस्; nom. voc. acc. sing. अहस्, loc. plur. अहस्सु, instr. dat. abl. dual अहोभ्याम्, but instr. sing. अह्ना, etc. In the Veda occurs also अहभिस् (instead of अहोभिस्). The nom. voc. acc. sing. अहस् becomes अहर् before all sonant letters, contrary to the Exc. to § 28.

When अहन् is the last member of a compound adjective, the nom. voc. sing. masc. is derived from अहस्, but the acc. sing., the nom. voc. acc. dual, and the nom. voc. plur. masc. from अहन् in the strong form (§ 221, III.), the rest as in the neuter, *e.g.* sing. nom. दीर्घाहास्, voc. दीर्घाहस्, acc. दीर्घाहाणम्, etc.

When the last member of a compound, it frequently becomes अह and अह्न (*cf.* my V.G. § 639); in the latter instance the loc. sing. may be derived also from अहन्, therefore ऽअह्ने or ऽअहनि or ऽअह्नि.

17. आत्मन् m. 'breath, soul, one's self,' drops in the Veda its initial आ particularly in the sing. instr. dat. loc. and even acc. (at the same time without lengthening the penultimate अ contrary to § 221, III.), *e.g.* त्मना, त्मनम्.

18. आसन्, see आस्य in No. 14.

19. उक्थशास्, see No. 12.

20. उदन्, see उदक in No. 14.

20*b*. उदीच्, see § 221, I.

21. उशनस्, see No. 6. Besides it may reject its final in the vocative sing., or substitute न्, उशनस्, उशन or उशनन्. Locative sing. उशने (*cf.* § 238, 1).

22. उषस् f. 'the dawn,' मास् m. 'the month' (*cf.* No. 14), स्ववस्

'voluntary,' स्वतवस् 'by one's own power,' have in the Veda before the terminations beginning with भ्, द् instead of their final, *e.g.* उषद्भिस्. The last two make in the nom. sing. masc. स्ववान्, स्वतवान् (*cf.* § 221, V.).

23. ऋत्विज्, see No. 10.

24. ऋभुक्षिन् masc. 'a name of Indra,' पथिन् m. 'a path,' मथिन् m. 'a churning stick,' derive their strong cases, except the nom. and voc. sing., from ऋभुक्षन्, पन्थन्, मन्थन्, the weakest (§ 220) from ऋभुक्ष्, पथ्, मथ्. The sing. nom. and voc. is ऋभुक्षास्, पन्थास्, मन्थास्; the acc. ऋभुक्षाणम्, instr. ऋभुक्षा, dual nom. voc. acc. पन्थानौ, instr. dat. and abl. पथिभ्याम्, gen. and loc. पथोस्, plur. nom. and voc. पन्थानस्, acc. पथस्, instr. पथिभिस्, loc. पथिषु.

25. ओषधि fem. 'a plant,' has in the Veda °धी as its base, except in the nominative singular..

26. करभू, कारभू, दृन्भू m. 'thunderbolt,' पुनर्भू f. 'a virgin widow re-married,' वर्षाभू m. 'a frog,' change their final before vowels to व्.

27. क्रुञ्च् m. f. 'a curlew,' changes ञ्च् in the nom. voc. sing., the loc. plur., and before भ् to ङ्, *e.g.* nom. voc. sing. क्रुङ्, but acc. क्रुञ्चम्, instr. क्रुञ्चा, instr. dat. and abl. dual क्रुङ्भ्याम्, instr. plural क्रुङ्भिस्, loc. क्रुङ्षु or क्रुङ्क्षु.

28. क्रोष्टु m. 'a jackal,' derives the strong cases, except the voc. sing., necessarily and the weakest (§ 220) optionally from क्रोष्टृ, sing. nom. क्रोष्टा, voc. क्रोष्टो, instr. क्रोष्टुना or क्रोष्ट्रा, dat. क्रोष्टवे or क्रोष्ट्रे, etc., dual nom. voc. acc. क्रोष्टारौ, instr. dat. abl. क्रोष्टुभ्याम्, gen. loc. क्रोष्ट्वोस् or क्रोष्ट्रोस्, plur. nom. voc. क्रोष्टारस्, acc. क्रोष्टून् or क्रोष्टॄन्, instr. क्रोष्टुभिस्.

When it forms the last member of a compound adjective, in the neuter क्रोष्टु alone is used.

29. जरा f. 'decrepitude,' may use also as crude form जरस्, except in the nom. and voc. singular, instr. dat. and abl. dual and plur., *e.g.* sing. nom. जरा, voc. जरे, but accus. जराम् or जरसम्, dual instr. dat. abl. जराभ्याम्, gen. loc. जरयोस् or जरसोस्.

30. जलासाह् in the Veda changes its स् to ष् in the nom. voc. acc. singular, loc. plural, and instr. dat. abl. dual and plural, therefore sing. nom. and voc. जलाषाट्, acc. जलाषाहम्, but instr. जलासाहा.

31. तन्वी, see No. 13.

32. तरी, see No. 13.

33. तिरस्, तिर्यञ्, see § 221, I.

33*b*. त्मन्, see No. 17.

34. दधन्, see दधि in No. 2.

35. दन्त्, see दन्त in No. 14; it is also used as second member of many compound adjectives, *e.g.* सुदन्त् *su-dant*, m. n. सुदती *su-dat-í*, f. 'having beautiful teeth.'

36. दिव् f. 'the day,' changes the final इव् to उ in the instr. dat. abl. of the dual and plur. and in the loc. plur., and makes in the nom. and voc. sing. द्यौस्, *e.g.* द्युभ्याम्, द्युषु, but acc. sing. दिवम्, etc.—In the Veda also acc. plur. masc. द्यून्, and nom. voc. acc. dual द्यावा.

When it is the last member of a compound, the nom. voc. acc. singular of the neuter is ऽद्यु.

37. दृन्भू, see No. 26.

38. ऽदृश्, when the final of a compound, *e.g.* सदृश् 'like,' makes in the nom. voc. sing. in the Veda दृङ्.

39. दोषन्, see दोस् in No. 14.

40. द्यु, द्यौस्, see No. 36.

41. धन्वासहस्, see No. 6.

42. ऽध्वस् (from the verb ध्वंस् 'to fall') and ऽस्रस् (from स्रंस् 'to fall'), forming the last member of a compound, change their final स् to त् in the nom. and voc. sing. and loc. plur., and before भ् to द्, *e.g.* nom. voc. sing. पर्णध्वत्, loc. plur. पर्णध्वत्सु, instr. dat. abl. dual पर्णध्वद्भ्याम्.

43. नस्, see नासिका in No. 14.

44. निश्, see निशा in No. 14.

45. नी m.f. 'a guide,' when standing alone or when forming the

last part of a compound, *e.g.* ग्रामणी 'a chief,' takes in the locative singular the termination आम्, before which ई in the simple word becomes इय्, in the compound य्, नियाम्, ग्रामण्याम्.

46. नृ m. 'a man,' may leave its final short in the genitive plural नृणाम् or नॄणाम्.

47. पति m. 'a master,' and सखि m. 'a friend' (except when forming the last member of a compound, and पति in the Veda also when governing a genitive) make in the sing. instr. पत्या, सख्या, in the dat. पत्ये, सख्ये, in the abl. and gen. पत्युस्, सख्युस्, in the loc. पत्यौ, सख्यौ.

सखि besides makes in the sing. nom. सखा, in the acc. सखायम्, in the dual nom. voc. acc. सखायौ, in the nom. and voc. plur. सखायस्.

The rest is regular, *e.g.* voc. sing. पते, सखे.

48. पथ्, पथिन्, पन्थन्, see No. 24.

49. पद्, see पाद् in No. 14 and No. 50.

50. पाद् f. 'a foot,' when it is the last part of a compound, becomes पद् in the weakest cases (§ 220), and before the affix of the femin. ई, *e.g.* द्विपाद्, adj. 'having two feet,' instr. singular द्विपदा, but nom. voc. sing. द्विपाद्, acc. sing. द्विपादम्, instr. dat. abl. dual द्विपाद्भ्याम् (Siddhânta K., 48*b*); fem. with ई द्विपदी, without it द्विपद् or द्विपाद्.

51. पाद्, see No. 14.

52. पुंस् m. 'a man,' has as base of the voc. sing. पुमंस्; of the other strong cases पुमांस्; of the instr. dat. abl. dual and plur. and loc. plur. पुम्, in the weakest cases (§ 220) पुंस्. In the nom. and voc. sing. the final स् is dropped and the penultimate Anusvâra changed to न् (*cf.* §§ 221, V. and 243); in the loc. plur. the final म् becomes Anusvâra.

Sing. पुमान्, पुमन्, पुमांसम्, पुंसा, पुंसे, पुंसस्, पुंसि.

Dual पुमांसौ, पुम्भ्याम्, पुंसोस्.

Plur. पुमांसस्, पुंसस्, पुम्भिस्, पुम्भ्यस्, पुंसाम्, पुंसु.

When the last member of a compound adjective, *e.g.* सुपुंस्, it makes in the nom. voc. acc. sing. of the neuter सुपुम्, in the nom. voc. acc. dual सुपुंसी, in the nom. voc. acc. plur. सुपुमांसि; the rest is like the masculine.

53. पुनर्भू, see No. 26.

54. पुम्, पुमांस्, see No. 52.

55. पुरुदंशस्, see No. 6.

56. पुरोडाश्, see No. 12.

57. पूषन्, see No. 9. Besides, the weakest cases (§ 220) may be derived from पूष्, *e.g.* instr. sing. पूषा or पूष्णा.

58. पृत्, see पृतना in No. 14.

59. भगवन्त्, see No. 3.

60. मघवन् m. 'a name of Indra,' युवन् m. 'a young man,' and श्वन् m. 'a dog,' derive the weakest cases (§ 220) from मघोन्, यून्, and शुन्; the rest is regular (§ 221, III.), sing. nom. मघवा, युवा, श्वा, voc. मघवन्, युवन्, श्वन्, acc. मघवानम्, युवानम्, श्वानम्, instr. मघोना, यूना, शुना, etc., dual nom. voc. acc. मघवानौ, etc., instr. dat. abl. मघवभ्याम्, etc., gen. loc. मघोनोस्, etc.

The feminine is according to § 210, मघोनी, but also (from the original form °मघवन्त्) मघवती, यूनी and (from the original form युवन्त्) युवति (with a short final), शुनी.

61. मथ्, मथिन्, मन्थन्, see No. 24.

62. महन्त्, महान्त्, see § 221, II.

63. मांस्, मांस, see No. 14.

63*b*. मास्, मास, see No. 14.

64. यकन्, see यकृत् in No. 14.

65. युञ्ज् adj. 'joining.' This form is employed in the strong cases (§ 220) and changes its compound final in the nom. and voc. sing. of the masculine and feminine to ङ्; in the weak cases the nasal is rejected. Thus sing. nom. voc. m.f. युङ्, acc. युञ्जम्, nom. voc. acc. of the neuter युक्, instr. m.f.n. युजा; dual nom. voc. acc. m.f. युञ्जौ, of the neuter युजी; instr. dat. abl. m.f.n. युग्भ्याम्, gen. loc. युजोस्; plur. nom. voc. m.f. युञ्जस्, acc. युजस्, nom. voc. acc. of the neuter युञ्जि, instr. m.f.n. युग्भिस्, etc.

66. युवन्, यून्, see No. 60.

67. यूष्, यूषन्, see No. 14.

68. ऽरि, neuter of adjectives, compounded with ऽरै, 'wealth,' according to § 210*b*, *e.g.* सुरै masc. and fem. सुरि neuter, 'having much wealth,' changes its final in the cases, the terminations of which begin with भ्, and in the loc. plur. to आ, सुराभ्याम्, सुरासु; also in the gen. plural, according to some grammarians, and with inserted ण्, सुराणाम्.

69. लक्ष्मी, see No. 13.

70. वर्षाभू, see No. 26.

71. वातप्रमी m.f. 'a swift antelope,' may form the sing. acc. वातप्रम्यम् or °प्रमीम्, the loc. °प्रम्यि or °प्रमी, the plur. acc. °प्रम्यस् or °प्रमीस्; the rest follows the analogy of जलपी, § 231, I. 2.

72. ऽवाह् as last member of a compound, when preceded by अ or आ, becomes in the weakest cases (§ 220) ऊह्, which combines with the preceding अ or आ to औह्, *e.g.* भारवाह् 'bearing a load,' instr. singular भारौहा.—But when preceded by another vowel and in the compound श्वेतवाह् this change is optional, *e.g.* भूवाह् in the instr. sing. either भूवाहा or (भूऽऊहा contracted to) भूहा, श्वेतवाहा or श्वेतौहा.

श्वेतवाह् besides forms its nom. voc. sing., loc. plur., and the cases, the terminations of which begin with भ्, according to the analogy of the nouns in No. 12, as if the crude form was श्वेतवस्, thus nom. and voc. sing. श्वेतवास्, instr. dat. abl. dual श्वेतवोभ्याम्, loc. plur. श्वेतवस्सु.

73. विवस्वन्त्, see No. 10.

74. विश्वराज् (विश्वऽराज्) m. 'a universal king,' lengthens the final अ of its first member in the nom. voc. sing., loc. plur., and before the terminations beginning with भ्, *e.g.* nom. and voc. sing. विश्वाराट्, loc. plur. विश्वाराट्सु, instr. dat. abl. dual विश्वाराड्भ्याम्.

75. शकन्, शकृत्, see No. 14.

76. शिरस्, शीर्षन्, see No. 14.

77. शुन्, श्वन्, see No. 60.

78. श्वेतवस्, श्वेतवाह्, श्वेतौह्, see No. 72.

79. सक्थन्, सक्थि, see No. 2.

80. सखाय्, सखि, see No. 47.

81. सानु, see No. 14.

82. स्त्री f. 'a wife,' is declined like देवी (§ 230) in the sing. nom. स्त्री and voc. स्त्रि; in the dative it forms स्त्रियै, in the abl. and gen. स्त्रियास्, in the loc. स्त्रियाम्; in the plur. gen. स्त्रीणाम्; in the sing. accus. स्त्रीम् or स्त्रियम्; and likewise in the plur. acc. स्त्रीस् or स्त्रियस्; in the rest it follows the analogy of श्री (§ 230), *e.g.* instr. sing. स्त्रिया.

When forming the last part of a compound adjective, it becomes ऽस्त्रि (§ 210), *e.g.* अतिस्त्रि m.f.n., and makes in the sing. accus. masc. either ऽस्त्रिम् (analogously to अग्नि, § 229) or ऽस्त्रियम्, in the dual. nom. voc. acc. masc. ऽस्त्रियौ, in the gen. loc. ऽस्त्रियोस्; plur. accus. masc. either ऽस्त्रीन् or ऽस्त्रियस्; in the rest it follows the analogy of अग्नि (§ 229). In the feminine the last part of the compound is formed as in the masculine in the sing. acc. ऽस्त्रिम् or ऽस्त्रियम्, dual nom. voc. acc. gen. and loc. ऽस्त्रियौ, ऽस्त्रियोस्, and even in other cases, viz., the instr. sing. ऽस्त्रिया, and optionally in the dat., abl. gen., loc. sing., *e.g.* ऽस्त्रियै or ऽस्त्रये (like मतये, § 229), ऽस्त्रियास् or ऽस्त्रेस्, ऽस्त्रियाम् or ऽस्त्रौ; the acc. plur. is either ऽस्त्रीस् or ऽस्त्रियस्; the rest follows the analogy of मति (§ 229), *e.g.* nom. voc. plur. ऽस्त्रयस्.

83. स्नु, see सानु in No. 14.

84. हृद्, see No. 14.

85. ऽहन्, see No. 9. Besides in the weakest cases ह is changed to घ्, *e.g.* वृत्रहन्, instr. singular वृत्रघ्ना.

2. Degrees of Comparison.

§ 240. The comparative is generally formed by subjoining to the crude form the affix तर *tara*; the superlative, by suffixing तम *tama*, *e.g.* नृ *nṛi*, 'a man,' नृतम *nṛi-tama*, 'most man-like.'

The adjectives and nouns which imply an agency (*nomina agentis*) sometimes form the comparative with ईयंस् *îyaṁs*, the superlative with इष्ठ *ishṭha*, *e.g.* पृथु *pṛithu*, 'broad,' comparative पृथुतर *pṛithu-tara* or प्रथीयंस् *prath-îyaṁs* (§ 242, 3), superlative पृथुतम *pṛithu-tama* or प्रथिष्ठ *prath-ishṭha*. Sometimes both affixes are combined, *e.g.* पाप *pâpa*, 'bad,' पापीयस्तर *pâp-îyas-tara*, पापिष्ठतम *pâp-ishṭha-tama*. तर *tara* may also be added to the superlatives ending in इष्ठ *ishṭha*, श्रेष्ठतर *çreshṭha-tara* from the superlative श्रेष्ठ *çreshṭha*, 'the best' (§ 242, 3).

The comparatives and superlatives formed by *tara* and *tama* have the accent of their bases, *e.g.* *nṛí*, *nṛí-tama*; *pṛithú*, *pṛithú-tara*, *pṛithú-tama*; those which are formed with *îyaṁs* and *ishṭha*, put the accent on their first syllable, *e.g.* *práth-îyaṁs*, *práth-ishṭha*.

§ 241. The crude forms undergo before तर *tara* and तम *tama* the changes prescribed in §§ 193, 2 and 27. But those in इस् *is* and उस् *us* change their final स् *s* to ष् *sh*, after which the initial त् *t* of the affix becomes ट् *ṭ*, *e.g.* सर्पिस् *sarpis*, n., 'molten butter,' सर्पिष्टर *sarpish-ṭara*.

The nouns which have strong and weak forms attach (conformably to § 193, 2) the affixes to that which they have before the termination of the locative plural, *e.g.* प्राञ्च् *prâñch*, loc. plur. प्राक्षु *prâk-shu*, comparative प्राक्तर *prâk-tara*; युनन्त् *yunant*, 'joining,' युनत्सु *yunat-su*, युनत्तर *yunat-tara*; राजन् *râjan*, 'king,' राजसु *râja-su*, राजतर *râja-tara*; धनिन् *dhanin*, 'wealthy,' धनिषु *dhani-shu*, धनितर *dhani-tara*; loc. plur. of the participle of the reduplicated perfect रुद् 'to cry,' रुरुद्वत्सु *rurudvat-su*, comparative रुरुद्वत्तर *rurudvat-tara*.

In the Veda some nouns in न् retain their final, some ending in vowels insert न्, *e.g.* सुपथिन्, सुपथिन्तर; मधु, मधुन्तम.

Feminine substantives and adjectives, corresponding to masculines which differ from them only in the gender, attach the affixes of the comparative and superlative to the crude form of the masculine, *e.g.* काली *kâlî*, f., 'a female black,' corresponding to the crude form of the masculine काल *kâla*, 'black,' forms its comparative and superlative from the latter, कालतरा *kâla-tarâ*, कालतमा *kâla-tamâ*. Many feminines ending in ई *î* and ऊ *û* optionally shorten the final, ब्रह्मबन्धू *brahmabandhû*, 'a female relation of a Brahman,' ब्रह्मबन्धूतरा *brahmabandhû-tarâ* or °बन्धुतरा *°bandhu-tarâ*.

§ 242. Some peculiar changes take place before the affixes ईयंस् *îyams* and इष्ठ *ishṭha*.

1. They cause the affixes तृ *tṛi*, मन्त् *mant*, वन्त् *vant*, वल *vala*, विन् *vin*, and इन् *in* to be dropped, *e.g.* दोग्धृ *dogdhṛi* = दोह् *doh* + तृ *tṛi* (*cf.* § 98, 3), comparative दोहीयंस् *doh-îyams*, superlative दोहिष्ठ *doh-ishṭha*. When after the rejection of तृ *tṛi*, an ए *e*, or ओ *o*, becomes the final, the first is changed to अय् *ay*, the latter to अव् *av*, *e.g.* जेतृ *jetṛi* जयीयंस् *jay-îyams*, स्तोतृ *stotṛi* स्तविष्ठ *stav-ishṭha*.

2. Polysyllabic crude forms reject their last vowel together with the consonant or consonants by which it may be followed, पटु *paṭu*, 'sharp,' पटीयंस् *paṭ-îyams*. This rule applies also to those which reject one of the affixes mentioned in 1, *e.g.* वसुमन्त् *vasu-mant*, वसीयंस् *vas-îyams*.

In the Veda यंस् occurs instead of ईयंस्, *e.g.* वस्यंस् from वसु 'good.'

3. Sometimes these affixes are attached to anomalous modifications of the nouns. The following is a list of these anomalous comparatives and superlatives:—

COMPARATIVE.	SUPERLATIVE.	POSITIVE.
कनीयंस्	कनिष्ठ	अल्प 'little,' or युवन् 'young.'
क्रशीयंस्	क्रशिष्ठ	कृश 'meagre.'
क्षेपीयंस्	क्षेपिष्ठ	क्षिप्र 'quick.'
क्षोदीयंस्	क्षोदिष्ठ	क्षुद्र 'small.'
गरीयंस्	गरिष्ठ	गुरु 'heavy.'
ज्यायंस्	ज्येष्ठ	प्रशस्य 'praiseworthy' and वृद्ध ['old.'
त्रपीयंस्	त्रपिष्ठ	तृप्र 'satiated.'

COMPARATIVE.	SUPERLATIVE.	POSITIVE.
दवीयंस्	दविष्ठ	दूर 'far.'
द्रढीयंस्	द्रढिष्ठ	दृढ 'firm.'
द्राघीयंस्	द्राघिष्ठ	दीर्घ 'long.'
नेदीयंस्	नेदिष्ठ	अन्तिक 'near.'
परिव्रढीयंस्	परिव्रढिष्ठ	परिवृढ 'august.'
प्रथीयंस्	प्रथिष्ठ	पृथु 'broad.'
प्रेयंस्	प्रेष्ठ	प्रिय 'beloved.'
बंहीयंस्	बंहिष्ठ	बहुल 'manifold.'
भूयंस्	भूयिष्ठ	बहु 'much.'
भ्रशीयंस्	भ्रशिष्ठ	भृश 'frequent.'
म्रदीयंस्	म्रदिष्ठ	मृदु 'soft.'
यवीयंस्	यविष्ठ	युवन् 'young.'
रजीयंस्	रजिष्ठ	ऋजु 'straight.'
वरीयंस्	वरिष्ठ	उरु 'broad.'
वर्षीयंस्	वर्षिष्ठ	वृद्ध 'old.'
वृन्दीयंस्	वृन्दिष्ठ	वृन्दारक 'beautiful.'
श्रेयंस्	श्रेष्ठ	प्रशस्य 'praiseworthy.'
स्थवीयंस्	स्थविष्ठ	स्थूल 'large.'
स्थेयंस्	स्थेष्ठ	स्थिर 'firm.'
स्फेयंस्	स्फेष्ठ	स्फिर 'much.'
ह्रसीयंस्	ह्रसिष्ठ	ह्रस्व 'short.'

§ 243. The feminines of the affixes तर *tara*, तम *tama*, and इष्ठ *ishṭha*, according to § 210, are तरा *tarâ*, तमा *tamâ*, and इष्ठा *ishṭhâ*.

The masculines and neuters are declined after the models in § 225; the feminines in accordance with that in § 226.

The feminine of ईयंस् *iyaṁs*, according to § 210 (*cf.* the instrumental singular of the masculine ईयसा *iyas-â*) is ईयसी *iyas-î*.

The rules for the declension of the masculine and neuter of ईयंस् *îyaṁs*, have been given in § 221, VI. I shall now give the paradigm गरीयंस् *gárîyaṁs*. The feminine गरीयसी *garîyas-î* follows strictly the analogy of देवी *devî* in § 230.

SINGULAR.

	m.n.	m.	n.
N.	—	गरीयान् *garîyân*	गरीयस् *garîyas* (N.V.Acc.)
V.	—	गरीयन् *garîyan*	
Acc.	—	गरीयांसम् *garîyâṁs-am*	
I.	गरीयसा *garîyas-â*	—	—
D.	गरीयसे *garîyas-e*	—	—
Abl. G.	गरीयसस् *garîyas-as*	—	—
L.	गरीयसि *garîyas-i*	—	—

DUAL.

	m.n.	m.	n.
N.V. Acc.	—	गरीयांसौ *garîyâṁs-au*	गरीयसी *garîyas-î*
I.D. Abl.	गरीयोभ्याम् *garîyo-bhyâm*	—	—
G. L.	गरीयसोस् *garîyas-os*	—	—

PLURAL.

	m.n.	m.	n.
N.V.	—	गरीयांसस् *garîyâṁs-as*	गरीयांसि *garîyâṁ-si* (N.V.Acc.)
Acc.	—	गरीयसस् *garîyas-as*	
Instr.	गरीयोभिस् *garîyo-bhis*	—	—
D.Abl.	गरीयोभ्यस् *garîyo-bhyas*	—	—
Gen.	गरीयसाम् *garîyas-âm*	—	—
Loc.	गरीयस्सु or गरीयःसु *garîyas-su* *garîyaḥ-su*	—	—

In the same way is declined लघीयंस् *laghîyaṁs*, comparative of लघु *laghu*, 'light.'

3. PRONOUNS.

§ 244. The pronouns have no vocative, and those of the first and second persons are declined as follows:—

SINGULAR.

N.	अहम् *ahám*, 'I.'	त्वम् *tvám*, 'thou.'
Acc.	माम् *mā́m* and मा *mâ*, 'me.'	त्वाम् *tvā́m* and त्वा *tvâ*, 'thee.'
I.	मया *máyâ*, 'by me.'	त्वया *tváyâ*, 'by thee.'
D.	मह्यम् *máhyam* and मे *me*, 'to me.'	तुभ्यम् *túbhyam* and ते *te*, 'to thee.'
Abl.	मत् *mát*, 'from me.'	त्वत् *tvát*, 'from thee.'
G.	मम *máma*, and मे *me*, 'mine' 'of me.'	तव *táva* and ते *te*, 'thine' 'of thee.'
L.	मयि *máyi*, 'in me.'	त्वयि *tváyi*, 'in thee.'

DUAL.

N.	आवाम् *âvā́m*, 'we two.'	युवाम् *yuvā́m*, 'you two.'
Acc.	the same and नौ *nau*, 'us two.'	the same and वाम् *vâm*, 'you two.'
I.	आवाभ्याम् *âvā́bhyâm*, 'by us two.'	युवाभ्याम् *yuvā́bhyâm*, 'by you two.'
D.	the same and नौ *nau*, 'to us two.'	the same and वाम् *vâm*, 'to you two.'
Abl.	आवाभ्याम् *âvā́bhyâm*, 'from us two.'	युवाभ्याम् *yuvā́bhyâm*, 'from you two.'
G.	आवयोस् *âváyos* and नौ *nau*, 'of us two.'	युवयोस् *yuváyos* and वाम् *vâm*, 'of you two.'
L.	आवयोस् *âváyos*, 'in us two.'	युवयोस् *yuváyos*, 'in you two.'

PLURAL.

N.	वयम् *vayám*, 'we.'	यूयम् *yûyám*, 'you.'
Acc.	अस्मान् *asmā́n* and नस् *nas*, 'us.'	युष्मान् *yushmā́n* and वस् *vas*, 'you.'
I.	अस्माभिस् *asmā́bhis*, 'by us.'	युष्माभिस् *yushmā́bhis*, 'by you.'
D.	अस्मभ्यम् *asmábhyam* and नस् *nas*, 'to us.'	युष्मभ्यम् *yushmábhyam* and वस् *vas*, 'to you.'
Abl.	अस्मत् *asmát*, 'from us.'	युष्मत् *yushmát*, 'from you.'
G.	अस्माकम् *asmā́kam* and नस् *nas*, 'ours,' 'of us.'	युष्माकम् *yushmā́kam* and वस् *vas*, 'yours,' 'of you.'
L.	अस्मासु *asmā́su*, 'in us.'	युष्मासु *yushmā́su*, 'in you.'

§ 245. There are five pronouns of the third person, तद् *tád*, 'he, she, it,' त्यद् *tyád*, 'that,' इदम् *idám*, 'this,' एतद् *etád*, 'this,' and अदस् *adás*, 'that.' The relative pronoun is यद् *yád*, 'who,' 'which,' or 'what,' and the interrogative pronoun किम् *kím*, 'who' or 'what.'

§ 246. These pronouns are declined in the three genders and substitute various forms as their inflectional bases.

तद् *tád* has as inflectional base in the nominative singular masc. स *sá*, in the fem. सा *sấ*. The other cases are derived in the masculine and neuter from त *tá*, in the feminine from ता *tấ*.

त्यद् *tyád* substitutes in the nom. sing. masc. स्य *syá*, in the fem. स्या *syấ*; in all the other cases in the masc. and neuter त्य *tyá*, in the fem. त्या *tyấ*.

इदम् *idám* substitutes: 1. In the sing. nom. masc., dat. abl. gen. loc. m.f.n., in the dual instr. dat. abl. and plur. instr. dat. abl. gen. loc. masc. and neuter अ *a*.—2. In the dual instr. dat. abl. and plur. instr. dat. abl. gen. loc. fem. आ *á*.—3. In the sing. nom. and acc. neuter इ *i*.—4. In the sing. nom. fem. ई *í*.—5. In the sing. acc. masc., dual and plur. nom. acc. of the masc. and neuter इम *imá*, in the fem. इमा *imấ*.—6. In the sing. instr., dual gen. loc. masc. and neuter अन *aná*, in the fem. अना *anấ*.—7. The base of the acc. sing., dual, and plural, of the instr. sing., and of the gen. and loc. dual sometimes is in the masc. and neuter एन *ena*, in the fem. एना *enâ*.

एतद् *etád* substitutes in the sing. nom. masc. एष *eshá*, in the fem. एषा *eshấ*; in all the other cases in the masculine and neuter एत *etá*, in the fem. एता *etấ*. एन *ena* and एना *enâ* are sometimes used as in the preceding rule, No. 7.

अदस् *adás* substitutes:—1. In the sing. nom. masc. असौ *asáu*, fem. असौ *asáu*.—2. In the sing. nom. and acc. neuter अदः *adáḥ*.—3. In the sing. acc. masc. and fem., in the whole dual, and in the plur.

nom. fem. neut., acc. m.f.n., instr. dat. abl. gen. and loc. fem., in the masc. and neuter अमु *amú*, in the fem. अमू *amū́*.—4. In the plur. nom. masc. and in the instr. dat. abl. gen. and loc. masc. and neuter अमी *amī́*.

यद् *yád* derives all its cases in the masc. and neuter from य *yá*, in the fem. from या *yā́*.

किम् *kím* substitutes in all cases of the masc. and neuter—except the nom. and acc. singular of the neuter—क *ká*, in the fem. का *kā́*; in the nom. and acc. sing. neuter कि *kí*.

§ 247. In the dative, ablative, and locative singular the masculine and neuter subjoin स्म *sma* to the base, the feminine adds स्य् *sy* in these cases as well as in the genitive singular.

The inflectional terminations differ in some instances from those of the nouns; instead of the final द् *d* in तद् *tad*, etc., appears त् *t* (*cf.* § 13).

1. तद् *tád*.

	SINGULAR. masc.	neut.	fem.	DUAL. masc. neut. fem.	PLURAL. masc.	neut.	fem.
N.	सस् *sás*	तत् *tát* (N. Acc.)	सा *sā́*	तौ *táu*, ते *té*, ते *té* (N. A.)	ते *té*	तानि *tā́ni* (N. A.)	तास् *tā́s* (N. A.)
Acc.	तम् *tám*		ताम् *tā́m*		तान् *tā́n*		
I.	तेन *téna*		तया *táyā*	ताभ्याम् *tā́bhyām* (I. D. A.)	तैस् *táis*		ताभिस् *tā́bhis*
D.	तस्मै *tásmai*		तस्यै *tásyai*		तेभ्यस् *tébhyas* (D. A.)		ताभ्यस् *tā́bhyas* (D. A.)
Abl.	तस्मात् *tásmāt*		तस्यास् *tásyās* (Abl. G.)				
G.	तस्य *tásya*			तयोस् *táyos* (G. L.)	तेषाम् *téshām*		तासाम् *tā́sām*
L.	तस्मिन् *tásmin*		तस्याम् *tásyām*		तेषु *téshu*		तासु *tā́su*

2. त्यद् *tyád.*

	SINGULAR. masc.	neut.	fem.		DUAL. masc. neut. fem.		PLURAL. masc.	neut.	fem.
N.	स्यस् *syás*	त्यत् *tyát* (N. Acc.)	स्या *syā́*	N. A.	त्यौ *tyáu*, त्ये *tyé*, त्ये *tyé*	N.	त्ये *tyé*	त्यानि *tyā́ni* (N. A.)	त्यास् *tyā́s*
Acc.	त्यम् *tyám*		त्याम् *tyā́m*			A.	त्यान् *tyā́n*		
I.	त्येन *tyéna*		त्यया *tyáyâ*	I. D. A.	त्याभ्याम् *tyā́bhyâm*	I.	त्यैस् *tyáis*		त्याभिस् *tyā́bhis*
D.	त्यस्मै *tyásmai*		त्यस्यै *tyásyai*			D. A.	त्येभ्यस् *tyébhyas*		त्याभ्यस् *tyā́bhyas*
Abl.	त्यस्मात् *tyásmât*		त्यस्यास् *tyásyâs* (Abl. G.)						
G.	त्यस्य *tyásya*			G. L.	त्ययोस् *tyáyos*	G.	त्येषाम् *tyéshâm*		त्यासाम् *tyā́sâm*
L.	त्यस्मिन् *tyásmin*		त्यस्याम् *tyásyâm*			L.	त्येषु *tyéshu*		त्यासु *tyā́su*

(In the singular, the neuter shares the masculine forms from the Instrumental onwards; in the dual, masc., neut. and fem. are alike from the Instrumental onwards; in the plural, the neuter shares the masculine forms from the Instrumental onwards.)

3. इदम् *idám.*

	SINGULAR. masc.	neut.	fem.		DUAL. masc. neut. fem.		PLURAL. masc.	neut.	fem.
N.	अयम् *ayám*	इदम् *idám*	इयम् *iyám*	N.	इमौ *imáu*, इमे *imé*, इमे *imé*	N.	इमे *imé*	इमानि *imā́ni*	इमास् *imā́s*
Acc.	इमम् *imám* एनम् *enam*	इदम् *idám* एनत् *enat*	इमाम् *imā́m* एनाम् *enâm*	A.	इमौ *imáu*, इमे *imé*, इमे *imé* एनौ *enau*, एने *ene*, एने *ene*	A.	इमान् *imā́n* एनान् *enân*	इमानि *imā́ni* एनानि *enâni*	इमास् *imā́s* एनास् *enâs*
I.	अनेन *anéna* एनेन *enena*		अनया *anáyâ* एनया *enayâ*	I. D. A.	आभ्याम् *âbhyā́m* आभ्याम् *âbhyâm*	I.	एभिस् *ebhís* एभिस् *ebhis*		आभिस् *âbhís* आभिस् *âbhis*
D.	अस्मै *asmái* अस्मै *asmai*		अस्यै *asyái* अस्यै *asyai*			D. A.	एभ्यस् *ebhyás* एभ्यस् *ebhyas*		आभ्यस् *âbhyás* आभ्यस् *âbhyas*
Abl.	अस्मात् *asmā́t* अस्मात् *asmât*		अस्यास् *asyā́s* अस्यास् *asyâs* (Abl. G.)						
G.	अस्य *asyá* अस्य *asya*			G. L.	अनयोस् *anáyos* अनयोस् *anayos* एनयोस् *enayos*	G.	एषाम् *eshā́m* एषाम् *eshâm*		आसाम् *âsā́m* आसाम् *âsâm*
L.	अस्मिन् *asmín* अस्मिन् *asmin*		अस्याम् *asyā́m* अस्याम् *asyâm*			L.	एषु *eshú* एषु *eshu*		आसु *âsú* आसु *âsu*

(The neuter shares the masculine forms from the Instrumental onwards.)

4. एतद् *etád.*

	SINGULAR m.	SINGULAR n.	SINGULAR f.		DUAL m.	DUAL n.	DUAL f.		PLURAL m.	PLURAL n.	PLURAL f.
N.	एषस् *eshás*	एतत् *etát*	एषा *eshā́*	N.	एतौ *etáu*	एते *eté*	एते *eté*	N.	एते *eté*	एतानि *etā́ni*	एतास् *etā́s*
Acc.	एतम् *etám*	एतत् *etát*	एताम् *etā́m*	A.	एतौ *etáu*	एते *eté*	एते *eté*	A.	एतान् *etā́n*	एतानि *etā́ni*	एतास् *etā́s*
	एनम् *enam*	एनत् *enat*	एनाम् *enâm*		एनौ *enau*	एने *ene*	एने *ene*		एनान् *enân*	एनानि *enâni*	एनास् *enâs*
I.	एतेन *eténa*, एनेन *enena*		एतया *etáyâ*, एनया *enayâ*	I.	एताभ्याम् *etā́bhyâm*			I.	एतैस् *etáis*		एताभिस् *etā́bhis*
D.	एतस्मै *etásmai*		एतस्यै *etásyai*	D.				D.	एतेभ्यस् *etébhyas*		एताभ्यस् *etā́bhyas*

etc., like तद् *tád,* paradigm 1 ; only in the genitive and locative dual एतयोस् *etáyos,* and एनयोस् *enayos.*

5. अदस् *adás.*

	SINGULAR m.	SINGULAR n.	SINGULAR f.		DUAL m. n. f.		PLURAL m.	PLURAL n.	PLURAL f.
N.	असौ *asáu*	अदस् *adás*	असौ *asáu*	N.	अमू *amū́*	N.	अमी *amī́*	अमूनि *amū́ni*	अमूस् *amū́s*
Acc.	अमुम् *amúm*	अदस् *adás*	अमूम् *amū́m*	A.	अमू *amū́*	A.	अमून् *amū́n*	अमूनि *amū́ni*	अमूस् *amū́s*
I.	अमुना *amúnâ*		अमुया *amuyā́*	I.	अमूभ्याम् *amū́bhyâm*	I.	अमीभिस् *amī́bhis*		अमूभिस् *amū́bhis*
D.	अमुष्मै *amúshmai*		अमुष्यै *amúshyai*	D.	अमूभ्याम् *amū́bhyâm*	D.	अमीभ्यस् *amī́bhyas*		अमूभ्यस् *amū́bhyas*
Abl.	अमुष्मात् *amúshmât*		अमुष्यास् *amúshyâs*	A.	अमूभ्याम् *amū́bhyâm*	A.	अमीभ्यस् *amī́bhyas*		अमूभ्यस् *amū́bhyas*
G.	अमुष्य *amúshya*		अमुष्यास् *amúshyâs*	G.	अमुयोस् *amúyos*	G.	अमीषाम् *amī́shâm*		अमूषाम् *amū́shâm*
L.	अमुष्मिन् *amúshmin*		अमुष्याम् *amúshyâm*	L.	अमुयोस् *amúyos*	L.	अमीषु *amī́shu*		अमूषु *amū́shu*

6. यद् *yád.*

<table>
<tr><th></th><th colspan="3">SINGULAR.</th><th colspan="3">DUAL.</th><th colspan="3">PLURAL.</th></tr>
<tr><th></th><th>m.</th><th>n.</th><th>f.</th><th>m.</th><th>n.</th><th>f.</th><th>m.</th><th>n.</th><th>f.</th></tr>
<tr><td>N.</td><td>यस् *yás*</td><td rowspan="2">यत् *yát*</td><td>या *yā́*</td><td rowspan="2">यौ *yaú*</td><td rowspan="2">ये *yé*</td><td rowspan="2">ये *yé*</td><td>ये *yé*</td><td rowspan="2">यानि *yā́ni*</td><td rowspan="2">यास् *yā́s*</td></tr>
<tr><td>Acc.</td><td>यम् *yám*</td><td>याम् *yā́m*</td><td>यान् *yā́n*</td></tr>
<tr><td>I.</td><td colspan="2">येन *yéna*</td><td>यया *yáyâ*</td><td colspan="3" rowspan="3">याभ्याम् *yā́bhyâm*</td><td colspan="2">यैस् *yaís*</td><td>याभिस् *yā́bhis*</td></tr>
<tr><td>D.</td><td colspan="2">यस्मै *yásmai*</td><td>यस्यै *yásyai*</td><td colspan="2" rowspan="2">येभ्यस् *yébhyas*</td><td rowspan="2">याभ्यस् *yā́bhyas*</td></tr>
<tr><td>Abl.</td><td colspan="2">यस्मात् *yásmât*</td><td rowspan="2">यस्यास् *yásyâs*</td></tr>
<tr><td>G.</td><td colspan="2">यस्य *yásya*</td><td colspan="3" rowspan="2">ययोस् *yáyos*</td><td colspan="2">येषाम् *yéshâm*</td><td>यासाम् *yā́sâm*</td></tr>
<tr><td>L.</td><td colspan="2">यस्मिन् *yásmin*</td><td>यस्याम् *yásyâm*</td><td colspan="2">येषु *yéshu*</td><td>यासु *yā́su*</td></tr>
</table>

7. किम् *kím.*

<table>
<tr><th></th><th colspan="3">SINGULAR.</th><th colspan="3">DUAL.</th><th colspan="3">PLURAL.</th></tr>
<tr><th></th><th>m.</th><th>n.</th><th>f.</th><th>m.</th><th>n.</th><th>f.</th><th>m.</th><th>n.</th><th>f.</th></tr>
<tr><td>N.</td><td>कस् *kás*</td><td rowspan="2">किम् *kím*</td><td>का *kā́*</td><td rowspan="2">कौ *kaú*</td><td rowspan="2">के *ké*</td><td rowspan="2">के *ké*</td><td>के *ké*</td><td rowspan="2">कानि *kā́ni*</td><td rowspan="2">कास् *kā́s*</td></tr>
<tr><td>Acc.</td><td>कम् *kám*</td><td>काम् *kā́m*</td><td>कान् *kā́n*</td></tr>
<tr><td>I.</td><td colspan="2">केन *kéna*</td><td>कया *káyâ*</td><td colspan="3" rowspan="3">काभ्याम् *kā́bhyâm*</td><td colspan="2">कैस् *kaís*</td><td>काभिस् *kā́bhis*</td></tr>
<tr><td>D.</td><td colspan="2"></td><td></td><td colspan="2"></td><td></td></tr>
<tr><td>A.</td><td colspan="2"></td><td></td><td colspan="2"></td><td></td></tr>
</table>

etc., like the preceding.

Obs. The final स् *s* of the nominative singular masculine सस् *sas* (सः *saḥ*), स्यस् *syas* (स्यः *syaḥ*), and एषस् *eshas* (एषः *eshaḥ*) are rejected before all letters, except अ *a*, before which it undergoes the change prescribed in § 28, Exc. 1.

§ 248. भवन्त् *bhavant,* properly a noun signifying 'man, master,' is frequently applied in polite speech instead of the pronoun of the second person, and is construed with the third person of the verb. It is declined like other nouns in वन्त् *vant* (*cf.* § 221, II., Exc. 2), *e.g.* masc. nom. भवान् *bhavân,* voc. भवन् *bhavan,* acc. भवन्तम् *bhavant-am,* instr. भवता *bhavat-â,* etc. The feminine, according to § 210, is भवती *bhavat-î,* and follows the declension of देवी *devî* (§ 230).

§ 249. The reflective pronoun is expressed:

1. By स्वयम् *svayam,* 'self,' which is indeclinable and may be combined with the three persons, *e.g.* स स्वयम् *sa svayam,* 'he himself.'

2. By आत्मन् *âtman,* masc., properly 'the soul,' and declined according to § 211, III., Exc. 1, *e.g.* sing. nom. आत्मा *âtmâ,* voc. आत्मन् *âtman,* acc. आत्मानम् *âtmân-am,* instr. आत्मना *âtman-â,* etc., *cf.* § 239, 17. It is used in this signification in the singular only, *cf.* Daçakum. in my Chrestomathie, p. 189, 9, आत्मानमात्मनोद्धरन्ति सन्तः *âtmânam âtmanoddharanti santaḥ,* 'the brave men save themselves by themselves.'

CRUDE FORMS FOLLOWING MORE OR LESS THE PRONOMINAL DECLENSION.

§ 250. The nouns अन्य *anyá,* 'another,' अन्यतर *anyátara* (its comparative), इतर *ítara,* 'another,' कतर *kátara* (comparative of the interrogative pronoun), 'who or which of two,' कतम *kátama* (superlative of the interrogative pronoun), 'who or which of these,' ततर *tátara* (comparative of the pronoun तद् *tad*), ततम *tátuma* (its superlative), यतर *yátara* (comparative of the relative pronoun), यतम *yátama* (its superlative), and एकतम *ékatama* (superlative of एक *éka,* 'one') follow the declension of यद् *yád* (§ 247, paradigm 6), but they may also form vocatives.

I here give the paradigm अन्य *anyá.*

	SINGULAR. m.	n.	f.		DUAL. m.	n.	f.		PLURAL. m.	n.	f.
N.	अन्यस्	अन्यत्	अन्या	N.	अन्यौ	अन्ये	अन्ये	N.	अन्ये	अन्यानि	अन्यास्
V.	अन्य	अन्यत्	अन्ये	V.				V.			
Acc.	अन्यम्	अन्यत्	अन्याम्	A.				A.	अन्यान्		
I.	अन्येन		अन्यया	I.	अन्याभ्याम्			I.	अन्यैस्		अन्याभिस्
D.	अन्यस्मै		अन्यस्यै	D.				D.	अन्येभ्यस्		अन्याभ्यस्
Abl.	अन्यस्मात्		अन्यस्यास्	A.				A.			
G.	अन्यस्य			G.	अन्ययोस्			G.	अन्येषाम्		अन्यासाम्
L.	अन्यस्मिन्		अन्यस्याम्	L.				L.	अन्येषु		अन्यासु

Obs. अन्योन्य *anyònya*, इतरेतर *ítaretara*, 'one another' (§ 208), and in the Veda इतर 'another,' make in the nom. acc. sing. of the neuter अन्योन्यम्, इतरेतरम्, इतरम्, and have in the vocative the crude form.

§ 251. एक 'one,' एकतर (comparative of एक) 'one of two,' उभय 'both' (has no dual), विश्व 'all,' सम, सिम (in the Veda with the acute on the final), सर्व 'all,' त्व 'another,' differ from the preceding paradigm only in the nom. voc. and acc. sing. of the neuter, which follow the nominal declension, *e.g.* sing. nom. masc. सर्वस्, neuter सर्वम्, fem. सर्वा, voc. masc. and neuter सर्व, fem. सर्वे; त्व may optionally make in the sing. nom. acc. neuter त्वम् or त्वत्, voc. त्व or त्वत्.

नेम 'half,' follows the declension of सर्व, except in the nom. voc. plur. masc., where it may optionally use the nominal inflexion नेमे or नेमास्.

§ 252. अन्तर signifying 'outer,' and 'an under-garment,' अधर 'inferior,' अपर 'another,' अवर 'posterior,' उत्तर 'above,' दक्षिण

'on the right hand,' पर 'behind,' पूर्व 'before,' and स्व 'own,' follow the rule of the preceding paragraph, except in the abl. and loc. sing. masc. and neuter and in the nom. voc. plur. masc., where they may optionally use the nominal inflexions, *e.g.* sing. nom. masc. अधरस्, neut. अधरम्, fem. अधरा, dat. masc. neut. अधरस्मै, fem. अधरस्यै, etc., but abl. masc. neut. अधरस्मात् or अधरात्, loc. masc. neut. अधरस्मिन् or अधरे, plur. nom. voc. masc. अधरे or अधरास्.

§ 253. द्वितीय 'the second,' and तृतीय 'the third,' may optionally follow the pronominal or nominal declension in the sing. dat. abl. gen. and loc. *e.g.* dat. masc. neut. द्वितीयस्मै or द्वितीयाय, fem. द्वितीयस्यै or द्वितीयायै, abl. masc. neut. द्वितीयस्मात् or द्वितीयात्, gen. m. n. द्वितीयस्य, abl. gen. fem. द्वितीयस्यास् or द्वितीयायास्, loc. m. n. द्वितीयस्मिन् or द्वितीये, fem. द्वितीयस्याम् or द्वितीयायाम्. The rest follow the nominal declension.

§ 254. प्रथम 'the first,' चरम 'the last,' अर्ध 'half, part of,' अल्प 'little,' कतिपय 'some,' and the numeral adjectives formed by the affix तय, as पञ्चतय 'fivefold,' may take the pronominal or nominal terminations in the nom. and voc. plur. masc., *e.g.* प्रथमे or प्रथमास्. The rest follow the nominal declension.

§ 255. The pronominal derivatives which are not mentioned in the preceding paragraphs follow the nominal declension, *e.g.* मदीय *madíya*, the possessive pronoun of the first person 'mine,' follows in the masc. and neuter § 225, and its feminine, मदीया *madíyá* (§ 210), follows § 226. But कति *kati*, 'how many' (interrogative), यति *yati*, 'how many' (relative), and तति *tati*, 'so many,' which are declinable in the three genders, but only in the plural, differ from § 229 in the nom. voc. acc. plur., which take no termination, therefore *e.g.* nom. voc. acc. कति, instr. कतिभिस्, dat. abl. कतिभ्यस्, gen. कतीनाम्, loc. कतिषु.

4. NUMERALS.

CARDINALS.

§ 256. The crude forms of the simple cardinals are:—

१ एक *éka*, 'one.'
२ द्वि *dví*, 'two.'
३ त्रि *trí*, 'three.'
४ चतुर् *chátur*, 'four.'
५ पञ्चन् *páńchan*, 'five.'
६ षष् *shásh*, 'six.'
७ सप्तन् *sáptan* (in the Veda सप्तन् *saptán*), 'seven.'
८ अष्टन् *áshṭan*, 'eight.'
९ नवन् *návan*, 'nine.'
१० दशन् *dáçan*, 'ten.'

The numerals from 'eleven' to 'nineteen' are formed by compounding the first nine from एक to नवन् with दशन् 'ten.' 'Nineteen' may also be formed by prefixing ऊन (*cf.* § 258) to विंशति 'twenty.' The numerals in न् drop their finals before दशन्. The modifications which the first members of eleven, twelve, thirteen, sixteen, and eighteen undergo, may be explained by their being inflected forms.

११ एकादशन् 'eleven.'
१२ द्वादशन् 'twelve.'
१३ त्रयोदशन् (ved. *tráyo°*) 'thirteen.'
१४ चतुर्दशन् 'fourteen.'
१५ पञ्चदशन् 'fifteen.'
१६ षोडशन् 'sixteen.'
१७ सप्तदशन् (ved. सप्तद°) 'seventeen.'
१८ अष्टादशन् 'eighteen.'
१९ नवदशन् or ऊनविंशति 'nineteen.'

The numerals from 'twenty' to 'hundred' are formed in a similar manner:—

२० विंशति *vim̃çáti*
२१ एकविंशति
२२ द्वाविंशति
२३ त्रयोविंशति
२४ चतुर्विंशति
२५ पञ्चविंशति
२६ षड्विंशति
२७ सप्तविंशति
२८ अष्टाविंशति
२९ नवविंशति or ऊनत्रिंशत्
३० त्रिंशत् *trim̃çát*
३१ एकत्रिंशत्
३२ द्वात्रिंशत्

३३ त्रयस्त्रिंशत्
३४ चतुस्त्रिंशत्
३५ पञ्चत्रिंशत्
३६ षट्त्रिंशत्
३७ सप्तत्रिंशत्
३८ अष्टात्रिंशत्
३९ नवत्रिंशत् or ऊनचत्वारिंशत्

४० चत्वारिंशत् *chatvârim̃çát*

४१ एकचत्वारिंशत्
४२ द्वाचत्वारिंशत् or द्विचत्वारिंशत्
४३ त्रयश्चत्वारिंशत् or त्रिचत्वारिंशत्
४४ चतुश्चत्वारिंशत्
४५ पञ्चचत्वारिंशत्
४६ षट्चत्वारिंशत्
४७ सप्तचत्वारिंशत्
४८ अष्टाचत्वारिंशत् or अष्टचत्वारिंशत्
४९ नवचत्वारिंशत् or ऊनपञ्चाशत्

५० पञ्चाशत् *pańchâçát*

५१ एकपञ्चाशत्
५२ द्वापञ्चाशत् or द्विपञ्चाशत्
५३ त्रयःपञ्चाशत् or त्रिपञ्चाशत्
५४ चतुःपञ्चाशत्
५५ पञ्चपञ्चाशत्
५६ षट्पञ्चाशत्
५७ सप्तपञ्चाशत्
५८ अष्टापञ्चाशत् or अष्टपञ्चाशत्
५९ नवपञ्चाशत् or ऊनषष्टि

६० षष्टि *shashṭí*

६१ एकषष्टि
६२ द्वाषष्टि or द्विषष्टि
६३ त्रयष्षष्टि or त्रिषष्टि
६४ चतुष्षष्टि
६५ पञ्चषष्टि
६६ षट्षष्टि
६७ सप्तषष्टि
६८ अष्टाषष्टि or अष्टषष्टि
६९ नवषष्टि or ऊनसप्तति

७० सप्तति *saptatí*

७१ एकसप्तति
७२ द्वासप्तति or द्विसप्तति
७३ त्रयःसप्तति or त्रिसप्तति
७४ चतुःसप्तति
७५ पञ्चसप्तति
७६ षट्सप्तति
७७ सप्तसप्तति
७८ अष्टासप्तति or अष्टसप्तति
७९ नवसप्तति or ऊनाशीति

८० अशीति *açītí*
- ८१ एकाशीति
- ८२ द्व्यशीति
- ८३ त्र्यशीति
- ८४ चतुरशीति
- ८५ पञ्चाशीति
- ८६ षडशीति
- ८७ सप्ताशीति
- ८८ अष्टाशीति
- ८९ नवाशीति or ऊननवति

९० नवति *navatí*
- ९१ एकनवति
- ९२ द्वानवति or द्विनवति
- ९३ त्रयोनवति or त्रिनवति
- ९४ चतुर्नवति
- ९५ पञ्चनवति
- ९६ षण्णवति
- ९७ सप्तनवति
- ९८ अष्टानवति or अष्टनवति
- ९९ नवनवति or ऊनशत

१०० शत *çatá*, masc. and neuter.—१००० सहस्र *sahásra*, masc. neut.—१०,००० अयुत neut.—१००,००० लक्ष neut., and लक्षा fem.—'One million' प्रयुत neut.—'Ten millions,' कोटि fem.—'Hundred millions' अर्बुद masc. neut.—'Thousand millions' महार्बुद (अब्ज, न्यर्बुद) neut.—'Ten thousand millions' खर्व neut.—'Hundred thousand millions' निखर्व neut., etc.

§ 257. The numbers 'two hundred,' 'three hundred,' etc., up to 'a thousand,' and 'two thousand,' 'three thousand,' up to 'ten thousand' are expressed either by conjoining the first ten cardinals as attributives with the duals and plurals of शत 'hundred' and सहस्र 'a thousand,' or by compounding them with both; the compounds are singular neuters, *e.g.* द्वे शते (dual neut.) or द्विशतम् (nom. sing. neut.) 'two hundred,' त्रीणि शतानि (plur. neut.) or त्रिशतम् 'three hundred.'

दशशती fem. sing. 'ten hundred,' occurs for सहस्र 'a thousand.'

When any number from 'eleven' to 'fifty' is to be added to शत 'a hundred,' or सहस्र 'a thousand,' the numeral implying the additional number is changed to an adjective by affixing an अ, before which final अन्, अति, and अत् are dropped. These adjectives agree with the numeral which expresses the larger number, in gender, number, and case, and are placed before them, *e.g.* एकादशं (from एकादशन् + अ) शतम् 'one hundred and eleven.'

The word अधिक 'increased (by)' is compounded with other numerals in order to denote addition, *e.g.* पञ्चाधिक 'increased by five.' These compounds either agree with शत, सहस्र, etc., in case, number, and gender, or are compounded with them, *e.g.* पञ्चाधिकं शतम् or पञ्चाधिकशतम् 'hundred and five.'

§ 258. In order to denote subtraction, the subtrahend is compounded with following ऊन 'diminished (by),' पञ्चोन 'diminished by five.' These compounds (*cf.* § 257) are either joined to the minuend as adjectives or compounded with it, *e.g.* पञ्चोनं शतम् or पञ्चोनशतम् 'hundred diminished by five' = 'ninety five.' But when a number is diminished by one, the word एक 'one' is generally left out and ऊन prefixed to the minuend, *e.g.* ऊनविंशति 'twenty diminished (by one)' = 'nineteen.'

§ 259. The first four numerals are declinable in the three genders. एक *eka*, the crude form of the masc. and neuter, has in the fem. एका *ekâ*. द्वि *dvi*, 'two,' has in the masc. and neuter as crude form द्व *dva*, in the fem. द्वा *dvâ*. त्रि *tri*, 'three,' is the crude form in the masc. and neuter, and substitutes in the fem. तिसृ *tisṛi*. चतुर् *chatur*, 'four,' likewise substitutes in the fem. चतसृ *chatasṛi*.

The following numbers up to नवदशन् 'nineteen' are used as adjectives with the same terminations in all genders, agreeing in case with the corresponding substantives, *e.g.* पञ्चसु ग्रामेषु 'in five villages.'

The numerals from ऊनविंशति 'nineteen' up to नवनवति 'ninety nine' are substantives of the feminine gender; ऊनशत 'ninety nine' has the same gender as शत, which as well as that of the following numerals is mentioned in § 256.

The objects numbered by these numerals are generally put in the genitive plural, *e.g.* 'twenty sons' विंशतिः पुत्राणाम्, but sometimes also in the same case as the numeral, *e.g.* नवतिं पुरः 'ninety towns,' or the numeral even takes the terminations of the plural, *e.g.* षडशीतयस् 'eighty-six.'

§ 260. The declension of the numerals up to नवदशन् *nava-daçan*, 'nineteen,' has some irregularities.

एक *eka*, 'one,' as already mentioned (§ 251), follows in a great number of cases the pronominal declension. The dual is wanting and the plural signifies 'some.'

SINGULAR.

	masc.	neut.	fem.
N.	एकस्	एकम्	एका
V.	एक	एक	एके
Acc.	एकम्	एकम्	एकाम्
I.	एकेन	एकेन	एकया
D.	एकस्मै	एकस्मै	एकस्यै
Abl.	एकस्मात्	एकस्मात्	एकस्यास्
G.	एकस्य	एकस्य	एकस्यास्
L.	एकस्मिन्	एकस्मिन्	एकस्याम्

PLURAL.

	masc.	neut.	fem.
N.	एके	एकानि	एकास्
V.	एके	एकानि	एकास्
A.	एकान्	एकानि	एकास्
I.	एकैस्	एकैस्	एकाभिस्
D.	एकेभ्यस्	एकेभ्यस्	एकाभ्यस्
A.	एकेभ्यस्	एकेभ्यस्	एकाभ्यस्
G.	एकेषाम्	एकेषाम्	एकासाम्
L.	एकेषु	एकेषु	एकासु

द्व 'two' follows the nominal declension (§§ 225, 226) and is used in the dual only. The remaining numerals up to नवदशन् are declinable in the plural only and have many irregularities. I shall give पञ्चन् as the model of those which end in न्.

	m.	n.	f.
N.V.A.	द्वौ	द्वे	द्वे 'two.'
I.D.A.	द्वाभ्याम्	द्वाभ्याम्	द्वाभ्याम्
G.L.	द्वयोस्	द्वयोस्	द्वयोस्

	m.	n.	f.
N.V.	त्रयस्	त्रीणि	तिस्रस् 'three.'
A.	त्रीन्	त्रीणि	तिस्रस्
I.	त्रिभिस्	त्रिभिस्	तिसृभिस्
D.A.	त्रिभ्यस्	त्रिभ्यस्	तिसृभ्यस्
G.	त्रयाणाम्	त्रयाणाम्	तिसृणाम्
L.	त्रिषु	त्रिषु	तिसृषु

	m.	n.	f.
N.V.	चत्वारस्	चत्वारि	चतस्रस् 'four.'
A.	चतुरस्		
I.	चतुर्भिस्		चतसृभिस्
D.A.	चतुर्भ्यस्		चतसृभ्यस्
G.	चतुर्णाम्		चतसृणाम्
L.	चतुर्षु		चतसृषु

	m.f.n.	m.f.n.	m.f.n.
N.V.A.	पञ्च 'five.'	षट् 'six.'	अष्ट or अष्टौ 'eight.'
Instr.	पञ्चभिस्	षड्भिस्	अष्टभिस् or अष्टाभिस्
D.A.	पञ्चभ्यस्	षड्भ्यस्	अष्टभ्यस् or अष्टाभ्यस्
Gen.	पञ्चानाम्	षण्णाम्	अष्टानाम्
Loc.	पञ्चसु	षट्सु	अष्टसु or अष्टासु

ऊनविंशति 'nineteen' up to नवविंशति 'twenty-nine,' and the numerals from षष्टि 'sixty' to नवनवति 'ninety-nine' and कोटि 'ten millions' follow the paradigm मति (§ 229).

ऊनत्रिंशत् 'twenty-nine' up to नवपञ्चाशत् 'fifty-nine' follow the rules given in §§ 212 and 213, II., *e.g.* sing. nom. voc. त्रिंशत्, accus. त्रिंशतम्, instr. त्रिंशता, etc.

ऊनशत 'ninety-nine' and the rest ending in अ follow § 225.

ORDINALS.

§ 261. The ordinals, except the equivalent of 'the first,' are derived from the crude forms of the cardinals, as will be shown by the following list.

m.n.	f.	
प्रथम *prathamá*	प्रथमा °*má*, or	'the first.'
अग्रिम *agrimá*	अग्रिमा °*má* or	
आदिम *ádimá*	आदिमा °*má*	
द्वितीय *dvitíya*	द्वितीया °*yá*, 'the second.'	
तृतीय *tṛitíya*	तृतीया °*yá*, 'the third.'	

m.n.	f.	
चतुर्थ *chaturthá*	चतुर्थी °*thí*, or	‘the fourth.’
तुरीय *turíya*	तुरीया °*yá*, or	
तुर्य *túrya*	तुर्या °*yá*	
पञ्चम *panchamá*	पञ्चमी °*mí*, or	‘the fifth.’
पञ्चथ *panchathá*	पञ्चथी °*thí*	
षष्ठ *shashṭhá*	षष्ठी °*ṭhí*, ‘the sixth.’	
सप्तम *saptamá*	सप्तमी °*mí*, ‘the seventh.’	
अष्टम *ashṭamá*	अष्टमी °*mí*, ‘the eighth.’	
नवम *navamá*	नवमी °*mí*, ‘the ninth.’	
दशम *daçamá*	दशमी °*mí*, ‘the tenth.’	
एकादश *ekádaçá*	एकादशी °*çí*, ‘the eleventh,’	

and so on up to

नवदश *navadaçá*	नवदशी °*çí*, or	‘the nineteenth.’
ऊनविंश *únaviñçá*	ऊनविंशी °*çí*	
विंश *viñçá*	विंशी °*çí*, or	‘the twentieth.’
विंशतितम *viñçatitamá*	°मी °*mí*	

and so on up to

नवनवत *navanavatá*	नवनवती °*tí* or	‘the ninety-ninth.’
नवनवतितम *navanavatitamá*	°मी °*mí* or	
ऊनशततम *únaçatatamá*	°मी °*mí*	
शततम *çatatamá*	°मी °*mí*, ‘the hundredth,’	

and so on.

The masculines and neuters ending in अ are declined according to § 225; the feminines ending in आ according to § 226, and those ending in ई analogously to देवी in § 230. But प्रथम, द्वितीय, and तृतीय may use in some cases the pronominal terminations, as already stated in §§ 253 and 254.

CHAPTER III.—INDECLINABLES.

§ 262. The indeclinables comprise—1. A few nouns (*cf.* § 211). 2. The adverbs, particles, and interjections. 3. The conjugational inflexions.

§ 263. I. Adverbs and particles are derived from nouns and pronouns by the following affixes :—

1. तस् *tas.* This affix signifies 'from' (ablative), *e.g.* ग्राम *grâma,* 'a village,' ग्रामतस् *grâma-tas,* 'from the village.'

The pronouns तद्, त्यद्, and यद् subjoin this affix to their inflective bases त, त्य, and य (§ 245), *e.g.* ततस्. The pronoun इदम् to इ, इतस्; अदस् to अमु, अमुतस्; किम् to कु, कुतस् 'whence;' एतद् forms it from अ, अतस्.

This affix is also added to the prepositions अभि and परि, अभितस्.

2. सात् *sât.* When the adverbs formed by this affix are connected with the verbs अस् 'to be,' भू 'to become,' and कृ 'to make,' they signify that some other object is, or has become, or has been changed to that which the noun expresses, *e.g.* अग्निसात् *agni-sât* (from अग्नि *agni,* 'fire') कृ *kṛi,* 'to change entirely to fire.' The स of this affix is never changed to ष (contrary to § 17).

3. वत् *vat* signifies 'like,' ब्राह्मणवत् *brâhmaṇa-vat* 'like a Brahman.'

4. शस् *ças* signifies 'fold' and 'successive order,' *e.g.* द्विशस् *dvi-ças,* 'two-fold,' पादशस् *pâda-ças,* 'foot by foot.'

5. धा *dhâ* is added to numerals to imply 'partition' and 'kind,' द्विधा *dvi-dhâ,* 'in two parts,' 'of two kinds.'

6. कृत्वस् *kṛitvas* is likewise attached to numerals to signify 'times,' *e.g.* पञ्चकृत्वस् *pañcha-kṛitvas*, 'five times.' एक *eka*, 'one,' is represented by स *sa* and the affix by कृत् *kṛit*, सकृत् *sa-kṛit*, 'once;' स् *s* is added to द्वि *dvi*, त्रि *tri*, and चतुर् *chatur*, द्विस् *dvi-s*, 'twice;' after चतुर् the स् is dropped, चतुर् 'four times.'

7. त्रा *trâ* is added to some words in the sense of a locative, पुरुषत्रा *purusha-trâ*, 'amongst men;' also after स 'one,' सत्रा 'with.' When added to pronouns it shortens its final, and the pronouns substitute their inflective bases, as in No. 1, तत्र *ta-tra*, 'in that (place),' अमुत्र, कुत्र, यत्र; इदम् subjoins ह in the same signification, इह 'here;' in the same way also कुह is derived from किम्, and सह 'with,' from स, which may affix also त्रम्, सत्रम् 'with.'

8. दा *dâ* and र्हि *rhi* are added to pronouns to signify 'time;' the bases of the pronouns are the same as in No. 1 and 7, यदा *yadâ*, यर्हि *yarhi*, 'when.' The forms तदा and इदा, of which the latter occurs only in the Veda, add also नीम्, तदानीम्, इदानीम्.

9. था *thâ* is likewise added to pronouns to denote 'manner;' the bases of the pronouns are the same as in Nos. 1, 7, and 8, तथा *ta-thâ*, 'in that manner.' But इदम् substitutes इत् and takes the affix थम्, इत्थम्. The same affix occurs also in कथम्, from किम् 'in what manner.'

10. तात् *tât* is subjoined to words expressing space and time without changing the signification, *e.g.* प्राञ्च् *prâñch*, 'in front,' प्राक्तात् (*cf.* §§ 193, 2, and 221, I., *prâk-shu* in the locative plural). Some forms ending in अ insert स् before this affix, *e.g.* अवर अवरस्तात् 'behind;' similarly from उपरि 'above,' उपरिष्टात् with ष्ट instead of स्त after इ as in § 241.

§ 264. II. As adverbs are used further:—

1. The accusatives singular neuter of all adjectives, *e.g.* मृदु 'softly.'

2. A kind of adverbial compounds, called अव्ययीभाव 'indeclinables,' the first part of which is an indeclinable, *e.g.* a preposition, अति 'over,' whilst the last part has the form of an accusative singular neuter, *e.g.* यथाशक्ति 'according to (यथा) one's power (शक्ति).' The last members are modified according to §§ 210*b* and 225, *e.g.* अधि with गोपा 'cowherd' makes अधिगोपम् 'amongst the cowherds.' For सह 'with,' when first member, is substituted स, *e.g.* सचक्रम् 'with the discus (चक्र).' When the second member as simple word ends in a consonant, except nasals, semi-vowels, and sibilants, अ sometimes must, sometimes may be added, *e.g.* ऽअनडुह् 'beast of burden' must become ऽअनडुहम्, but ऽसमिध् 'fuel' may become ऽसमिधम्, *e.g.* with उप, उपसमित् or उपसमिधम्. For further details *cf.* my V.G. § 682.

3. Many words, for which *cf.* my V.G. § 783, III. and the dictionary.

§ 265. III. The particles are:—

1. The prepositions which serve to determine more precisely the sense of the cases. As prepositions are used:—

(*a*) The greater part of the prepositions enumerated in § 189, viz., अति 'beyond,' with the accusative, in the Veda also with the genitive.—अधि 'over,' with the locative, in the Veda also with the accusative, instrumental, and ablative; when doubled, अध्यधि, with the accusative.—अनु 'after,' in the significations 'to,' 'for,' 'with,' etc., with the accusative and ablative; in the Veda also with the genitive.—अप 'off,' 'from' with the ablative.—अभि 'towards,' with the accusative in the same significations as अनु.—अव 'down,' in the Veda with the ablative.—आ 'to' with the ablative; in the Veda 'near to' with the locative, 'till to' with the accusative.—उप 'over,' 'near,' with the locative; 'under,' with the accusative.—परि 'around,' with the accusative; in the Veda also with the instrumental; in the sense of 'except' with the ablative, in the Veda also in the signification 'over.'—प्रति 'towards' with the accusative; 'in return for' and 'like' with the ablative.—सम् 'with' with the instrumental in the Veda.

(*b*) Some other particles and adverbs. With the *accusative:* अधोधस् 'near;' अन्तर् 'between,' in the Veda also with the genitive and locative; अन्तरा and अन्तरेण 'between,' 'in,' 'outwards;' तेन 'in that direction,' 'there against;' येन 'where against;' अभितस् 'on both sides;' उपर्युपरि 'over;' उभयतस् 'on both sides;' धिक् 'fie,' also with the vocative; निकषा 'near,' 'between;' परितस् 'round about;' समया 'with,' 'near,' 'in;' सर्वतस् 'from all sides;' हा 'woe!'

With the *accusative, ablative,* or *genitive*: words signifying 'far,' or 'near,' like दूरम् 'far,' अन्तिकम् 'near.'

With the *accusative* or *genitive:* अधरेण 'under,' उपरि 'over,' उत्तरेण 'to the north (of),' दक्षिणेन 'to the south (of),' ऋते 'without' (also with the ablative).

With the *accusative* or *locative:* तिरस् 'across.'

With the *instrumental:* the words signifying 'with,' अमा, जोषम्, सजूस्, सचा (also with the ablative and locative), सत्रम्, सत्रा, समम्, सह, साकम्, सार्धम्, and in the Veda स्मत्.

With the *dative,* in the Veda also with the locative: अलम् 'enough,' but, when prohibitive 'away with,' with the instrumental; नमस् 'veneration,' वषट्, स्वधा, and स्वाहा, words used at sacrifices, स्वस्ति 'hail' (well-being).

With the *dative* or *genitive:* शम् 'hail.'

With the *ablative:* आरात् 'far,' बहिस् 'out,' 'outwards,' the accusatives of the neuter gender of nouns ending in अञ्च्, *e.g.* प्राक् 'before;' उत्तराहि 'from above,' दक्षिणाहि 'from the right side,' प्रभृति 'beginning with,' etc.

With the *ablative* or *genitive:* उत्तरा 'from above,' दक्षिणा 'from the right side,' पश्चात् 'behind.'

With the *genitive:* अधस् 'below,' also with the ablative and in the Veda with the accusative; अन्ति (vedic) 'opposite,' अवस् 'below,' पुरस् 'before,' 'to the east,' अवरतस् 'from behind,'

उत्तरतस् 'from the north,' परतस् 'behind,' अधरात् 'below,' उत्तरात् 'to the north,' दक्षिणात् 'to the south,' and all the adverbs ending in अस्तात्.

2. Some few words which modify the signification of the preceding word,' *e.g.* अपि 'even,' after numerals 'all,' चत्वारो पि 'all four,' सर्वे पि 'all together;' इत् (vedic), ईम् (vedic), घ (vedic), ह 'just;' एव 'only,' 'truly,' to the pronoun तद् it gives the signification of the Latin *dem* in *idem*, स एव 'the same;' कम् (vedic) 'well;' चन and चित्, following cases or derivatives of the interrogative pronoun, give them the signification of indefinite pronouns, *e.g.* किं चित् 'something.'

3. The conjunctions.

(*a*) Copulative conjunctions are: अथ 'now,' 'and,' अथो 'then,' अपि 'moreover,' आत् (in the Veda) 'then,' उत 'and,' च 'and' (following the word to which it belongs, like the Latin *que*), तत् 'then,' 'thus,' तथा 'thus,' 'also,' 'and,' किं च 'farther.'

(*b*) Disjunctive conjunctions are: वा 'or' (following the word to which it belongs), वा ... वा 'either ... or' (following the word to which they belong).

(*c*) Adversative conjunctions are: अथ वा 'but no,' तु 'but,' किं तु 'but.'

(*d*) Conditional conjunctions are: चेत् and यदि 'if.'

(*e*) Causal conjunctions are: हि, तत्, तेन, तस्मात् 'for this reason,' 'for.'

(*f*) Interrogative conjunctions are: आहो स्वित्, उताहो, किम्, किमु, कच्चित्, etc.

(*g*) Affirmative conjunctions are: अङ्ग 'indeed,' अथ किम् 'yes,' अद्धा 'truly,' तथा 'thus,' ओम्, नूनम् 'certainly.'

(*h*) Negative conjunctions are: न 'no,' ननु, नहि, नहिकम्, etc.

§ 266. There are a great number of interjections, *e.g.* for 'calling,' अहह, भगो, भो, etc., *cf.* the dictionary and my K.G. § 521.

§ 267. The indeclinables may form comparatives and superlatives. In the comparative तराम् is affixed, तमाम् in the superlative, *e.g.* from अव 'away,' अवतराम्, अवतमाम्; from उच्चैस् 'high,' उच्चैस्तराम्, उच्चैस्तमाम्; from पचति, third person singular of the present Parasmaipada of पच् 'he cooks,' पचतितराम्, पचतितमाम्.